C000231109

Arthur Janov, PhD, practised insight therapy for seventeen years, both as a psychologist and as a psychiatric social worker, before formulating the theory of Primal Therapy. A member of the American Psychological Association and the Californian State Psychological Association, he has been a consultant on the State of California Narcotic Outpatient Programme and has been on the staff of the Psychiatric Department of Los Angeles Children's Hospital. Dr Janov now divides his time between directing The Primal Institute in Los Angeles and supervising research at The Primal Research Laboratory. Dr Janov is the author of *The Primal Revolution, Primal Man, The Anatomy of Mental Illness* and *The Feeling Child*.

Also by Arthur Janov and available in Abacus

PRISONERS OF PAIN

Arthur Janov

The Primal Scream

Primal Therapy: The Cure for Neurosis

AN ABACUS BOOK

First published in Great Britain by
Abacus in Sphere Books Ltd 1973

1st reprint 1974	6th reprint 1982
2nd reprint 1976	7th reprint 1987
3rd reprint 1977	8th reprint 1988
4th reprint 1978	9th reprint 1990
5th reprint 1980	

Published simultaneously in hardback
by Garnstone Press Ltd 1973

Copyright © 1970 by Arthur Janov

All rights reserved.
No part of this publication may be reproduced,
stored in a retrieval system, or transmitted, in any
form or by any means without the prior
permission in writing of the publisher, nor be
otherwise circulated in any form of binding or
cover other than that in which it is published and
without a similar condition including this
condition being imposed on the subsequent
purchaser.

Printed in England by Clays Ltd, St Ives plc

ISBN 0 349 11843 4

Sphere Books Ltd
A Division of
Macdonald & Co (Publishers) Ltd
Orbit House, 1 New Fetter Lane, London EC4A 1AR
A member of Maxwell Macmillan Pergamon Publishing Corporation

This book is dedicated to my patients, who were real enough to recognise that they were sick and wanted to end the struggle, and to the youth of the world – the real hope of mankind

The author wishes to notify readers that the Paris address of the Institute Primal Europeen is as follows:

Institut Primal Europeen
17, Square de l'Avenue Foch
75016 Paris
France

Telephone - - (1) 500.81.30

Acknowledgments

For their help in the preparation of this book, I want to thank Mrs Karol Markley, my research assistant, and Mrs Ann Farnell Blow who helped in the editing. Thanks, too, to my children, Ricky and Ellen, who helped keep me straight about how to rear children. They taught me what being 'real' meant. I want to thank as well Tony Velie, whose editorial assistance was invaluable. There is one person who truly made this book possible: my wife, Vivian, whose work as director of training for the Primal Institute helped clarify and develop many crucial theoretical ideas.

INTRODUCTION

The Discovery of Primal Pain

Some years years ago, I heard something that was to change the course of my professional life and the lives of my patients. What I heard may change the nature of psychotherapy as it is now known – an eerie scream welling up from the depths of a young man lying on the floor during a therapy session. I can liken it only to what one might hear from a person about to be murdered. This book is about that scream and what it means in terms of unlocking the secrets of neurosis.

The young man who emitted it will be called Danny Wilson, a twenty-two-year-old college student. He was not psychotic, nor was he what is termed hysteric; he was a poor student, withdrawn, sensitive, and quiet. During a lull in our group therapy session, he told us a story about a man named Ortiz who was currently doing an act on the London stage in which he paraded around in diapers drinking bottles of milk. Thoughout his number, Ortiz is shouting, 'Mommy! Daddy! Mommy! Daddy!' at the top of his lungs. At the end of his act he vomits. Plastic bags are passed out, and the audience is requested to follow suit.

Danny's fascination with the act impelled me to try something elementary, but which previously had escaped my notice. I asked him to call out, 'Mommy! Daddy!' Danny refused, saying that he couldn't see the sense in such a childish act, and frankly, neither could I. But I persisted, and finally, he gave in. As he began, he became noticeably upset. Suddenly he was writhing on the floor in agony. His breathing was rapid, spasmodic; 'Mommy! Daddy!' came out of his mouth almost involuntarily in loud screeches. He appeared to be in a coma or hypnotic state. The writhing gave way to small convulsions, and finally, he released a piercing, deathlike scream that rattled the walls of my office. The entire episode lasted only a few minutes, and neither Danny nor I had any idea what had happened. All he could say afterwards was: 'I made it! I don't know what, but I can feel!'

What happened to Danny baffled me for months. I had done standard insight therapy for seventeen years, both as a psychiatric social worker and as a psychologist. I was trained in a Freudian psychiatric clinic, as well as in a not-so-Freudian Veterans Administration department. For several years I had been on the staff of the psychiatric department of the Los Angeles Children's Hospital. At no time during that period had I witnessed anything comparable. Since I had taped the group session that night, I listened to the recording frequently over the next several months in an effort to understand what had happened. But to no avail.

Before long I had a chance to learn more about it.

A thirty-year-old man, whom I shall call Gary Hillard, was relating with great feeling how his parents had always criticised him, had never loved him, and had generally messed up his life. I urged him to call out for them; he demurred. He 'knew' that they didn't love him, so what was the point? I asked him to indulge my whim. Half-heartedly, he started calling for Mommy and Daddy. Soon I noticed he was breathing faster and deeper. His calling turned into an involuntary act that led to writhing, near-convulsions, and finally to a scream.

Both of us were shocked. What I had believed was an accident, an idiosyncratic reaction of one patient, had just been repeated in almost identical fashion.

Afterwards, when he quieted down, Gary was flooded with insights. He told me that his whole life seemed to have suddenly fallen into place. This ordinarily unsophisticated man began transforming himself in front of my eyes into what was virtually another human being. He became alert; his sensorium opened up; he seemed to understand himself.

Because of the similarities of the two reactions, I began listening even more carefully to the tapes I had made of Danny's and Gary's sessions. I tried to analyse what common factors or techniques produced the reactions. Slowly some meaning began to emerge. Over the next months I tried various modifications and approaches in asking the patient to call for his parents. Each time there occurred the same dramatic results.

I have come to regard that scream as the product of central and universal pains which reside in all neurotics. I call them Primal Pains because they are the original, early hurts upon which all later neurosis is built. It is my contention that these pains exist in every neurotic each minute of his later life, irrespective of the form of his neurosis. These pains often are not consciously felt because they are diffused throughout the entire system where they affect body organs, muscles, the blood and lymph system and, finally, the distorted way we behave.

Primal Therapy is aimed at eradicating these pains. It is revolutionary because it involves overthrowing the neurotic system by a forceful upheaval. Nothing short of that will eliminate neurosis, in my opinion.

Primal Theory is an outgrowth of my observations about why specific changes take place. Theory, I must emphasize, did not precede clinical experience. When I watched Danny and Gary writhing on the floor in the throes of Primal Pain, I had no idea what to call it. The theory has been expanded and deepened by the continuing reports of one patient after another who has been cured of neurosis.

This book is an invitation to explore the revolution they began.

Contents

14 Contents

The Primal Scream

Primal Therapy: The Cure for Neurosis

1

The Problem

A theory is the meaning we give a certain observed sequence of reality. The closer the theory meets this reality, the more valid the theory. A valid theory is one that enables us to make predictions because it fits the nature of what is being observed.

Since the days of Freud, we have had to rely on post-dictive theories – that is, we have used our theoretical systems to explain or rationalise what has gone on before. As the observable data increased in complexity, our observations have led us into a maze of different theoretical systems or schools. In psychotherapy today, fragmentation, specialisation abound; neurosis seems to have developed so many forms over the last half century that not only is the word 'cure' no longer mentioned among psychologists, but the word 'neurosis' itself has been broken down into a number of problem areas. Thus, there are books on sensation, perception, learning, cognition, etc., but none on what can be done to cure the neurotic. Neurosis seems to be whatever anyone with a theoretical propensity thinks it is – phobias, depressions, psychosomatic symptoms, inability to function, indecision. Since Freud, psychologists have been concerned with symptoms, not causes. What we have lacked is some kind of unified structure that would offer concrete guidelines on how to proceed with patients during each and every hour of therapy.

Before coming upon what was to grow into Primal Theory, I knew in a general way what I expected from my patients. Nevertheless, a lack of continuity from session to session bothered me, just as it bothers some of my colleagues. I seemed to be doing a patch-up job. Wherever a leak appeared in a patient's defence system, I was there, like the legendary Little Dutch Boy. One day I might analyse a dream; another day, encourage free association; the next week focus on past events; and at other times, keep the patient in the 'here and now'.

Like many of my colleagues, I was staggered by the complexity of the problems presented by a suffering patient. Predictability, that cornerstone of a valid theoretical approach, often gave way to a kind of inspired faith. My unspoken credo: With enough insight, sooner or later, the patient will come to know himself well enough to control his neurotic behaviour. I now believe, however, that neurosis has little to do with *knowing* in and of itself.

Neurosis is a disease of feeling. At its core is the suppression of feeling and its transmutation into a wide range of neurotic behaviour.

The dazzling variety of neurotic symptoms from insomnia to sexual perversion have caused us to think of neurosis in categories. But different symptoms are not distinct disease entities; *all* neuroses stem from the same specific cause and respond to the same specific treatment.

Genius that he was, Freud bequeathed us two most unfortunate notions which we have taken as gospel truth. One is that there is no beginning to neurosis – that, in other words, to be born a member of the human race is to be born neurotic. The other is that the person with the strongest defence system is necessarily the one who can best function in society.

Primal Therapy is based on the assumption that we are born nothing but ourselves. We are not born neurotic or psychotic. We're just born.

Primal Therapy involves the dismantling of the causes of tension, defence systems and neurosis. Thus, Primal Theory indicates that the healthiest people are those who are defence-free. *Anything that builds a stronger defence system deepens the neurosis.* It does so by encasing neurotic tension in layers of defence mechanisms that may enable the person to function better outwardly but cause him to be ravaged by inner tension.

I do not console myself with the rationalisation that we live in an age of neurosis (or anxiety), so it is to be expected that people will be neurotic. I would like to suggest that there is something beyond improved functioning in socially acceptable ways, something beyond symptomatic relief and a more thorough understanding of one's motivations.

There is a state of being quite different from what we have conceived: a tensionless, defence-free life in which one is completely his own self and experiences deep feeling and internal units. This is the state of being that can be achieved through Primal Therapy. People become themselves and *stay* themselves.

This does not mean that post-Primal patients will never again be upset or unhappy. What it does mean is that, despite what they may undergo, they will confront their problems realistically in the present. They no longer cover reality with pretence; they do not suffer from chronic, inexplicable tension or fears.

Primal Therapy has been applied successfully to a wide range of neuroses, including heroin addiction. Primal sessions are interrelated, and for the most part, the Primal Therapist can predict the course of his patient's therapy. The implications of this statement will become increasingly important, for if we can cure neurosis in an ordered, systematic manner, we also may be able to isolate those factors that will prevent it.

2

Neurosis

We all are creatures of need. We are born needing, and the vast majority of us die after a lifetime of struggle with many of our needs unfulfilled. These needs are not excessive – to be fed, kept warm and dry, to grow and develop at our own pace, to be held and caressed, and to be stimulated. These Primal needs are the central reality of the infant. The neurotic process begins when these needs go unmet for any length of time. A newborn does not know that he should be picked up when he cries or that he should not be weaned too early, but when his needs go unattended, he hurts.

At first the infant will do everything in his power to fulfill his needs. He will reach up to be held, cry when he is hungry, kick his legs, and thrash about to have his needs recognised. If his needs go unfulfilled for a length of time, if he is not held, changed or fed, he will suffer continuous pain either until he can do something to get his parents to satisfy him or until he shuts off the pain by shutting off his need. If his pain is drastic enough, death may intervene, as shown in studies of some institutional babies.

Since the infant cannot himself overcome the sensation of hunger (that is, he cannot go to the refrigerator) or find substitute affection, he must separate his sensations (hunger; wanting to be held) from consciousness. This separation of oneself from one's needs and feelings is an instinctive manoeuvre in order to shut off excessive pain. We call it the *split*. The organism splits in order to protect its continuity. This does not mean that unfulfilled needs disappear, however. On the contrary, they continue throughout life exerting a force, channelling interests, and producing motivation towards the satisfaction of those needs. But because of their pain, the needs have been suppressed in the consciousness, and so the individual must pursue substitute gratifications. He must, in short, pursue the satisfaction of his needs *symbolically*. Because he was not allowed to express himself, he may be compelled to try to get others to listen and understand later in life.

Not only are unattended needs that persist to the point of intolerability separated from consciousness, but their sensations become relocated to areas where greater control or relief can be provided. Thus, feelings can be relieved by urination (later by sex) or controlled by the suppression of deep breathing. The unfulfilled infant is learning how to disguise and change his needs into symbolic ones. As an adult he may not feel the need to suck his mother's breast owing to abrupt early weaning but will be an incessant smoker. His need to smoke is a symbolic need, and the essence of neurosis is the pursuit of symbolic satisfactions.

Neurosis is symbolic behaviour in defence against excessive psychobiologic pain. Neurosis is self-perpetuating because symbolic satisfactions cannot fulfill real needs. In order for real needs to be satisfied, they must be felt and experienced. Unfortunately, pain has caused those needs to be buried. When they are buried, the organism goes into a continuous state of emergency alert. That alert state is tension. It propels the infant, and later the adult, towards the satisfaction of need in any way possible. This emergency alert is necessary to ensure the infant's survival; if he were to give up hope of ever having his needs fulfilled, he might die. The organism continues to live at any cost, and that cost is usually neurosis – shutting down unmet bodily needs and feelings because the pain is too great to withstand.

Whatever is natural is a real need – to grow and develop at one's own pace, for example. This means, as a child, not being weaned too soon; not being forced to walk or talk too early; not being forced to catch a ball before one's neurological apparatus can do so comfortably. Neurotic needs are unnatural ones – they develop from the nonsatisfaction of real needs. We are not born in this world needing to hear praise, but when a child's real efforts are denigrated virtually from birth, when he is ready to feel that nothing he can do will be good enough for him to be loved by his parents, he may develop a craving for praise. Similarly, the need to express oneself as a child can be suppressed, even by the lack of anyone listening. Such denial may turn into a need to talk incessantly.

A loved child is one whose natural needs are fulfilled. Love takes his pain away. An unloved child is the one who hurts because he is unfulfilled. A loved child has no need for praise because he has not been denigrated. He is valued *for what he is*, not for what he can do to satisfy his parent's needs. A loved child does not grow up into an adult with an insatiable craving for sex. He has been held and caressed by his parents and does not need to use sex to satisfy that early need. Real needs come from inside out, not the reverse. The need to be held and caressed is part of the need to be stimulated. The skin is our largest sense organ and requires at least as much stimulation as other sense organs. Disastrous consequences can occur when there is insufficient stimulation early in life. Organ systems may begin to atrophy without stimulation; conversely, as Krech has shown,[1] with proper stimulation they may develop and grow. There must be constant mental and physical stimulation.

Unfulfilled needs supersede any other activity in the human until they are met. When needs are met, the child can feel. He can experience his body and his environment. When needs are not met, the child experiences only tension, which is feeling disconnected from consciousness. Without that necessary connection, the neurotic does not feel. Neurosis is the pathology of feeling.

Neurosis does not begin at the instant a child suppresses his first feeling, but we might say that the neurotic *process* does. The child shuts down in stages. Each suppression and denial of need turn the child off a bit more. But one day there occurs a critical shift in which the child is primarily turned off, in which he is more unreal than real, and at that critical point we may judge him to be neurotic. From that time on, he will operate on a system of dual selves; the unreal and real selves. The real self is the real needs and feelings of the organism. The unreal self is the cover of those feelings and becomes the façade required by neurotic parents in order to fulfill needs of their own. A parent who needs to feel respected because he has been humiliated constantly by *his* parents, may demand obsequious and respecting children who do not sass him or say anything negative. A babyish parent may demand that his child grow up too

[1] D. Krech, E. Bennett, M. Diamond and M. Rosenzweig, 'Chemical and Anatomical Plasticity of Brain', *Science*, Vol. 146 (30 October 1964), pp. 610–19.

fast, do all the chores, and in reality become adult long before he is ready – so that the parent may continue to be the cared-for baby.

Demands for the child to be unreal are not often explicit. Nevertheless, parental need becomes the child's implicit command. The child is born into his parents' needs and begins struggling to fulfill them almost from the moment he is alive. He may be pushed to smile (to appear happy), to coo, to wave bye-bye, later to sit up and walk, still later to push himself so that his parents can have an advanced child. As the child develops, the requirements upon him become more complex. He will have to get A's, to be helpful and do his chores, to be quiet and undemanding, not to talk too much, to say bright things, to be athletic. What he will not do is be himself. The thousands of operations that go on between parents and children which deny the natural Primal needs of the child mean that the child will hurt. They mean that he cannot be what he is and be loved. Those deep hurts I call Primal Pains (or Pains). Primal Pains are the needs and feelings which are repressed or denied by consciousness. They hurt because they have not been allowed expression or fulfilment. These Pains all add up to: I am not loved and have no hope of love when I am really myself.

Each time a child is not held when he needs to be, each time he is shushed, ridiculed, ignored, or pushed beyond his limits, more weight will be added to his pool of hurts. This pool I call the Primal Pool. Each addition to his pool makes the child more unreal and neurotic.

As the assaults on the real system mount, they begin to crush the real person. One day an event will take place which, though not necessarily traumatic in itself – giving the child to a baby sitter for the hundredth time – will shift the balance between real and unreal and render the child neurotic. That event I call the major Primal Scene. It is a time in the young child's life when all the past humiliations, negations, and deprivations accumulate into an inchoate realisation: 'There is no hope of being loved for what I am.' It is then that the child defends himself against that catastrophic realisation by becoming split from his feelings, and slips quietly into neurosis. The realisation is not a conscious one. Rather, the child begins acting around his parents, and then elsewhere, in the manner expected by them. He says *their* words and does their thing. He acts unreal – i.e. not in accord with the reality of his own needs and desires. In a short time the neurotic behaviour becomes automatic.

Neurosis involves being split, disconnected from one's feelings. The more assaults on the child by the parents, the deeper the chasm between real and unreal. He begins to speak and move in prescribed ways, not to touch his body in proscribed areas (not to feel himself literally), not to be exuberant or sad and so on. The split, however, is necessary in a fragile child. It is the reflexive (i.e. automatic) way the organism maintains its sanity. Neurosis, then, is the defence against catastrophic reality in order to protect the development and psychophysical integrity of the organism.

Neurosis involves being what one is *not* in order to get what doesn't exist. If love existed, the child would be what he is, for that is love – letting someone be what he or she is. Thus, nothing wildly traumatic need happen in order to produce neurosis. It can stem from forcing a child to punctuate every sentence with 'please' and 'thank you', to prove how refined the parents are. It can also come from not allowing the child to complain when he is unhappy or to cry. Parents may rush in to quell sobs because of their anxiety. They may not permit anger – 'nice girls don't throw tantrums; nice boys don't talk back' – to prove how respected the parents are; neurosis may also arise from making a child perform, such as asking him to recite poems at a party or solve abstract problems. Whatever form it takes, the child gets the idea of what is required of him quite soon. Perform, or else. Be what they want, or else – no love, or what passes for love: approval, a smile, a wink. Eventually the act comes to dominate the child's life, which is passed in performing rituals and mouthing incantations in the service of his parents' requirements.

It is the terrible hopelessness of never being loved that causes the split. The child must deny the realisation that his needs will never be filled no matter what he does. He cannot live knowing that he is despised or that no one is really interested in him. It is intolerable for him to know that there is no way to make his father less critical or his mother kind. The only way he has of defending himself is by developing substitute needs, which are neurotic.

Let us take the example of a child who is being continually denigrated by his parents. In the schoolroom he may chatter incessantly (and have the teacher come down hard on him); in the schoolyard he may brag nonstop (and alienate the other children). Later in life he may have an uncontrollable craving for and loudly demand something as patently symbolic (to the onlooker) as the 'best table in the house' in an expensive restaurant.

Getting the table cannot undo the 'need' he has to feel important. Otherwise, why repeat his performance every time he eats out? Split off from an authentic unconscious need (to be recognised as a worth-while human being), he derives the 'meaning' of his existence from being greeted by name by various maîtres d'hôtel in fancy restaurants.

Children are born, then, with real biological needs[2] which, for one reason or another, their parents do not fulfill. It may be that some mothers and fathers simply do not recognise the needs of their child or that those parents, out of a desire not to make any mistakes, follow the advice of some august authority in child rearing and pick up their child by the clock, feed him by a timetable an airline would envy, wean him according to a flow chart, and toilet train him as soon as possible.

Nevertheless, I do not believe that either ignorance or methodological zeal accounts for the bumper crops of neurosis our species has been producing since history began. The major reason I have found that children become neurotic is that their parents are too busy struggling with unmet infantile needs of their own.

Thus a woman may become pregnant in order to be babied – which is what she has actually needed to be all her life. As long as she is the centre of attention, she is relatively happy. Once delivered of her child, she may become acutely depressed. Being pregnant would serve *her* need and have nothing to do with producing a new human being on this earth. The child may even suffer for being born and depriving his mother of the one time in her life when she could

[2] Many parents make the mistake of not picking up their child sufficiently out of fear of 'spoiling' him. By ignoring him, this is precisely what they do, and later they will be swamped by the child's insatiable demands for symbolic substitutes – until the day they crack down on him. The consequences of *that* are both inevitable and dreadful.

make others care. Since she is not ready for motherhood, her milk may dry up, leaving her newborn with the same raft of early deprivations which she herself may have suffered. In this way the sins of the parents are visited on the children in a seemingly never-ending cycle.

The attempt of the child to please his parents I call the struggle. The struggle begins first with parents and later generalises to the world. It spreads beyond the family because the person carries his deprived needs with him wherever he goes, and those needs must be acted out. He will seek out parent substitutes with whom he will play out his neurotic drama, or he will make almost anyone (including his children) into parental figures who will fill his needs. If a father was suppressed verbally and was never allowed to say much, his children are going to be listeners. They, in turn, having to listen so much, will have suppressed needs for someone to hear them; it may well be *their* own children.

The locus of struggle shifts from real need to neurotic need, from body to mind, because mental needs occur when basic needs are denied. But mental needs are not real needs. Indeed, there are no purely psychological needs. Psychological needs are neurotic needs because they do not serve the real requirements of the organism. The man in the restaurant, for example, who must have the best table in order to feel important is acting on a need which developed because he was unloved, because his real efforts in life were either ignored or suppressed. He may have a need to be recognised by name by the maître d' because early in life he was referred to only by category – 'son'. This means he was dehumanised by his parents and is trying to get a human response symbolically through others. Being treated as a unique human being by his parents would obviate this so-called need to feel important. What the neurotic does is put new labels (the need to feel important) on old unconscious needs (to be loved and valued). In time he may come to believe that these labels are real feelings and that their pursuit is necessary.

The fascination of seeing our names in lights or on the printed page is but one indication of the deep deprivation in many of us of individual recognition. Those achievements, no matter how real, serve as a symbolic quest for parental love. Pleasing an audience becomes the struggle.

Struggle is what keeps a child from feeling his hopelessness. It lies in overwork, in slaving for high grades, in being the performer. Struggle is the neurotic's hope of being loved. Instead of being himself, he struggles to become another version of himself. Sooner or later the child comes to believe that this version is the real him. The 'act' is no longer voluntary and conscious; it is automatic and unconscious. It is neurotic.

The Primal Scenes

There are two kinds of Primal Scenes – major and minor. The major Primal Scene is the single most shattering event in the child's life. It is that moment of icy, cosmic loneliness, the bitterest of all epiphanies. It is the time when he begins to discover that he is not loved for what he is and will not be.

Prior to the major Primal Scene, the child has had countless minor experiences – minor Primal Scenes – in which he has been ridiculed, rejected, neglected, humiliated, driven to perform. Eventually the day comes when all these deleterious events begin to make sense to the child. One crucial event seems to summarise the meaning of all these past experiences: 'They don't like me as I am'. That meaning is catastrophic. It is denied and buried. What takes its place is the struggle by the unreal self. From then on, experience will be buffered by this front so that the child often will not know when he is suffering. His struggle will cover his Pain.

Some patients can recall one crucial scene that was the sum of all previous minor scenes. For others, there was simply a slow, monotonous accretion of small traumas, each insignificant in itself, which one day built into a major rend. Whether the rend is dramatic in the form of one major scene or simply the result of the accumulation of minor scenes, a day comes when the child becomes more unreal than real.

The split occasioned at the major scene spells the end of the child as an integrated and connected human being.

The major Primal Scene usually occurs between the ages of five and seven. This is when the child learns to generalise from concrete experience. This is the time when a child can begin to understand the significance of each disparate event that has happened to him before.

The major scene is not necessarily traumatic from an objective point of view. It need not be an auto or air crash. Rather, it is an understanding – a quick, terrifying glimpse of the truth which hits the child during what may be a rather ordinary event. One patient, for example, remembers calling out for his mother early in his life, and his father, whom he feared, came instead. The flash was: 'My mother is never going to come when I need her.' The basis for this was the many times he would go to bed at night and call his mother to bring him a glass of water. She never came. Only his father came. One day it dawned on him that his mother was not going to come when he needed her. He was pulled in two because to want his mother was to bring on the feared father who castigated him for calling; thus, to want was to get what he did not want. He never called again for her, pretending he did not need a mother – until that day in my office when he cried out in pain for his 'mommy'.

Minor scenes are simply the small events that strike at the real self – criticisms, humiliations – until one day at the major scene that self cracks from the strain.

It is possible that a major Primal Scene can occur in the earliest months of life. This happens when an event takes place that is so intrinsically shattering that the young child cannot defend himself and must split away from the experience. This event produces an irreparable rupture that will last until it is relived again in all its intensity. Being wrenched away from one's parents and sent to an orphanage in the beginning months of life is such an example.

Key Primal Scenes are significant because they represent many hundreds of other experiences, each of which meant pain. For this reason, when these scenes are relived during Primal Therapy, they bring in their wake a flood of associated memories. What ties all the events together is a feeling (such as 'There's no one to help me').

Let us look at some examples of Primal Scenes. The following is Nick's major scene. When he was six years old, the Second World War had just ended and his father had come back from the Army. That Christmas, the first one his family had had together since Pearl Harbor, was to be very festive. Nick had been looking forward to it as only a small boy can. He bought his father a necktie, which he wrapped as best he could, attaching a card he himself had made. By two in the afternoon all the presents had been opened, except the one he had given his father. By three everyone was enjoying a stuffed turkey, except Nick. His father had completely ignored his present.

Finally, someone noticed it still under the tree and brought it into the dining-room. As Nick tells it: 'My father was drunk, and no sooner did he see it than he started acting. "Why, what on earth's this? Is it an automobile? Is it a boat, do you suppose? No. It's an aeroplane. Crudely wrapped, of course, but I can tell it's an aeroplane." Everybody laughed; I felt like crawling under the table. He made me feel ashamed I'd even got him a present. He went on, running the thing into the ground. When he was drunk, he could be remorseless. He pretended he didn't know who it was from, although the card I'd made read "Daddy" and I'm an only child. Finally, he consented to open the package, and then he came over to where I was sitting and slobbered all over me. "Light of my life," he said, "of all the two hundred and ten neckties in my wardrobe, this one will henceforth and forever more be my very special favourite. ..." Crap like that. He just piled insult on injury. Finally, when he said, for about the fifth time, "You shouldn't have wasted your money on your poor old pa," I couldn't take it any longer and got up and ran from the table, thinking: *Goddamn right I shouldn't have!*'

Objectively, in a world whose daily fare is nuclear bombs, concentration camps and genocide, very little happened that Christmas afternoon. Nevertheless, it went far, as a last straw can, towards condemning a man to almost a quarter century of nervous disorders, sexual aberrations, and severe bouts of depression. For Nick, that Christmas necktie symbolised the feeling that 'Nothing I can ever do will be good enough to get you to love me, Daddy'.

The major Primal Scene, then, brings into focus hundreds and even thousands of incidents which meant hopelessness to a child. From the day it occurs onward, real feelings will galvanise the unreal self so that the child no longer recognises many of his feelings. (Thus, after attaining puberty, Nick disguised his need for a warm father and replaced it with homosexual fantasies.) The unreal self furthermore keeps those same real feelings suppressed so that they cannot be connected and finally resolved. ('Objectively', Nick felt only contempt for his father who is an alcoholic.)

The major Primal Scene is a qualitative leap into neurosis.

Before Christmas Day, 1946, Nick had been tense. After it, his tension did not evaporate, just as his denied needs and feelings did not simply pass away. They remained inside him, coded in the brain in the form of repressed memories which permeated his entire bodily system. They kept him tense. His tension kept him unaware of behaving as he did and impelled the struggle to fill the need symbolically (homosexually).

It can readily be seen, therefore, that the kernel of the neurotic struggle is *hope* – hope that what the neurotic does will bring comfort and love. The hope of the neurotic must, however, be unreal because it forces him to try to get via the neurotic struggle something from the world that simply does not exist: feeling parents. The neurotic is trying to convert the world into caring, interested, warm parents, if they really had been good, feeling people, the struggle would be unnecessary.

After the crisis of the major Primal Scene, many more thousands of harmful experiences occur in the course of family life. Each widens the gap and deepens the neurosis; each makes the child more unreal. Another of my patients' Primal Scenes was more dramatic.

Four-year-old Peter was spanked often by his father for a variety of minor offences. He experienced his spankings, felt he must have done something pretty terrible to deserve them, and went on his way. One day, while he was out with his mother, an accident occurred and the family car was wrecked. When Peter and his mother arrived home, his father was waiting, and he was furious. 'How could you be so stupid!' was his opening remark. Still shaken from the collision, Peter's mother began to cry, further enraging the father. Finally, he hit her and knocked her down. Screaming, the little boy rushed to his father and grabbed his arm, which was drawn back for another blow. Peter's father seized him, shook him roughly, and slammed him against the wall. At that instant, Peter realised that his father could kill him if provoked.

From that day on, the little boy had to watch everything he said around his father, every move he made. His childhood became a time of terror, because he was so busy placating his father. Still, he had his mother to turn to. Before long, however, she couldn't take life with her brutal husband and began to drink heavily, so heavily that she had to be committed to an asylum. After she was taken away, Peter knew that it was 'the end'. And so it was, of himself as a normal, integrated human being. For the next two decades he behaved symbolically with everyone he met. What he was acting out was the feeling 'Please don't hurt me, Daddy', and this feeling infected every aspect of his life.

Another example of the beginning of neurosis as a state of being seems innocuous. Nevertheless, it is Anne's major Primal Scene.

One day, when she was six, Anne was caught out in the rain. A woman in the neighbourhood found her soaking wet and shivering. She took the little girl inside her house and warmed her by an open fire, cuddling her. Anne suddenly felt 'strange,' 'funny' – and, without a word to the nice woman, raced out of her house and ran all the way home in the rain. In her room she sobbed for approximately an hour. Anne's mother came to see what the matter was, but the child didn't know. She just felt uncomfortable. Later she wiped her tears away and went down to help her mother get dinner ready.

That's all there is to it, her major Primal Scene. Nevertheless, it was more traumatic than any beating because it could not be integrated and understood.

Before the day of the rainstorm, Anne had been spanked for getting dirty or saying nasty words or pulling her dress up – all the usual things that happen to most of us. In each case she felt she had done wrong, made her apology dutifully, and continued to live her life. But she experienced totally what happened. The day it rained, however, she hadn't done anything wrong; there was no apology to be made, nothing to focus on to make her feel the way she did.

The warmth of that neighbour pointed up the emptiness of her life. She received a glimpse of what she had never got at home, time spent on *her*, kindness, reassurance, simple humanity, and she realised that she could never be what she was and still have her mother love her. She ran home to sob away this realisation before its total impact hit her, before that devastating *never* was felt.

After the cry, when the little little girl went downstairs to help Mommy, her real life ceased. Outwardly, she became polite, sweet, and helpful. Inwardly tensions were building.

She tried to work off her discomfort by constantly helping her mother, who was sick half the time. She volunteered to take care of her little brother. She struggled; the tension deepened, as did her neurosis. She didn't want to take care of little brother, *she* wanted to be cared for and hugged; she didn't want to do the dishes, *she* wanted to play. But she gave in to what Mommy wanted and denied herself. She spent a lifetime trying to convert her mother into that kindly neighbour who offered her love without a *quid pro quo*. The struggle kept her from feeling the truth that her mother was never going to be the warm person she needed. The little girl was caught.

If she stopped acting meek and polite, she would have set off her mother's resentment at having to *be* a mother to begin with. Being meek was Anne's way of avoiding total rejection, so she let Mommy become the little girl while she adopted her mother's role in life. It was because of unreal hope[3] that Anne shouldered this burden. Someday, she hoped, there would be something for her, and so she struggled for her mother's imaginary love, but all she ever got was the dishes.

The Primal Scene, then, is an event which is *not* fully experienced. It remains disconnected and unresolved. This does not mean that there is only one time in our lives that produces neurosis, but that that one time – i.e. the major Primal Scene – sets an unalterable course, and each new trauma widens the gap between the real and unreal selves.

The major Primal Scene is a time when the accumulation of small hurts, rejections and suppressions congeal to form a new state of being – neurosis. It is the time when the child starts to understand that in order to get by, he must forgo part of himself. This understanding, too painful to withstand, is never made fully conscious so that the child begins to act neurotically without a flicker of recognition of what has happened to him.

As we have seen, some Primal Scenes can be dramatic. Others need not be – when Mother says, 'If you ever do that again, I am going to send you away'. It is not the scene as

[3] The hope is largely unconscious and is usually not even felt. Rather, it is acted out in the struggle.

such; it is the *meaning* to the child that makes it devastating. An apparently minor threat or mild spanking can be subjectively as traumatic as being sent away to an orphanage.

THE REAL AND UNREAL SELVES

Though I shall refer to the real and unreal selves, we must remember that they are aspects of a single self. The real self is the true self, what we were before we discovered it was not acceptable to our parents. We were born real. Being real isn't anything we try to be.

The shell we build around the real self is what the Freudians would call a defence system. But the Freudians believe that a defence system is necessary for humans and that a 'healthy, well-integrated person' is the one with the strongest defence system. I see a normal as a totally defenceless person, someone without an unreal self. The stronger a person's defence, the sicker he is – that is, the more unreal.

An example of the literal way in which the real feeling self is suppressed is the yogi who walks over hot coals or goes to sleep on a bed of nails. Every day in my therapeutic practice, I see patients who have managed to split themselves completely away from feeling as a buffer against Pain, and who can no longer feel their psychological hurts any more than the yogi can feel physical pain.

Occasionally, the neurotic may get a glimpse of himself. An illness or a vacation leaves him with few opportunities to practise his struggle, and he is thrown into himself. Sometimes this leads to psychiatric symptoms – he suddenly feels 'depersonalised,' 'strange,' as though he had been going through the motions of life. This depersonalisation is often the beginning of reality, but because the neurotic believes that his unreality is reality, he comes to feel that his real self is some alien force. Generally, he'll retreat into his accustomed unreality and in no time be feeling like his 'old self' again. If he could take a step farther, if he could go all the way and feel the reality of his unreality, I believe that he could become real.

In the neurotic, then, the real feeling self is locked away with the original Pain; that is why he must feel that Pain in order to liberate himself; feeling that Pain shatters the unreal self in the same way that denying the Pain created it.

Because the unreal self is a superimposed system, the body seems to reject it as it might any foreign element. The pull is always towards being real. Because neurotic parents will not allow us to be real, we choose circuitous – i.e. neurotic – routes to get to the reality. Neurosis is no more than the unreal way we try to be real.

It is the unreal system that pulls the body out of shape, resulting in cramped growth and stunted development. It suppresses the real endocrine system or overstimulates it beyond necessity. It puts undue strain on various vulnerable organs, causing periodic 'blowouts'. In short, the unreal system is total; it is not simply a behaviour here or there. To be neurotic means not to be totally real; thus, no part of us can function in a smooth and normal way. Neurosis is as infinite as normality; it is in everything one does.

There is a way for the neurotic to get below the surface of his symbolic struggle and into those Pains that drive him. I call that way Primal Therapy. It is the systematic assault on the unreal self which eventually produces a new quality of being – normality – just as the original assaults on the real self produced a new state of being – neurosis. Pain is both the way in and the way out.

DISCUSSION

Primal Theory regards neurosis as the synthesis of two selves, or systems, in conflict. It is the function of the unreal system to suppress the real one, but because real needs cannot be eradicated, the conflict is unending. Trying to find satisfaction, these needs become transmuted by the unreal system so that they can be satisfied only symbolically. The real feelings which have become painful because they were not fulfilled must be suppressed so that the child is not overcome with Pain. Yet, paradoxically, those needs cannot be fulfilled until they are felt.

If we think of those denied needs and feelings as energy which is driving the organism, we see that the neurotic is very much like someone who has his motor switched on for life. Nothing he can do will shut that motor off until those needs and feelings are felt in all their agony exactly for what they are. This means somehow that the unreal system must be overthrown so that the real one can find expression.

A simple example of not being allowed to cry early in life might clarify this discussion. Where do those tears go? For some people, they become diverted into stuffed sinuses and postnasal drip (which disappear when, in Primal Therapy, the person cries with every fibre of his being). For others, that suppressed sadness finds its way into the droop of the lips or in a melancholy look. The real need is never felt, in any case, because it is acted out symbolically. And it is this acting out that keeps a person from feeling his need and finally resolving it. Thus, the neurotic continues to deny himself fulfilment of what he really needs.

The unreal system transforms real needs into sick ones. A person may stuff himself with food in order not to feel his emptiness. Food symbolises love. Overeating, then, is an example of acting out symbolically.

Once real needs have become perverted into sick ones, they cannot be fulfilled. This means that once the major disconnection has taken place at the major Primal Scene, two selves in constant dialectic contradiction have been created. The unreal self will prevent the real need from emerging and being fulfilled. This is why, for instance, the love and affection of a second-grade teacher can be only meliorative, that the child will not hurt for the moment he is being caressed or paid attention to by a caring teacher. But the teacher's behaviour cannot mend the split which was produced by day-in, day-out deprivation of the omnipotent parents during the first crucial years of the child's life. Once the split occurs, a teacher's hug often brings on Pain for what the child never had.

Primal Pains are disconnected from consciousness because consciousness *means* intolerable pain. Primal Pains are what the child experiences when he cannot be himself. Tension arises when Pains are disconnected from consciousness. It is the Pain diffused. It is the pressure of denied, disconnected feelings surging for release. Tension produces the driving businessman, the narcotics addict, the homosexual, each of whom suffers in his own way but who develops a life-style or 'personality' to attempt to minimise and eventually dull that suffering. The addict is often more honest than either of the other two examples cited. He usually knows that he is in Pain.

Primal Pain are unresolved Primal needs. Tension is the

feeling of those needs disconnected from consciousness. Tension operates in the mind as incoherence, confusion, and lack of memory and in the body as tight musculature and distortions of the visceral processes. Tension is the hallmark of neurosis. It drives the person on towards resolution. Yet there can be no resolution until Primal Pains are felt – that is, experienced consciously.

The neurotic struggle is endless because those early needs remain unresolved. The struggle is the constant attempt to stop the organism from needing. Yet it is that struggle which keeps us from feeling the great Pain of the real need and so finally resolving it. A person can be held by dozens of lovers and never resolve the need for warmth from a parent. A person can lecture to thousands of students and still have a desperate need to be listened to and understood by his parents – an unfelt need which will drive him on to more and more lectures. The struggle is unfulfilling precisely because it is symbolic and not real.

Any real need or suppressed feeling which derives from the early relationship with one's parents much be acted out symbolically as long as it is not directed towards them. The function of Primal Therapy is to help make people real by getting below the symbolic activity and into their real feelings. This means to help the person want what he needs. A normally developing infant wants what he needs because he feels those needs. As he becomes neurotic, his wants and needs split (because he cannot have what he needs) so that he wants what he does not need. For an adult, this may show up in a craving for alcohol, drugs, clothes, money. These are sought to ease the tension of nonrecognised real needs. But there will never be enough alcohol, drugs, clothes, or money to fill the void.

3

Pain

How we react to pain is important in order to understand
Primal Theory and Primal Therapy. I shall indicate, briefly,
research investigations which have been helpful in the formulation of the theory.

E. H. Hess, investigating pupillary contraction and dila-
tion in response to certain stimuli,[1] found that the pupil
dilates when the stimulus is pleasant and contracts when it is
unpleasant. When experimental subjects were presented
with pictures of torture scenes, their pupils contracted; when
the subjects were asked to *remember* these painful scenes,
there was an automatic and involuntary pupillary constriction. I believe that the same thing happens, but in an
overall manner, when a child faces unpleasant scenes. That
is, withdrawal from pain is a total organismic response that
involves sense organs, cerebral processes, muscle systems,
etc. – as was the case in the Hess experiment.

I contend that turning away from great pain is a human
reflexive activity that ranges from withdrawing fingers from
a hot stove to averting the eyes at a particularly gruesome
scene in a horror movie to hiding painful thoughts and feelings from the self. I believe that this principle of pain is
intrinsic to the development of neurosis.

At the Primal Scene, then, the child's organism shuts
down against full realisation and becomes unconscious of
this realisation in the same manner that sufficient physical
pain can render even the staunchest of us unconscious.
Primal Pain is unexperienced hurt, and neurosis can be seen
from this point of view as a reflex: the instantaneous response of the entire organism to Pain.

T. X. Barber has tested subjects physiologically while under
hypnosis.[2] The subjects while apparently awake, yet in-

[1] E. H. Hess and J. M. Polt, 'Pupil Size in Relation to Interest
Value of Visual Stimuli', *Science*, Vol. 132 (1960), pp. 349–50.

[2] T. X. Barber and J. Coules, 'Electrical Skin Conductance and
Galvanic Skin Response During Hypnosis', *International Journal of
Clinical and Experimental Hypnosis*, Vol. 7 (1959), pp. 79–92.

formed hypnotically that they would feel nothing, were given pain stimuli; they reported feeling no pain, although all the physical measures indicated that they were reacting to it. In other experiments, electroencephalographic (brain-wave) changes occurred in hypnotised subjects under pain who reported feeling nothing.

What this would indicate in terms of Primal Theory is that the body and brain are constantly reacting to pain even while the person is unaware that he is being ravaged. Physiologic measures show the bodies of subjects are still reacting to painful stimuli even after they have been given pain-killing drugs.

To react physically to pain and to be *aware* of that pain can be two distinct phenomena.

When the body shuts down against intolerable pain, then, it requires something to keep the Primal Pains hidden and suppressed. Neurosis serves this function. It diverts the sufferer away from his Pain and towards hope – i.e. what he can *do* to fill his needs. Because the neurotic has such urgent, yet unfulfilled needs, his perceptions and cognitions must be diverted away from reality.

The concept of the blockage of Pain is important to my hypothesis, because I believe that feeling is unitary, a total process of the organism, and when we block off such large critical feelings as Primal Pains, we prevent our ability to feel at all.

Primal feelings are like a giant tank from which we draw. Neurosis is the lid to that tank. It serves to suppress nearly all feeling, pleasure as well as Pain. This is why post-Primal patients uniformly report after their therapy that 'I can feel again'. They talk of really feeling pleasure for the first time since they were children.

This notion of a tank of Pain inside the neurotic is more than simply a metaphor; often it is what the Primal patients report in one way or another (carrying a septic tank of hurt around inside them). For example, each time Daddy hits the child, the feeling is: 'Daddy, please be nice to me! Please don't make me so afraid!' But the child does not say this for a number of reasons. Usually, he is so locked into the struggle that he is not aware of his feelings, and if he were, such honesty ('You make me afraid of you, Daddy') might so threaten the parent that it could bring on more castigation. So the child acts out what he cannot say by being more tentative, apologetic, less intrusive, and more well behaved and polite.

Primal Pains become stored one by one, laminated into layers of tension surging for release. They can be released *only* through connection to their origins. Each incident need not be relived and connected, but the general feeling underlying many experiences must be felt. In the case above, when the feeling is connected to Daddy, the person will be bombarded with one memory after another (stored in the 'tank') when his father made him afraid. This is evidence of the existence of key Primal Scenes, scenes which are representative of many experiences, each bound to the central feeling. The Primal process is a methodical emptying out of the tank of Pains. When the tank is empty, I consider the person real, or well.

Underlying Primal Pains is the need to survive. The young child will do what he has to in order to please his parents. One patient put it this way: 'I took me away from me. I killed little Jimmy because he was rough and wild and boisterous and they wanted something tame and delicate. I had to get rid of little Jimmy in order to survive with those crazy parents of mine. I killed my best friend. It was a bad deal, but it was the only deal I could make.'

Because we were unified human beings, the real self will constantly press to surface and make those mental connections. If there were no intrinsic need to be whole, then the real self could be put away for good; it would lie peacefully within us and never make any attempt to intrude into our behaviour. What drives neurosis is the need to be whole again, the need to be our natural selves. The unreal self is the barrier, the enemy which must finally be destroyed.

It takes a considerable effort on the part of the Primal Therapist to force the organism into those early Pains again. No matter how much the patient may want to get well, there is always resistance against feeling the hurtful feelings. In fact, most patients fear 'going crazy' when they are on the verge of feeling those Pains.

For our purposes, the most significant aspect of Primal Pain is that it remains encapsulated internally as pristine

and intense as the day it began. It remains untouched by
the life circumstances and experiences of the person, whatever they be. Forty-five-year-old patients experience those
early hurts with wracking intensity, as if they were going
through the experience – which may have happened forty
years before – for the first time. And, indeed, I believe they
are. The Pain was never fully experienced; it was aborted
and covered before its total impact could be felt. But that
Pain is terribly patient. It nudges and reminds us of its existence in various subtle ways every day of our lives. Rarely
will it shout for release.

What is more usual is that the Pain becomes woven into
the personality system so that it continues to be unfelt and
largely unrecognised. The neurotic system then acts the Pain
out.

It does so automatically because the Pain must have a
release of some kind, recognised or not. The release may
come in the perpetual smile that says, 'Be nice to me', or in
the physical ailment that importunes, 'Take care of me'. Or
acting loud or boisterous or being clever in a social gathering in order to say, 'Pay attention to me, Daddy!' No matter
what position a man has attained in life, no matter how
sober or 'mature', his defence, when one scratches a bit, I
have found a hurt child beneath the veneer.

I want to stress that the Primal Pain experience is not just
knowing about the Pain; it is *being* the Pain. Because we are
psychophysical entities, I believe that any approach that
separates that unity cannot succeed. Diet clinics, speech
clinics, and even *psycho*therapeutic clinics are examples of
isolating symptoms and treating them as separate from the
total system. Neurosis is neither an emotional nor a mental
illness; it is both. To become whole again, it is necessary to
feel and recognise the split and scream out the connection
that will unify the person again. The more intensely that split
is felt, the more intense and intrinsic the unifying experience.

It is the Primal hypothesis that all present-day hurts that
are inordinate or that are out of keeping with reality, refer to
the Primal Pool of Pain. The existence of this pool is what
makes uncomfortable feelings linger long beyond the moment of an otherwise trivial unpleasantness or criticism.

We are all probably acquainted with a hostile or fearful person, someone who seems to wake up each morning as hostile and fearful as the day before without apparent provocation. Where do these feelings spring from every day? I believe they draw on the Primal reservoir of feelings.

Anything that ruptures the unreal front will touch this pool and produce ascending Pain. For example, a patient whose looks never seemed to satisfy her mother was told by her boyfriend, in a casual way, that her pretty blue eyes didn't seem to go with her jet-black hair. This seemingly minor comment elicited the entire feeling of being rejected, and she could not stop this feeling even though she 'knew' that her boyfriend meant no harm. Discussing this current situation was used as a means of getting into her Pain. Feeling that Primal Pain I call a Primal.

One can receive dozens of compliments in an evening, but one small criticism makes all the compliments unimportant because it has set off lifelong feelings of being worthless, inadequate, unwanted, etc. Often neurotics are drawn to critical people *just because* they can struggle symbolically with critical parent surrogates so as to finally resolve and overcome criticism. This is the same dynamic process by which someone will become involved with a cold, aloof person in order symbolically to make (through him) one's parents warm. This is the essence of neurotic struggle – to set up the original home situation and attempt to resolve it, to marry a weak man and try to provoke him to be strong, or to find a strong man and to chop him unmercifully so that he will be weak and without power. Why do people symbolically 'marry' their 'mommies and daddies'? In order to make them into real, loving people. Since it cannot happen, it only ensures that the struggle will continue.

One may question at this point, 'How do we know that the neurotic is indeed suffering from some great pain?' In every case I have seen, irrespective of psychiatric diagnosis, the Pain has surfaced once the defence has been crushed. The Pain is always there; only it is spread out in the body in a generalised tense state.

A further question may well be, 'How do we know that the person is not simply responding to the hurt imposed by the therapist?' First of all, the therapist is not *imposing* a hurt. The attack on the defence *allows* the patient to feel himself, his needs, wants, and hurts. Second, once the major part of the thought-feeling barrier is destroyed, feeling erupts constantly in a spontaneous manner. Third, the hurt immediately leads the patient back into his life and almost never centres on the therapist.

By a curious twist of reason, we have come to believe that he who tolerates pain best is the strongest and the most virtuous. The person who suffers in silence is the 'real man', the one who can 'take it'. Yet it is the unreal man who can take it 'best' because he is inured to pain. What we seem to be saying is that he who denies himself most, he who suffers best, is the winner of the American Neurotic Sweepstakes. There seems to be a direct relationship between self-denial and virtue in Western man, not only in our religious life where renunciation is extolled, but also in the ways of every-day man who works hard to support his family and who may die prematurely from his sacrifice. The person who hasn't had any time for himself, who has been self-sacrificing, ends up literally sacrificing himself. It is in this sense, alone, that I believe we could say that unreality kills.

4

Pain and Memory

When the neurotic first becomes split, there seems to be a division in the memory system. There are real memories, stored away with the Pain, and memories associated with the unreal system. The function of the unreal system is to screen, filter, or block memories which might lead to the Pain. Each new Primal Scene forces the young child to blot out more of his experience, so that each major Pain has around it a cluster of associations which are blocked off from full consciousness. The greater the trauma, the more likely it will affect some aspects of memory.

It is the Primal hypothesis that this memory is stored with the Pain and is restored by feeling the Pain. Primal patients are consistently surprised by the way the therapy breaks open the memory bank. In one case, a woman began her therapy reliving experiences at six months of age, and on each succeeding day of treatment she would relive the subsequent year of her life until she went through her entire life. During each of these sessions, her memory would expand greatly, but would not extend beyond the age she was dealing with during a particular day. So when she recalled being left in the crib, she also remembered the house she lived in at that time, when the grandparents came to play with her, when her brother pinched her while she lay helpless.

Memory is intimately associated with Pain. What will tend to be forgotten are those memories too painful to be integrated and accepted consciously. So the neurotic will have incomplete memories in some critical areas.

Here are some sessions in which patients relived Primal Scenes. Scene one: A thirty-five-year-old schoolteacher goes through the scene in increased frenzy: 'She's being wheeled down the hall. It's dark. She's being lifted on to the bed. She's alone. It's scary ... Ooh! (Here she doubles up as if hit in the stomach.) My God! *I'm* being put to bed for three years. I can't stand it! I can't stand it!'

This scene took place in her memory during the fourth month of therapy. She came in upset that day and didn't know why. As she began talking and feeling, her disturbance increased, and she began talking in the third person: 'She's being wheeled down the hall.' Suddenly she doubled up when she made the shift from the third person, 'She', to the first person, 'I' – the shift from the split self to the single self. As she said, 'I can't stand it!' she was screaming and writhing in Pain. The day she was talking about was the day it was discovered she had rheumatic heart disease and was put to bed at the age of five for a period of three years. It was such an experience of doom that she split to make it tolerable, and from then on she saw herself going through the motions of living as though she were two people. It was as if she were saying, 'It's not happening to *me*; it's happening to *her*.'

(As indicated above, not every Primal Scene involves the parents *directly*. But if parents are loving and kind, then no matter what the trauma, I believe there will be no neurotic split. I recall one woman who remembered the bombs falling on her orphanage on the Yugoslav-Italian border. The principal feeling *still* was: 'Mama, I'm afraid. Where are you? Come back and protect me, please!' She discussed this point after the Primal and said that the war was totally overwhelming for her because there was no one there to explain what it meant, no one to shelter her and make her feel protected. She could not hold up under that early stress on her own.)

The scene described by the woman with rheumatic heart disease was only a hazy recollection before. There were memories of colouring books, sipping milk in bed, etc., but nothing substantial: Pain had borne the deeper aspects of the memory with it into a submerged realm. After reliving this scene, she reported feeling the deep muscles in her legs and the bones of her feet. She suddenly knew why she had avoided even wanting to do anything physical in her life. She had effectively numbed not only the conscious desire, but the limbs that were to carry out those instinctive desires to run and play.

It took four months of therapy to produce this memory. When it happened, it was practically automatic, as though the body were now ready for even greater Pain and would be able to hold together against its impact. The memory came in the reverse way from how it began. First the memory was of a split experience in which she is describing 'her' and what is happening to 'her'. Then fragmented and discrete pieces of the experience were remembered: being wheeled down the hall, being carried into bed, etc. These disjointed memories were like a fuse, one setting off another until there was that one, whole, explosive moment when the split itself was experienced (when 'her' became 'I') and she was *one* again.

Scene two: A twenty-three-year-old woman remembers this during her second week in therapy: 'I was seven. I was taken to see my mother in a hospital or something. I can see her blue robe and the white stiff sheets. I see her frizzly hair as though it weren't combed. I sit upon the bed . . . I don't know. That's all I can remember.' I urge her into the feeling and ask her to look. She goes on: 'I think I sat next to Mother. I'm looking at her . . . Ooh! Her eyes! Her eyes! She doesn't know who I am. Mother is crazy; she's crazy!'

This memory opened up a great deal. She always thought that she dreamed that her mother once tried to kill her but later could remember that her mother did indeed have a breakdown in which she tried to kill the children. Her memory of the situation immediately expanded. She knew that it was a mental sanitorium in which her mother had been placed. She always could remember selected aspects of the scene – going to the hospital, riding up the elevator, etc. – but never could remember actually seeing her mother and the truth of her condition.

The splits that took place in these scenes can be likened to amnesic states, not as dramatic or complete as the amnesia we sometimes read about, but if the situation is completely unacceptable, rape by a father, for example (taken from one of our Primal cases), there may be great areas where the Pain has blotted out a year or two surrounding an event. Sometimes hypnosis is able to retrieve some of these old memories by suppressing the Pain factor, but I do not think that hypnosis can touch areas and memories in which the Pain is overwhelming. The patient who was raped by her father at an early age could come to that memory only after some thirty Primal sessions – and then only in stages.

A twenty-seven-year-old man was reminiscing about his childhood during therapy when he stumbled on a memory about being hit with a swing which he had completely forgotten. The memory was not commensurate with the Pain he suffered at the moment. He relived it in this order: 'I don't know why I feel so bad. There's a swing, and it's going to hit me. It really clobbers me. Gee! There must be more. Where's Mama? Mama, Mama! That's it. No one came. No one ever came. I was always alone, and no one even cared where I was. Ooh, Mama, Mama, care about me, please!' He said that the reason he forgot all about those days in that neighbourhood was that he never wanted to face how all alone and rejected he was: 'So I just forgot about that swing episode'. The memory of the swing hitting him was not important in and of itself. The meaning surrounding the incident was catastrophic, and it was this meaning that no one cared about him which was denied and then acted out in his attempts throughout his life to get people to care. When he became ready to face the fact that his mother, whom he imagined to be loving, really didn't care about him and never had, his memory of the swing became conscious, total and real.

The neurotic's memories are often dreamlike, and the person may have as much trouble remembering his early childhood as he does remembering some of his dreams. I believe that for concrete memory to exist, there must be concrete experience – that is, the individual must be totally involved in his experience and not split away from it by fear and agitation. Some patients have wandered through life almost completely unaware of what was going on about them. They often complain that life didn't happen to them. It happened to *unreal them*. They were marching through life not 'all there'. They usually lived inside some kind of barrier which filtered out the impact of experience and allowed in only what was comfortable. As a Primal patient digs down into this barrier, he can begin to see what some of his experiences and behaviour, previously blunted by Pain, really meant.

I would suggest that memories are suppressed to the degree that they echo elements similar to the key Primal Scene Pains. If a current insult sets off an old suppressed hurt – say, of feeling stupid – that event may be forgotten or only remembered hazily. How much will be remembered will depend on how similar the situation and the feeling are to the old hurt.

There are several implications to the notion that the unreal memory system begins at the initial major Primal

Scene. For example, a neurotic can have a phenomenal memory about dates, places, and historical facts, even about his own life, yet his memory may serve only to shore up the unreal front that says, 'Look how brilliant and aware I am'. The deeper aspects of his memories may be totally blocked. The memories of the unreal self are selective and stick in the mind to ease tension, to bolster the 'ego'. This means that often a so-called good memory of a neurotic is only a defence against *real* memory.

One case may help clarify the relationship of Pain to memory. A young woman in her early twenties was doing well in Primal Therapy, had had two Primals, and was quite insightful. At the end of the second week she was involved in a serious auto crash. She fractured a number of bones and was diagnosed as a traumatic brain concussion case. After she regained consciousness, she had no memory of the accident. Her physicians doubted that she would regain memory of the trauma and told her that if she didn't remember the accident within a few weeks, chances were that it would be lost to her forever.

After several weeks she recovered sufficiently to attend therapy again. Before her visit she began to have stomach cramps and could not move her bowels for three days. After a Primal about a major Pain in her early childhood, she was automatically led without any direction to her most recent pain – the auto accident. She went through the entire trauma from beginning to end in every detail without conscious effort to remember. She saw the car coming, heard the crash, felt the blow to her head, and screamed the terrifying scream she never got out at the time. She could discuss every detail of the accident without any haziness of thought.

What this indicates is that the physical effects of concussion alone may not be responsible for obliterating memory; the accompanying Pain may help shut down memory of catastrophic events. If this assumption is correct, it will be possible to put a person through a Primal in cases of severe trauma, such as rape, and regain memory of the event.

I do not think it is possible for a neurotic to have a complete memory system so long as he has Primal Pain. Once he has had Primal Therapy, there seems to be a sharp increase in memory, and most of these patients find themselves easily going back to the first months of life to recall one incident after another. It is as though the whole memory system had been thrown wide open with the experience of Pain.

5

The Nature of Tension

In Primal terms, there is no neurosis without tension. By that I mean unnatural tension, which has no place in the psychologically normal human, not natural tension, which each of us needs to move about. Unnatural tension is chronic and is the pressure of denied or unresolved feelings and needs. Whenever I discuss tension, I am referring to neurotic tension. What the neurotic feels in place of real feelings are degrees of tension. Less tension usually feels good; more tension feels bad. What the neurotic tries to do with his behaviour is feel better.

Where does tension come from, and what is its function? I believe that tension, as part of neurosis, is a survival mechanism which mobilises the body towards the fulfilment of need or protects the organism against feeling catastrophic feelings. In both cases, it attempts to maintain the continuity and integrity of the organism. For example, when we are not fed, tension is aroused which galvanises us towards finding food and satisfying the need. If we are not held or stimulated, the need spurs us into action. If the need persists in our early months and years, the lack of satisfaction becomes painful and intolerable, and to suppress the hurt, the need is suppressed – and remains in the form of tension. It will remain as tension until it is connected into consciousness and resolved. A suppressed movement (stop running, sit still, etc.) will also remain in the form of tension until connected and resolved.

In short, any critical suppression of a movement or feeling early in life becomes a need until it is felt and expressed and thereby resolved. The disconnection is maintained by fear. Fear signals when Pain (the need or feeling which may bring Pain) is near consciousness. Fear provokes the defence system into action, producing all the varied machinations to keep the need away. Fear is an automatic response that is part of the survival mechanism. It prepares the organism to ward off the blow in the same way that we tense up when we are going to get an injection. When the system cannot ward off the Pain successfully, there is conscious fear – i.e., anxiety. Fear, too, is usually not consciously felt. It becomes part of the general pool of tension.

Anxiety is felt but not correctly focused fear. Anxiety is evoked when the defence system is weakened, allowing the feared feeling to near consciousness. Because the feeling is not connected, the anxiety is often unfocused. The basis of anxiety is the fear of not being loved. Most of us stave off anxiety by developing the kinds of personalities that keep us from feeling how unloved we are.

Personality develops as protection. The function of personality is to fulfil the child's need. This means he is going to try to be what 'they' want so that *he* can finally be loved. Trying to be 'them' is what makes tension. Being oneself is what eliminates it. Being oneself means to be whole – to be connected body and mind. Let us suppose that a young boy needs to be held by his father but his father thinks that 'men' do not hold and kiss. The boy, trying to be a man for his father, denies his need and acts rugged. This rugged personality both produces and binds tension. Then this boy grows up and has an ulcer and is sent for psychotherapy. Sometime soon in his treatment I call him a fag. Now he is anxious. I have found him out – that is, I have put my finger on his suppressed need which may have turned into latent homosexual feelings. He may become angry at my name-calling, but that anger is a cover for the real hurt – a defence against feeling his real need. His anger is a way of releasing tension. The reason that the boy became rugged in the first place was to be loved by his father, but this motivation has long since been buried. Not allowing him to be rugged is to face him with the loss of love and approval – the Primal hopelessness.

Any behaviour in the present which is based on past-denied (unconscious) feelings is *symbolic*. That is, the person is trying through some present confrontation to fulfil an old need. Any present behaviour based on these unconscious needs I call symbolic acting out. In this sense, the personality is the symbolic acting out in the neurotic. The way he holds himself, the way he looks and walks are behaviours in response to old buried feelings.

Nothing else but connection can stop chronic, neurotic tension. Other activities *relieve* tension momentarily but do not resolve it. There is no innate or basic tension, in my opinion, or a basic anxiety. These are only developments growing out of early neurotic conditions. A neurotic is tense whether he is conscious of the fact or not.

Neurosis is not synonymous with defences. Neurosis is a broader term indicating the way one's defences are linked together; neurotic types are simply the peculiar constellation of a person's defences. Since a neurotic can use all sorts of defences in his everyday life, there can be no pure type. Usually, he will settle on a style (being over-intellectual, for example) which, for convenience, we may label a certain kind of neurosis. Any neurosis means that an unreal system exists converting real feelings into tension. Most human feelings and needs are pretty much the same. What gets complicated is how we defend against them. There is no need to deal with these complications, however, if we can get to what lies below.

So long as Primal Pains are there, the neurotic must be tensed up against them. His personality is the more or less stabilised way he has found to defend himself. To remove those Pains is to 'remove' the personality.

Let us think of this in terms of energy. We know by the law of conservation of energy that energy cannot be destroyed; it can only be transformed. I view the original Primal feelings as essentially neuro-chemical energy which is transformed into kinetic or mechanical energy impelling constant physical motion or internal pressure. The aim of Primal Therapy is to change this transformed energy back into its original state, so that there will no longer be an inner force pushing the person towards compulsive action. That feeling of pressure is why so many neurotics feel agitated or upset, why they can't sit still, why they must forever be *doing something.* We must keep in mind that tension is a total bodily phenomenon. Each new blocked feeling or unfilled need adds weight to the inner pressures which affects the total system.

It is possible to work off tension mechanically – to play tennis, handball, or to run. Indeed, most people who run on 'nervous' energy are running off their tension. But there is no way to 'run off' those Primal feelings, so tension seems to be perpetual. I liken those people who are busily engaged in running off tension to a decapitated chicken still in motion.

The neurotic is decapitated, in a sense, until he can connect what his body is doing with the specific reasons for those actions.

Because of the extent of the body's responses to tension, there are any number of ways to measure it. One investigator, E. Jacobson, defined tension in terms of muscular contraction.[1] He believes that tension prepares the body for some kind of locomotion (flight), and this results in the shortening of muscle fibres. The changes in muscle fibres result in an increase of voltage or electrical pressure, which can then be measured by an electronic instrument known as the electromyograph. The electromyograph, however, is as yet an imprecise instrument that cannot measure very minute changes in muscle fibres. Nevertheless, the point Jacobson is making is that our total musculature becomes involved in tension and fatigues the individual whether awake or asleep. This helps explain why the neurotic so often awakens more exhausted than when he went to sleep.

Not only is tension a total phenomenon, but it also tends to concentrate in vulnerable areas. Malmo in his investigations found that most of us have specific target areas of organs that show increases in tension levels under stress.[2]

If a person had chronic pain on the left side of his neck, for example, a stress situation would create a much larger tension score on this side than on the right one.

Though tension is the inner pressure that results from the denial of feelings, each of us experiences it differently. It can be a shakiness, a knotting of the stomach muscles, a tautness of the skeletal muscles, a band across the chest, a grinding of teeth, a queasiness, a feeling of impending doom, a stab of nausea, a lump in the throat, or butterflies in the stomach. Tension keeps the mouth moving, constricts the jaw muscles, flutters the eyelids, starts the heart pounding, the mind racing, the foot tapping, the eyes darting. There is no

[1] E. Jacobson, 'Electrophysiology of Mental Activities', *American Journal of Psychology*, Vol. 44 (1932), pp. 627–94; 'Variation of Blood Pressure with Skeletal Muscle Tension and Relaxation', *Annals of International Medicine*, Vol. 13 (1940), p. 1619; 'The Affects and Their Pleasure-Unpleasure Qualities in Relation to Psychic Discharge Processes', in R. M. Loewenstein, ed., *Drives, Affects and Behavior* (New York, International Universities Press, 1953).

[2] R. B. Malmo, in A. Bachrach, ed., *Experimental Foundations of Clinical Psychology* (New York, Basic Books, 1962), p. 416.

need to labour the point. Tension is intolerable and shows up in many various ways.

So many of us experience tension that we have come to believe it is just one of the exigencies of being human. I am sure that this is not the case. Unfortunately, however, a number of psychological theories have based their suppositions on the inevitability of tension. The Freudian system, for example, posits a basic anxiety around which we must place defences if we are to keep healthy. I believe that this anxiety is solely a function of the unreality of the person.

There have been a number of experiments with both animals and humans in which a buzzer went off whenever a mild electric shock was given the subject. Later the sound of the buzzer alone produced the same kind of anticipated threat and high level of physical activation. This kind of experiment is called conditioning the subject to something which ordinarily should hold no threat – a buzzer. Subjects likewise may be deconditioned by pairing the harmless stimulus (buzzer) with a reward or non-shock situation.

Primal Theory also deals with shock. Often, this shock is an early *realisation* which if fully felt would be catastrophic. The shock is repressed and acted on, producing tense behaviour years after the danger is past. A six-year-old with parents who despise him (this is sensed, since such hatred rarely is openly displayed) may be in great danger both physically and psychologically, but a thirty-six-year-old who understands now that his parents used to despise him is actually no longer in any danger – even though most of his adult behaviour has been based on fear of that feeling.

To understand why thirty years after being faced with a shocking realisation a person is still reacting to it, we must bear in mind that the young infant is wide open. He is defenceless, and this means that he can perceive in a direct feeling way. What he may perceive in his earliest months or years may be too much to bear. So he covers. He may develop symptoms or dull his senses, yet the painful perception is still there waiting to be felt. In one case a patient at the age of two and a half saw the deadness in his parents' faces. He began to perceive the utter lifelessness of the existence of those around him and of his own existence. He did not feel that feeling completely. He developed asthma. *That deadness around him could be experienced only later when he was safely out of it.* For that deadness meant that he had to be 'dead' in order to survive with his parents. It took many Primals to feel that feeling in its entirety. Feeling the deadness brought him to life.

The original psychological shock evoked fear. Fear converted the feeling into generalised, vague tension. The person discussed above was not consciously anxious. He acted lifeless as an unconscious means to avoid anxiety. His 'dead' movements and his 'deadpan' expression were the ways he found to get by with his parents. So long as he was 'dead', he was tense but not anxious. Having to act alive produced anxiety. For the most part, neurosis (symbolic acting out) binds tension so that the neurotic does not even know he is tense.[3] The distinction between fear and anxiety is a matter of context and not physiology. The physiological processes of fear and anxiety may be identical, but in fear the person is reacting to the present situation, while with anxiety he is reacting to the past *as if* it were the present. It is at the point when tension becomes felt anxiety that a person usually comes for psychotherapy.

Real fear is feeling life threatened. It occurs without tension or a dulling of the senses and mind. With real fear the organism is completely prepared to face the threat. Primal fear dulls because it is a catastrophic scare. Primal fear remains because the Primal Pain ('They don't love me') remains. This means that the old threat stays in the present, making fear anxiety. Anxiety is the old fear not connected because connection means catastrophic Pain. (This will be discussed in greater detail in the chapter on fear.) Reacting to a truck bearing down on us is fear. Feeling that a truck *might* bear down on us is anxiety.

---

[3] It is likely that very early in life the infant cannot distinguish between physical and emotional harm, when his conceptual level has not sufficiently matured to allow him to make fine distinctions between a psychological and physical hurt. By the time he can distinguish between the two he may have already covered his Primal Pains with his neurosis. For example, a very young child may not know that he is being humiliated, only that he feels uncomfortable when his parents say certain things in certain ways to him. The experience, then, is undifferentiated pain. It may only be later in Primal Therapy that he will first feel those vague pains again and be able to conceptualise their meaning.

An infant and young child feel fear directly and behave according to their feelings. But as time goes on, even showing fear may be criticised by neurotic parents ('Now stop that crying. You know there's nothing to be afraid of') so that fear becomes denied and then takes its place in the Primal Pool as more tension. This denied fear means that the person cannot act directly and *appropriately* on his feelings. He must invent objects of fear (Negroes, militants, etc.) in order to focus his feelings and relieve tension.

It is when we force the neurotic patient to feel, rather than act out his Primal fears that we can help him understand the feelings that are terrorising him. It is at the point where we take him into and beyond his fears that we move him into his Primal Pains.

A study reported in *Psychology Today* (June 1969) by Martin Seligman relates to this notion of early shock. Seligman describes an experiment by R. L. Solomon in which dogs were strapped into a harness and then given electric shocks. Later the dogs were put into a two-compartment box where they were supposed to learn to escape the shock by simply jumping across a low barrier from the shock section to the non-shock section. It was found that if a dog were first shocked while harnessed so that he could not escape, something 'bizarre' happened. During later shocking episodes, even while free to jump across the barrier, the dog would stay in the shock section until he was actually dragged away. Other dogs who were not harnessed (helpless) when first shocked quickly learned to jump to freedom. In many respects, the young child is harnessed into an inescapable situation of trauma and is as helpless as those harnessed dogs. The child, too, cannot do anything appropriate to escape incessant Pain and often cannot learn later how to act in situations to avoid hurt. When no response a child can make will alter his situation, he often has little else to do but turn off internally, to remain as passive and hurting as those harnessed dogs who could not escape the first major shock they had experienced in their lives. We note from Solomon's experiment that if dogs were first shocked in a situation where they could escape (do something about their predicament) and then later harnessed and shocked, when they were again shocked and allowed to respond freely, they learned to escape that shock normally. Seligman points out that if an infant cries to be fed and there is no one around to feed him, then crying becomes an irrelevant response and may be stamped out in time solely because crying did nothing to alter a hurting or uncomfortable situation. Primal Theory indicates that the continued Pain of not getting, of never having one's earliest needs satisfied, tends to shut off the response until the individual goes back and dares cry again as that infant.

The effects of Primal Pains are considered permanent until felt (I use the term 'felt' to mean 'totally experienced'). This means that Primal Pains cannot be conditioned out of the organism. Thus, though one may punish or reward the surface manifestations of the Pains (smoking, drinking, addiction), one will not change the Pains themselves. They will still require neurotic outlets of one kind or another until they are completely felt.

The neurotic engages in unreal, symbolic behaviour to ease tension. Thus, he may have compulsive sex in order to feel loved without ever recognising early feelings of being unloved.

Though tension is felt everywhere, there seems to be one organ that is focal – the stomach. Clenching the muscles of the stomach (and the entire abdominal area) seems to be the neurotic's internal painkiller. Wilhelm Reich made this discovery decades ago.[4] Reich developed much of his early therapeutic methods around easing the patient's abdominal tensions.

The stomach is where nearly all neurotic patients report the focus of their tension. American folklore testifies to its significance with sayings such as: 'I had to swallow my words!' 'I can't stomach that!' 'I hate your guts!' 'Let's have some gut [meaning "real"] talk!' Evidently when words are swallowed, it is more than a simple, symbolic gesture.

Words seem to have been literally choked down into the gut, tying the person in knots. Most often, the pre-Primal patient isn't aware of the amount of his stomach tension until we begin to wrench it loose. During Primal Therapy we often watch the tension leave the stomach and work its way

[4] Wilhelm Reich, *The Discovery of the Orgone* (New York, Noonday Press, 1948).

up. The person will report in sequence, a tightness across the chest, a constriction of his throat, a grinding of his teeth, an aching in his jaw – and then, when the important words have been said, there is no more of this.

I hesitate to say, 'We can watch the Pain rise from the stomach to the mouth'; nevertheless, we have documented on videotapes the phenomenon of ascending tension. During Primal Therapy. the feelings which begin their rise cause the entire abdominal area to quiver and shake. It is as though the feelings are being jarred loose from their encased abdominal vice. They move up the body and out of the mouth in the form of Primal Screams. When this happens, patients report feeling their stomachs unblocked for the first time. Before, the stomachs were evidently clogged with tension, tension that would not allow food to be completely digested.

Tension does not always cause the inability to eat. In some cases the opposite happens – the person stuffs his feelings back down with food. There is a dual phenomenon at work – descending and ascending tension. Ascending tension occurs when the defence system is weakened and the feelings become close to consciousness. Ascending tension (anxiety) often makes it difficult to eat. Descending tension, on the other hand, enables the neurotic to keep his feelings at bay with food so that tension does not become an anxiety state. As a general rule, the very overweight person has a deep and hidden set of Pains. His layers of fat seem to form a buffer of insulation against them – descended tension.

6

The Defence System

The concept of a defence system is found in many psychological theories beginning with the Freudian. Primal Theory indicates that *any* defence is neurotic and that there is no such thing as 'healthy' defences. The belief in healthy defences is based on the supposition of a basic anxiety that must be contained – something inherent in all humans. Primal Theory does not recognise the notion of basic anxiety in normal individuals. This will be discussed in detail later. The last point of difference in regard to defences between Primal Theory and some other theories is that it views defences as psychobiologic phenomena and not simply mental actions. Thus, a constricted blood vessel may be as much a defence as compulsive talking.[1]

In Primal terms, a defence is a set of behaviours which automatically function to block Primal feelings. When the abdomen automatically tightens, when an individual swallows a feeling, when the face tics under pressure, the body is clamping down against feeling.

There are involuntary defences and voluntary ones. Involuntary defences are the automatic responses of the mind and body to Primal Pain – fantasising, bed wetting, gagging, blinking, tightening the muscles. These are usually the first defences utilised. These are the child's inbuilt defences. Clamping of the respiratory apparatus, for example, will affect the tone and timbre of his voice. The clamping process and the resultant squeezed voice become interwoven into part of the personality system. In this way, the personality becomes built around and is an integral part of the defences.

Involuntary defences are of two types – tension building and tension releasing. Knotting the stomach muscles holds

---

[1] Anna Freud, in her *Ego and the Mechanisms of Defence*, p. 75, states, 'The efforts of the infantile ego to avoid "pain" by directly resisting external impressions belong to the sphere of *normal* [my emphasis] psychology. Their consequences may be momentous for the formation of the ego and of character, but they are not *pathogenic* [my emphasis again].'

the feelings down, resulting in tension. Wetting the bed at night (when conscious defences are lessened) is an involuntary release of the tension. Other involuntary release forms are grinding the teeth, sighing, having nightmares (more on this later).

Voluntary defences come into play when involuntary release mechanisms fail to do the job. Smoking, drinking, drug use, and over-eating are examples of voluntary defences. They can be stopped by a force of will. Voluntary defences are needed to relieve excess tension – an angry word by a cashier at a restaurant may sufficiently disrupt the pleasing façade of a neurotic to create the need for a drink. The purpose of both defence forms – voluntary and involuntary – is to block the real feeling.

Defences operate continuously, night and day. An effeminate male does not suddenly become masculine while asleep. His effeminacy is a psychophysical event which goes on awake or asleep; it is built into the organism. This means that unnatural actions become the norm because the person cannot feel his natural inclinations. He will not be able to walk, talk, or conduct himself in any other way until he can regain his natural self.

Defences are, by and large, what the parents demand from the child. One child may talk continuously and use big words while another plays it 'dumb'. Both are responding to a sensed demand by their parents, both are closing off part of themselves.

Defences spring into action as an adaptive mechanism to keep the organism going. In this way, neurosis is viewed as part of the inherited adaptive equipment we all share. Because neurosis is adaptive, we cannot simply blast away neurosis with a shock machine. Defences must be dismantled in an orderly sequence a bit at a time until the person is ready to do without them entirely.

The child shuts himself off in his earliest months and years because he usually has no other choice. A loud and talky child may not long be tolerated by repressed parents who want a polite, meek son or daughter. They will spank or castigate him until he shuts off that avenue of behaviour. Thus, the child must sentence part of himself to death for life. He must play their game, not his. This same kind of behaviour may result from parents who do too much for the child so that he has to make no effort on his own behalf. He has been smothered by their kindness.

If the unreal front does not work, if it cannot arouse a human response in parents, then the child is going to have to adopt more desperate defences. He may shut off everything about himself in order not to displease them or to make them warm and kind. He may talk in a rigid, programmed, computer-like way. His thoughts may become constricted and narrow and his eyes but a squint; in short, he has de-humanised himself in an attempt to make his parents human. He may eventually turn himself inside out for them – a boy who becomes a 'girl'.

Total response is a crucial concept. The need for love is not just something cerebral which can be changed by changing ideas. That need pervades the entire system, distorting the body and the mind. That specific distortion is the defence.

If the personality cannot bind tension, symptoms will result. The child may masturbate, suck his thumb, bite his nails, or wet his bed. These are avenues for more relief. Too often, mistakenly believing they are helping the child, parents will try to stop up these spillways for tension and thus compound the problem, forcing the child to find more hidden means. One patient told me that he passed gas constantly because his parents believed that he had a stomach disorder. He said, 'Farting was the only thing they would accept because they thought it was involuntary.'

A young child cannot understand that it is his parents who are troubled. He does not know that their problems exist apart from anything he can do. He does not know that it is not his job to make them stop fighting, to be happy, free or whatever. He is doing what he can so that he can live. If he is ridiculed almost from birth, he must come to believe that something is wrong with him. He will try any measures to please, but tragically, what he must do is left vague and indistinct because his parents do not know what to do to make themselves free and happy. Because they do not make him feel better, he must rely on himself. He will eat everything in sight, suck his thumb when no one is looking, masturbate, and, later, shoot himself with drugs to ease the suffering which no one else would soothe for him. He is no longer just being neurotic; neurosis is his being.

The drug addict is an example of someone who has run out of inner defences. He is usually the one who has cancelled out so much feeling that he is almost dulled out of existence. Because he cannot manage to defend himself as other neurotics do, he develops a direct relationship with the needle: Pain ... needle ... relief. Remove the needle, and there is the Pain. The penis serves the same purpose for the homosexual. Both represent relief from tension. An external connection developed to take the place of the internal connection that was not made.

Irrespective of the pain involved in the use of the needle or in intercourse as practised by male homosexuals, the symbolic feeling is pleasure or, more correctly, relief. Real, physical pain, the pain experienced by the real self, is filtered through the defence system where it is interpreted as pleasure.

The varieties of ways the neurotic has defended himself have been classified by professionals and categorised into diagnostic states. I want to stress again, however, that the defence system is only important insofar as it masks the Pain. What matters, in terms of the Primal hypothesis, is the Pain.

For the neurotic, all his experience must wend its way through the labyrinth of his defences where what is happening is not seen, is misinterpreted, or is exaggerated. The same distortive process influences his bodily activity so that, finally, he is unable to interpret or understand the kinds of changes that are going on in his own body. He must then place himself in the enigmatic situation of going to a stranger (professional) to help him understand what he is feeling inside himself.

Defence systems become more intricate depending on the family situation of the child. When the parents are brutal, the defence is direct and on the surface. When the family interaction is more subtle, the defence system becomes more subtle.

Those individuals who have developed layers of subtle, intellectual defences (who have fled to their 'head') are the most difficult to cure. Insight therapy has been the central treatment of the intellectual class; any method that further engages the 'head' of these neurotics only helps worsen their problem.

Reich gave us insight into bodily defences decades ago: 'We can say that every muscular rigidity contains the history and meaning of its origin. It is thus not necessary to deduce from dreams or associations the way in which muscular armour developed; rather, the armour, itself, is the form in which infantile experience continues to exist as a harmful agent.'[2]

Reich explained that muscular rigidity is not simply a result of repression but represents the 'most essential part of the process of repression'. He pointed out that repression was a dialectic process in which the body not only became tense through neurosis but perpetuated the neurosis via the tense musculature. He did not make clear what kept the body tense year after year, but he did believe that neurosis could be significantly affected by certain exercises or techniques designed to reduce muscle tension – more specifically, abdominal tension.

According to the Primal view, needs and blocked feelings begin virtually with birth and very often before the time we can verbalise about them. A child who is not held sufficiently in his first months does not consciously know what he is missing, but he hurts, nevertheless. He hurts all over his body, which is exactly where the need is. The need, then, is not just something mental stored away in the brain. It is coded into the tissue of the body, exerting a continuous force towards satisfaction. That force is experienced as tension. We may say that the body 'remembers' its deprivations and needs just as the brain does. To be rid of the tensions, the person is going to have to feel the needs at the nucleus of those tensions – in other words, organismically – which is exactly where those needs are. The needs are found in the musculature, organs and blood system.

Simply to know one's unconscious feelings and needs is not enough. Much of modern psychotherapy operates on the assumption that making unconscious feelings conscious is sufficient to change a person. I see it differently – that consciousness is the result of an organismic feeling process and that it is the *feeling* process, not simply *knowing* what those needs are, which changes someone. Knowledge of need, in my opinion, does not get rid of it. We have under-

[2] Wilhelm Reich, *The Discovery of the Orgone* (New York, Noonday Press, 1942), pp. 266–67.

estimated how much deprivation goes on in the first months of life and how that deprivation affects us for the rest of our lives. The Reichians recognise that much to do with feeling is non-verbal, and they attempt to deal with repressed feelings physically through bodily manipulation.

The point of Primal Therapy is to connect the body's needs with the stored and unconscious memories and so unify the person. Dance therapy, yoga, body movement therapy, or exercises designed to free the body of tension would be of no avail because these tensions (unconscious early blockages and deprivations) are woven inextricably with Primal memories into unitary organismic events. Encouraging insights splits the individual in one way, and body movement therapy splits him in another. What we need is something total – a joining together *at once* of the body and mind. There is no way to permanently massage away memories from a tense shoulder when those memories innervate that shoulder below the level of consciousness.

It may help us understand this if we consider how we develop. The infant has little ability to abstract or to reason about his predicament. He cannot transform his needs into specific fantasies, nor can he act them out during infancy in symbolic ways. His body must make his defences. So for him it isn't a matter of the mind's controlling the body; the infant doesn't seem to have developed the mental capacity in the first few months to do that. Rather, what seems to happen is that some children must defend themselves physically almost from the time they are born.

I recall one patient who was born in an orphanage where there was hardly anyone to take care of her. During her later experiences in therapy, she relived being in a crib in the orphanage and remembered crying for a long time with no one coming. She relived what she did then. She remembered sitting up at about eight months after crying for many minutes, looking around and seeing that there was no one, feeling her body dull, and lulling herself into sleep. Soon this became a habit. She would wake up uncomfortable, start to cry, shut off, and lie back in her crib, numb. This dulling became automatic in the first two years of her stay in the orphanage. Later, when out of the orphanage, it took the form of numbing herself whenever she was uncomfortable or frightened. She said, 'It was like sucking myself back inside and being dazed. I deadened every part of me so that I was half-asleep even walking around.' This apathy and life-lessness, incidentally, are noted by many investigators in regard to institutionalised children. I think they have to deaden themselves and create a barrier in order to survive.

What happened to this woman back in that orphanage was the result of a protective system of the body. That bodily defence which followed her for a lifetime developed because her trauma and split began before the development of intellect and the possibility of intellectual defences. I do not believe that any amount of exercise later would limber up and activate her muscle system. After her therapy, in which she relived those infantile traumas which rigidified and suppressed the freedom of her musculature, she felt lib-erated and 'light'. For the first time she could dance freely without that automatic lifeless and heavy feeling which had plagued her for most of her life. Feeling her deadness made her come alive.

Recently we saw a weight lifter in Primal Therapy. He was addicted to looking at his body in the mirror. What he saw was carefully constructed tension. He was watching his defence system and trying to build it physically – all to keep from feeling weak and unprotected. His unconscious atti-tude went like this: 'There is no one to watch out for me. I'll have to be strong so I can protect myself.' The symbolism is: 'If I act and look like a man, I'll be a man.' In Primal Ther-apy, he began to feel like the weak and unprotected little boy he was. We had to get him to stop lifting weights – that is, to unprotect himself enough in order to feel that weakness.

Cure of neurosis must always deal with the total system. We therapists have spent decades talking to the unreal front of our patients, thinking we could convince that front to give up the needs and Pains that produced it. There is no power on earth that can do that.

One might ask, 'What difference does it make? If I feel all right, isn't that what matters? Do I have to give up how I feel now for someone's idea of a more ideal state?' Obvi-ously, the answer is no. But I do think that many people, homosexuals, for example, have come to terms with their sicknesses because they honestly believe that they have no alternatives. Although most neurotics are not content, they suffer only a vague malaise as long as their defences work.

But the neurotic should know that there is an alternative; a state of being beyond his present imagination. He may have taken LSD at one time in his life and experienced feelings of unbelievable magnitude. Perhaps he attributed these feelings to the drug. I would disagree. Drugs do not feel. People do! That is, unneurotic people feel, and I believe the greatest contribution of Primal Therapy is to allow people to experience their own feelings.

DISCUSSION

Neurotic behaviours are the idiosyncratic ways each of us finds to release tension. To alter or suppress specific surface behaviour does not change neurosis. Developing 'good' habits (not eating too much, for example) must always be an effort when neurosis exists, because the person is trying to drown Primal Pain.

Neurosis is frozen Pain. In the ordinary course of our lives we encounter many hurts which we get over, but there is no end to Primal Pain because it is not felt. Nevertheless, one can often see that Pain frozen onto the faces of neurotics, pinching and contorting those faces out of shape.

Though the neurotic usually is not aware of his hurts, he is a nervous wreck. He may be that physician racing from one treatment room to another, or the woman with one vague complaint or another. The neurotic is usually too busy trying to be himself to realise that he isn't.

Neurosis begins as a means of appeasing neurotic parents by denying or covering certain feelings in hopes that 'they' will finally love him. No matter how many years of disappointment go by, hope is eternal. It must be because the needs are eternal. Those needs drive him to believe in irrational ideas and to act in irrational ways because rational truth is so painful. So long as a person has not felt his Pains completely, he cannot give up hope. In Primal Therapy, a person feels the childhood hopelessness, thereby dashing unreal hope, which is the foundation for neurotic struggle.

When does neurosis begin? At almost any early age – one, five, or ten. What is important is that it has a beginning – the time when the child splits away from his real self and leads a dual existence. Does this mean that one scene or one event makes one neurotic? Obviously not. The one major scene is but the culmination of years of deleterious parent-child relationships. Many neurotics turn off at about the age of six or seven because it is then that they can make sense out of what is going on in their lives. They become dissociated or split and cannot put themselves back together (that is, undo neurotic tension) by any conscious effort.

Neurosis can begin at the age of one if the trauma is severe and the past history warrants it. Obviously, the split in many individuals has occurred before the age of six because the stutterers I have seen complain that their speech defects began at the time they started talking – between the ages of two and three. Others report becoming finally split at the age of twelve. One patient said that he managed fairly well until the age of thirteen. It was then that his parents divorced and his father remarried. The boy was required to call his stepmother 'Mother' and treat her like a real mother. Instead of facing the loss of his real mother, he closed off inside.

Why does neurosis begin earlier, rather than in one's teens, for example? Because in the earliest months and years the child is so utterly helpless and dependent on his parents. They *are* the world to him. What they do sets the child on a course which soon becomes rigidified, determining how he will meet the world.

Usually by the time he begins school he is disconnected and neurotic, and that neurosis affects the way he acts towards teachers and peers. A child made into a 'stone', who was made shy and obsequious by his overbearing parents, will tend to carry on that pattern with others. The split is usually not a big bang, a cataclysmic event. One day the child simply becomes more unreal than real. The reason it happens earlier than in the teens is, as a rule, that if a child could make it to his teens without neurosis, he could find other support, love from a girlfriend, for example, or an understanding teacher who would help him withstand the pressure and turmoil at home. Usually, by the time he has reached his teens he has already developed a neurotic personality that cannot be undone by such help, only temporarily palliated. Why doesn't rejection by a social club, failing a class, or being turned away by a lover produce neurosis? Because single events, even in the home, do not produce reactions so strong as to cause us to split. A normal child, rejected by a teacher, would attribute it to her own problems or to his poor work or misbehaviour, say; he would feel *that* and not become split from his feeling. Trauma, in Primal terms, is not a hurtful event such as being rejected by a social club at school. Trauma is what is *not* experienced. That is, it is a reaction so strong and overpowering as to cause part of the event to be blotted out of consciousness. Sobbing over social rejection with a comforting mother is very different from realising that one is hated by his mother and has no one to turn to with his feelings. No family conference later will undo that. A child can understand *why* his mother rejected him earlier, but that understanding will not change his early, deprived needs.

Does the Primal Scene mean that you are neurotic then and there and forevermore? The Primal Scene represents the qualitative leap, the shift into a new state – neurosis. No amount of loving, reassurance, or caring from then on will undo the neurosis. It deepens with each new trauma or suppression by parents. If, when the child was eight years old, say, a loving parent were suddenly to appear, the previous damage still would have to be resolved. Such a loving parent does help, of course, because he does not deepen the neurosis, but he cannot undo neurosis. Only Pain can do that – feeling the Pains that required parts of the real self to be covered.

7

The Nature of Feeling

The central demand of the body is to be felt. We begin to feel when all our early needs are met, when we are held and kissed, allowed free expression and free movement, and permitted to develop at a natural pace. When basic needs are met, the child is ready to feel whatever there is to feel each new day. When they are not met, the needs will supersede anything else and prevent the child from feeling the present. The present for the neurotic is but a trigger, setting off old needs and hurts and an attempt to resolve them.

There are two reasons needs and feelings from the past are unconscious. Often the feeling developed before the use of concepts so that the feeling is unrecognisable. (An infant doesn't know that he should not be weaned too soon, for example.) Second, even though feelings were once recognisable before the Primal Scene, they may have been continuously suppressed by neurotic parents so that in time the child comes not to know what he is feeling. If a child is not permitted to cry, either because of an oversolicitous parent who can't stand an instant of sadness in his child or because of parental derision about being a 'baby', before long he may not even know that he wants to cry. Indeed, he too may grow to deride tears as weakness.

The suppression of feeling does not necessarily have to be a direct act by a parent. Denial of feeling may occur in infancy before a child is old enough to compromise his feelings and put up a good front. The simple lack of having a parent around to hold it may create so much Pain that after a time the child shuts off his Pain by shutting off his need. He stops *feeling* his need. The need lingers on, however, minute after minute, year after year. The need remains fixed and infantile because it *is* an infantile need. A neurotic cannot have adult feelings when infantile needs importune. He may later have compulsive sex, for example, not out of true sexual feelings but out of an early need to be held and loved. When he has felt all the old needs for what they are, he can then feel truly sexual – which is a very different feeling from what the neurotic thinks of as sexuality.

What the neurotic is acting out in the instance of compulsive sex is an old, possibly non-conceptualised need. He may put a new label (sex) on it, but the need is to be held. When this fact hit one patient in the middle of his sex act, he lost his erection (his symbolic sexual feeling) and asked his wife just to hold him. When this man *stopped* his sex act, he was truly feeling. (This insight was not appreciated by her!) He was conceptualising his real need and no longer acting it out symbolically. Thus, we see that feeling is sensation conceptualised. This means correctly conceptualised. A gnawing sensation in the stomach may be the feeling of the hollowness of one's life. The neurotic may transmute this feeling into the sensation of hunger.

Neurosis masks painful bodily sensations from proper recognition ('They don't love me'), leaving the person to suffer constantly. He may try to relieve those sensations in one way or another (sex, in the example above), but that sensation cannot be relieved until it is correctly connected – *when it becomes a feeling.*[1]

Primal Pains are the *sensations* of pain. In Primal Therapy they become feelings through connection – connection to the specific traumatic origins. Only *connection* changes a sensation of pain into a true feeling. Conversely, the disconnection of the thought from its feeling content early in life produced continuous uncomfortable sensations – headaches, allergies, backaches. They persist because they were not connected. It is as though the painful feeling were cut off from the knowledge ('I am all alone; there is no one who will understand'), and takes on a life of its own inside the

---

[1] Feeling is not synonymous with emotion. Emotion may be the expression of feeling – the motions one goes through when feeling. True feeling requires little emotion. Most emotion is but going through the motions of feeling sans the feeling. Unfortunately, many neurotics have viewed emotion as a sign of feeling, and unless someone is effusive and overreacting, they tend to believe a person is not really feeling. Neurotic parents seldom are happy with a grateful thank-you for gifts they have given; they need a profuse display of emotion to make sure they are appreciated. In these subtle ways children cannot be themselves and react naturally; rather, they must overreact because honest reactions are too often taken by parents as a sign of rejection.

body, alighting here and there in the form of aches and hurts.

When a pain becomes a felt Pain, it is no longer painful, and the neurotic can feel. Anything which elicits true feelings in a neurotic must evoke Pain. Any purportedly deep feeling experience that does not bring up Pain is a pseudofeeling – a non-connected acting out.

A number of patients later in their treatment report that the sex act often leads involuntarily into a Primal. One man explained it as follows:

'Before therapy, I had all kinds of suppressed feelings which I let out through sex. I thought I was sexy. I could do it all the time. Now I know that my high sex urge was all those other feelings trying to get out in any way they could. I shot them out of the end of my penis. It was no wonder that orgasm often was painful for me. I used to think that it was natural for the climax to be painful. I climaxed early in sex because the pressure of all those other hidden feelings were pushing for release faster than I could control them. Early in my life it took the form of wetting the bed. But it wasn't control I needed to learn either in my bed wetting or in premature ejaculation. I needed to feel all those suppressed feelings and so to rid myself of all that horrible constant pressure.'

When he could no longer make those old feelings sexual, he became much less sexually motivated and his sex drive diminished radically. That same pressure could just as easily (given the right early conditions) produce the constant need to talk – to use the mouth as a spillway for great tension. The person does not talk out of feeling like talking; he talks out of tension. You can sense the difference because it is easy to lose interest in someone who is yakking to fulfil an old inner need and hard to lose interest in someone who truly feels what he is saying. The neurotic talker is not talking to anyone else; he is talking to his need (really to his parents). Here again, we see the cruel paradox. A person *must* talk because he was never listened to, and his neurotic talk alienates people and only heightens his need (and compulsion) to talk all the more. He cannot feel what he says until he can stop talking out of old need, and he cannot do that until he *feels* the great Pain of that need.

The neurotic is sensation-bound until he feels. He will

either seek pleasant sensations to ease the unconscious painful ones or will suffer those painful sensations here and there in his body, believing he has a real physical malady. Those who drink liquor to ease the knot in their guts may be keeping away something more serious (such as an ulcer). Those with few acting-out outlets to ease inner pain may have to suffer those pains physically. The neurotic may not drink liquor but uses another pain-killer, pills, to ease his suffering. It is all the same. It is the same because all suppressed feelings are painful, by definition. So whether the neurotic is enjoying the weightlessness of SCUBA diving, the colour of a painting, the euphoria of alcohol, or the relief from a pill, he is in the constant process of exchanging one (painful) sensation for another. Until he connects that tight sensation in his neck (which becomes pain soon enough) with the more profound feeling, he must spend his life in the sensation exchange.

The sensation exchange is largely what is behind compulsive sex or compulsive anything. Orgasm for the neurotic becomes a narcotic, a sedative. Take away that symbolic acting out (the sedative) and the organism suffers.

Why is it that the neurotic is sensation-bound? Because nobody recognised his feelings. Children may suffer *allowable hurts*. They may have stomach aches, for example, but not emotional aches – being sad. So the child must hurt where he is directed to hurt; he must act out symbolically when all he is trying to say to his parents is 'I'm sad'.

To illustrate my point, let us examine an incident in the life of one of my patients. A young man is getting married. At the wedding reception he is suddenly seized by an older man, an old friend, who hugs him tenderly and wishes him well. The young man is inexplicably overcome by a deep sadness and weeps uncontrollably while clutching the older man. The young man has no idea of what has happened to him.

Primal Theory would suggest that the hug by the older man touched off an old hurt in the younger man. This patient reported never having had a warm father who would hold him or wish him well – someone who cared and who would be truly happy at his happiness. The deep void had been carried around by the young man without feeling it until warmth set off his Pain.

What the young man was feeling was a fragment of a total feeling which, if felt completely, would have inundated him with Pain beyond the deep sadness he felt at the moment. Though he received the warmth that day, it will not alter that Pain until the man is able to lie down and feel every bit of the feeling, and more important, conceptualise his hurt. His struggle began when he first glimpsed that he could not have a warm daddy. He began to act independent, as though he really didn't need warmth from his father. As long as he could avoid warmth (exactly what he needed), he could avoid hurt. The sudden warmth of the older man caught him unawares at an emotional and vulnerable moment– his wedding.

Another patient described what happened to her feelings in this way:

'It is as if I drew a circle around that image of me that was not wanted, not to be seen or heard, and confined it to forgetfulness. But it was all my own feelings that went with that pain of not being wanted. Along with my feelings went love, strength and desire. I no longer existed. When I turned to look for that self, there was an emptiness, a nothingness. I died in their hate and rejection. Reality to me was feeling the reality of myself despised.'

When the neurotic becomes disengaged from his Pain, I believe he stops feeling in a complete way. The neurotic, until he really feels again, doesn't know that he isn't feeling. Thus, it is not possible to convince a neurotic that he is unfeeling. Feeling again seems to be the sole convincing factor. Until that happens, the neurotic might properly reply that he recently saw a tragic scene in a movie that moved him to tears. 'Surely, that is feeling', he might say. But the person was not feeling his own personal sadness, and therefore, it would not be considered a full feeling. If he were to relate that movie scene to the exact conditions of his life, he might have a Primal right in the theatre. Indeed, many Primals have begun when a patient discusses a movie scene that made him cry. However, the feeling in the theatre and the subsequent feeling in the office are two disparate phenomena.

Tears in a movie are a fragment of the denied past of the neurotic. They are generally the result of the release of feeling rather than the expansion into total Primal feelings. The release process is what helps make the complete feeling unfelt. It vitiates and aborts the feeling and thus mitigates the hurt.

The same explanation applies to the person who blows up frequently. Surely, he is feeling anger and expressing it, isn't he? But unless that anger, which is being siphoned off in bits and pieces each day against *apparent* targets, is felt and connected to its initial context, it cannot be feeling in the Primal sense.

Take the individual who explodes because he has been kept waiting the slightest amount of time. He might well be the adult whose parents constantly kept him waiting when he was a child. Later in life anything that simulates his parents' earlier inattention might well set off an anger vastly out of proportion to the situation. Unfortunately, similar lack of attention from other people will continue to produce anger until he is able to experience the correct context of his initial angry feelings.

Until then the anger cannot be considered a real feeling since its targets are only symbols and do not constitute the reality that gave rise to the anger. His blow-ups, therefore, are symbolic, neurotic acts.

Feelings follow the all-or-none principle, in my view. Anything that evokes feeling will cause it to be felt all over the body. To a neurotic, however, eroticism will often provide localised sensations in the genitalia, rather than full bodily sexual feelings which are felt from the head to the toes. The fragmentation of the neurotic accounts for his choked laughter, his suppressed sneezes, and speech which seems to ooze out of the mouth without any relation to the rest of the face. Not every neurotic suffers in these precise ways, but the fragmentation process will find some form to express itself.

There are a number of expressions that are commonly called feelings, but which I do not believe are. The 'feeling' of *guilt* is one. A neurotic might say, 'I feel just horrible about that lie; I'm so guilty!' I would view guilt as the flight from feeling (Pain) because it sets in motion behaviours designed to ease tension. A healthy person who has done wrong would feel the full impact of that wrong and try to correct the situation.

I believe that at its base guilt is no more than *fear* of loss of parental love. One patient during a Primal said that he was furious at his father for having left him early in his life. He said that he felt like an angry lion in his belly and like a cowed pussy in his mouth. Guilt, he said, kept him from screaming his anger. When he felt what it really was, he found that he was afraid to tell off his father once and for all for fear of never getting him back. Guilt motivation, then, is seen as behaviour in response to fear.

Depression is often thought of as a feeling. Post-Primal patients do not report depressions. They have feelings of sadness at one event or another, but those feelings are specific to a situation. In my observation, depression is a mask for very deep and painful feelings which cannot be connected by the person. Indeed, some neurotics are willing to kill themselves before they would feel those feelings. Depression is a *mood*, close to the Primal feelings, but still remains experienced as uncomfortable bodily sensations ('I'm down. I feel black. There's a weight on my chest, a tight band across my chest,' etc.) because there is no connection to the early source of the mood. Connection changes moods to feelings, and this is why post-Primal patients have no moods, only feelings. When depressions are measured with an electromyograph, they exhibit a very high level of tension, which shows that depression is a *disconnected* feeling. Recently, Dr Frederick Snyder of the National Institute of Mental Health recorded the sleep pattern of depressive patients. Depressives begin their dream activity almost as soon as they fall asleep, and the sleep is truncated and fragmented. Depressives tend to sleep less than others, additional evidence of the tension involved in depression.[2]

Any trivial event might trigger a depression. One patient went to a party and left early, depressed. No one had talked to her or seemed interested enough to sit with her. The depression lasted for days and it became clear that she was no longer responding to something at the party. The party had evidently set off an old, covered feeling that her parents were never interested enough in her to sit down and talk to her. When she had a Primal in which she begged them to do it,

[2] G. B. Whatmore, 'Tension Factors in Schizophrenia and Depression', in E. Jacobson, ed., *Tension in Medicine* (Springfield, Ill., Charles Thomas, 1967).

her depression disappeared. Some may push themselves out of depression by going shopping, by making plans for a date or a party, but the depression will lurk, waiting until these activities are over. Depression will continue to plague the person until the real feelings weighing him down are felt.

There are other pseudo-feelings. Here is an example of 'rejection':

During a training session, I criticised a young psychologist's written report as inaccurate. He began a wave of defences. 'I didn't mean it the way you took it. Besides, that report is not finalised,' etc. etc. When I asked him what he felt, he said, 'Rejected'. What he really felt were old buried feelings of rejection by his father ('Nothing I could do is good enough to get you to love me'). To keep from feeling that whole hurt, however, he threw up a smokescreen of explanations, projections, excuses to ward off that Primal hurt. He did not discuss the inaccuracies in his report. Those errors meant to him that he was no good and that he would not be loved. The incipient feeling of rejection was not fully felt. Rather, it started behaviour in motion to cover feeling.

What the young psychologist was really doing was covering the *old* feeling triggered off by the *current* criticism. There was nothing so inherently painful in writing an inaccurate report which would justify all those denials and excuses. He made excuses about his report to keep Primal Pain away. He did start to feel something – rejected – the old, real rejection, but he covered *feeling*, and this is why I say the neurotic does not fully feel. He is split off from his childhood and his childhood feelings so he cannot have a total feeling experience. Each new insult or criticism he receives as an adult sets off fragments of the old Pain. But to feel really rejected means to be writhing in pain during a Primal – to feel utterly alone and unwanted as that child. Once that is felt, there are no more feelings of 'rejection' – only feelings about what is going on in the current moment. Thus, when a woman snubs him at a social gathering, the person will feel: 'She didn't like me', or 'She is really uptight today'; he will not feel 'rejected' in the neurotic sense of the term. This means that there is no history of rejection to make a snub an all-day upset.

Shame is another pseudo-feeling. Let us say a grown man cries and then feels ashamed for what he did. He really feels that he won't be approved of for acting 'weak'. He tries to cover his act ('I feel so ashamed') with an apology for misbehaviour so that he *won't* feel unloved. In this sense, the unreal self, having absorbed the values of parents (and later of society), is putting down the real self.

Pride is the unreal self succeeding. Pride is a non-feeling. It is pointing to something, some act, which, often unconsciously, makes 'them' proud. It is the performance for them. Feeling people do not need a performance in order to feel. What the neurotic does to feel proud changes with his age. At two it is keeping his diapers dry, and at thirty it is killing an elephant. The same need may drive both behaviours. The need remains constant. What we do as we grow older is spin ever-widening circles of defences around the need until we are lost in a maze of symbolic activities.

When the neurotic thinks he is having tremendous feelings about some current situation in his life, the intensity of that feeling is the added weight of the Primal Pool. When that pool is emptied out methodically in Primal Therapy, the person discovers how non-intense his feelings really are. When his clothes are not cleaned properly at the cleaners, he may be annoyed, but not furious. The emptied-out neurotic will also learn how few are the feelings of man. Stripped of shame, guilt, rejection and all the other pseudo-feelings, he will understand that the pseudo-feelings are but synonyms for the covered great Primal feeling of being unloved.

Even when a neurotic thinks he is having a great emotional experience, in a standard therapy group, for example, he has no conception of the tremendous power and range of neurotic suppressed feeling. Tears and sobs in conventional group therapy are but the tiny affluvia of that gigantic, still-dormant inner volcano composed of thousands of denied and compacted experiences pressing for release. Primal Therapy unleashes that volcano in steps. Once those denials are felt, there are no longer these great emotional depths we have come to expect in man. The Primal view of a feeling tends to be at polar opposites from the usual lay view. Terribly emotional people are usually acting out suppressed feelings from the past and do not feel the present. Normal people, bereft of the past suppressions, feel only the present, and that present is not nearly as volatile as neurotic emotionality because there is no repressed force behind it.

Thus, the neurotic may laugh explosively because there *is* an explosion inside. Or, he may not be able to laugh at all spontaneously because he is still back there in some kind of sadness. In the first case, the neurotic has covered a feeling and diverted it into laughter; in the second instance, laughter (as well as sadness) may have been suppressed by a person who has flattened out *all* his emotions. What the layman has often come to see as real feelings are but strong reactions to hurt – anger, fear, jealousy, pride and so on.

In standard therapy, even the position of sitting up in a chair facing the therapist would militate against having these convulsive feeling experiences. Nor are these feelings the result of some kind of therapeutic confrontation between patient and therapist. The only confrontation in Primal Therapy is between the real and unreal selves.

The fact is that the neurotic is a totally feeling person; only his feelings are kept locked away by tension. He is constantly full of these old unresolved feelings surging for final connection, which emerge as tension. For the neurotic to fully feel again, he must go back and feel what he wasn't. Thus, he may try hugging and physical touching in a special therapeutic encounter group and believe that he is breaking down the barriers between himself and others or having a warm experience – a 'getting the feel of others'. But there is no way for an unfeeling person to get a feel of anyone else, no matter how much hugging goes on. First we learn to feel ourselves; *then* we can feel ourselves feeling others. A blocked person could conceivably touch someone else all day long and feel nothing. Not exactly 'nothing' – he will feel the old hurt, perhaps of not having any warmth early in his life; only he won't know that is what he is feeling. Being sensual, in my sense of the word, is to have one's total sensorium open to stimuli. When this is lacking, we find such instances as a frigid woman hopping into bed with any number of men and *still* feeling nothing.

The point is that feeling barriers are usually not *between* people, except in an indirect way; the barriers are internal. The barrier, shield, or 'membrane' which so many neurotics live behind is the result of thousands of experiences where feelings and responses were suppressed. That barrier has grown thicker as each new feeling has been shut off. There is no single dramatic way to break that barrier. There is only going back and feeling each major denied hurt and in this way chipping away at the dam of denials until one day there is no more barrier – no more unreal self to filter and fog vivid experience. Thus, the closer one is to oneself, the closer one can become to others.

Symbolic ways of breaking the barriers which people have erected internally cannot resolve *real* feelings. For example, one popular technique is to have people gather in a circle with one person in the middle. He learns to 'break out' by crashing through the circle of people who are arm in arm. I suppose the person is theoretically learning how to be free by this act. One rationale often given is that the person is learning how to liberate himself. This seems to be magic: 'If I do this ritual, I will solve my real problems.' I suppose that this ritual is designed to enable the person to feel truly free. But until he feels what is really constricting him, I believe that this ritual is encouraging the neurosis by encouraging symbolic acting out. It seems to be no different from the neurotic who is skydiving in order to *feel free*. I am sure that there is a momentary release of tension through the symbolic ritual, but it scarcely can dent the rigid defence system.

What this all amounts to is that actions of a neurotic, no matter what they are, cannot undo neurosis. The neurotic may touch but not feel, listen but not hear, see but not perceive. He may go in for sensitivity exercises such as fondling others to develop his sense of touch. But only when he can feel these experiences will he have real meaning, and by then he won't need special sensitivity exercises to help him feel.

The Primal view of feeling is considerably different from other views. If, during a sensitivity training session, someone were to hold another person's hand in an empathic gesture, it would normally be simply a warm interpersonal experience. But what happens to the neurotic in such a situation is that the touch sparks, but does not fully ignite, powerful Primal needs which have no name but which make the person often feel 'zapped'. Why? Because what is a simple human affectionate act, a nice sensation, becomes plunged in the deep emotional bank of a neglected, sterile childhood, adding extraordinary resonance and power to the experience. Because that power is not conceptualised, it tends to be an isolated experience in which the person may be overcome with emotion or in which he feels some ineffable mystical sensations which he may label a peak experience. Primal Therapy both ignites that stored powerhouse of feeling and *couples it with conceptualisation.* After that, the experience can be what it is – a touch – and not what a history of neglect has made it into. Here we see how exaggerated, neurotic response (what the neurotic *thinks* is real feeling) is what is created by unfulfilled need.

I believe that there are levels of defences or, rather, layers of defences which allow some people to be closer to their feelings than others. It depends on how the family constellation aligned itself, the cultural milieu, as well as the general constitutional makeup of the person. There are some families in which no feeling at all is allowed; others in which sex but no angry feelings are permitted. Generally, however, neurotic parents are anti-feeling, and how much of themselves they have had to cancel out in order to survive is a good index of how much they will attempt to cancel out in their children. Often it isn't a deliberate stamping-out process. It may be the constant shushing when children are exuberant, the look in the parent's eyes when the children grumble or complain, the embarrassment when the children discuss sex or when the daughter shows her body in the bath. It may be in the no-nonsense approach of a father who pooh-poohs his son's fears or his daughter's sadness. It may be the mother so beaten by life that she cannot tolerate or permit her own daughter to express her helplessness and need for protection. It's in the 'Don't you ever talk that way again!', the 'Don't dwell on failure, my boy, think success', or in the 'What's the matter, sissy? Can't you take it?'; it is found in the thousands of trivial experiences in which children can never be allowed to be grumpy, critical, excitedly happy, or furious. Or, more tragically, it may be in the simple fact that there was no one there to tell one's feelings to – a working mother, a sick parent too ill to help or listen, or a father too preoccupied with making a living to pay attention. It all adds up to the same thing – the real hurt self locked away by Pain.

I believe that in the field of psychology there has been a good deal of confusion over whatever happened to the neurotic's feelings. Some say that he never really developed the full capacity to feel. Others believe that the early feelings are buried and cannot be retrieved. It is my contention that the ability to feel cannot be irrevocably damaged. Indeed, the neurotic seems to be a walking Primal in the sense that his feelings are with him each minute of the day. They show up in his high blood pressure, his allergies, his headaches, in the tight skeletal muscles, in the set of his jaw, the squint of his eyes, the frown on his face, the sound of his voice, the way he walks. What we previously have not been able to do is retrieve those fragmented feelings from the symptomatic spillways and piece them back together into one complete and clear feeling.

I believe the way to retrieve those feelings is through the Primal Method, which shall be discussed next.

8

The Cure

New Primal patients are prepared in advance for the fact that this is not an ordinary treatment procedure. In a telephone conversation they describe the nature of the problem and provide a quick history of previous physical problems. The patient is then asked to get a thorough physical examination to rule out any physiological contra-indications for Primal Therapy such as organic brain pathology. If any psychosis is suspected, a personal interview is held. The patient is asked to write a letter about himself in which he describes his life, family history, problems, previous therapy, and why he wants Primal Therapy. In most cases, no personal interview is given before the treatment begins. Usually, it is not necessary because the person has been referred either by a friend who has been through Primal Therapy or by his physician, who explains the therapy to him. By the time he begins he already knows a good deal about what to expect.

After our first phone contact and receipt of the letter, the patient is sent a list of instructions (see Appendix B). These instructions specify that he must give up all alcohol, cigarettes and drugs for the duration of Primal Therapy, a period of several months. He is told he will have three weeks of individual treatment where he is seen daily, followed by several months of group sessions. He is asked not to work or go to school during his first three weeks. He will need all his energy for the therapy; he will also often be too upset to work even if he wanted to.

The new patient will be *the only person seen* for individual therapy during the three weeks. He will be given all the time he needs each day; only his feelings will determine when the session ends. Generally, sessions last between two to three hours; rarely is anyone seen for fewer than two hours or more than three and a half. Primal Therapy is much more economical than conventional insight therapy – not only in financial terms but also in the time involved. The total financial outlay is about one-fifth the cost of a psycho-analysis.

Twenty-four hours before we begin, the patient is isolated in a hotel room and asked not to leave that room until his therapy hour the following day. He may not read, watch television, or make phone calls during this twenty-four-hour period. He is permitted to write. If we have reason to believe that this is a well-defended patient, we ask that he stay up all night. This technique may be used occasionally during the first two weeks of individual therapy.

The isolation and sleeplessness are important techniques which often bring patients close to a Primal. The aim of the isolation is to deprive the patient of all his usual outlets for tension, while the sleeplessness tends to weaken his remaining defences; he has fewer resources to fight off his feelings. The aim is not to allow the patient to become distracted from himself. One patient told me, 'Halfway through the night I began doing push-ups. Every time I stopped and looked out of the hotel window I began sobbing and I didn't know why.' Another patient had a panic attack and had to call me at midnight for reassurance that she wasn't going crazy. Aloneness often can make the neurotic desperate. For many patients that night in the hotel room is the first time in years that they have sat still, been completely alone, and thought about themselves. There is no place to go and nothing to do. There is no place to act out the unreality. One of the important functions of keeping the patient awake during the night is to prevent him from acting out his unreality in his dreams. Lack of sleep helps crumble defences, partly because plain fatigue renders the person less able to carry on his act, but mainly because he cannot act out symbolically via his dreams, and thus is unable to relieve tension. By stopping this symbolic act, awake and asleep, we bring the person closer to his feelings. In addition to this point, a number of research studies have found that isolation itself lowers one's threshold for pain.

THE FIRST HOUR

The patient arrives suffering. He is neither smoking nor taking tranquillisers, and he is tired and apprehensive. He is not sure what to expect. He may be kept waiting five to ten minutes beyond his appointed time in order to allow more tension to build. The soundproof office is semi-darkened; the phone is off the hook. The patient lies on the couch. He is instructed to lie spread-eagled because I want the body in as defenceless a physical position as possible. The importance of position and carriage was brought home to me by observing new jailbirds who often spend their first days in jail with their legs crossed, arms folded across the abdomen and body hunched over their knees, as if to protect themselves against their aloneness, despair and hurt. What happens from this point, of course, depends on the individual patient. The following is a typical example:

The patient will discuss his tension and problems; his impotence, headaches, depression and general unhappiness. He might say, 'What's the use of it all?' or 'Everyone is so sick; there's no one left!' or 'I'm tired of being alone! I can't make friends, and when I do, I tire of them!' The point is that the patient is unhappy and suffering. If he is very tense and afraid, I will ask him to let that feeling overtake him. If he gets panicked, I encourage him to call one of his parents for help. On occasion that will produce a painful feeling within the first fifteen minutes of his first session. I will ask him to discuss his early life. He will say that he cannot remember very much. I push for whatever can be remembered. The patient will then begin to talk about his early life.

As he speaks, I am gathering information. The patient is revealing his defence system in two ways. First, in the way he talks. He may be intellectualising, showing almost no feeling, using abstractions, and, in general, acting as though he were an observer of his life rather than someone who has lived it. Because he is using his 'personality' (or unreal self) to describe his life, we look carefully for what *it* is saying. The cautious person, who hedges and modifies the therapist's questions, may be saying, 'Don't hurt me any more. I won't feel until you stop hurting me.'

As he talks the patient is also telling us about how he handled things at home: 'I used to clam up when he said that.' 'I wouldn't give him the satisfaction of knowing he hurt me.' 'Mother was such a baby I had to take over and pretty much be the mother.' 'Dad was always so accusatory that I had to have fast answers.' 'I could never be right.' 'There was no affection.'

The patient is encouraged to sink into an early situation that seems to have evoked a good deal of feeling in him. 'I was sitting there, letting him beat up my brother and – Gee, I feel tense ... I don't know what it is ...' He is again encouraged to sink into the feeling. He may not discover what the feeling is, or he may say, 'I think I began to feel that this thing could happen to me if I spoke back like my brother did ... Ooh, I've got a knot in my stomach. Was I afraid?' The patient begins to twitch a bit. He moves his legs and hands. His eyelids flutter, and his brow is furrowed. He sighs or grinds his teeth. I urge him to: 'Feel that! Stay with it!' Sometimes he will say, 'It's gone. The feeling has passed.' This sparring process may go on for hours or days, but here I will telescope the situation and assume that the feeling stays so we can go on to the next stage.

'I feel tight all over. Yeah, I think I was really afraid of the old man' may be the patient's next statement. At this point, when I see that he is into the feeling and is holding on tight, I will ask him to breathe deeply and hard from the belly. I will say, 'Open your mouth as wide as possible and keep it that way! Now pull, pull that feeling from your belly!' The patient will begin to breathe deeply, writhing and then shaking. When the breathing seems to be happening automatically, I will urge, 'Tell Daddy you're afraid!' 'I'm not going to tell that son of a bitch anything!' he may answer. I urge him on. 'Say it! Say It!' Usually, during the first hour, as simple as that task seems, the patient will not be able to say it. If he does scream it out, it will usually bring a stream of tears and stomach-wrenching gasps. He may immediately begin talking afterwards about the kind of person his father was. Chances are good that he will also have several insights as he speaks.

This initial reaction is called the pre-Primal. The pre-Primals may go on for several days or even a week or so. It is essentially a chipping-away process, the aim of which is to open up the patient and get him ready to have him surrender his defence system. No one simply comes in and allows that to happen. The body gives up neurosis in begrudging stages.

After possibly fifteen minutes the patient is calm again and may start 'rapping', his usual style of non-communication: *his* talk, devoid of feeling. Again, he is led into a particularly painful situation from his past. The therapist is also challenging every display of the patient's defence. For example, if the patient is talking softly, he is made to speak up. If he is intellectual, his intellectualisation is called at every turn. For the patient who is far from his feelings, who lives 'in his head', it usually isn't possible to get at a pre-Primal for several days. Nevertheless, we make constant stabs at it throughout each session.

The intellectualiser's first hour, for example, may be much like a standard therapy session: discussion, history, questions and clarification. In no case are ideas discussed. We do not discuss Primal theory or its validity, as many patients would like to do. Each day an attempt is made to widen the hole in the defence system until the patient can no longer defend himself. His first few days of therapy seem to parallel the first few years of the patient's life, before the occurrence of the Primal Scene that shut him down. He experiences isolated and discrete events in bits and pieces. As each fragment combines into a meaningful whole, the patient goes into his Primal.

If the patient is being bright, humble, polite, obsequious, hostile, dramatic – whatever the front he presents – it is forbidden in an effort to get him beyond the defence and into the feeling. If the patient raises his knees or turns his head, he is made to lie straight. He may giggle or yawn as feelings rise, and this is immediately pointed out with impatience. He may try to change the subject, and that is stopped. Or he may literally swallow the feeling, as is true with many patients who swallow each time a feeling starts to come up. This is one reason we keep the mouth open.

As the patient discusses a new, early situation, we continue watching for signs of feeling. The voice may tremble slightly as if jostled by tension. We repeat the process of urging the patient to breathe and feel. This time, which may be an hour or two later, the patient is shaken. He won't know what the feeling is, just that he feels tense and 'uptight' – that is, tightened up against the feeling. I start the pulling and breathing process. The patient swears that he doesn't know what the feeling is. His throat becomes tight, and his chest feels as though there were a band around it. He begins gagging and retching. He says, 'I'm going to throw up!' I inform him that it is a feeling and that he won't throw up. (No patient has actually vomited despite long periods of gagging.) I urge him to say the feeling even though the patient doesn't know what he is feeling. He will start to form a word only to begin thrashing about and writhing in Pain. I urge him to let it out, and he will continue to try to say something. Finally, out it will come: a scream – 'Daddy, be nice!' 'Mommy, help!' – or just the word 'hate': 'I hate you, I hate you!' This is the Primal Scream. It comes out in shuddering gasps, pushed out by the force of years of suppressions and denials of that feeling. Sometimes the scream is only 'Mommy!' or 'Daddy!' Just saying those words brings with it torrents of Pain since many 'mommies' would not even permit their children to call them anything but 'Mother'. Letting down and being that little child who needs a 'mommy' helps release all the stored-up feeling.

The scream is at once a scream from the Pain and a liberating event where the person's defence system is dramatically opened up. It results from the pressure of holding the real self back, possibly for decades. It is largely an involuntary act. That scream is felt all over the body. Many describe it as a lightning bolt that seems to break apart all the unconscious control of the body. I discuss the scream and its meaning in greater detail in a later chapter. Suffice to note here that the Primal Scream is both the cause and result of a crumbling defence system.

During the first hour I will sometimes have the patient talk only to his parents. To tell me *about* them automatically removes the patient one step from his feelings, very much like two grown-ups having a discussion. So the patient may say something like, 'Dad, I remember when you were teaching me how to swim and you yelled at me because I was afraid to put my head underwater. Finally, you dunked me under.' At this point, the patient might turn to me with anger and say, 'Can you imagine that stupid son of a bitch dunking a six-year-old under the water?' I say, 'Tell him what you feel!' and he does, unloosing a tirade and screaming his fear as that six-year-old. This will lead to other associations, and he is now into some feeling. He will begin to discuss how his father tried to teach him other things and how fearful he was: 'Once there was this big horse and I didn't know how to ride and he made me get up anyway. The horse bolted and started to run away. The guide caught up with us and stopped the horse. My dad

didn't say a word.' Again, I direct him to tell his father his
feelings. His associations may keep him on the lessons in his
life or the fearful situations where his father refused to let
him be afraid. Or it may suddenly switch to his mother.
'Why didn't she stop him? She was so weak. She never protected me from him.' The patient now learns and directs
himself to her. 'Mommy, help me, I need help. I'm afraid!'
This may give way to even deeper feelings: sobs, tears and
an abdominal wrenching. More associations about the time
she never protected him from the 'monster'. More insights
about how childish and fearful Mother was. How she was
too weak to help out and so on. After two or three hours of
this the patient is exhausted, and we stop for the day.

The patient returns to his hotel room. He knows that I am
on constant call should he need me, and during the first
week he may want to come back again for another session
later in the same day because of his high level of anxiety.
After the first week, this is less the case. He still may not
watch television or go to the movies. He really does not
want to because he is consumed with himself.

THE SECOND DAY

The patient walks in spouting insights. 'It's like my whole
mind exploded,' he may say. 'I figured so much out last
night. I hardly slept, and I don't feel like eating. When I did
sleep, I dreamed and dreamed.' He begins right in because
everything is coming up. He tells me about memories he has
forgotten, talks about more painful situations that he
neglected to mention in the first hour. He may begin weeping within the first ten minutes and again is discussing memories and insights interchangeably. He seems in great pain,
yet will say, as nearly every patient says, 'I couldn't wait to
get here today'. Again, we are stabbing at the defence
system. He is not allowed to wander off the subject if we
suspect he is avoiding something. Nor is he allowed to sit up
and 'rap'. We again hook into a painful memory: 'Once
Mother took me shopping with her and two women friends,
and she put a bow in my hair and said to her friends, "Don't
you think he'd be a beautiful girl?"' 'I'm a boy, you
dummy!' he'll scream. And then he'll discuss the ways that
his mother tried to make him feminine. More memories,

insights and feelings aimed at her. Then he'll discuss her
background. What made her the way she is. Why she married such an effeminate man. Then, another memory. 'I was
going off to the Army, and she was kissing me good-bye. She
stuck her tongue in my mouth. Can you imagine? My own
mother. My God! She always wanted me instead of Father.
Mother! Leave me alone! Leave me alone! I'm your son!'
Then he might say, 'Now I see why she was down on my
girlfriends. She wanted me for her. God, is that sick! Now I
remember when we went on a picnic and we ran away and
hid from my father and she put her head in my lap. I felt
funny. Sick, kind of. Ooh! Mother was seducing me. I got
sick and threw up and didn't know why. Now I know. She
turned me against my father. The one decent thing in my
life. Ooh, you bitch! you bitch!' Now the patient may be
rolling on the floor, writhing and gasping, 'Hate, hate, hate,
hate. Ooh, ooh!' He screams how he wants to kill her. '*Tell
her*,' I say. He begins pounding the floor, out of control with
rage which may go on for fifteen or twenty minutes. Finally,
it ends. He is exhausted, too tired to talk, and we end the
second session.

THE THIRD DAY

The patient is becoming defenceless. Sometimes he begins
crying while he is walking into the office. Other times I find
him on the floor of the waiting room sobbing. 'I can't take
all the pain', he will complain. 'It's too much. I can't read
anything because I'm awash in memories and insights. How
long does this go on?' Back again we go to the process of
evoking feelings. 'I remember once my dad got mad at me
because I wouldn't do what my mother had asked. I was
only eight. I told him to shut up. He warned me never to say
that to him again. I said it again. He picked up the broom
and began to swing it at me. I ran. He chased me and caught
me and began to thrash me. My God! He's going to kill me.
Daddy hates me. He wants me out of the way. Stop, Daddy,
stop!' The patient may be totally engulfed by the feeling
now. He has rolled off the couch onto the floor and is
screaming, amid violent abdominal convulsions, that his
father is going to kill him. He may be gagging and perspiring, trying to scream, but he can't get it out. More gag-

ging and retching and screaming that he is going to die. Finally: 'I'll be good, Daddy, I won't talk bad!' And he doesn't again. He becomes a good little boy. What he underwent was a Primal. *A total feeling-thought experience from the past.* It is over in a matter of minutes and appears to be inordinately painful. That patient is not discussing his feelings. He is feeling them.

A Primal is a totally engulfing experience. The patient is almost unaware of where he is at the moment. What he experienced during the first two days of his therapy are what I call pre-Primals. They are major feelings from the past, yet not completely engulfing. This is not to say that a total Primal does not happen in the first hour. While possible, it is not the rule. Sometimes a full Primal does not take place for weeks. When it does happen, it seems to crack open the thought-feeling barrier, the person becomes open to all sorts of feelings and begins to have spontaneous Primals outside therapy. From that point on the patient is on the road to health.

As each day passes, he is likely to have deeper experiences until he reaches that point where the critical balance between the unreal and real selves is altered in favour of the real self, allowing a complete feeling experience. From that time on he will be engulfed by past painful situations and have many more Primals extending over a period of months. This is not to say, however, that the person is completely real. Each Primal lessens the unreal self and broadens the real self. When the Major Pains have been felt, there will be no more unreal self, and we can say that the patient is normal. Our job is to evoke Pains in order to produce a real feeling person.

AFTER THE THIRD DAY

The process of treatment during the ensuing three weeks continues largely as already described. There are plateaus on which the patient doesn't seem to be feeling much or has 'gone dry'. Sometimes he is simply in a refractory period in which the body is resting from days of Pain. The organism is an excellent regulator of Pain, and we take care not to push a patient into more hurt while he is in the refractory period.

Sometimes the patient is simply resisting facing his feelings, his defence system still being obdurate. Though the patient has left the hotel room after the first week, as a rule, we may again ask him to return there and have him stay awake all night. The attempt is to weaken the defences again.

Each new day of therapy is described by some patients as a stripping away of layers of defences. This process gains momentum because feeling one bit of Pain paves the way for the patient to tolerate more. Each Primal seems to break open new hidden memories leading to additional Primals. Succeeding Primals may increasingly envelop the whole organism as more defences are lost. The body will allow itself to feel only so much Pain at a time, so if the patient is not hurried, Primals will take place in an ordered and safe sequence. Forcing a patient to try to feel more than he can handle will only result in having him shut off again.

What usually happens in the Primal sequence is that as the days go on, the patient goes farther back into his childhood. It is common to hear the exact voice of the age being relived – the lisp, the baby talk, and, eventually, the infantile cry.

Observing all this led me to understand the relationship of Pain and memory, because once Pain is out of the way, memories of post-Primal patients begin within a few months of birth. These observations also led me to understand the enormous impact of the first three years of life. This is not a new discovery; Freud made this known at the beginning of this century. But the nature of the trauma is so subtle: being left wet in a crib, helpless; being picked up and handled abruptly; neglected and left to cry and cry for hours; lying in a crib exposed (defenceless) to strident parental voices that constantly disrupt the child's calm; not being fed when hungry; not being allowed to nurse – and when allowed, not being allowed to wean in a natural way, but weaned by a timetable.

And the trauma results from a difficult birth itself, which will require us to take a new look at Otto Rank, who wrote about birth trauma early in this century. Only Rank believed birth itself is traumatic (leaving the warmth and security of the womb behind), while I believe that it is *traumatic* birth which is traumatic. Birth is a natural process, and I do not believe that anything natural can be traumatic.

I have seen a Primal where a woman was bunched up in a ball, gurgling, almost choking, spitting up fluid, and then straightening out and wailing like a newborn. When she came out of it, she felt that she had relived her very difficult birth, in which she was indeed filled with fluid and almost choked to death. Another person relived his long birth (his mother was in labour some twenty hours). After feeling what a struggle it was to come alive, he knew that his struggle began at birth and never ended: 'It was like my mother was going to make it hard for me from the beginning,' he said.

Another Primal I observed was instructive in this regard. A woman kept having the feeling that she was uncomfortable and unhappy and didn't know why. She kept wailing, 'I can't cry, I can't cry'. Suddenly, she relived an experience, and tears gushed out of her eyes; that experience was having an operation on her tear ducts at the age of one year to remove a blockage which had occurred after birth. This woman was now in her thirties and able to cry; yet while reliving events before the age of her operation, she could not shed a tear in my office.

This indicates that even in preverbal state, trauma exists. It isn't just how the mother or father screamed at the child which produces neurosis; trauma seems to be laid down in the nervous system and remembered *organismically*. The physical system 'knows' it is being traumatised even when there is no accompanying consciousness. And again, it is not enough to *know* about these occurrences; if they were traumatic, they must be relived and *experienced* fully in order to be resolved from their continuing effect on the organism.

Beginning with the second of the three-week period, Primals will usually occur almost daily. There is a primal style which is unique for each person. Some patients need to talk their way into feeling; others will start with a bodily feeling which is momentarily inexplicable and later hook it up with some memory. Just before the main connection which is so painful, some patients will grasp the couch, others will clutch their stomachs, and still others will begin to roll their heads, teeth chattering and perspiring profusely. Some patients will double up with the Pain, others will curl in a corner of the couch, and some will fall off the couch onto the floor convulsing.

No two Primals are alike even for the same person. There are angry and violent ones, fearful ones and quiet, sad Primals. Whatever form it takes, the therapy is aimed at old unresolved feelings.

It is difficult to describe in words how different feelings can feel. One patient who had had conventional therapy said that although she had cried a great deal, it was a completely different experience from crying during a Primal. She used to cry to ease her hurt and make herself feel better, to protect the hurt self. She cried now *out of* her hurts, and those feelings are far more intense and enveloping. During a Primal, she said, she could feel her cry all the way to her toes.

Patients quickly learn during their therapy how to get into feelings. A patient may discuss a dream from the night before, tell it as though it were happening right then, feel the feeling of fright or helplessness, and quickly be out of control and connecting the feeling to its source. Being totally out of control permits connection because self-control nearly always means suppression of self. The patient wants that Pain because he knows that is the *only* way out of his neurosis. 'It's me hurting,' said one patient, 'and if I can feel me, that is all I want.'

After a while, there is little for the therapist to do except remain silent. When the patient is into a feeling, he is 'back there' reliving it – smelling the aromas, hearing the sounds and going through the bodily processes which occurred and were blocked in that early time. A patient who was loved for being so controlled and for almost never wetting his diaper at the age of one and a half suffered from the same terrible need to urinate during his Primal as he had while an infant. It must be remembered that the patient is totally into that past scene, and any talk by the therapist in the present may bring him out of it. Left alone, the feeling will transport the patient back to its beginnings, which cannot happen when the feeling is being *discussed* by the therapist and the patient.

There are a number of signs that are characteristic of a Primal. One is vocabulary. If the person uses words of young children, as is most often the case, it means that he is involved in a Primal. One PhD, for example, said during his Primal, 'Daddy, I ascared.' To me, this indicated that he was not playacting. If, however, the patient yells profanity, such as 'Daddy, you bastard!' during a Primal, there is a good chance that this is pre-Primal.

Another quality of the Primals is the way in which feeling more and more of one's infancy and childhood produces great maturity. This occurs because getting the past out of the system allows the person to be truly grown-up, not just *acting* adult. In short, he becomes what he is. Often a patient in a Primal will be into his infancy, wailing and crying like a year-old baby, and then come out of it with a new kind of voice, deeper and richer, instead of the thin, infantile voice he had before therapy.

When a patient has been reliving his past during a Primal, he tends to lose track of time. Patients will say something like 'It seems years ago since I came into the office this morning.' When I ask a patient to estimate how long he has been in the office, he may answer, 'I guess I've been here thirty years.' He seems not to have been living present time for the minutes or hours he was back in his former environment.

Patients describe these Primals as a conscious coma. Though they could come out of them any time they want, they prefer not to do so. They know where they are and what is going on, yet when inside the Primal, they are reliving past history and are engulfed by it. They have always been engulfed by this past, but they acted it out, rather than felt it. Even their dreams were usually dealing with the past. The Primal, then, puts the past back where it belongs, allowing the patient finally to live in the present.

THE PRIMAL SCREAM

The Primal Scream is not a scream for its own sake. Nor is it used as a tension release. When it results from deep, wracking feelings, I believe it is a curative process, rather than simply a release of tension. It is not the scream that is curative, in any case; it is the Pain. The scream is only one expression of the Pain. The Pain is the curative agent because it means that the person is feeling at last. At the moment that the patient feels the hurt, the Pain disappears. The neurotic has hurt because his body has been constantly set for the Pain. It was the tense apprehension that hurt.

The real Primal Scream is unmistakable. It has its own quality of something deep, rattling and involuntary. When the therapist suddenly removes any portion of defence and the patient is left naked with his Pain, he screams because he is wide open to his truth. Though the scream is the most usual reaction, it is neither the sole nor the perennial response to sudden vulnerability to Pain. Some people moan, groan, writhe and thrash about. The results are the same. What comes out when the person screams is a single feeling that may underlie thousands of previous experiences: 'Daddy, don't hurt me any more!'; 'Mama, I'm afraid!' Sometimes the patient just needs to scream at first. He screams for the hundreds of shushes, ridicules, humiliations and beatings. He screams now because often he was wounded and wasn't allowed the luxury of bleeding. It's as though someone kept jabbing him with a small pin and he could never once yell 'Ouch!'

THE RESISTANCE

Primal Therapy doesn't go as smoothly as I may have indicated. Defences themselves are resistance against feeling. Therefore, there is always a resistance of one kind or another as long as any part of the defence system remains. Many patients refuse to call out to parents. They may have had years of analysis and will say, 'Look, I worked that out years ago. I know what they are; there's no point to what you're asking.' I submit that they really don't know until they call. Patients are embarrassed by this 'puerile exercise'. 'It's pretty simplistic, don't you think?' was the comment of a young psychologist. Yet to know in the head that you were unloved is a split experience – a semi-experience in which the body does not take part. To ask for love is another matter. The neurotic struggle began because the child could no longer safely ask for love; asking brought rejection and Pain. Since the struggle is the continuous symbolic asking for love, to bring the person back to the straight question, 'Please love me, Mama,' is to push back the struggle and uncover the Pain.

Sometimes the resistance is physical. The person is asking

to breathe, and he does so backward. He seems to be pushing the air down instead of up and out. This inability to breathe out is often found in neurotics, particularly those repressed ones who had to hold everything in. The physical resistance seems to be automatic. The throat tightens up, the body doubles up, the patient rolls over and curls into a ball – all to shut off feeling. The point is that, no matter how uncomfortable it seems, no one simply lies down and sheds his neurosis.

If the patient persists in shallow breathing, I may occasionally press on his abdomen. This is rarely necessary, however. In no case would it be done until the patient is securely fastened into some feeling, because it is not the breathing we are after, but the feeling.

THE SYMBOLIC PRIMAL

Because excessive pain seems to be shut off automatically by our system, what seems to happen in the first few days of therapy is what I would call the Symbolic Primal. This is particularly true of older people with reinforcing layers of defence. The physical part of the Pain may be galvanised at first, but the patient cannot make a mental connection. He may, instead, feel a terrible pain in his back (symbolic of someone's being 'on his back'), or he will become partially paralysed (symbolic of his helplessness), or he may feel a weight on his shoulder (the burden he has been carrying, perhaps). The symbolism varies. One patient could not move his left side for half an hour: 'It's all that dead weight I've ben carrying around all of my life,' he said, soon after he began making connections.

When the patient has his neurotic behaviour curtailed by the Primal Therapist, the neurosis seems to retreat to the next line of defence, physical symbolism – that is, psychosomatic complaints. Here again, we find that physical pains are the result of early mental pain, and when those hurts are felt, the physical afflictions drop away.

Psychosomatic afflictions trouble almost every Primal patient early in his therapy, even those who have been relatively healthy before. One patient had diarrhoea after his first major Primal. He told me, 'Things are coming out of me faster than I know what they are.' When he knew and felt what they were, his diarrhoea stopped. When crucial feelings are blocked, the Pain seems to move against areas or parts of the body first. This is how we know that Pain is on the rise. As connections are made, psychosomatic hurts quickly fade.

One patient felt literally pulled in half during his second pre-Primal. His fists were clenched, and his arms were rigidly outstretched, taut and trembling. To watch this patient, one could see him being pulled from side to side. Yet this was symbolic behaviour – symbolic of feeling (and being) split but being un·ble to connect up to the causes of the split. Later he felt what was happening. He was reliving a scene when his parents were divorced. He felt how he wanted to go with his father but dared not feel that for fear of displeasing his mother . . . He felt how much he hated his mother but had to squelch the feeling because he would have to live only with her and be completely dependent on her . . . He felt the anger at his father for leaving that he had to cover in order to make his father come back and visit him . . . All these contradictions resulted in a physical pull of his body. They became physical because he dared not feel them directly. The feelings, then, were coded into the muscle system in terms of their *symbolic* value; he really was being torn in half by these conflicting feelings because feelings are real, physical things. To solve the pull, he had to go back and feel each separate element of the contradiction. It was not enough to 'know' that he was in conflict about the divorce.

The Primal explanation for the above is that denied memories – that is, happenings too painful to fully face – are laid down in the brain and stored below the level of awareness, sending messages to the body. Thus, a never-expressed impulse to strike back at a tyrannical parent may instead take the form of taut arm muscles. During an early Primal, when a patient remembers being struck by his parent, he may feel this tautness in his arms but not know why. Later he will connect this muscle tightness to its proper context (anger, wanting to hit), and the muscle tightness will finally be resolved.

One patient was a constant teeth grinder. It was an automatic and unconscious behaviour occurring day and night (in his sleep). He began thinking about the time his father had broken his promise about taking him to a baseball game, and he unconsciously began grinding his teeth furiously. Expressing anger was forbidden in his household. In my office he finally screamed out his rage, and the grinding stopped. That one incident did not cause him to grind his teeth. That one incident, a salient memory, simply represented and triggered all of the patient's anger for the whole host of broken promises which my patient was never allowed to complain about in the home.

We all see symbolic behaviour around us but probably do not call it that. When a child leaves school without permission, he is acting impulsively. What he may be doing is acting out symbolically a freedom he cannot feel. What is imprisoning him may not be school at all but old feelings. To feel those feelings is what will free him from having to act out his freedom by leaving school. This child could be made to *act* better by school administrators or by a helpful therapist who points out the necessity of being responsible in school, but the impulse to be free will remain, driving symbolic and often sociopathic behaviour.

The symbolic stage is a necessity in Primal Therapy. The patient feels part of a feeling because there is too much hurt to feel it all – the body then shuts down for the time being, and the patient acts out (or acts in) the remaining part of the feeling. This acting out need not be anything specific. It can be just in the form of vague tension which keeps parts of the old personality intact.

The symbolic stage must not be hurried. The system is facing Pain in small doses and will continue to do so in an orderly process with lesser degrees of symbolism occurring as more feeling is experienced. This also shows up in the decrease of symbolism in his dreams.

As the patient moves out of the symbolic stage and into his feelings in a more direct way, he finds himself less interested in symbolic things. Symbolism seems to be a total phenomenon, and unfortunately the neurotic often spends his life in this symbolic never-never land. His 'raging' headaches may be telling him how angry he is, and despite years of headaches, he seldom seems to make sense out of them. One patient after a particularly vehement Primal put it this way: 'I think all that pressure in my head was angry feelings that couldn't spread out and hook up to my bodily feelings.

It was like I had to tuck even my ideas into some compartment that was already overloaded.'

The worst time in Primal Therapy seems to be the first week. The patient is anxious and miserable and will usually say, 'My God, when does this all end? It's been a week and seems like a lifetime!' He has been in great turmoil. One patient said, 'It's like from the minute I walked in here, you grabbed me by my feet, held me upside down, and shook everything out of me.'

He feels more tense than ever before because he has fewer neurotic defences against the feelings that are surfacing. Once he is wide open, there is an urgency to his needs that makes it mandatory for the therapist to be available constantly.

By the end of the third week the major work of dismantling the defence system is done. The patient is not yet well, however. He has a good deal of residual tension – old hurts and feelings that have not come up or have not been triggered for one reason or another. Because it isn't economical or necessary to keep the patient in individual therapy, he is placed in a post-Primal group. The patient may still need an individual hour occasionally, but the major work is left for group therapy.

When I say that the major work has been done after the first few weeks, I mean that by then major changes in personality and symptomatology are noticeable. When I practised conventional therapy, it used to take me three weeks just to get a patient's history and do a psychological test battery. Now in this length of time we see things such as a lifetime of high blood pressure dropping dramatically to normal (and staying there). There is a change in the way one speaks, the tone of voice, and in the 'look' – dead faces become mobile and alive. The person's ideas change radically in that short period, and this occurs without any patient-therapist discussion. This is because unreal ideas must accompany unreal systems.

The key aim, of course, is to break down defences in the three weeks, and this is what most often happens. The person can scarcely talk about anything meaningful without a good deal of emotion. Even the way he walks is different – especially true of swishy men. Many of these changes are noted in detail in the case histories written by my patients.

VARIATIONS IN PRIMAL STYLES

Primals can vary in a number of ways. One patient, for example, started her Primals with what appeared to be birth. During the first day of her therapy she hunched in a ball, began contracting and releasing her body, said that she felt cool air hitting her, and then wailed exactly like a newborn. She had no idea of what she was going through at the time and reported that it was a totally involuntary process. Other patients never get that far back. A patient who had no memory before the age of ten began to relive experiences at the age of fourteen and worked her way down the age ladder until she relived a terrible event that caused the final split at the age of ten. After this, however, she continued to have Primal experiences earlier and earlier in her life until she reached the age of three, when she came to feel the 'pure need' of wanting her parents' love. She later said that this was her most painful Primal – to feel that physical need meant to feel the continuous Pain of something that was never fulfilled. There were no words during this Primal, just a completely internal experience with a bunching up of the body, writhing and groaning, clenching of the fists, and grinding the teeth.

Primals vary, depending on the age of the split and the depth of the Pain. Some patients are able to go directly to the major scene in which they felt the split; others take months to get there. Some report that they never get to one specific scene; many scenes seemed to have equal weight in producing their neurosis. If the split is early and the Pain great, the patient may relive one scene many times over. For example, one patient has recently relived being left for many weeks as a child of nine months in the crib in a hospital. His parents were unable to visit him because he had a communicable disease. The next day he went back to that scene and knew that it was some kind of hospital. Then he saw the face of his mother; last, he saw his parents leave and felt the abandonment. His lifelong neurotic acting out was to find someone, lately a girlfriend, to hang onto and to do everything he could to keep her from leaving him. He had no idea that much of this behaviour was based on something that had happened so early in his life; in fact, he had no memory of the early experience at all. He came in the first time filled with tension because his latest girlfriend had abandoned him. Sinking into this feeling took him back to the crib. While reliving the crib scene, there were only baby cries. He had several wordless Primals. The last Primal of this sequence was a loud, shrill wail for his parents to come back – something that he dared not do for some reason back there in the crib.

We can usually tell when a person is coming out of a Primal. He opens his eyes and blinks as though he has come out of some kind of coma. Sometimes it isn't as dramatic as that; there will be a shift in the tone of the voice back to the adult voice, and we know that the person is out of the early feeling. What is continuously surprising is the way tension often sets in when the organism has had enough Pain for one day. After feeling a great Pain, the person will inexplicably feel tension and say that he cannot remember any more. Or if he has felt the entirety of one experience, he will feel completely relaxed. We know there is more feeling to be resolved if the person ends up tense after a Primal. Residual tension after a Primal is dramatic evidence that neurosis was our early friend and benefactor. It took over and kept us safe when life became too painful to bear, and it takes over and makes the patient tense when he has had enough Pain for one day.

There are times when Primals are predominantly physical; one patient near the end of his therapy went into a Primal in which his body began twisting from right to left in strange and bizarre postures. He was lying on his abdomen and his legs were drawn up towards his back while his head was raised off the floor, neck thrown back. This went on for almost an hour in involuntary fashion. He then stood up straight and said that he felt that his hunched back, which had plagued him for most of his life, was gone. He described it this way:

'I think that it wasn't only my mind that was twisted, it was my body too. It seemed to be running off some kind of sequence where first it was all contorted – like what I made myself into – and then it began automatically putting itself back together. Just before I went into this, I kept telling myself I was going crazy. Something snapped in my head and then this physical sequence began. What I think happened is that when my mind finally let go of the struggle and all that unreality (kind of letting itself go to pieces), the body could finally get real and straight with itself at last. I'm standing and walking now loose, like a different human being. Never in my life have I been able to cross my legs fully like I can do now or, strange as it seems, for the first time I can move my neck all the way around to the side. I can only say that I was not only in a mental straitjacket, thinking narrow thoughts, I was like in some kind of physical mould, like a die that kept me all pressed into some strange shape.'

We have all become so used to watching the 'normal' range of emotion that it is difficult to convey the tremendous power of Primals. Their depth and range of feeling are almost beyond description. Their great variety and often strange quality are likewise difficult to portray. Suffice it to say that when a feeling can convulse a human being, when it can produce earth-shaking screams, it testifies to the enormous pressure the neurotic must be under continually. What is astounding is that so many neurotics cannot feel it directly; they feel it instead in a pressured chest, a bloated stomach, or a head that feels as though it will explode.

The Primal process takes patients into a realm rarely if ever seen, even in the offices of psychotherapists. It is more rarely understood. It is a systematic trip, not a random, hysterical flight, but a step-by-step, ordered journey of man into himself. When patients finally get down to the early catastrophic feeling of knowing they were unloved, hated, or never to be understood – that epiphanic feeling of ultimate aloneness – they understand perfectly why they shut off and how a young child could not withstand that feeling and go on living. To observe these patients in paroxysms of pain when they strike that feeling is to see the depths of human feeling. In all my years of doing conventional therapy, I never observed or even understood what feeling really was. I saw a great deal of crying and agony, of course, but there is a universe of distance between crying and a Primal experience.

Here is how one patient described his Primal experiences:
'The feeling in a Primal that is associated with a childhood experience any time after the split is a piece of the real self, a real self that cannot be totally experienced unless you

go back before the split. That is why reliving childhood experiences or scenes in Primal Therapy is so important. They help you feel pieces of your real self by associating the pain with specific incidents, until you can *be* the essence of your real self. For example: If I am having a Primal about my mother's pushing me away, I will probably say, "Don't push me away, Mommy." The pure feeling in that Primal really has no words. The feeling *is* my real self, and the words are really saying, "I feel bad, Mommy, please take my pain away," and this is a defence against *being* that feeling. The many times that this feeling is associated with specific incidents will take the patient, I think, to finally being that feeling totally and experiencing his *essence*, and this only happened once before, just before the split. At this point there is nothing to say and no scenes to be connected to. You are being you. For me it was what total deprivation did to me. I cannot hope to communicate in words what that experience actually feels like for me, and that I can't is further testimony to the fact that there are no words . . .'

Reliving Primal Pains seems almost indescribable in intensity. When one watches patients during Primals, one is convinced that they are in agony. I was so convinced of this that I never bothered to ask a patient if it hurt until months after I started doing Primal Therapy. Much to my surprise, patients reported that despite all that groaning, screaming and convulsing, the Pain *did not hurt*! One patient described it this way:

'It isn't as though you have cut your hand and you look at it and say, "Oh, my, my hand hurts!" During a Primal you don't even think about whether it hurts. You are just feeling a miserable feeling everywhere. But it doesn't hurt. If anything, you could say that it hurts nice because it's such a relief to finally be able to feel.'

What I think he means is that during a Primal there is no reflecting on what you are doing, no processing of the happening, no reasoning the need, so to speak. There is only a self *totally* engaged in something for the first time since childhood. The person is the feeling. One of the reasons that he can be completely engaged in the feeling process is that he is not simply sitting constricted in a chair remembering something. His whole body is engaged in the process just as the young child was totally engaged in a feeling before he was shut off. Patients remember how in their first years they expressed their anger – lying on the floor, kicking their feet, flailing their arms and wailing. They were wholly involved, and if you asked that child who was having a tantrum if he hurt (if he could understand the question), I doubt if he would have answered yes.

Here is another description of a Primal which occurred towards the end of a patient's therapy. I quote it here because it helps explain this phenomenon of a non-painful Pain:

'I guess the best way I can describe what this experience was like is to say that I was not conscious of the feeling and its connections, I don't really think I was conscious of anything. I simply was my pain, and there was no connection needed (nothing separate that says, "You hurt"). The only thing that was needed was for my being to accept the experience and not split away from it as I did once before when I finally went neurotic. This was being my real self.'

What is significant about the Primal Pain experience is that it indicates that feelings, in and of themselves, do not hurt. Tensing up against the feeling is what seems to hurt. This does not mean that there are no unpleasant feelings, but when they are felt for what they are, they will not become transmuted into Pains. Sadness doesn't hurt. But if one is deprived of his sadness, if he isn't permitted his misery, *then* he will hurt. *Feeling, then, is the antithesis of Pain.* The dialectic of the Primal method is that *the more Pains one feels, the less pain one suffers.* You cannot really hurt the feelings of a normal person, but you can hurt a neurotic by triggering off denied feelings.

THE GROUP EXPERIENCE

Post-Primal groups meet twice weekly for three or more hours. The group is composed of patients who have had individual Primal Therapy. Its major function is to stimulate group members into new Primals. The general emotional atmosphere of group is conducive to more Primals. One person's Primal may trigger two or three other persons' Primals. It isn't uncommon for two to take place at once because one patient, now defenceless, has a hard time holding off for a half hour or so while another patient has his Primal.

When two Primals go off at once, it can be bedlam. The only people who aren't affected by the chaos are the ones doing their Primals. They seem oblivious to what the other person is doing. It is not uncommon for there to be six or seven Primals at once during a single three-hour group session.

Because the whole Primal process is unsettling, to say the least, the group has another function. It is comforting to patients, who can meet and know other people who are undergoing the therapy. This group process goes on for several months, depending on the patient.

Because I did standard group therapy for many years prior to Primal Therapy, I want to point out that the Primal group is a very different kind of experience. Patients who have had other kinds of group experience, ranging from marathon groups to analytic groups, report on the difference as well. In the Primal group there is very little interaction. There is almost none of the here-and-now, give-and-take of the usual group therapy. There is little questioning of one another about motivations, and there is no exchange of insights. Seldom is either anger or fear shown to one another. The focus is internal. When someone spends his time looking at others, watching their reactions, it is a good sign that for that moment he is not feeling. There are many reasons for this, I believe, but the key one is that Primal Therapy is not an interacting process. It is a personal feeling process where insights flow almost unceasingly when a Pain has been deeply felt. (See the section on insights.)

The second difference is that patients understand that whatever the inordinate reactions that occur in group, they relate to *old* experiences.

Third, the group period is the time of great defencelessness. Patients come in and vie to get on the floor because they cannot seem to hold back their feelings for another minute. No one has to prompt them into a feeling. They are, so to speak, a mass of feeling. Patients in group have a great deal of respect and patience for what is happening on the floor, and there have been times when two hours have been taken up with a single Primal. Frequently, as I have stated, what is occurring on the floor – 'I could never say I was afraid' – will evoke similar feelings in those watching, and despite an observer's best efforts at self-control, he may have a Primal in his seat or in another corner of the room.

Three hours is a short period for Primal groups. After a Primal in group – the average Primal lasts about half an hour – the patient may lie there for another hour or so, making connections silently while other Primals are going on. It is not unusual for six or eight patients to be on the floor at once. Whatever is going on with the other patients seems not to disturb anyone else who is into his feelings and memories. At the end of each group there is a discussion period in which people talk about what happened to them. They discuss how a particular feeling, for example, during their Primal has previously produced specific kinds of neurotic behaviour.

BECOMING WELL

After seven or eight months of group therapy, a patient may still be having Primals. They are infrequent, and by the time someone has reached his eighth month he is generally well. What does this mean? It means that whatever painful feelings he has, he can now feel wherever he is without help. There is no major defence left to hide his feelings and produce acting out. It means the end of symbolic behaviour. It definitely means the end of physical (psychosomatic) symptoms which are symbolic Pains. It also means the end of obvious neurotic behaviour such as smoking and drinking. Even if they wanted to, patients cannot do anything unreal. They cannot get back their old headaches because their headaches were a part of the defence which kept feelings blocked. There are no more defences. They cannot smoke without getting revolted. The harshness of cigarette smoke gets to them immediately. They cannot act out sexually (compulsive sex) because there are no old impulses to be channelled through sex. They have no desire to overeat because they are not stuffing back feelings with food.

Does this hold up over the passage of time? Yes. Thus far, unreal behaviour (and that includes physical symptoms) has not returned in graduate patients. How could it? The person has become himself; to revert to his unreal behaviour, he would have to become someone else again. Current adult events cannot produce a split which would make a person into two people. It happens to young children because they are so fragile and so dependent on parents for life. They have to become what parents demand or else. This is rarely the case for an adult. No one can make a real adult into someone unreal. He will not struggle with an unruly boss or an impossible work situation.

Let me make clear that the finished patient is not ecstatic or even 'happy'. Happiness is not a goal of Primal Therapy. Finished patients may still have many more hurts to feel because they have a lifetime of unfelt hurts behind them. So they will have their moments of misery after therapy, but as one patient put it, 'At least it is *real* misery with some kind of end to it.'

Being well doesn't necessarily mean different interests; many patients find that they now can do the same old things with an entirely different feeling. Being 'well' means feeling what is happening 'now'. Patients know when they are finally fully feeling because they have no residual tension and they feel completely relaxed. Nothing makes them tense. Events upset them, and they feel the upset – not tense.

Many patients finish before the eight months; some remain in therapy for ten or eleven months. It all depends on how sick they were to begin with – how repressed and unconscious they were before treatment. No matter how many Primals a person has had, if there are significant remaining denied or blocked feelings, these feelings will be acted out symbolically *in perpetuity* until they are felt and resolved. This means that the person may still be neurotic even after a number of Primals.

One patient who returned to college in his third month of therapy found that he suddenly could not understand his lectures. He began acting and even appearing stupid in class, unable to understand the simplest instructions by the professor. He came into group and talked about how he was derided by a teaching assistant because he did not understand something on an exam paper. He sank into the feeling as he talked: 'Explain it to me, Daddy. Take some time with me!' His father had derided him when he did not understand something immediately. He tried his best to comprehend things instantly to please his father and ward off the hurt.

This was a simple feeling, yet laden with intense effect. The hurt was in feeling stupid and trying to cover it by catching on quickly. As his therapy went into its third month, his defence of being quick mentally began to fall apart, and he acted stupid. The stupidity was saying, 'Explain it to me.' He would go on acting stupid until he felt its source.

DISCUSSION

I believe that the only way to eliminate neurosis is with overthrow by force and violence: the force of years of compressed feelings and denied needs; the violence of wrenching them out of an unreal system.

Just as neurosis results from a gradual shutting-off process, becoming healthy involves a gradual turning on again. Since Pain will not permit too fast a trip into those Primal feelings, they must be felt in stages. Until they all are felt, there is the likelihood of symbolic acting out.

Primal Therapy is like neurosis in reverse. Each day in a young child's life, hurt after hurt closes off more of his feelings until he is neurotic. In Primal Therapy the patient relives those hurts, opening himself up until he is well. One hurt does not make a neurosis, and one Primal does not make a normal. It is the accretion of hurts and feeling the hurts that finally change quantity into new qualities of either sickness or health. I believe that the process of getting well is inevitable in Primal Therapy so long as the person stays in treatment. Once the major defence system is broken, the patient has no choice but to get well. This inevitability is analogous to the young child who remains in a traumatic environment where there is constant suppression. His neurosis, the final closing down of the real self and the construction of a lasting defence, is a foregone conclusion. Take the child out of the traumatic environment before the major split, and serious neurosis can be avoided. Take the patient out of the therapeutic circumstance before he has mended the split, and health might not be inevitable.

Why is it that early neurosis cannot be undone by loving parents, teachers? A number of patients did have new stepmothers and stepfathers in their teens with whom they got along very well, who were often warm and kind, and still these individuals needed therapy later. Those kind step-mothers and stepfathers *never* undid lifelong stuttering, tics, allergies, etc. Speech therapists did not undo speech disorders. Leaving home in the late teens, finding decent loving boyfriends and girlfriends did not undo tension and long-lasting symptoms such as psoriasis (something which seems to respond to Primal Therapy, by the way). If kindness and love and interest could undo neurosis, certainly psychotherapy as practised by warm therapists should have been able to reverse many neuroses, which I think is not the case.

Neurosis cannot be placated, reasoned, threatened, or loved out of existence. Its pathological processes seem to gobble up anything in its path. You can feed neurosis insights, and it will absorb them handily as it lumbers on. You can cut off one neurotic outlet after another only to find new and better hidden ones. Neurosis can be allayed by drug after drug, but it will be as strong as ever once the drugs are removed. Driving neurosis is one of the great energy sources – the need to be loved and to be real, in body and mind.

Having been well grounded in scientific caution, I am aware as I write how dramatic and 'otherworldly' all this sounds. It may be that some readers will want to dismiss Primal Therapy as a treatment applicable only to special kinds of neurotics. However, it applies to all neurosis and, as shall be discussed later, possibly to psychosis as well. Patients who had first been treated by me with standard therapy never experienced anything like a Primal. After discovering Primals, however, I asked some of my former patients to return for treatment with Primal Therapy, and we did not fail to find their Pain. After years of engagement with their rational façade, it seemed incredible to us that so much unexplored feeling lay beneath.

Neurosis becomes understandable, though, when we consider the thousands of experiences in which a child was prevented from acting in a real way. Indeed, it is a wonder of the human system that the real way still waits to be felt; the system seems to require reality.

The patient is an ally in Primal Therapy. His Pain has waited a long time, and it usually wants to surface. His compulsive behaviour seems to have been an unconscious search for the right connection so that it could get out. When the opportunity is presented, it cannot be stopped, and I think that this accounts for our success with a wide variety of neurotic types.

Primal Therapy draws forth an ambivalent reaction in some neurotics, depending on how close they are to their Pain. When they are close, they seem to be drawn to it immediately because it *feels* right. When they are not close to their feelings, they may dismiss it as primitive, unsophisticated and oversimplified. The neurotic who has had to twist himself out of shape to get anything worthwhile from his parents may feel that a therapy that does not involve a prolonged and 'agonising' struggle over a period of years cannot be worth much.

Primal Therapy may seem so simple, however, that I must post this warning: NO ONE WHO IS NOT A FULLY TRAINED PRIMAL THERAPIST SHOULD ATTEMPT IT! The results might be quite harmful. A training group has now been in progress for many months. It is the judgment of both the psychological trainees and myself that they have yet to master the fundamentals of the theory and the technique. I stress this point to emphasise the possible danger involved in the use of Primal Therapy by untrained personnel.

While practically no details of technique have been included in this book, I wish to stress that Primal Therapy is not a haphazard methodology. It is a planned programme. There are specific objectives to be attained during the first three weeks and certain results to be expected from month to month. We have a good idea of how the patient will be eating and sleeping during his therapy and what this means. Given certain therapeutic conditions, different therapists will follow almost the identical course.

This therapy requires a good deal of trust in the therapist. If the therapist is not real, it cannot be accomplished. If he is real, patients will sense it. Many of us are willing to let a surgeon slice into our bodies after only a handshake, so it should not be surprising that a patient will allow a Primal Therapist to cut into his Pain soon after their meeting.

The end of neurosis is very much like its beginning. It is not a big bang, some last great insight, or some tremendous emotional experience. It is just an ordinary day in which the patient has felt another feeling that had previously welded him to the past. Here is the end of neurosis in the words of one patient: 'I don't know what I expected out of all this. I suppose I wanted something dramatic to happen to even the score for all those years of misery. Maybe I expected to become my neurotic fantasy – that someone special who would finally be loved and appreciated. All there seems to be is me . . .' And there is just unneurotic him.

Kathy

The following is a portion of a diary of several weeks of Primal Therapy by a twenty-five-year-old woman. The diary is presented in order to give the reader some idea of what patients feel day by day in treatment. This woman entered therapy because she was having frightening hallucinations resulting from a 'bad trip' on LSD. These hallucinations hung on for months after her drug trip. At the present writing her therapy has terminated with all symptoms gone. She thinks of herself as a new person.

What follows is an account of my first five weeks in Primal Therapy. These notes, aside from a few changes made for purposes of clarity, appear as I wrote them following each session.

I spent my first ten years living with my mother, father, older sister and uncle. My parents were then divorced, and until sixteen I lived with my mother, sister and another woman. I was married for two years and divorced at twenty-three. I spent four years in college, but received no degree. I'm twenty-five years old.

Shortly before going into therapy, I began having visual fantasies of knives and razors coming towards my head. I started to panic when driving, imagining that cars were going to run into me. I never let the knives get at me in the fantasies, but became afraid I was really going to hurt myself. I decided I needed help.

Wednesday

The beginning is trying to remember my childhood. I'm shocked to find that I have almost no memories. I remember feeling abandoned and rejected at the girls' school my sister and I were sent to when Mom had a breakdown. I was about four years old, and I remember sitting on the floor and crying and crying. I remembered the house on W—— being dark, lived there till five years old. Coming home to the house of D——, wondering if Mommy would be home. She's told me she'd come home to find me sitting and burning up matches. I lied a lot, stole things at parties, cut up my sister's underwear and today saw all of that related for the first time. I was cheating Mommy and Daddy back for not giving me what I needed – for cheating me. They weren't there for me, weren't real. They pretended everything was all right when it wasn't. That we were a family when we weren't. And I pretended, too. That's why I've always remembered my childhood as being happy – I pretended to be a happy little girl because I couldn't face the reality of it.

I remember seeing Daddy cry on D——. Then and after the separation, he showed how sad he was – he always looked pained. The night I came home from summer camp (ten years old), right before I found out about the separation, he told me he loved me, looking pained, wanting to insure the bond between us before the split. But Mommy didn't expose herself. She pretended I needed her. I felt lost. Something wasn't real – maybe everything. I didn't tell them how I felt. I only buried it all and then burned matches.

At the end of the session I felt dizzy and weak. I went back there, to my childhood, a little – but it's all so disconnected and spotty. How can I remember so little? It's like I wasn't really there.

Thursday

A rough beginning today – struggling to find memories that aren't there. I started to feel panic – why can't I remember? I am lost; first I felt it as I am now, then lost as a child. I tried to call out for Mommy. It felt unreal. Then I called – felt her holding me. But as she held me, there was no comfort, only the feeling of being alone before she got there. I began to realise I was pushing with my hands. I felt like I was a baby in my crib, pushing and waving my hands. I felt alone. I really was there in the darkness of the house on W—— where my crib was. I was a little baby alone. I wanted my mommy, but couldn't call her. Then I realised I hadn't called out for her even when I was a baby. I lay quietly and felt the sadness of that and cried. Then I got freezing cold, went into foetal position to get warm. Suddenly I felt like I was falling in space. I was floating, terrified. I was afraid I would fall and bump against something and get hurt. My body, still curled up, began contracting in and out. I became unaware of what was happening but felt the fear and struggle and cried out. Finally, I felt myself squeezing through a smaller area. I could feel sides around me. I was afraid when I squeezed through I would be hurt, but as I did get out, I realised I was being born and had come out all right. I popped out and felt cool air around me. My body uncurled a little. I felt happy and exhausted. I was born! While in the womb, I felt as though I was aware of the whole thing when I shouldn't have been aware yet. Like I was experiencing something I should have slept through. Art[1] said I was contracting for fifteen minutes; it only seemed like a few minutes to me. It's fantastic.

I saw all my fears of height, of falling, of the ocean. I looked out the window and all around the office. Everything looks different – like a layer of film has been removed. I leave the office feeling great.

This evening, listening to music, I start crying. I feel how sad Daddy felt – how badly they both felt – and what a sad little girl I was. I tried to picture Mom. I see her at the piano, but her face keeps dissolving into something from a horror comic book. I try to see her now, but keep seeing that sad, sick face from twenty years ago. I feel terrible, realising for the first time how sick and pitiful she was.

Friday

I begin by looking at Mom at the piano, as I saw her last night, and again her face dissolves into horror. I can't hold the image and look at it. Then I see her at about thirty years old. She's looking out of the corner of her eyes, paranoid, panicky. I cry out, 'She crazy.' I cry and cry. She's crazy and unreal. A mask. She wasn't there for me as a child because she was crazy. She has to keep running around, then and now, to keep from going crazy. It must have driven her crazy to have to just stay home with my sister and me. Poor

[1] Author's note: Since 'Art' is the nickname by which my patients call me, it will appear frequently in their case histories.

Mommy. Suddenly, I became little – standing and looking at my family. Daddy is sad; Mom is crazy and afraid; my sister is angry – each of us all alone. I tried to make it better by dancing wildly and being funny. I was bewildered, too little to comprehend or accept it. They were pitiful and frightening and no help to a little girl. I could feel Mommy's craziness. I understand her pretending. She thinks if she acts 'healthy', does 'healthy' things, she'll be okay. That's what all her therapy did for her. I cried for my sister, who also tried to make it okay by pretending and performing.

Saturday

Still no childhood memories, so I talked about my acid trips. The first two joyous, ecstatic, mystical, totally unreal and very visual trips. During the three months between the second and third trips I began using a lot of amphetamines and codeine. The third time I took acid I was unhappy, and I wanted it to make me feel better. I was afraid to take it alone but did. The first couple of hours were like the other trips. Some friends visited me for a short while, and when they left, I became anxious. I tried to remember why I was afraid to take it alone but only became confused. I couldn't remember what acid was. I couldn't remember anything real. The hallucinations became frightening and overwhelming. Minutes seemed unending; the clock melted. My mind wouldn't work. I couldn't remember who I was. There were no references left. I was crazy, felt I would never come back to the real world. Terrified, I found I could still use the phone and called my sister to come over. I was so relieved to hear her 'real' voice that I'd 'regained' myself quite a bit by the time she arrived. The rest of the trip was alternately fun and sad, but I knew I'd never be the same after feeling that insanity. About three weeks later, with much Methedrine and codeine in between, I woke up feeling very depressed. I lay on the beach all day, got a sunburn, and felt terribly depressed. I went to my mother's and began crying hysterically and gasping for air. She gave me a tranquilliser, which put me to sleep. I woke up still crying and hyperventilating. The next day she took me to the Neuropsychiatric Institute at UCLA. After speaking to the acid expert doctor there, he assured me I wasn't really sick but was only reacting to the various drugs I was taking and the acid. If I stopped taking them, he said, began to live a normal life, I would surely be okay. He put me on enough Mellaril to knock out a cow and advised me to return to work as soon as possible and stay with people at all times. Everything that he advised took me further away from my real feelings, helped me to cover them up again just when they were ready to be exposed and felt. I stayed highly depressed, crying, sleeping and hyperventilating for about one month. Then I began putting myself back together again, pushing down my feelings so I could function.

During the session today I realised I went crazy because I couldn't face the feelings of aloneness the acid had uncovered. My current fantasies of knives and razors coming at me are related. If I ever let them get at me, they would rip me open and let my feelings out. The fear of hurting myself is the same as exposing myself and feeling the pain I've buried. I'm beginning to feel all the sadness and hurting in me. Twenty-five years of burying the hurt, the fear, the aloneness. I see the gasping for air is fighting to keep the feelings down when they start to come up, as they did after the acid trip. I cry and cry and cry. It seems like it will never stop. I feel the pain in my stuffed-up head. I want to vomit it all out. I am afraid and alone.

I realise those first two acid trips and the other times in my life when I've felt all right about being alone, it's only because I'd covered my feeling so well. I pretended everything was okay (just like I did as a child) because I couldn't face feeling helpless and alone. Even now after my session, I pretend I don't feel anything because I can't face feeling shitty and alone all day. I'm still burying my feelings except during my sessions.

Tuesday

Today I came in with strong feelings in my stomach. It came out in shuddering screams from the gut, but no words. Finally, I realised I was terrified because I was alone; Mommy and Daddy weren't there. I couldn't make it alone; I was too little. I saw Mom as she was after the sanitorium when I was four and as she is now: coming on to people, pretending to be gay, phony, a mask. Then I realised why I feel so repulsed by her showing her body, her ugliness, because I am like her, all covered over – a mask over my feelings and fears. That's why I saw her pain as a child, even though I couldn't face it then. My legs are fat because I pushed my feelings down that far, like she did. My breasts are big because I acted grown-up. I feel tension now, all over my body and want to get it out. I sink into the tension and feel that it is pain. All my tension is pain that I'm not feeling. I feel it now and cry.

Also realised today that my concern for my sister's well-being is displaced concern for myself, because she's acted out the hurt and pain that I've kept locked inside.

Wednesday

I walked in this morning with my stomach upset, nervous, excited. All the talking seemed wrong, so I sank down into the feeling. I was little, lying in my crib. I looked up and saw Mommy alone with me. She looked pained, terrified and crazy. I was horrified, felt just like she looked. Even as a baby – I saw her, what she was. It was too painful. I was too little to have to see that. It wasn't fair. I couldn't stand it. That's why I had to push my feelings down from the very beginning. A little baby having to see that her mother is crazy and helpless.

Then I tried to remember Daddy. I got littler but felt proportionately bigger (like when I have a fever). I was a little baby in my crib (first seemed like an incubator because there was a plastic dome above me). I saw only darkness and felt I needed Daddy to hold me. Then I saw him standing there, much higher than me. He was a statue staring at me. I couldn't get through to him. I called quietly but he couldn't hear. He just couldn't hear me. I cried, 'What's the matter with you, Daddy?' I couldn't move. I couldn't call out. Then I saw Mommy next to him. They were both waxen statues, empty shells just looking down at me, not seeing me or feeling anything. Then my sister was on my right, a phony smile on her face, reaching in to poke me. I wanted them all to go away – they were horrible and unreal. It was frightening. I closed my eyes and turned on my left side, hoping they would think I was asleep and go away.

My childhood was hideous and frightening from the be-

ginning, but I hid from it. I set my jaw against the feeling –
and it's still set there.

Thursday

I started with tension in my stomach again. I became a baby,
feeling a huge need with no words. I tried to call Mommy,
but it was no good. Then I saw her but didn't want her to
hold me because she looked crazy. I wanted her and Daddy
not to be crazy and waxen. I felt sad because I couldn't just
feel the need without also needing them to change first. I
begged them not to be crazy, and it felt very real. Then I felt
the rage that lay under that reality. I screamed to them, 'I
needed you, and you were no help to me – you were too
insane.' Who wants to call for their parents and have two
crazy people come? I thought the rage would last forever,
but one scream and it seemed to be all out.

I felt sad all day and night after the session – felt cheated
and locked into my unhappy baby self.

Friday

I was little again and felt the need for Mommy and Daddy. I
was afraid and terribly cold. I lay there paralysed, freezing
my fear that they wouldn't take care of me, hold me. I
couldn't call out, because I still couldn't bear to look at
them. When I screamed for them and finally screamed out
like a baby from my stomach, it hurt my left ear. Maybe
opened it up because I could feel the scream going out
through my ear. It was a real little baby scream, sounded
like a goat to me when it came out. When I was lying there
frozen I felt how tight my stomach was, braced against the
feeling. My stomach muscles are still tight as a rack to this
day.

Monday

Feeling pains in stomach, cramps, headache over weekend
and this morning. Had sinking feeling in stomach that I've
always had (and has always reminded me of the past).
Trying to get into that feeling – felt dizzy (like when too
high or with a fever). Spinning feeling with sort of sideways

motion. My left arm began to feel paralysed like someone was holding it down really hard, squeezing into the muscles. I screamed, 'Let me go, let me go,' but it wasn't right. Then suddenly the dizziness felt like someone was rocking my baby carriage too hard, trying to scare me. My brain said it might be my sister, but then I pictured Mom, her face distorted. But that didn't seem right. I felt my arm again. I felt sick in my stomach. My parents were holding me, twisting me, scaring me. I yelled and finally broke my arm away. I felt a rush of feeling into it. But I was terrified and confused. I didn't understand what had happened. Finally I called out, 'I don't understand,' and that was it. I was about five years old and confused and bewildered by my parents. They weren't taking care of me. Everything they did confused and hurt me. They were crazy and making me crazy. I hated them for it, and I needed them. They didn't love me. It made me crazy trying to figure out what was going on. And I acted out being crazy: the wild dancing, the grimaces to cover the feeling. I was too little to understand – but more capable of understanding than the baby me. It was terribly painful. My head stuffed up always, my ears, nose, throat – all that shit and confusion bottled up inside. I screamed some more infant-type screams and felt a little better. When I sat up, the melody of 'The Farmer in the Dell' popped out of my mouth real quietly – almost unaware. Maybe that's how simple I wanted it to be.

Tuesday

Sank immediately into feeling little. I was paralysed, standing in doorway between kitchen and dining-room – looking into the living-room. Mom and Dad are there, then not there – they're transparent. I need them but can't call out. I'm paralysed between wanting them and being afraid of their unrealness. I was alone, very alone. I pretended I didn't need them. I didn't ask them for anything ever. I never asked Daddy even to help me cut my meat like my sister did. Today I called out, 'Daddy, where are you? I don't even see you around the house.' I felt I wanted to talk to Mommy then; I wanted to tell her that it was hurting in my head. I did finally, and it was very real. Also I called to her, 'I needed you,' which changed into 'I need you'. I felt no matter how many lights were turned on in that house, it was still dark and empty. I was alone and little, pretending to be big and independent. They weren't really there for me even when they were there. I felt cheated. Why didn't you take care of me? Even if I'd yelled and stomped, they wouldn't have heard me or seen me.

Wednesday

Felt anxious this morning. Started remembering the house on D—— more clearly. Then feeling little – I stood just inside the back door, afraid of the empty house. I couldn't breathe, felt I couldn't walk through the house, but kept picturing all the downstairs rooms. Finally, I started walking through the house and even remembered what was in the closets. I was really afraid to go upstairs, afraid of finding some horrible secret that was causing the anxiety. I forced myself to go up, step by step. I looked into my uncle's room – nothing there. I turned down the hall to my parents' room, heart pounding. At the door my heart sank as I looked into the empty room and realised that's all it was. I was afraid because the house was empty; there was no one there for me; I was alone. I felt sadder than I've ever felt. I realised I never did walk around the house then. I couldn't face the fear and pain then, alone – so I went and sat in front of the TV and covered it with anger. I burned matches to let out the anger, and by the time Mommy got home I could pretend nothing was wrong. I reacted like a baby inside but refused to act like one on the outside.

Thursday

All last night I felt panicky – couldn't breathe, stomach in knots like cramps. This morning I couldn't have a session, so I decided to try getting to it myself – kept seeing the house on —— where we lived when I was ten. Looked into Mom and Dad's room and had a feeling of violence, anger – imagined a fight, but it wasn't real. Finally found myself in den. Remembered the night I came home from camp when I knew something was wrong. The next day I asked Mom if they had ever thought of getting a divorce. That night I thought I heard them fighting upstairs while I was in the den. I remembered Daddy with me while I was taking a bath telling me he loved me, looking sad, letting me know everything wasn't all right by his expression. I cried. I must have cried in pain for two hours today. I knew that night that the pretending was going to be over. That it would soon be unavoidable. There was no family. I had to face that it wasn't right, never was – after ten years of all of us pretending. I felt panic – I wouldn't be able to face it. I wanted to beg them – I cried no, no, no. All the pain I had hidden as a child I had to hide from again that night. Mommy could have made it all right – if she'd kept on pretending we could have all gone on pretending. It was horrible – the end of the world – our pretend world.

Friday

Still feeling headache and stomachache. I didn't get it all out yesterday. Repeated it all in the session today. All that was left was the screaming I didn't feel free to do at home. I screamed no over and over and felt relieved.

Monday

Still in pain most of the day. In session I sank way down into my fears of being alone trying to find the terror. But the terror is all in the anticipation. Once I felt the aloneness, instead of pushing it away, it was just feeling alone and sad. Not pleasant, but bearable. I sank into the pounding in my stomach and brought it up into my head, but I couldn't name the feeling. I started crying hard – screaming from the stomach trying to get the feeling out. I called to Mommy: 'I need you. I'm afraid. Take care of me.' It didn't help. I became panicky. I wouldn't be able to get it out. My nose was stuffed up, and I was choking. I couldn't name the feeling. I started going in circles in my head, getting confused and crazy. It felt like the acid trip – trying to put something simple into words, but something I couldn't face. I kept grabbing for answers, trying to figure it out, getting angry. Finally gave up, went home afraid and confused.

Tuesday

Decided to go back over the Primal and see what I couldn't

face – all the yelling I did and need I felt had been unconnected. I went back to the day after the night I came home
from camp. Mom and I were driving to Glendale. I asked
her if they'd ever thought of getting a divorce. Then felt
frozen before she responded, started floating out of the car,
feeling dizzy, falling. I realised I was removing myself from
reliving that situation. I forced myself back into it. I was
back in the car, facing her. I asked again, felt the pounding
in my stomach. She said yes. I sank; it was like a punch in
the stomach – impossible. She said yes. I felt pushed against
the door, they were pushing me away – she was. Finally, it
hit me like it hit me then: 'She doesn't love me.' If she loved
me, she wouldn't say yes – she'd lie to me, protect me, be
unreal for me. I needed her to say no. That's the feeling I
couldn't face. At twenty-five I'd go crazy before I'd face that
at ten years old and probably all my life I'd felt my Mommy
didn't love me.

Saturday

Started with crying. Saw house on O—— Street after the
divorce. My bedroom – my lying on bed feeling so alone. I
screamed and cried for Mommy. Couldn't stand feeling so
alone. It was more of the feeling that she didn't love me or
she wouldn't have gotten the divorce, shattered the fantasy.

Wednesday

Started with throbbing in stomach and choking in throat. I
saw house on B—— Street. The hallway between den and
kitchen. Walked around house looking for something. Saw
Mom and my sister in different places, but they were posed
like immobile statues. I needed something from them but
couldn't get it. I was cut off and alone. I needed to really be
with someone, Mom, and be warm. I needed her to love me.
I hurt – my arms and head hurt. Then felt paralysed like a
baby. The only two ways I knew how to get love. I saw the
three of them in living-room. They looked sick, in their eyes,
afraid. I kept wanting to close door – like I always did. I
went to my room. Or hid by reading. I realised the lifetime
connection I've made between love and pain and for being a
helpless baby, hence never fallen in love with someone

unless it included this struggle with pain. And the need, owing money to Mom and Dad – had to get something from them. When I tried to ask for love, I found my mouth was frozen. Finally could ask for love, over and over again.

Thursday

Throat so tied up this morning I couldn't even talk when I came in. Feeling that all my childhood hurt was like a punch in the stomach. Cried out, 'Mommy, why don't you love me? Please love me.' Felt I wanted her to take care of me and protect me then: 'Mommy, please, don't hurt me,' over and over. None of the calling helped; then came: 'You hurt me, I'm sick, you're making me sick.' I rolled over feeling nauseous. Now: 'You can't help me?' Sank into that feeling – terrorised of being alone and feeling the pain. Deep breathed some of it out of my stomach. Just felt sad in a bigger way, a bigger pain and terror in there than I'd faced before.

I cried some more. Then my body felt tingly, my stomach wracked, but calmer inside. When I sat up I touched my face, and it felt different like I'd never really felt under the skin before – my terrified frozen mask had cracked.

Friday

The feeling still there in my stomach and throat. Finally, today I really felt the pain and aloneness. But couldn't make a connection. Where is that huge pain from? I can't get it out. I'm finally feeling it all the time – not just during sessions. But I feel I've got to get it out.

Saturday

The feeling sits there in the group. Finally, an uncontrolled scream comes out. I cry and cry and then: 'I knew Mommy wasn't there for me all along. I knew she couldn't help that I was alone.' Momentary relief that it came out when it had to. But it's not all of it. Just another piece of the Pain.

9

Breathing, the Voice, and the Scream

Freud believed that dreams were the 'royal road to the unconscious'. If there is a 'royal road', it may lie in deep breathing. For some patients, the use of deep breathing techniques, together with other methods, does help release the tremendous power of the Pain inside the body.

A research study done almost a quarter of a century ago suggested a possible connection between breathing and unpleasantness.[1] A group of subjects who had been instructed to think pleasant thoughts were suddenly asked to think about unpleasant things. There was a significant increase in sighing respirations. More recently, an investigation into the problem of hyperventilation found that breathing dysfunctions were highly correlated with anxiety. Furthermore, during hyperventilation tests, the researcher pushed on the lower portion of the person's chest with his palm to encourage deeper excursion. In nearly all cases this resulted in an accompanying emotional release, along with weeping and the revelation of important historical material.[2]

Wilhelm Reich made the observation that the inhibition of respiration was associated with the inhibition of feeling: 'For it has become clear that the inhibition of respiration was the physiological mechanism of the suppression and repression of emotion, and consequently, the basic mechanism of neurosis.'[3] Reich believed that the respiratory disturbances in neurotics were the result of abdominal tension and went on to describe how this produces shallow breathing and how in fright one holds in the breath with the help of abdominal clenching.

Thus, the technique of deep breathing is used during Primal Therapy to get the patient closer to his feelings. Many of my patients reported the differences in

[1] J. E. Finesinger, 'The Effect of Pleasant and Unpleasant Ideas on the Respiratory Pattern in Psychoneurotic Patients', *American Journal of Psychiatry*, Vol. 100 (1944), p. 659.

[2] B. I. Lewis, 'Hyperventilation Syndromes; Clinical and Physiological Evaluation', *California Medicine*, Vol. 91 (1959), p. 121.

[3] Reich, *op cit.*

their breathing after therapy; only after they had begun to breathe deeply did they understand how shallow their breathing had been previously. Now they say they can feel the air go 'all the way down' when they breathe. In the Primal context this means that they do not dip into their Pain in the ordinary course of events, which suggests that one of the functions of shallow breathing is to prevent the egress of deep Pain.

Proper breathing should be instinctual – the most natural thing in the world – yet the neurotics I have seen rarely breathe correctly. This is because they have enlisted breathing to push down feeling; in short, breathing becomes part of the unnatural system. Neurotic breathing is a good example of how the unreal system suppresses the real one, because after Primals these patients automatically breathe deeply and properly.

Because neurotic breathing is designed to clamp down against the Pain, forcing the Primal patient to breathe deeply often helps lift the lid of repression. The result is the emission of explosive force, something which previously had been diffused throughout the body, in the form of high blood pressure, elevated temperature, shaky hands, or whatever. Primal breathing techniques become the *via regia* to the Pain, unblocking memories along the way. In this important sense, they are the pathways to the unconscious.

It is tempting to minimise the Primal experience as simply a result of the hyperventilation syndrome (that is, breathing heavier than the system requires, resulting in increased oxygenation and decrease of carbon dioxide in the bloodstream). But to do so is to disregard two important factors. The first is that research studies have indicated that feeling pain or unpleasantness, in and of itself, deepens the breathing process – a phenomenon which has been noted by scientific investigators but not explained. I believe that Primal Therapy explains the connection of pain with the depth of breathing. Second, in most cases of hyperventilation there is an accompanying dizziness or lightheadedness. This is not the case during a Primal. Indeed, if a patient reports dizziness, we know he is *not* having a Primal.

I do not believe that breathing techniques, by themselves, have any intrinsic power to transform a neurosis. They may, like a sigh, ease tension for a time, but then they would be considered a defence like any other tension reliever.

In the majority of cases, breathing techniques are either not necessary or rarely used after the first few days of therapy. It must be remembered that it is the *Pain* we are after and that breathing is one of many devices we use to arrive at it.

Breath and the voice that rides astride it seem to be a significant indicator of neurosis. The nervous guest on a television interview show often seems unable to catch his breath. This may be ascribed to trying to present an image which isn't in accord with his real self.

The tense patient about to begin his therapy may be in the same predicament. He is frequently terrified and comes in licking his lips, swallowing and gasping for air.

After the Primal Therapist goes to work on his defence system, the gasping increases. The Pain that seems to be ascending from the knotted stomach cannot rise above the chest barrier, however (often experienced as a tight band). The deep breathing has begun to smash at the barrier. The patient is asked to pull from below at the same time he says 'Aah'. As soon as the 'Aah' hooks into the ascending feeling, the patient is on his own. The power below, finding an opening, seems to push up automatically, and the patient enters into the state I call conflict-breathing.

It is at this point that the major breakthrough is about to take place – the patient is about to shift from being predominantly unreal to predominantly real. Conflict-breathing usually occurs after a number of Primals, just prior to the major connection which will unify the person, keeping him awash in feelings and insights thereafter.

Conflict-breathing is an involuntary stage of the Primal in which the patient begins heavy panting that sounds animalistic. The breathing becomes increasingly rapid and heavy until at times it sounds very much like a locomotive. Because he is so involved with the feeling, the patient is often unaware of the nature of his breathing. Conflict-breathing seems to be the result of the push from below of all the denied feelings against the neurotic forces holding them down. The breathing process can go on for fifteen or twenty minutes, and the person looks as if he were running a race for his life, needing every bit of air he consumes. Under ordinary circumstances, a patient would pass out.

Once the breathing takes on a life of its own, there is little for the therapist to do but watch. Conflict-breathing is a pathognomonic sign that the Primal has begun. Patients report feeling helpless before the onrush of the Pain. During it they somehow know that they could stop if they wanted, but not once in Primal Therapy has a patient aborted his Primal during this stage.

As the breathing broadens and deepens, we can sense that the climax is only seconds or minutes away. The stomach is quivering; the chest is heaving; the legs are bending and unbending; the head is moving from side to side; he is gagging and, in general, seems to be in his last-ditch flight from his Pain. Suddenly, in one large convulsion, the connection seems to be made – and explodes out of the mouth in the form of the Primal Scream. He then breathes fully and easily; one patient said, 'I've just breathed myself back to life.' Patients report then feeling 'cool' 'cleaned', 'pure'.

After the major connection, we find an effortless flow of air, unlike the jerky, sporadic kind of breathing the patient suffered at the beginning of the hour. One patient, a college sprinter, reported that he had never had that kind of full breathing experience even after running a mile.

The Scream has a number of side effects. Patients who could never utter a 'peep' during their home lives, sense a feeling of power. The Scream itself seems to be a liberating experience.

When one listens to Primals on tape, one is always aware of the changes in breathing that accompany the various stages of the Primal experience. The sound of the breathing is critical; a patient cannot be defending part of himself while engaged in a breathing process that encompasses the whole body.

On rare occasions a patient will fake the Scream. It seems to come off the top of the lungs and nearly always comes out as a shriek. The fake Scream seems to be the continuation of unreal hope. Because the Primal Scream signifies an end to the struggle, it is unlikely to be heard from someone still engaged in the struggle.

Though we often talk about deep feelings, we rarely specify where 'deep' may be. From my experience, I think 'deep feelings' involve the total organism, particularly the area of the stomach and diaphragm. Some of us get the idea early in life that our parents do not want us to be exuberant and really alive, and soon learn to go around almost holding our breath out of fear of doing or saying the wrong thing, being too loud or boisterous, laughing too unroariously. Sooner or later this fear strangles the feeling into a taut throat, a tight chest, and a clenched stomach. Because of this clamping-off process, the voice tends to be higher-pitched; it is a voice *not connected* to the whole body.

In many cases, neurotic speech can best be compared to a ventriloquist's dummy – the mouth moving mechanically, dehumanised without any seeming ties to the rest of the system. Because it rests on a layer of tension rather than on a solid foundation of feeling, the tense voice is often shaky.

The mouth also seems quite involved in the neurosis. Patients after Primal Therapy often report feeling the tension they used to have about their lips. One patient, after her Primal, felt her upper lip for the first time in years. She said that her lip had always been numb: 'Maybe because I grew up in a family nurtured on clichés like "Keep a stiff upper lip".' What I am suggesting is that our entire system seems to reflect the Pain. When one is angry, for example, one will usually draw the lips back into a thin line; when the anger persists, the set of the lips may persist.

Not only do the face and jaw relax after the Primals, but the voice drops. It is possibly one of the more obvious and dramatic signs of someone who has been through the therapy. Thin-voiced, baby-talking women find a new depth and fullness to their voices. There is a richer quality to their speech.

Neurotic speech often lacks nuance because it reflects a constant state of tension. One patient said, 'I used to speak in a rush, off the top of my head. I never had any feeling that I was talking. All that pressure inside used to push everything out in hunks. Now I can feel myself talking.' Perhaps the phrase 'torrent of words' is an apt analogue to the notion that neurotic speech is the spillway of tension.

A patient who always had a small voice said after his Primal, 'I think everything about me was small. I had a feeling there was a strong voice around somewhere, I just never had the guts to use it.' Another patient who spoke nasally before said, 'All my life I thought I had something wrong with my nose. Now it seems that I was just whining and didn't know it. I was filtering all my feelings through my nostrils instead of being open and direct about things.'

One indication that speech can be a rather accurate mirror of the self is that when we imagine ourselves with someone else's voice (bereft of our defensive speech) it often produces anxiety. For this reason I will sometimes have the patients in group swap voices as a means of lowering their defences.

Clearly, I consider the speech of the neurotic to be a defence mechanism. The soft-voiced person may be acting out through his inaudible phrases the fear of drawing any more attention, and therefore, he may be keeping the lid on a scream.

When the Primal Therapist slows down the rapid speaker and makes him 'take pains' with his speech, he is cutting into a defence mechanism. So long as there is a pool of denied feelings, they colour and shape each word out of the neurotic's mouth, as well as the structure of the mouth itself. When the patient speaks during his first few hours, we are listening to his defence at work. Here, at least, 'the medium is the message'.

I think that speech is but one facet of the total defensive operations of the person. When we find babyish speech, it has been my experience that we find immaturity in sexual relationships *and*, often, in body build (where there is a little girl's or boy's frame). In terms of the above, one would not expect to find a problem in one area without finding it elsewhere as well. The same thing that is inhibiting a full voice may be affecting the patient's inability to achieve full orgasm.

An example: A young boy is criticised for everything he says and does and at the same time is not allowed to talk back or express his anger. The suppressed anger stays on and colours his facial set as he grows. Later he has children. Each word out of his mouth has an angry tone and is an implicit and perpetual threat to his child. The child subdues all facets of his own behaviour out of fear of setting off the old volcano in Father. His speech is subdued; his movements are tight and restricted. This constriction may affect all bodily processes, possibly even the growth process. The fear of saying the wrong thing and causing an explosion in his father may produce a speech problem in the child. Each word will have to be examined for its possible danger. Stammering and stuttering may be the result.

One former stutterer explained his speech problem in this manner: 'My stuttering was really the struggle. It was like the "not me" was talking to keep the real me from getting out. I always had to choose my words carefully since the time I began speaking. I ended mouthing my parents' thoughts and words. I spoke what they wanted to hear. It's like I held onto them with my mouth. As long as the real me didn't say what it felt, I could get by with them.'

This man never stuttered during a Primal when he was being his real self. Stuttering seems to be graphic evidence of the conflict between the two selves and the symptoms that the conflict engenders. This patient's stutter-free Primals also indicate how feeling does away with the neurotic symptoms.

During a group session, while this man was discussing his symptoms, another member of the group pointed out to him that while he held onto his parents with his mouth, she held on by keeping her vagina frigid. In other words, she was suggesting that the locus of the struggle is that place where the growing child focuses his struggle. If a woman hopes to be good and pure for her parents, the struggle (the denial of feeling) may be channelled into the genitalia. Other times, as we have seen, it can be the mouth. In any case, when a child takes his parents' attitudes into his mind and operates on them instead of his own feelings, we can expect that the body will no longer function in a real, fluid way.

Speech is a creative process in which we produce something in each moment that did not exist before. The neurotic re-creates his past in his every word. The normal creates a continuously new present.

10

Neurosis and Psychosomatic Disease

Tension is the central motivant of the neurotic, constantly activating him. Because the activation is an unreal response, there is no feedback into the system that tells him when to stop. Muscles are taut, hormones are secreted, the brain is alert – all for a danger that no longer exists.

There is an experiment of John Lacey and associates that gives us more information about the mechanisms involved in the bodily reaction to stress.[1] The study dealt with the acceleration and deceleration of the heart under stress. It was found that the heart rate decreases when the subject is attentive and open to his surroundings – that is, when he wants to accept what is going on about him. The heart rate accelerates when the person wants to reject what is happening. Further, the heart rate accelerates during pain. The investigators believe that it speeds up in order to mobilise the body against the anticipated impact of pain. In addition, under pain there is an increase in arterial (blood) pressure.[2]

The significance of the study is that it may not be pain alone that causes heart rate increase, *but the need to reject it*. If the Primal Pain hypothesis is correct, it follows that the body, particularly the heart, would be affected adversely by attempts to reject such Pains. This would then help explain the great prevalence of heart and blood pressure syndromes so early in the lives of many of us. Our bodies are just working overtime, fighting unseen and unfelt enemies. The heart, as a muscle, must be responding in the same manner as the rest of our muscle system.

[1] John I. Lacey, 'Psychophysiological Approaches to the Evaluation of Psychotherapeutic Process and Outcome', in E. A. Rubenstein and N. B. Parloff, eds., *Research and Psychotherapy* (Washington, D.C., American Psychological Association National Publishing Co., 1959).

[2] Ernest R. Hilgard reported in the February, 1969, edition of the *American Psychologist* on his studies of pain and blood pressure ('Pain as Puzzle'). He states: 'When stressful conditions which normally lead both to reported pain and to an increase in blood pressure do not lead to an increase in blood pressure, it may be assumed that pain is absent.'

Tension as a total bodily experience must wreak havoc with all the organism, especially constitutionally weakened organs. Year after year of this stress must wear us down, accounting for the fact that the tension-free individual should live a good deal longer than his neurotic counterpart.

The symptom that develops depends on a number of factors. One, for example, is what the person's culture has come to regard as acceptable – headaches and ulcers are often 'expected' symptoms in the United States. But more critical is the symbolic meaning of the organ or area affected. Most neurotics cannot, or dare not, see their problems, so the message of the feeling is symbolised – myopia, for example, or the asthma that develops when a child is not even allowed to breathe on his own. (A patient who had previously had asthma as a child found it acted up again as he approached key Primal feelings during therapy.)

Literally symbolic of the neurotic split is the 'splitting' headache. This affliction is largely due to feeling one way and having to act another. 'There's shame in my head for what my body is feeling,' said one patient.

The neurotic then feeds himself aspirins and other pain-killers without understanding that the pain he is dealing with is Primal Pain. The headaches recur because the Primal Pain is there constantly. One patient put it this way: 'I used to say, "Mama, my head is killing me," without knowing what I was saying. My head was killing the real me. I had to pretend that my feelings didn't exist so I packed them away somewhere in my head until it felt like it was going to explode.'

Many of us spend so much time killing the wrong pains – taking stomach relaxants or muscle relaxants or pain-killers, trying in vain to dispel the symptomatic expression of real hurts inside. Those symptomatic pains have fought their way through the defence system to warn us, but because of that defence system, all that usually emerges is pure hurt, localised here or there, so the person does not know what is causing his suffering.

At a recent meeting of the New York Academy of Science, several scientists reported a possible link between emotions and cancer. A psychiatrist, Claus Bahnson of the Jefferson Medical College, reported: 'Most prone to cancer ... are those who deny their emotions.' His findings indicated that when individuals experienced personal tragedy, those who were cancer-prone tended to channel their emotional response internally through the nervous system. This, in turn, upset the hormone balance and thus played a role in the control of the growth of cancer. Bahnson also pointed out that cancer patients as a rule have had a 'poor, ungratifying, mechanical relationship to their parents'.[3] He went on to say that since these parents were unable or unwilling to respond emotionally, their children developed a tendency to repress rather than express their feelings.

Other research findings at this same meeting tended to corroborate these possibilities. W. A. Greene, of the University of Rochester, found in cancer patients a high degree of hopelessness and helplessness.[4]

(An interesting sidelight is that the Sioux Indians, who are known to vent emotions freely, have almost no incidence of cancer.)

Psychological literature is filled with volumes of psychosomatic medicine. We are particularly indebted to the pioneer Franz Alexander for his work on the symbolic meanings of somatic ailments.[5] It is not my intent to explore all the various kinds of psychosomatic ailments and their meanings. Suffice to note that many current diseases which have been considered purely physical must be understood in terms of afflicted bodies hooked into a *totally* sick system which, under otherwise ordinary circumstances, functions remarkably well and healthily.

When a child is young and his physical system is still strong, he can apparently withstand a good deal of tension. After years of chronic tension, vulnerable organ systems tend to break down. Only when individuals are ready to be grown-up, to be free of their childhood, can they become free to be the adults they are *physically* as well as mentally. Thus, maturity means maturity of limbs and organs, as well as mental maturity. (Personal growth means growth of the entire person.) One very short woman began growing after a Primal in which she felt the meaning of being little: 'I stayed

[3] Claus Bahnson, *Proceedings*. New York Academy of Science (Spring, 1968).

[4] W. A. Greene, *Proceedings*. New York Academy of Science (Spring, 1968).

[5] Franz Alexander, *Psychosomatic Medicine* (New York, Norton, 1950).

small so that my father would see that I was still his little girl waiting for him to take care of me. If I grew tall, he would never have realised (I thought) that I was still his baby.' My experience in conventional therapy never produced results of this kind.

Corroboration of the relationship of growth to mental status has recently come from a Johns Hopkins pediatric research investigator, Robert Blizzard. Lecturing before the Children's Division of County–USC Medical Center (Los Angeles, 22 September 1969), he has this to say: 'Many pediatricians used to call hogwash the notion that the psyche might control growth. But it's not hogwash.' Dr Blizzard noted that often when a six-year-old has the height of a three-year-old, the level of the growth hormone is far below what it should be. He pointed out that some small children will grow rapidly when taken out of a poor home environment, even when that move is to an orphanage. Within four or five days they will begin producing the normal flow of growth hormones, and some of these short children will grow ten inches in a single year. When these children were returned to their old environments, they immediately stopped growing again! Studies of the homes of these children indicated great deprivation in terms of love. Sometimes the mothers admitted hating their children. Dr Blizzard says the only help for stunted children is a new environment. For stunted adults, I suggest Primal Therapy.

Psychosomatic medicine is often a perplexing problem for the physician because, first, the patient often isn't aware that he is tense and, second, nothing may be happening in the patient's present life to indicate the cause of an affliction. So there is often no apparent psychological cause for a sudden illness. An example of this is the man on the go who finally has his first heart attack. His physician may attribute it to pushing himself so hard at work and say: 'You'd better take it easy from now on; try to relax and not be so active.' But this very behaviour may well hurry along his second coronary since being inactive is tantamount to removing the defence system, building tension and increasing the internal pressure. Thus, the second attack would be the result not of overwork but of *underwork*. More precisely, it would come about because the person had nothing to focus on to relieve his tension. Perhaps the early death we see in some men following retirement can also be ascribed to this removal of the work defence.

The physician may reason that the various problems which patients bring to his office are not psychosomatic because there is no visible emotional trauma. It is possible, however, that the symptom which confronts the physician is the result of accumulated tension. The necessity of having one's tension level measured periodically may be helpful in understanding and preventing many kinds of maladies. High continued tension means, *inter alia*, the possibility of hormone imbalance and the diseases resulting from that imbalance. Several patients who had hypothyroidism before therapy found themselves changed after therapy. When they stopped taking thyroid pills, they had none of the usual effects they had experienced from going off medication before.

I believe that neurosis must be considered a factor in nearly every disease. To block a feeling is to suppress aspects of one's physiology. I have rarely seen a neurotic who was physically healthy. Recent studies have shown that more anxious individuals are more susceptible to viruses, for example. I foresee the day when medicine will no longer be split between the body (internal medicine) and the mind (psychiatry). This split has caused medicine to deal with physical symptoms and psychiatry to deal with mental symptoms without a thorough understanding that those symptoms are an outgrowth of a psychobiologic system in conflict. In Primal terms, there is little difference between a mental symptom, such as a phobia, and a physical one, such as headaches. The symptom is but the idiosyncratic way the person resolves his conflict. To specialise in the treatment of symptoms is to deal in fragments of human beings. It must not be forgotten that symptoms are hooked into *systems*. To treat an ulcer or a depression apart from that system means to neglect causes. This does not mean that symptoms must not be dealt with, but alleviating symptoms is a temporary expedient.

THE DISAPPEARANCE OF SYMPTOMS

While symptoms – tics, ulcers, frigidity, headaches, sexual perversions, etc. – do disappear in Primal Therapy, this is true of many therapies. But one important difference is that in Primal Therapy, symptoms are usually the last to go. This is in contrast with my experience with standard therapy where I was sometimes able to alleviate symptoms rather quickly. This may be because by helping a patient function and keep busy, the standard therapy practitioner provides enough outlets for excess tension to diminish his patient's symptoms. In Primal Therapy, with outlets cut off, symptoms may initially become aggravated because along the therapeutic path he has lost many of his lesser defences. So long as any part of the unreal self exists, so long as there is a split, the symptom will continue. It will disappear at about the time the person is ready to leave therapy.

There are good reasons for the delayed loss of symptoms. First, the symptom – let us say overeating – usually has been the focal point of the patient's life and the central spillway for neurotic tension. The symptom is often the last to go because it usually has made an early appearance in the patient's life. Tics and allergies often begin before the age of five, but stuttering can begin with the beginnings of speech at the age of two or three. The symptom was how the young infant resolved his split.

Bodily symptoms such as constipation, stuttering, or tics should not be thought of as simple habits to be conditioned out of the organism. They are the involuntary physical reactions to the split (the feeling disconnected from thought) which produces bodily pressures that are beyond conscious will or control. These pressures produce symptoms. Suppressing a real thought (the mental counterpart of a physical feeling) can produce a mental symptom (an unreal idea or a phobia which is a more serious kind of unreal idea). Suppressing the physical counterpart of the real thought (the painful, Primal thought) can produce physical symptoms (minor gas pressure in the stomach, which sooner or later can become an ulcer or colitis).

It is important to understand that the severity of symptoms increases with the amount and longevity of the pressure. Initial mental pressure may produce a few unreal ideas or phobias. Eventually, it can produce delusions or hallucinations. Hallucinations would be only the end point of a process of developing unreal ideas which began in early childhood. As pressure of more and more denied feelings mounts, it provokes the mind to twist itself in more complex convolutions. At the same time, it puts more stress on vulnerable organs which help drain some of the tension. Should an organ system finally give way, the tension (pressure) will tend to become channelled there. If it cannot reduce enough of the pressure, more organ systems may be affected. So we may find (as is the case with one patient), first a post-nasal drip, then severe allergies, then asthma, then ulcers, and so on.

I wish to stress the unity of all neurotic symptoms, psychological and physical. A blocked feeling may result in accumulated tension eventually affecting the lining of the stomach, or that same feeling may be acted out masochistically, resulting in an externalisation of that same Pain. In both cases it is making the Pain real. Once it is real, something can be done about it. For ailments there are pills. For the masochistic ritual there is a beginning and an end. In both cases it is a relocation of Pain to something concrete, into something that can be controlled. Ailments are involuntary symptoms of Pain, while masochism is a voluntary symptom. Though they appear to be disparate phenomena, they are only different channels for blocked feelings.

Sadism is another variation in which Pain, in order not to be felt, is inflicted on another. Someone hits his wife when he really wants to hit his mother, and on a deeper level, he may want to hit his mother because he hurts from lack of love.

The dynamics in the choice of symptomatic acting out or acting in can be complex. (Psychosomatic symptoms are unreal behaviour.) They are the result of life circumstances and one's constitutional makeup. But to understand any symptom (in this case, masochism or psychosomatic afflictions), we must see that it is relocated behaviour. It is the focus, the way we pinpoint the apparent sources of suffering: 'My husband is cruel. Life would be different if he did not get drunk and beat me.' 'I would be fine if I could just shake the headaches.' Neither statement is usually true. Life would not be fine. Both behaviours fit into the life-style of the individual. They serve a purpose; they keep real Pain away.

Because symptoms keep real Pain away, they are defences. The reason significant symptoms are often the last to go in Primal Therapy is that the defence system, which came into being as a stable entity after the major Primal Scene, functions on an all-or-none basis. When there are still critical hurts to be felt even during the latter stages of Primal Therapy, the patient will frequently first revert to his entering symptoms. When he finally feels what made him split fully, it is unlikely that he will ever have symptoms again. If we see this in reverse, it becomes more understandable. When a young child splits at his major scene, the excess, unresolved tension finds a spillway – the symptom. This symptom 'handles' the feeling and resolves the conflict in an unreal way. Treating symptoms alone, then, means treating unreality. It is an endless job, whether those symptoms are mental or physical. This is why psychoanalysis of symptoms takes so long.

An insight into symptom formation is provided in a study by Barker and associates.[6] They had previously found that symptoms such as asthma, ulcers and hypertension became worse during sodium amytal interviews ,amytal is a barbiturate used to sedate or hypnotise). Patients speak more freely under amytal; the drug seems to relax some of the acquired inhibitions (the unreal front). The implicit question in the Barker study was: Why should someone get worse (develop symptoms) when he is less inhibited? During the course of their study into fits and epilepsy with patients under amytal, they described the following situation:[7]

> The patient [who had previous epileptic fits] sat in a semi-reclining chair with electrodes fixed to his scalp for brain-wave recording. It had been a 'tough week', he said, characterised by arguments with his wife and mother. Sodium amytal [was given] at the rate of one-and-a-half grains per minute for three minutes. The relaxation induced at the start of injection was, in this case, transitory. He began to display increased tension. Asked, 'What is the matter?' he replied, 'My m-m-m-mother.' He grimaced, growled and spoke rather

[6] W. Barker and S. Wolf, 'Experimental Production of Grand Mal Seizure During the Hypnoidal State Induced by Sodium Amytal', *American Journal of Medical Science*, Vol. 214 (1947) p. 600.

[7] Wayne Barker, *Brain Storms* (New York, Grove Press, 1968), pp. 105–6.

disconnectedly of his mother. He appeared alternately angry and in pain. Comments about his mother were interspersed with groans of, 'Oh ... Oh ... Oh ...!' Asked, 'How does your mother bother you?' he said, 'I wish I could get ahold of her. I'd k-k-kill her. She's no good ... She's always bothering me ... all the time ... all the time.' He seemed to be barely restraining great rage.

'My mother killed my father,' he continued. 'I'll kill her sometime. She drives me crazy.' He clenched his fists, raised them to his forehead, and appeared no longer able either to contain his rage or *express it* [my emphasis]. Suddenly his face went blank and he gave a short, strangled cry. Then a violent muscular spasm seized him; he went rigid; his face contorted in a great grimace; his back arched; his arms flexed strongly across his chest; his legs were straight and stiff. This rigid muscular spasm relaxed and returned in a series of alternating contractions and relaxations typical of a major convulsion. Brain waves during his two minute seizure were characteristic of a major convulsive fit. Hypnoidal *reliving of reactions to his mother had been aborted by the eruption of an epileptic fit* [again, my emphasis].

The researchers were frankly astonished by all this because sodium amytal has definite *anti-convulsive* properties. They concluded that the fit was brought on by a conflict between uncontrollable rage and the restrictions of conscience.

I shall quote just a bit more of what Barker has to say because it relates to the Primal concept. 'This was consistent with Freud's formulation ... a convulsive fit, in this view, reduces the level of discharge from that of a meaningful display to that of subpersonal meaningless neuromuscular activity.'

What his investigator is saying, in effect, is that blocked feelings resulted in a massive buildup of tension with the final convulsive release – an epileptic fit. If it were not a seizure he was describing, I would have thought he was writing about what happens in Primal Therapy. Clearly, one blocked feeling in one's life does not produce the epileptic syndrome, any more than it produces ulcers or stuttering or asthma. But when years of repressing feelings are involved, one must conclude that there is an accumulation of tension beyond the capacity of the organism to withstand it. Affected will be the area or organ of vulnerability. For a person born with a tendency towards allergy, a tension buildup may eventually become asthma; for one with a tendency to disorders of the brain, accumulated tension may lead to epilepsy. What would have happened if the patient were urged to scream his feeling? I believe that expressing his feeling would have prevented the development of a symptom (the resolution of the conflict). Blocking the feeling produced diffuse neuromuscular activity – tension.

It should be clear that expressing his feelings one time might have stopped only that one particular seizure; he would still be epileptic and, given enough stress, would have symptoms again. When all his past repressions were out of the way, we might then be able to say that he had a predisposition to epilepsy but not epilepsy. It is like being basically sensitive or allergic but having no allergies.

Barker goes on:

> Dr Herbert S. Ripley and I conducted [another] interview [a different patient]. At the induction of hypnosis the patient began spontaneously to relive a series of traumatic experiences (charged with aggressive urges, feelings of guilt, and feelings of helplessness), regressing in time as he went from one episode to another. It was as if he were spreading out in time, for our inspection, a dense complex of highly charged related experiences. The abreactive reliving of the series seemed to convey what he could usually only express convulsively.

Here Barker states almost word for word the Primal hypothesis. Indeed, this man had a Primal experience induced by a hypnotic process where conscious controls were removed. In this case Barker indicates that reliving strong emotional situations from the past headed off an epileptic fit. Or, conversely, it infers that strong unresolved, unexpressed feelings from the past build into convulsive fits. Many people build tension, some have ulcers, and still others have fits. The problem is the *tension*, not the release form. I would conclude from Barker's descriptions that hypnosis and amytal weaken the unreal, defensive self. What emerges are Primal feelings – feelings previously held in check by the front. A stage hypnotist may at one point reroute the front and make someone into something or someone else, but in the Barker experiments nothing more was done than easing the front. This is evidence again of how relaxation (a vacation, retirement, a brief illness) is a threat to some neurotics, a threat to their whole physical system. It helps explain why so few neurotics dare relax; to relax is to be overwhelmed and perhaps to die.

Barker's work has something else to say. Symptoms are necessary to the psychophysical economy of the individual. They resolve conflict. *To remove symptoms without removing causes is to leave persons susceptible to worse occurrences from accumulated tension.*

Barker later interviewed a ten-year-old boy. This boy had been persuaded by his mother to avoid fights at all costs. He was asked about this while hooked into a brain-wave machine: 'How did you feel when you had to turn the other cheek and it meant getting beat up or having to run away?' 'I didn't want them to think I was a coward, but mother would feel very bad and make me feel bad if I got into a fight. . . .' Barker then describes him as tense, and then the boy said, 'I couldn't get mad at my mother. She's my mother. She borned me!'

The brain-wave pattern was of tension, not unlike some minor epileptic readings. Barker concludes: 'Without the EEG [brain-wave machine], the presence of an epileptic component in this seemingly ordinary blocking of speech might not have been suspected. [This] establishes a connection between all epileptic and *non-epileptic* [my emphasis] fits.' Blocked feelings, in short, have the capacity (at least on the level of brain activity) to produce convulsions. This means that under upset the brain has convulsions at times even when the person doesn't. Those brain convulsions may then produce neurotic behaviour and symptoms which are no different in cause from epileptic fits (according to Barker, even flatulence can be a fit). Because there are convulsive brainstorms in many kinds of upsets, one must wonder whether a symptom such as stuttering is an epileptic equivalent. Is stuttering then, 'epilepsy of the mouth'?

Barker is indicating that blocked speech and the feelings that go with that speech build tension which finds its way to the brain. One wonders from this what the effect must be of years of repressing speech and feelings. What is significant about the Barker study is that if one were to study brain tracings alone, one would assume that symptoms of either epilepsy or, say, stuttering would be caused by brain-wave irregularities. To look further is to find out that those irregular brain tracings result from the accumulation of blocked feelings. We must always use care not to equate the cause of a disease with what we are measuring. Thus, if certain changes can be found in the chemical components of the blood or urine of schizophrenics, it must not necessarily be assumed that those urine and blood changes *cause* schizophrenia.

What Barker points out in his excellent book is that many disjunctive behaviours seem to have a correlation in the absence of smooth functioning of the brain and that these both may be the result of blocked feelings and the subsequent buildup of tension. This load 'embarrasses' (his term) the brain by giving it too much to do smoothly. In Primal terms, it means that brain functions break down when something happens to us which is more than we can integrate at one time – Primal Scenes.

What all this means is that when we cannot be ourselves in a situation, that situation does not simply end for us. It is internalised in the form of tension which finds its way to the brain, where functioning is disrupted. This could result in hazy thinking, stuttering, or epilepsy. Or in simply random acting-out behaviour such as keeping on the go.

The neurotic symptom is the idiosyncratic resolution of the person's internal struggle. The style, in this sense, is the man. The symptom, therefore, cannot have universal meaning; it can have meaning only within that person. So grinding one's teeth may have a myriad of meanings. For one patient it was holding on for dear life – 'by the skin of my teeth', as she put it. For another, it reflected rage which could never be expressed. But for each patient each symptom has *one* meaning – what it means to him and him alone. So we cannot say that there is a type who grinds teeth and that those who grind teeth are passive-dependent, aggressive, latent this, or latent that. Nor can we have universal definitions; only the patient can tell us what his symptom means.

There are neurotic symptoms which are not usually thought of as such – being short, for example. Now a person usually wouldn't go to a psychologist because he was short. But we find out after therapy that the person's development was retarded not only mentally but physically. We see that the patient has grown and thus may infer that his being short *was* indeed a symptom – his idiosyncratic resolution of the inner contradictions which plagued him.

Over the past two years, I have not known of any symptom which has returned in a person who has completed Primal Therapy, something I could never say about my work as a conventional therapist. Why? Because symptoms, in my estimation, depend on tension. The symptoms do not return because there is no Primal Pain to produce tension. There is no split pulling the body and mind apart. There is nothing, in short, which lies submerged creating pressure on the organism.

I could go on endlessly listing all the symptoms which Primal Therapy has eliminated, from menstrual cramps to asthma. But that would tend to make Primal Therapy seem some kind of panacea and thus lessen its credibility. 'At least if you told me about some of your failures, about some symptoms that *never* went away,' said one colleague, 'I'd be more ready to accept your outrageous claims.' But Primal Therapy *should* be able to do away with all symptoms or the premise – that symptoms are the result of Primal Pains – is not valid.

Perhaps the post-Primal patient, symptom-free and nontense, sounds like superman. But it is the neurotic who is trying to be superman; eating twice as much, working twice as hard, using twice the energy to accomplish twice the misery.

DISCUSSION

Every man is his truth. For the neurotic, those truths are Primal Pains. A lie of the mind means a hurt of the body. Though the neurotic's mind says there is nothing wrong, his body is telling the truth. Psychosomatic ailments are the truth of the body.

As time goes on, we may have to change many of our ideas about what is normal functioning. A patient who is a nurse has measured the pulse rates and blood pressures of other patients in the group and found these rates to be consistently lower than average. A number of patients have noted a constant drop in their resting body temperature. Some state that their temperature hovers near 96 degrees continuously. In general, Post-Primal patients are in excellent health, and I can ascribe this finding only to the absence of chronic tension.

When the neurotic doesn't fall prey to disease resulting from chronic tension, he may succumb to his tension-relief habit. Smoking, over-eating, pills, drinking – all take their toll. Even with the aid of these habits to drain tension, many neurotics still suffer from psychosomatic illnesses. The neurotic system is like a giant vessel spilling over the edge with symptoms. It has been our task to beat back the symptoms as best we can. But it must be clear that we need to drain the vessel of high tension if symptoms are to be eradicated. We can only do that if we understand that neurotic tension is not normal and has no place in a healthy system. Symptoms are the result of the body working against self, of the pressure between the unreal and real selves. Any lasting physical and mental health must involve eliminating this pull.

11

On Being Normal

It is the aim of Primal Therapy to make individuals real. Normal people are real by definition. Post-Primal patients become real because of their therapy. These patients still carry scars, however. They have been wounded many times over in their lives, and one cannot wash away their memories; one can only defuse them so that these memories no longer exert the force which made the neurotic act out symbolically. With so much deprivation as a neurotic, obviously the post-Primal person is not going to be a totally fulfilled human being. As a neurotic he could only struggle towards fulfilment. His therapy now frees him to fill his needs in the present.

When I talk about a normal human being, I am discussing a defence-free, tensionless, non-struggling person. My view of normality has nothing to do with statistical norms, averages, social adjustment scales, conformity, or non-conformity. When a person is himself, how he behaves may be as varied and infinite as the number of people in the world. The normal is himself. Primal Therapy makes someone into himself, rather than tries to have a person 'make something *out* of himself'.

I shall discuss the normal in contrast with the neurotic. Later I shall draw a composite picture of a post-Primal patient: how he feels, what he does, and the kinds of relationships he has.

Being satisfied makes the normal relaxed. The neurotic who is dissatisfied because he did not have his needs satisfied must search out apparent sources of his dissatisfaction. This keeps him from knowing what the real sources of his unhappiness are. So he dreams of getting a new job, going after another college degree, moving someplace else, or finding a new girlfriend. By focusing on his bad job, non-understanding wife, etc., he hopes the basic discontentment will be removed.

I recall one patient coming into therapy one day complaining about the political turn of events in this country.

He was obsessed with getting out and moving abroad. What he had to say about the political atmosphere seemed to be quite real. Nevertheless, when he felt his real discontentment, it did not change his ideas about the political situation, but it did alter his obsession to get out. What he felt was: 'There is no good home for me.' He had never had a good home. Bad home = bad homeland. His dream was of finding that good home elsewhere.

Because he is not where he is, the neurotic will never be content for any lasting period of time. He is using the present to work out the past. So he will buy a house and fix it up, and when he is done, he will want a new house. Or he will find a girlfriend and then leave her after he has 'conquered' her.

To the neurotic, the struggle, not the result, is important. Thus he often cannot complete what he starts. He justifies his inadequate jobs on the basis of having so much to do. But he has so much to do because he does not finish. To finish and feel unfulfilled is to hurt. This is why so many individuals have a hard time in the last months of working for an advanced degree. It is also why some people cannot rest content with money in the bank. Just after getting out of debt, they must borrow again so as to maintain the struggle. To feel 'I have arrived; I have money in the bank, and I still feel unhappy' is intolerable. The struggle takes care of that. Some neurotic housewives rarely get up early and finish their housework completely. Then they would have to face the emptiness of their lives. Instead, they have one or two rooms in constant disarray, in this way they maintain their struggles. They can *look forward to* having the house furnished or cleaned and that keeps them from feeling 'And now what?' once the chores are done.

The normal, who does not need struggle, who needs no obstacles in his path to keep him in that struggle, can get down to things. The neurotic, delaying the feeling of his Pain, delays much of the rest of his living. Indeed, feeling that Pain is the beginning of living for the neurotic. Until he feels it, he must be elusive, in terms of eluding not only what hurts but any unpleasantness as well. Because he is constantly on the move away from his real self, he tends to be flighty – if not physically, then mentally. His mind is filled with what he plans to do; he cannot sit still. He is on the move even in his sleep, thrashing about or perspiring. He may be so activated that he cannot sleep at all – obsessed with disturbing thoughts and unresolved business.

The normal can be with you completely. Part of him isn't locked away in 'reserve'; the normal, therefore, can be completely interested. The neurotic is too often a whirlpool of distractions; his eyes, like his mind, seem to dart from one subject to another, unable to focus for any length of time.

The normal, of course, is not split. This means that when he shakes your hand, his eyes are not looking elsewhere. He can listen completely, something which is rare in a neurotic society. The neurotic can really hear only what he wants to hear. Most of the time he is thinking about what he is going to say next. What he hears, as a rule, will be valued only if it refers to himself in one way or another. He cannot be objective and appreciate for itself what is outside him (and that goes for his children). Neurotic conversations can rarely transcend personal experience ('what I said', 'what he said to me') because neurotic interest is in the self which is unfulfilled. The normal is interested in his self in a different way. Everything in the world does not have to be related to it, but he is able to relate himself to the world. He is not using his outer world to cover the inner one.

The normal does not feel lonely; he feels alone, and that alone feeling is far different from what he felt before when alone. It is a separate, unattached experience devoid of fear and panic. Neurotic loneliness is a denial of being alone, a need to be with others in order to flee from the catastrophic Primal feeling of being rejected and really alone most of one's life. The inventors of Muzak and the car radio understood neurotic loneliness; these are like Pain relievers – defences provided gratis so that the neurotic will not have to feel his aloneness. For the normal, they are often considered an invasion of one's privacy.

The normal is straight, and one can sense it in the way he reacts. The neurotic leads an exaggerated life – he either overreacts or underreacts; since the time he found his true reactions unacceptable, he has had to react in phony ways or pretend not to react at all. For example, a patient had a neurotic friend over to see her new apartment. She asked her how she liked the decor. The friend said, 'Oh, I wish my rug looked as good as yours.' She only saw the room in terms of her own needs, and her reaction was a typically neurotic response. Or, if some neurotics hear a joke, instead of experiencing the humour and laughing, they will immediately counter with a topper.

Whenever someone must 'identify', rather than feel, we see this improper reaction. Thus, the normal reacts appropriately, not because he is trying to produce an effect or has studied a book of rules, but because he can feel what is appropriate. This means that to be a good parent, he need not endlessly study parent guidance manuals. He will be a natural person, allowing his children to be natural people.

Because the normal no longer must cover the feeling of unimportance, he does not have to struggle to be treated as someone special by waiters and hotel personnel. For the neurotic, this is often a full-time occupation. Part of the neurotic need is to surround oneself with people, not to feel alone, or to join clubs, to cover the feeling that one never belonged to a real family. All this incessant struggle is over for the normal.

When I think about the neurotic struggle, I remember a recent advertisement for a brand of scotch: 'It can be a small way of paying yourself back for all the years of struggle it took to get where you are.'

Neurotic struggles are manufactured. Thus, a woman can spend years shopping for bargains and never feel that what she bought was totally satisfactory. Probably it wasn't. If she could have got her parents' love without struggle, then perhaps bargains wouldn't be so important. Bargaining is the all-American neurosis. It's much the same as the magic diet pill; it's getting something good for little effort, like scotch. What makes bargaining especially delicious is the struggle. The greater the struggle, the more valued the prize, except that this is not the real prize desired for the great struggle of the person's life. It is but a lowly substitute because years of struggle for parental love came to naught. Bargaining is the analogue of the neurotic's life with his parents with one difference: The neurotic finally wins what he often doesn't want.

Walking into a store and paying the list price are difficult for many neurotics because to pay retail is not to be made 'special'. Anyone can pay retail, and if you do, you are just like anyone else. The normal is not a compulsive bargain hunter. He tries to make his life easy, not difficult.

Closely akin to bargaining is the way neurotics treat money. One patient said that he could never keep money in the bank before therapy because it meant that he didn't have to struggle any more. This man was in a constant struggle away from an early feeling of worthlessness. He had hoped (unconsciously) that money would make him feel worthwhile. But of course there was never enough money to do that. When he had money, he could not live with it because he still felt worthless, and so he was driven on to accumulate more. The normal is not using money symbolically to fill old needs. He feels worthwhile because he was valued just as he was by normal parents. Money is the natural preoccupation of so many neurotics because the neurotic, by definition, must feel worthless; he was not valued for what he was. Not being able to feel his true needs, he will always want more than he needs.

There are other neurotics who can never spend money. Their struggle was possibly to try to feel safe and secure. But again, money alone cannot make an insecure person secure. This kind of neurotic is constantly postponing life: 'Some-day, when things are right, I'll take my vacation.' He never lives. Instead, he clings to a fantasy of how life will be some-day. That fantasy is intimately associated with Pain, which helps explain why so many individuals postpone so much of their lives. The normal, on the other hand, can get to things now. He has no old Pains dragging him back and making him put off matters. His real feelings eliminate the need for unreal fantasies.

The normal is stable. He is content to be just where he is and doesn't have to imagine that real life is 'out there' some-where. One woman put it this way: 'I used to look in the mirror and see my wrinkles and get terrified. I ran to one beauty expert after another, tried special lotions, and when that didn't do it, I tried a face lift. I was in a desperate flight from feeling that my youth was over and I'd never have a chance to get what that little girl inside me needed. Seeing those wrinkles and some grey hair set off my hopelessness at ever being little again, and so I ran and ran. I went to parties and functions by the dozens. Tried to be "in" and attractive. "Run" was my middle name. I couldn't stop.'

The normal can accept his age because he is living now and has felt and experienced his youth. He is not trying each day of his life to recapture something lost decades before. He is neither excessively worried about the future nor perpetually reminiscing about his past because he is not living a time that doesn't exist.

With the neurotic, 'the personality is the message', to borrow from McLuhan's apothegm. The personality is warped towards the message it must convey. Thus, the laconic person may be saying, 'Daddy, talk to me. Draw me out'; the fumbling, disorganised sort is saying, 'Mommy, I'm lost. Direct me'; the hangdog look, 'Mama, ask me what hurts'; the depressive may be saying, 'Don't kick me when I'm down.'

Because the normal is no longer trying to say anything *indirectly*, he has no warped personality. Without old needs, people are just what they are. I am not sure how to explain this in any other way than to say that without a psychological frontispiece the normal just lives and lets live. As I have already pointed out, the body is part of that overall personality so that neurotics often look neurotic: we may find straight, thin lips closing down against the unacceptable words, narrowed eyes 'unable to see everything that is going on', as one patient put it. Or we will note drooping lips from unexpressed and unresolved sorrow and a jaw set in perpetual anger. The neurotic's entire organism is expressing the unconscious message. With no message to convey, we may expect a properly proportioned body in the normal, all else being equal. The physical changes I see in post-Primal patients lead me to conclude that some of what we believe is inherited may really be the results of neurosis.

The normal is able to enjoy himself. It is surprising how few neurotics are able to do that without artificial aid, such as liquor. As one patient put it, 'Fun torpedoes hope. I managed to turn everything into something not pleasurable. If the whole day went well, I would suddenly get irritable and pick a fight. I couldn't stomach a steady diet of goodness. It made me feel uncomfortable, like the axe was going to fall. I look back now, and I think that accepting all that goodness meant giving up my struggle to make my parents good people. If I accepted goodness wholeheartedly and really enjoyed life, I'd have to give up hope of having my misery recognised.' The neurotic isn't after pleasure *now*, he wants it to make up for *then*. The same can be said for affection. The normal enjoys affection without reservation. But for the neurotic to do so may mean, 'I don't need you any more, parents. I've found someone to love me.' It is terribly difficult for the neurotic to feel that he is never going to be that little boy or girl who is going to get from his parents what he missed.

An example of the difference between the normal reaction and the neurotic one was illustrated by a patient who, after Christmas, came in to say that he had got just 'millions of presents'. He needed to make it more than it was to fill the large lifetime void.

Over and over one reads that children need chores or jobs to learn responsibility. Children are pressed into service to earn money, even when there is no need. So, when a young child is asked by a neighbour child to play, the first question out of the parent's mouth may be, 'Have you done all your chores?' Somehow, parents fear that to let children do what they want means that they'll never do all the 'shoulds'. So they put obstacles in front of each want until the child comes to feel apprehensive about the simplest wants and he, too, eventually avoids them. Later in life this person may never be able to act spontaneously without the nagging question, 'What should I be doing first?' One patient told me, 'If I had fun one day and someone asked me to come over and spend the night the next day, my mother would always squelch it because it was "too much excitement!" – meaning pleasure. She was probably terrified that I had used up my allotment of fun without paying my dues.'

The normal's life is much easier in this respect. He does not keep himself from living the present, nor does he put his children into the struggle so that they feel guilty about being free and spontaneous.

Nothing is ever exactly right for the neurotic, because he was never right for his parents. It's an art form all its own never to say one praising word to a child, one phrase that means you're all right just the way you are, but patient after patient report they can never remember such a word. Instead, the neurotic parent must speak his Pain with every breath because that Pain is there every moment.

The result of being criticised for a lifetime takes many

forms. For example, you can buy some neurotics a present, and they will invariably find something wrong with it. Or they will find the bad in anything because only the bad was found in them. When the neurotic reads the news, he reads about bad news: what went wrong; who else is miserable or did bad things. In a neurotic society where people must project their misery outside themselves to make life tolerable, news becomes synonymous with bad news. The normal is not feasting off the misery of others. He feels their misery and wants to help end it.

When you try to fill a neurotic's void, you have to remember what a bottomless pit it is. The neurotic may need very expensive gifts to cover years of emptiness and lovelessness. But no gift can do that, no matter how expensive; there isn't enough fur in the world to warm a lifetime of coldness.

Even achieving long-sought goals is not always the answer. A patient of mine finally got his PhD and went into a severe depression. He thought that after eight years of terrible struggle the diploma was going to do something for him but he still didn't feel loved or important. He told me that getting that PhD was like producing the final miracle and he couldn't feel it. The normal is not hoping that something external will do anything for him, so he can let things be what they are.

For the neurotic, disappointment is the handmaiden of hope. Hope which obscures reality often ensures that the person will be hurt by his unrealistic expectations. The neurotic is bound to be disappointed by the Christmas party, for example, when somehow that party is expected to make him feel wanted and loved.

The normal is healthy. He doesn't have to run around telling doctors, 'I hurt', because he could never say it to his parents. Because there is no pull towards being unreal, no symbolic system to keep the body restless and fatigued, the normal is not only more healthy but much more energetic. His energy is used for the accomplishment of real tasks, not for struggling to achieve the impossible. And the normal finally knows when he feels good. One patient told me, 'I never even knew if I felt good. I was so far from my feelings. When someone asked me how I felt and I didn't feel bad, I had to deduce that since I wasn't feeling bad, there was only one thing left – I must feel good.'

The normal doesn't put anyone else in the struggle. He understands that children should be liked without having to earn it. *So he doesn't make his children struggle for anything.* Paradoxically, those children seem to do very well in life, contrary to the view that early struggle in life somehow prepares you for the later one. Many neurotics never even realise that they shouldn't have had to do anything to be liked by their parents. They have struggled for so many years to be liked that they can't imagine just being liked for being alive. The conditioning process of having to perform for approval begins almost at birth, where the child is 'kootchykooed' to try to get him to smile (look happy). Later he is asked to wave 'bye-bye' or to dance for the grandparents or to say this word or that, irrespective of how the child may feel at the moment. Almost every contact during infancy is one of performing at the will of someone else. This need on the part of parents and grandparents to get a constant response *to* them seems a subtle outgrowth of how little response they were able to get out of their own parents.

When one stacks the normal up against the neurotic, it's a wonder that neurotics last as long as they do.

If there were some key principle concerning real behaviour, it might be as follows: *Reality surrounds itself with other reality in the same way that unreality seeks out unreality.* Real or normal people will not have continuing relationships with unreal people, and the converse would also be true. Phoniness becomes intolerable to the normal. He isn't going to flatter, submit, pamper, or mollify a neurotic in order to get along. He also cannot be charmed, conned, or dominated by the neurotic, so that unless someone is fairly straight, the relationship will be difficult. The normal will not be ensnared in someone else's struggle. One patient reported that before, he had had to finish his wife's sentences. She would start a sentence and then look to him beseechingly, and he would immediately jump in and take care of her. The reaction was automatic and unconscious.

The neurotic isn't likely to continue a relationship where his neurotic needs are not being served. He has special requirements. He will tend to seek out those individuals who share his kind of unreal ideas and attitudes. We may often expect, therefore, a homogeneity of thought within his group of friends when it comes to economics, politics, people or general social phenomena. I am indicating that being unreal is an encompassing pattern. The neurotic must avoid reality until he is ready to face his own. Until that time he will create a comfortable but unreal cocoon around him in the job he has, the newspapers he reads, the friends he keeps.

The strength of the neurotic's social unreality will depend to some degree on how much of himself he is forced to deny. If a man was never loved by his father, he may have homosexual fantasies. Some may recognise these fantasies and accept them; others may deny them and possibly not even admit that they exist in their dreams and daydreams. The latter group would be more denied than the former. They may come to despise even seeing homosexuals and want to pass laws against them. In their social behaviour, then, they will demand abrogation of any rights of homosexuals – all because they want a daddy and can't say so. These same men might be so fearful of their 'weakness' that they come to despise it. Not only do they try to act strong and independent, but they will want to pass laws against 'welfare leeches' or any other group that can't be tough and Make It on Their Own. To repress one's own needs, in short, often means denying recognition of the needs of others.

To try to change the social philosophies of some neurotics is tantamount to changing their whole psychophysical systems. Neurotics believe what they have to believe in order to make life tolerable. To talk them out of their basic beliefs is like talking them out of their constitutional equipment.

The normal is not interested in the exploitation of others. There is nothing that he needs from people that is unrealistic. The neurotic, helpless before his Pain, often needs to exploit others in order to feel an importance he cannot feel. He must do this in order to cover himself. He tends to need others to say what is good about him, his child, his house, or his clothes.

Someone who is not normal cannot be giving of himself when that self is locked away inside. The neurotic may feign concern and interest in others and may convince himself that he is caring, but that self cannot care in any real sense until it can feel and express itself fully. So long as that real self is stuffed under fear and tension, so long as that self desperately needs, it cannot give.

The normal isn't likely to collect many friends as a buffer against feeling alone in the world. His friends tend to be neither trophies nor possessions. Post-Primal patients report that they can get along with other real people, irrespective of their personalities. It is their contention that real people are open and honest and undemanding and that idiosyncrasies don't seem to be a threat.

The normal doesn't need an appointment book full of Saturday night dates reaching months into the future in order to feel wanted or popular. A normal doctor wouldn't need a waiting room full of patients in order to feel needed. This last points seems to work in two ways. The neurotic patient may also become apprehensive when he is the only one in a doctor's waiting room and is taken in immediately. Because he has not struggled, waiting and squirming, he may feel that his doctor is not as good as the one who keeps people waiting an hour.

The normal, who acts realistically, will tend to be on time because he operates on real time, not on some time from the past. What this means is that he will not use time symbolically to feel something he cannot otherwise feel. He will not be late, for example, to try to feel important or to try not to feel rejected as in the case with the neurotic.

For example, being late can mean keeping unreal hope alive. It's one more way the neurotic is not straight with life. Or he will contrive a busyness that never leaves him time to feel. He keeps on the go, feeling a pressure from outside that really lies inside. Many neurotics manage their lives so that there is never time to live leisurely. They plan so many projects (time fillers) for the purpose of never having a free moment to feel or reflect. Pretty soon they have more to do than there are hours in the day. The result is that they are late to everything.

As discussed elsewhere, there are pseudo-feelings that no longer reside in the normal. This means that the normal would be neither jealous nor guilt-ridden. The normal, content to be what he is, would not envy others, want what they want, or demand what they have. I suppose that this is another way of saying that he can allow others – his wife, his children, his friends – to be themselves. He isn't living through their achievements and successes. He isn't busy stamping out their signs of happiness and life. The normal does not feel alienated because it is Pain that produces alienation of one part of the self from another. (Perhaps alienation from self is what enables leaders to discuss killing so readily. Divorced from their own humanity, they may not be able to feel for the humanity of others. Death is evidently not a real tragedy for those who do not feel life. It is in this sense that being 'dead' internally makes the actual death of others less real and, therefore, less horrifying.)

The normal seems to sense the pulse of life of others. He can be tactful, not out of a deep dishonesty, but because he can sense the Pain of others. He feels how much reality others may be capable of feeling.

The normal is sensitive in the true sense of the word. He not only is mentally acute to the needs and drives of others, but has a total organismic sensitivity where his mind and *body* are directly affected by stimuli. I would differentiate neurotic, mental sensitivity from the openness of the normal. I want to clarify this point because there are many neurotics who are acutely perceptive and who do see accurately into the personalities of those around them. What they cannot do, I believe, is *feel* the situations they are in because they are acting out *denied* feelings at the time. So, for instance, a brilliant man may be expounding on some philosophic point at a dinner table, acutely sensitive to the kinds of people who are his listeners, while being totally insensitive to the fact that he is dominating the conversation. He is too busy acting out his need for attention and importance. This is why it is crucial for a therapist not only to be trained in perceiving the personalities of others but to be normal. If he isn't, he may be acting out his need to be needed, for example, with his patients, thereby countervailing any good his insightfulness might bring.

The normal no longer suffers from 'looking forward to', in order to escape the emptiness of the present. One patient said, 'I used to rationalise that I wouldn't want to be rich because the rich must be unhappy. They can have everything they want and therefore have nothing to look forward to. I see now that if you can enjoy everything at each moment, you don't need anything to look forward to.'

The normal doesn't confuse hoping with planning. He may plan for a future situation, but he doesn't keep himself so full of plans that he has no present. It would seem that some neurotics keep things in the future so that they can never quite take pleasure now. I believe that this derives from early in a child's experience when to have led his life his own way, to do exactly what he wanted, would have meant rejection and possibly abandonment by parents who expected things done their way. He had to put off doing what he wanted, hoping for a future time when he could enjoy himself. This may go far to explain the idea many of us have had as children – 'When I grow up, I'm going to be so happy.' It would seem that some neurotics continue this pattern into adulthood. The normal, having given up unreal hope and the struggle to please, can lead his life as *he* pleases.

The neurotic 'wants'; the normal 'needs'. For the neurotic to want what he really needs is to feel Pain, so he must want substitutes – something attainable. The normal has simple needs because he wants what he needs, not some symbolic substitute. The neurotic may want a drink or a cigarette, prestige, power, high grades, or a fast car – all to cover Pains of emptiness, worthlessness, powerlessness, or whatever. There is nothing to cover in the normal, nothing to fill up.

Life seems to conspire against the neurotic. He wants so much because he got so little. Yet because he has had to twist his personality in strange ways to satisfy himself even minimally, he becomes the kind of person who turns people away. His cloying demands, his dependence and narcissism become intolerable to others. The normal, who *isn't* trying to fill a lifetime of personal neglect in each social contact, is often sought after and emulated.

The neurotic is a taker. No matter how much you may do for him, it may not matter because he must have those needs fulfilled over and over until they are properly connected and resolved – something usually that can only be done with Primal Therapy.

The normal operates on the 'musts' instead of the 'shoulds'. Neurotic behaviour, in the Primal context, means the abdication of personal need in deference to parental wants and needs. Parental wants become the child's shoulds. A 'bad' child is one who isn't doing his shoulds. The young child, trying to be good so he can be loved, tries to be what his parents demand. He does this with the implicit hope that finally they will fulfil his needs – that they will hold him, for instance. But parental needs can *never* be fulfilled by the child no matter how hard he tries. So the situation arises where the child is perpetually trying to satisfy his parent, to make him happy or pleased. It will never be enough; no child can make up for parental misery.

The shoulds of the child are the needs of the parents. Not to perform them means giving up hope for parental love. Neurotic children become so involved in the shoulds – being quiet, polite and helpful – that they lose sight of their personal needs. Having lost those needs, they want what they don't need.

The robbery of children's needs is often subtle. Neurotic parents will remind children, 'You *should* be happy. Stop complaining. Look at all we're doing for you. We've given you everything.' Often children are convinced. They look around and see material goods and believe that they have what they want, and they no longer even know that they need something desperately – love.

The tragedy of the shoulds is that in performing them, the child imagines that someday, when he does exactly what they want, his parents will shower a rainbow of love upon him. But since his parents themselves need what he can never give them, that day never comes.

To operate on the shoulds is not to function according to one's feelings. So the shoulds contain not only hope, but anger as well – anger at having to do what one does not feel. Having spent a lifetime doing what he did not want to do, the neurotic often has a difficult time doing what he must. The normal does what must be done because he acts in terms of realities.

The neurotic is often indecisive because he is split between repressed needs and doing the shoulds. The normal can decide for himself because he feels that self and what is right for it.

The neurotic relies on others to supply the shoulds. 'What should I order from the menu?' In this way, he manoeuvres his life so that people go on providing shoulds for him and he never allows himself to function according to his feelings. That simple question – 'What should I order?' – is often a sign of the neurotic's deadness. It is saying, 'I have no wants, no feelings, no life. Live my life for me.'

The normal is not in the search for the meaning of life, for meaning derives from feeling. How deeply one feels his life (the life inside him) is how meaningful it is. The neurotic who had to shut down against real catastrophic meaning early in his childhood must be in the search, conscious or unconscious. He may try to find meaning in a job or travel, and if his defences are working, he may imagine that his life is meaningful. Other neurotics sense that something is missing and set out on the quest for meaning. They may travel to gurus, study philosophy, steep themselves in religion or cults – all to find a meaning that lies but a deep breath away.

The neurotic must be in the search because real meaning is Pain and must be avoided. Thus, the search *becomes* the meaning; because the neurotic cannot fully feel his own life, he must find his meaning through others or things outside him. He may find it in his children or grandchildren, their accomplishments and successes. Or it may lie in holding important office or making big business deals. It is when the outside things are removed that the neurotic suffers. It is then that he may begin to feel, 'What's the use? What is it all for? What is the meaning of it all anyway?'

The normal lives inside himself and does not feel that something is missing; no parts of him are missing. The neurotic must feel this way if he ever stops his struggle because part of him *is* missing. One patient put it this way: 'I have a fascinating job. It's too bad it doesn't interest me.' It had no meaning for him.

The neurotic, unable to feel the full meaning of his life, must often invent a superlife or an afterlife – places where real living will go on. He must imagine that somewhere lie the real meaning and purpose of it all. He may think that savants can find it for him when only he can do that. The normal, by discovering his own body, has no need to conjure a special place where life really is going on. Implicit in the neurotic's seeking out psychotherapy is that possibly it will help him find a more meaningful life. It, too, becomes one long search. The normal has made a simple discovery:

Meaning is not something to be detected, only felt. He therefore does not race to weekend seminars on how to live the good life, find joy, or whatever.

The neurotic's search is exemplified by a patient who was formerly a philosophy major in college: 'I liked philosophy because I never had to know anything for sure. I never understood how much I wanted that state of limbo. I couldn't feel what was right in life, anyway, so limbo was perfect for me. I searched in the heavens and in the intellectual clouds for some supermeaning – all this so I didn't have to face that all my years of hassling at home had no meaning. It was senseless. Finding meaning in Descartes and Spinoza was a pleasant cover for all that.'

The normal is not trying to derive meaning from special occasions such as Christmas and Thanksgiving (Primal season, as one patient put it). The neurotic may be depressed during the holidays because the holiday gatherings did not make him feel loved or that he had a real, warm family.

The normal has no need to make life what it is not. He has no need for the broad philosophical search. He knows he is just alive and living, no more.

One could spend the rest of this book describing the normal. Normal is, simply, whatever normal people do – and not digging endless holes to climb out of.

12

The Post-Primal Patient

What kind of person has undergone Primal Therapy? There is no special kind of Primal patient. Primal patients range in age from seventeen to forty-eight with the greatest percentage in the mid-twenties. Their occupations vary from ex-monk to professionals of all kinds, including many psychologists and people in the arts. Whereas middle-class educational status is a plus factor in conventional insight therapy, non-intellectuals do just as well in Primal Therapy. Patients come from all religious backgrounds and from all parts of the country and from many sub-cultures.

The great bulk of my patients have had previous therapy ranging from many years of psychoanalysis, rational therapy, Gestalt therapy, existential therapy and Reichian treatment (Wilhelm Reich). With the exception of Reichian methods, the other schools have used a variety of techniques centring on the use of insight (to be discussed later). Though many of the patients are single, a number are married or divorced. The patient's marital status is often important. If he is older and has a family, he is going to be more difficult to treat. This is because he may have sunk his unreal roots into a relationship with a neurotic wife or may have chosen an unreal job and picked up unreal friends. In short, he has a lot to give up in order to become real; not many people are willing to do that when they have reached their forties and fifties. When an older person, entrenched in a neurotic marriage for one or two decades, becomes real, the spouse not in therapy may begin an undermining process which makes treatment unpleasant and difficult for the patient. Perhaps the ideal Primal patient is unmarried and fairly young without a vested interest in unreality. However, there are numerous middle-aged patients, open to change, who have had great success in this therapy.

Significantly, few Primal patients have any idea about what they are about to undergo. Therefore, our results seem less coloured by preconceived expectations. Despite its revolutionary form, patients are almost never put off by the

Primal approach. It seems to make immediate sense to them, irrespective of their backgrounds.

Let us look at this patient who has just completed his therapy. What is he like?

He functions in a new way. Often that means performing a different job. Many post-Primal patients physically can no longer do anything unreal; they cannot recapture a sales pitch or do the meaningless paper work required on some jobs. Two parole agents found it impossible to continue to supervise parolees instead of offering them the kind of help they needed in order to stay out of jail. Two psychologists waiting to enter training in Primal Therapy took menial jobs rather than pursue work in the field of psychology they believed was unreal. One had been a marriage counsellor who found it impossible to go back and deal with surface behaviour alone. A television producer gave up his hack job in order to write a more meaningful personal statement. One labourer decided to go to college because, as he put it, 'A college union card brings in more money than a working one.' He had no illusions about what he would learn in college. One schoolteacher had to leave her job and transfer to another school because working for a neurotic principal became impossible.

One of the usual indexes of normality among the other schools of psychotherapy is functioning. That is, the normal person is thought of as an efficient and productive member of society. The Primal view would be different. Post-Primal patients are no longer willing to drive themselves relentlessly. In Primal terms, the neurotic drives his *self* so that it can finally feel worthwhile, accepted or loved. Primal psychologists, for example, must go through therapy as part of their training. Though they are willing to work thirty or forty therapeutic hours before their treatment, they are not willing to carry such a load afterwards. They know that too often the neurotic derives his 'identity' from his functions instead of from his feelings – thus, a person may be PTA chairman or Hadassah president or fund drive co-ordinator and appear to be functioning and organising well, yet be quite sick. One patient who had finished Primal Therapy had this to say: 'I kept myself and everything around me well organised so as not to feel my real disorganisation. I had to keep functioning and planning and going, or else I would have come apart.' This person's functions became her life.

Many post-Primal patients decide that much of what they thought had to be done before really isn't so urgent. Thus, Sunday becomes a time to play with the children instead of cleaning out the garage. As one patient put it, 'Now that I know that I am all I've got in the world, there is no reason to try for "them" any more. I plan to be nice to myself and relax.'

With less drive (not being driven to find approval and love), the post-Primal patient does less in terms of struggle. But now he can do *more* in the realm of satisfying the self and therefore be able to give real love to his spouse and children.

Post-Primal patients do less, but what they do is something real so that the quality of their contribution to society is beneficial. Schoolteachers, for example, require much less of their students and teach them much more. They allow the students to express themselves and try to teach them things that are relevant to their lives (as much as is possible under the present educational system).

These patients are not selling things to people that they do not need. A studio labourer stayed on the job because what he was doing, building something, was real to him. He stopped working overtime when possible because he wanted to be with his family. He was no longer driven towards acquiring more and more gadgets, and he stopped gambling so that he was able to put his money to proper use. The money he saved on beer, he told me, was enough to take a vacation every year.

This question of motivation is an important one because so much of the world runs on neurotic motivation. One patient said that if people could harness the energy which lay inside the neurotic, they could drive trains with it.

I recall one patient after one of his last Primals being unable to lift his head off the floor for more than an hour. He was a swimming-pool cleaner, a hard worker all his life (greeted his friends with the neurotic salutation 'Keeping busy?'). After all his old neurotic motivation had been destroyed, he could not move a muscle. He took a long vacation after his therapy, and when he returned to his job, he found that he could no longer clean sixteen pools a day. He found it miraculous that he had ever been able to. Neurosis had inured him to how tired he really was. He hired a helper, made less money, but enjoyed life much more.

Too many neurotics produce in order to feel important, rather than do what is really important to them. One psychologist, after treatment, stopped running around delivering papers to learned societies. He said that all that energy was used not to communicate with his colleagues but to gain points on the ladder of prestige.

Perhaps the most dramatic changes which take place in post-Primal patients are physical. This is because it is a psychophysical therapy, not simply an insight approach. For example, about one-third of the moderately flat-chested women independently reported that their breasts grew; when they went shopping, they were surprised to discover that they needed new brassiere sizes. One woman who had flown in from a distant city for therapy returned home after several weeks of treatment. Her astonished husband was certain that she had received hormone injections. I have had many of these women measured by their physicians to verify the growth they report; in every case it has been corroborated.

Other indications of adult functioning were reported. Two male patients in their early twenties told of beard growth for the first time in their lives. Several others reported giving off an odour for the first time after perspiring. Several patients noted growth of hands and feet. These discoveries are not the result of any suggestion; no patient is given any idea of what to expect in the way of results. For example, one woman had no idea that her hands had grown until she tried on a new pair of gloves. She needed a size larger.

The explanation for all this necessarily must remain speculative until physiologic research can be conducted. One colleague, a biochemist, has indicated that much of this can be explained in terms of changes in hormonal output. This in turn may ultimately affect a genetic coding mechanism in the cells. He hypothesises that because of the suppression of the system and the alteration of hormonal output early in life, a certain genetic sequence is not run off; so, for example, beard growth would be delayed beyond the time it might ordinarily appear.

According to the biochemist, there may be a change in the *interactory* relationships of the entire hormonal system, permitting changes which might not occur with hormone injections.

The Primals may set off the proper growth sequence again. We shall await the results of physiologic research for a sound explanation of our observed phenomena.

While on the subject of hormonal changes, I would like to point out that in every case women who have had either premenstrual cramps or irregular menstrual periods have had these problems clear up completely in Primal Therapy.

Previously frigid women who had experienced painful intercourse find that the vagina lubricates well, sometimes even without obvious sexual provocation. One woman became concerned over what she called her continuous 'horniness'. For the first time in her life she knew what it was to really want sex. It had been a duty before, something her husband wanted.

Patients change in many ways – equilibrium, for example. One person described it as follows: 'In the past each step I took was carefully controlled and predictable ... and now when I raise my foot, I am not at all sure where or how it will land. It was the same pavement I walked on before I came in here, but it seems like a totally different experience. I feel loose and sense what my whole body is doing each moment. I'm not a robot any more.'

Post-Primal patients often report complete changes in their co-ordination – how they run, catch and throw a ball. A tournament tennis player found that he was beating opponents who could ordinarily trounce him with ease. Part of this can be explained by the absence of tension – the removal of the split which kept parts of his body and respiratory system from functioning in co-ordination. During one of his Primals, he could feel his breathing finally come into unison with the rhythm of his body.

Primals do not produce 'heightened' sensation; they produce real sensation which seems heightened because of the dulling process which has gone before (just as anything more than real sensation must be unreal). Tension dulls the sensory apparatus so that we are neurotic not only in our

166 of The Primal Scream

behaviour but in our sense of taste and smell. Thus, some neurotics require a lot of spice on their food in order to be able to taste anything.

One patient described the change in sensation this way: 'I never ate because I was hungry. And I never really tasted anything. The other night I had a charcoal-broiled steak and discovered I can't stand the taste of charcoal. I've had charcoal steaks for years and never even tasted them.' When life processes are dulled, life is dull.

Primals do not produce a new and special quality of sensation; they only permit the latent sensory capacity to be experienced fully. Two patients who required eyeglasses no longer do so. This increase in sensory status makes the post-Primal especially alert. He is acute to sounds in the voices of others or in music.

One patient described her Primal Therapy in the following way: 'My whole life has been out of focus. Primals gave me the lens so that I could bring it all into focus. Everything is sharp and clear now. I'm smelling smells I never knew existed. For the first time my husband's BO is noticeable to me and bothersome. My life before was just grey. Colours have come alive for me.'

Thermal changes occur frequently. One patient said, 'It's like I have felt cold all my life but not the coldness of my life.' When she did indeed feel the emptiness and coldness of her early family life, shivering convulsively for more than half an hour, she felt warm for the first time because she *felt*. Feeling, evidently, is a warming experience more than figuratively. There have been a number of conditioning experiments which show how blood vessels tend to constrict in anticipation of pain, leading us to assume that the same constriction goes on in anticipation of Primal Pain.

While many patients report this cold feeling (and are cold to the touch) when they are on the verge of a painful Primal feeling, some neurotics with a vascular vulnerability may respond differently to Pain. Their inner dynamics cause them to feel hot all the time. One patient said, 'I was always hot – hot under the collar. I mean mad. I was like a boiling cauldron of rage.' This man used to react to the world in terms of anger, not fear.

In Primal terms, constantly bundling up against the cold

is a symbolic process in many neurotics – the way they defend themselves against *feeling* cold and the way they *make* them*selves* warm. Conversely, never needing a sweater may be acting out 'I don't need warmth from anyone or anything.' This latter type is usually the hard, independent person who operates on total denial of his needs. To him, to need is to be weak.

The post-Primal patient cannot be unreal physiologically. He can no longer wear sweaters when the climate does not call for it because his body would soon tell him it was over-heated. To be unreal is a total systemic event.

The way one reacts in terms of anger or fear shows up in the body chemistry. For example, when two groups were divided into those who let their anger out and those who kept it in, differences were found in the ratio and kinds of hormones secreted. The group that held in their anger was more likely to secrete a hormone from the adrenal medulla called norepinephrine, while their opposites were more likely to secrete straight epinephrine. (Interestingly enough, biochemists sometimes refer to the norepinephrine hormone as the 'uncompleted' hormone.[1])

Let us look at the post-Primal patient in the light of some non-physical phenomena.

When I asked one graduate patient what changes he noted, he answered, 'I don't give a damn whether the Minnesota Twins win the pennant this season.' This was not a flip comment. Before Primal Therapy he was, as he put it, 'a baseball nut'. He knew the names of almost every player in the league, their batting averages, who was traded where, etc. For him, that interest was symbolic acting out. He had never been part of anything, and by knowing all the names and averages, he could make himself a part of something. Further, he 'identified' with the Twins, unconsciously hoping through them to become a winner – to cover the fact that he had been a loser all his life. When he solved his personal problems in a real way, he no longer had to act out symbolically. To be interested in a team is one thing; to live through it is quite another.

[1] I refer the reader to Hans Selye's work on hormones and stress, particularly *The Stress of Life* (New York, McGraw-Hill, 1950).

Another patient had been hooked on football. After his Primals he became acutely aware of the fantastic struggle situation on the playing field, and he was far less interested once the struggle inside him was removed.

A patient who used to like opera became a rock-and-roll fan after his Primals: 'More gutsy, more of the body,' he said. 'Now that I am alive I can't go with those operatic agonies any more. Rock for me is a celebration of life.'

Changes in intelligence are marked in post-Primals. One patient put it this way: 'If I were smart when I was young, I would have died because I would have known that they hated me. I had to be dumb to survive. I just shut off part of my brain. I've noticed the bright, alert look in very young children, and then something happens to change them. I think what happens is that they get the Primal message and make themselves not understand it.'

College suddenly becomes easy for these patients. They know that part of it is a game, going through obligatory motions, and they do so without anxiety.

They become articulate because they have finally articulated what they dared not say most of their lives. They are perceptive – 'super-straight', they call it. To be straight is not manifested only mentally; they walk straight instead of crouched or hunched.

No single behaviour can be pointed to as normal, as can be seen from these remarks of several women graduates. One said, 'I can go out now to other people's houses without fear. I can enjoy being social for the first time in years.' Another countered: 'I can stay home and read now. I used to be on the run, couldn't sit still for a minute. I like being alone.'

The post-Primal takes new pleasure in the smallest acts. He enjoys what he is doing now.

What happens to the creativity of the post-Primal patients? Does it wither with the neurosis? No. No one loses his ability to paint or compose music. What does change is the content of the art produced. We must remember that neurotic imagination means the symbolisation of what is unconscious. Thus, the neurotic must reveal himself in abstract, non-direct ways. The content of his art is the peculiar way that his feelings and thoughts join together artistically after detouring around the Pain. Obviously, without the Pain block, that content will change. The creative act of the neurotic is the way he keeps from knowing his feelings or, rather, feeling them. The post-Primal patient's artistic perspective changes; he sees and hears things differently. Neurosis is not a prerequisite for art.

What about relationships? A woman who finished therapy went out to dinner with her husband who had not been in treatment. When it came time to order, she would not let him order for her. To make matters worse, she cancelled the wine he had decided on and ordered the brand *she* liked. He became furious and left the table. There was quite a scene in which he accused her of 'castrating' him. He said, 'You refuse to let me be the man any more. You're trying to take my manhood away.' But all she had done was change from the sycophant her husband needed to feel manly into a person in her own right.

It is instructive to note that married couples who have both gone through Primal Therapy have *never* separated. They have no neurotic wants for someone else because they have felt their true needs. There is simply no reason for them not to get along. They do not make unreal demands on one another because they are not unreal. Each partner becomes a viable human being, content to live and let live.

Post-Primal patients cannot put up with unreal behaviour, and so they avoid many old friends. They tend to see a good deal of one another, and marriages within the group are common. The friendships are non-possessive; they are relaxed. This relaxation shows up in their faces. There are no longer the strained masks to cover feelings, the fearful eyes, the clamped lips. They are not putting up a face for the world, and so they have a natural look. They find that they do not need as much money as before. They eat less, go out less, lead more moderate lives. Avid readers, especially those who devoured novels, give up much of their reading. One patient said that her preoccupation with fiction was, for her, living vicariously and that she didn't feel the need to do that any more.

There is far less regimentation to their lives. They eat when they are hungry, buy clothes when they really need them, have sex when they are sexual rather than when they are tense. This means less but far more enjoyable sex. Almost all these patients listen to more music than before. When I asked some of these graduate patients what they did mostly, they said, 'We sit around a lot, relax and listen to music.' Many of them added that it was a feat of no small consequence just to be able to sit around without planning where to go next.

Are their lives dull? By neurotic standards, yes. But we must remember that excitement in the neurotic means excitation by *tension*. This means that the neurotic is constantly in a state of inner excitement, and he often manipulates his life to match that internal state. He *cannot* sit still, so he plans many things which look as if they would be exciting but which are often nothing more than outlets for his tension. Indeed, the neurotic often manoeuvres himself into more and more actions so that he *can* finally feel. He may fly, scuba dive, travel, go to parties and feel 'up' only for the moment. When the activities cease, he begins to be filled with tension again. The activities are exciting for him because they allow a channel for the release of tension, which the neurotic often regards as the ultimate state of pleasure.

In a way the post-Primal person is a new kind of human being. For example, he is never moody. Moods are gradations of tensions, of old unlabelled, unconceptualised feelings. The graduate patient is neither elated nor in the dumps. He just feels and knows what that feeling is. These people give off a definite aura: 'I am what I am, and you can be what you are.' It is very hard to look an unreal person in the eye because there is the feeling that one is communicating with someone who isn't there. Post-Primals are very easy to be around because one feels he is talking to real people.

The post-Primal person has a new feeling about being alone. Here is the statement of someone who has been out of treatment for two years: 'Alone? All the way but it no longer bothers me. Before therapy I was really alone – only me and my phantom (God), and now he's gone. But now I have *me*. So in that sense I have company – real company, and I suppose that's all any of us have. Wife, friends certainly exist "out there", but never to the same degree that I exist for myself.'

The post-Primal patient does not need liquor to be with people or to laugh (as so many neurotics do). He is a conscious person and needs nothing to deaden that consciousness: It's fine as it is.

The post-Primal is greatly relieved that he no longer has compulsions. He is delighted to be free of his allergies, headaches, backaches and other symptoms. He is truly in control of his life.

I have discussed the job situation earlier. It is true that many post-Primal patients change jobs. As one patient said, 'I used to live for my job; now I live for me.' Generally, their attitude is to find something they might like to do, without concern about its worth as a career. One person found being a cobbler more appealing than working his way up the ladder of an insurance company. He liked working with his hands, but because he had white-collar aspirations (coming from a proper middle-class home), he could not bring himself to do physical labour. While looking for work, he told me he was relaxed about being unemployed for the first time in his life.

Overwork, unrealistic intellectual ambitions are not part of the post-Primal patient. Perhaps this is a reaction to a society where self-sacrifice is apotheosised. Yet not all careers are thrown over. One dental student still wanted to continue in dentistry, and some teachers stayed in teaching, while others left the profession. It all depends on how neurotic the motivation for the choice of career was in the first place.

The lack of urgency about jobs and careers is due to another factor as well. For years, possibly decades, the neurotic's body and mind have been harassed. He needs time to regroup. He needs a healing period not only from being neurotic but from the therapy, which is not an easy experience. Suddenly to become unneurotic after years of walking this earth in an unreal state is a whole new experience. He needs time to savour it.

RELATIONSHIPS TO PARENTS

One of the more predictable post-Primal changes is the patient's relationship to his parents. When the son or daughter, irrespective of age, stops struggling for the parents' love, the parents begin their struggle for the child's love. The more normally the offspring acts, the more desperate the parents become. We must remember that the neurotic child *is* the defence for the parent. He was used to quell *their* Pain. He was their foil so that they could feel cared about. He was the one they could demean in order to feel superior. She was the dutiful daughter who took care of her mother. Without a child to phone, to write, to visit them, the parents begin to feel their own Pain, their own unfulfilled empty lives. So they begin the struggle to make the child back into what he used to be. For it is the neurotic parent who is really the small child who needs advice and comfort and all the things he never got from his own parents.

Why is it that children become the symptoms of neurotic parents? Why don't the parents take it out on others? Because their children are the most defenceless, parents have to be less defended around them. This means that the parent is more apt to let out his old, repressed feelings on a child who has no power and who can in no way threaten him. I believe that the way to find out what a person is really like is to watch his relationship to his children. If the parent was made to feel worthless and wrong about almost anything he did as a child, then each day of his life as a parent he may try to feel right (by making his children 'wrong') and worthwhile (by making his children feel unimportant). Or he may take a different, though equally destructive route. He may push his child to become important so that he (the parent) can finally feel worthwhile. Whether it be harsh criticism or gentle but firm suggestion, the result is to use a helpless child as an instrument for the fulfilment of old parental hurts. The end of this process is that the child loses the recognition of (is split from) his own needs in his urgent desire to fill those of his parents.

Dramatic things happen to the parents of post-Primal patients. Mostly they become depressed, angry, or sick. One mother of a woman in her twenties became seriously ill and had to be hospitalised with a complaint that could not be diagnosed – until her daughter flew to her side. Then the complaint disappeared. The mother of one previously effeminate man became enraged at his aggressiveness and wondered aloud to him. 'What's happened to my sweet boy?' Another mother went into a deep depression because her daughter stopped visiting every week and decided to go away to school. This mother had lived out her life through her daughter and the thought of being alone in the world overwhelmed her.

It becomes extremely difficult for the post-Primal patient to tolerate all the unreality of the parents, and he tends to stay away from them in order to avoid the inevitable conflict. Neurotic parents do not care about their children *as they are* because they are shaping them into what they need to quell their own pain. One patient said, 'I was an orphan with parents. They were parents to the invented, phony me, while no one took care of that real me.'

The difficulty begins during the Primal when the patient first finds out what he wants, which, unfortunately, often isn't what the parent wants. It is a tragic and difficult period for both patient and parent. The patient doesn't become deliberately cruel. He doesn't confront the parents with their sins. That would be hope again, of having them see their wrongs and becoming loving parents, which isn't going to happen. The patient can now let them be what they are. He is going to lead his own life, which is all any of us can do. I am reminded of one woman who spent a lifetime being the intermediary between her mother and father, who fought constantly. When she stopped shouldering the burden of being the pacifier, she found that, for the first time, they got along.

What sometimes happens is that children become more valuable to the parent when that parent has to struggle for their love. So long as children could be taken for granted, they were not valued. So as the post-Primal patient becomes real and independent, he finds his parents calling and visiting more often. The parents do not realise that when their child, who may be a forty-year-old man, allows them to lead their own lives, good or bad, he is in fact giving them real love. Before therapy, parents relied on quantity to measure 'love'; how many invitations, how many phone calls, and how expensive the presents. When the child no longer deals in quantities but offers the quality of feeling, neurotic parents often do not know how to respond, because their children's feelings never counted for them.

The post-Primal patient can relate to his parents, if he chooses, in non-struggle terms. Once he can accept himself, he can accept his parents. He realises that to have to act neurotically is a life sentence and that no one chooses to do so voluntarily. He has a deep understanding of his parents' pain because of what he has been through. He knows that they, too, were victims.

It is a difficult job being a parent because it involves moulding someone into himself, not into what you need for yourself. Unmet needs inside a parent will dictate whether he can be a creative parent. It doesn't matter if that parent is a psychologist or psychiatrist; if those buried needs are still there, the child will suffer. How much the child will suffer depends on how much the parent had to cancel himself out in order to get by with his parents. What the parent will see in his child is his own need and the hope of fulfilment of that need. The child will not be seen for what he is – something that begins with the very name the child is given. A child named Percival already represents certain expectations by the parents even at birth.

Or a parent can be a decent soul, who tries hard with his children but, because of his past needs, has to 'yak' constantly. One patient had a Primal about just such a parent 'Stop talking! Let my senses rest so I can have thoughts all my own!' This parent talked so much to the child that the child could not have his own private thoughts. Indeed, when there was a silence for even a moment and the child looked as if she were thinking, the parent would nearly always have to know what her thoughts were.

Because the neurotic parent sees his own need in his child, the child who suffers most is the one with the parents who need most. The parent who destroys is not that 'kooky' eccentric but the one who has aspirations and ambitions for his child. Those aspirations are not going to allow the child to be himself; he is going to be busy filling that parent's needs. The destructive parent, in short, is the one the child has had to 'deal' with: 'I'll do this if you do that.' This is conditional love, and the condition for love is that the child become neurotic.

The post-Primal person is going to hurt again, especially by the violence and sickness he sees all around him, but he is not going to be neurotic again. He will be affected by what happens to him, but he will not be split off from those experiences. In short, he will react with feeling and not with tension. He is a vulnerable human being, directly affected by stimuli in the world, but he cannot be overwhelmed because he has himself at all times. I believe that he is going to make a new world in which to live – a real world designed to solve the real problems of its inhabitants.

Gary

The following case of Gary is included in detail to show the process of Primal Therapy at work. Even so, much of it had to be edited owing to space requirements.

Gary was quite paranoid early in treatment. His first group was marked by an argument with another group member; Gary thought the other person and I had conspired against him to make him feel left out. He covered his feeling of not belonging with anger. We stopped the anger, and this led him to his hurt and away from the paranoia. I call Gary the 'street fighter' because this was his main occupation in his teens. Now he 'cannot get angry'. This change is reflected in his speech and in his face. When he first came to me, he used to talk and look like a tough guy. Now his appearance and manner of speech can only be called 'gentle'. Before therapy he was markedly round-shouldered, which resulted in a back problem. Now his back problem has disappeared and he has erect posture.

February 25th

Today I exploded for the first time. The feeling is one of having a great weight lifted from your chest, and you become an outpouring of yourself. Everything spilled out of me in waves, gushes and torrents. At no time can I remember consciously wanting to hold it back; I am not sure if I feel purged – I'm not sure that's the right word anyway – but I feel like lightened, unburdened just a little, a little less ill at ease. Afterwards I felt drained, sapped of energy, less hostile, certainly very unangry at anybody.

The whole outpouring seemed to get started by itself; at least I can't remember what it was that Janov or I did to get it started – but I'm sure the whole damn thing has been getting started and squelched by me over the past eighteen years or so. And then I was in it, riding it like you'd ride an orgasm, squeezing out every moment of it, filling it with screeching-angry-hurt-lamentations-curses-moans-yelling. There were things I spewed out that I thought I had long ago put out of my mind and had accepted, but now I know that I had simply stored them up in my gut and that they had been eating me up all these years. There were things I said that I've wanted to say probably a million times before, but I had them beaten out of me.

Now, tonight, I feel some of the loneliness and hurt that I've tried to fight off. I know now that hurt is a physical thing, that when you are forced to bring it up, you gag on it because it is so nauseating to have to live it again; the hurt I've got stored up in me inside must be rotten, putrified and poisonous after all these years, and I know I've got to get it out of me so I can have a decent chance of living a decent life for a change.

I still find it difficult to be with myself. Today, I slept-dozed for about an hour until one and then generally stayed with myself for the rest of the day until dinner. I still can't induce myself to really feel things; I find myself ruminating through my mind looking for something to occupy my mind like a snatch of a poem or song. I'm still fighting myself, I guess, from feeling feelings. Being alone is the most difficult; I guess I'm learning that I'm a drag to be with.

The rest of the afternoon wasn't too bad. I stayed on my back for the greater part of the day, trying to relive again what I had lived through today, but I couldn't. Went to the group in the evening, got there ten minutes late and caught some shit for that from Janov, who said, 'I don't mean neurotic time'. I never thought of it in that way. The group was something else; now I know how sick I am because there were all these people who were unafraid and unashamed to get down on that floor and do their thing. One guy got me all tight inside, and I could feel myself struggling uncomfortably inside my gut, but I couldn't get out there. Like *I'm* not really sure that anybody there really brought up anything in me. I'm becoming increasingly more aware that I'm fighting myself from feeling things – the tightness in my gut is all of the clue I need to tell me that. When I got back to the motel, I tried to pull off my own Primal thing. I couldn't, just a few tears. I tried to re-create the conditions that would enable me to have one – couldn't. I knew I was aching because there was a horrible tightness in my gut, I mean really tight this time. I tried the Daddy thing — nothing. Finally, a little later I beat off, felt better. Felt so better, I beat off a second time about an hour later. I tried the Primal thing again but couldn't make it; the tightness was there still but not quite so bad. All this lasted from about ten to twelve thirty.

February 26th

Again, for the third night in a row I cannot sleep soundly; no dreaming, just a lot of tossing and turning and waking up a few times. I woke up about 2, 6.45, and 8.15 without an alarm; got out of bed at 8.30. Light breakfast, listened to *Bolero* once, typing this, and am going to be alone with myself until today's appointment at noon.

Today's Primal was devastating. I was amazed at how much hurt was stored up in me. That's the thing about this therapy — you are constantly being amazed at how much poison you've stored up in your body. I think that in my case what I'm doing now is saying to a lot of people 'Fuck You' as loud as I can and with as much venom as I can. I couldn't do this when I was a boy because I was defenceless. The other thing that Primal Therapy does, is that it proves to you that feelings/Pain is a real physical thing: It's right there in your gut, tearing you to pieces, or it's between your shoulder blades or in your chest. When you open your mouth to breathe, it makes you gag — Pain is a nauseating thing. Today I felt like I was going berserk. I couldn't stop raving at my foolish old lady or old man. Then I started in on the kids; I'm glad — relieved, unburdened — that I screamed what I did at them. I am so damn sick it's disgusting. I am really a mentally sick person. I've got to get myself together.

After a light lunch I drove out to the beach. I guess I've been to the beach hundreds of times, but this time it was just me and the beach together and alone. I walked along the waterfront for a couple of miles, scrounging among shells and driftwood, getting my feet in the cloddy-cold damp sand. The wind was the greatest — a gusty wind that cut through my coat, my skin, into my bones. It was delicious when I breathed it in; it roughened my cheeks. I can't say why, but today out there I felt alive, like I hadn't felt in quite a long time. I just felt plain alive.

The being alone part isn't too bad now. I find I can sit alone for longer periods of time without growing fidgety, and I can stay more interested in what's going on in my body for a longer period of time. I don't need props like a radio or a book now. But still I can't go like for hours that way. Tonight alone again. Hope I can sleep, but maybe it's better if I have another rotten night because that's the only way I'm ever going to get some good nights.

It just occurred to me that when I'm raving, my speech degenerates into obscenities, but that's not the interesting part; what really interests me is that my speech becomes the urban-ghetto English I used to speak; it has all the curious interjections, fragmented question-statements and slang. It's almost like I'm purposefully choosing the kind of language that I know they'll understand. I think also that the speech is really real – now there's no need to search for the proper word; the word that is ready to fly out of my guts has to be the right word.

I just thought of something that seems significant: When I'm going through a Primal with either one of the old folks, I'm punching outwardly, actually flaying my fists in their faces; but today with my brothers, I can't remember doing that. I did punch the couch to death, but I think it's significant that I didn't aim my fists at them. Also, if I remember accurately, I didn't call any of them any dirty words. Something else that bothers me is that when I'm emphasising something to the old man, I tend to strike myself a lot and hard. While I never hurt myself, it sort of bothers me to think I'm hitting myself for what? Probably guilt; I have so much guilt that I actually found myself making excuses for my parents today, trying to explain away what they are. But whatever they are or were, Art is right when he says that they hurt me, and that's real enough. I know because I have the Pain.

February 27th

Last night wasn't bad at all. I had a good sound night's sleep. I don't know if that's good or bad for the therapy. I was alone for one long stretch of little more than four hours,

and they passed with relatively little uneasiness. I tried to induce myself into a Primal thing several times, but the most I could bring up was tears. Today's session I thought was okay. I didn't go through any of the violent stuff, as I have been the previous three days. Still, there's a lot of screaming and thrashing and punching the air. I seem to be able to make more 'connections' in the past two days. I don't know if I'm supposed to be making them, but I find myself coming to a realisation about a certain thing and then being able to link it up with something that has relevance to it. No crying outbursts today; there just wasn't any *feeling* to cry. When I say 'feeling', I think I'm describing a sense of physical urgency that is actually 'living' inside me. I say 'living' because when I let myself sink below that urgency and when I let it overtake me, it swooshes out of me like a river, alive with pulsating immediacy. I'll never again doubt or question the fact that *feelings* are real physical happenings which are happening inside me and which can be allowed to happen outside of me if I allow myself to feel them and let them out. The strange thing is this: Once I have felt that feeling many times, it sort of leaves me. For example, today I didn't seem to have any feeling to cry about loneliness, while over the past few days that feeling has brought on tremendous tears. Today I just sort of talked it. I'm a little confused as to what that means. It could mean (1) that I was blocking the feeling, which I doubt because Janov could have seen that; or (2) that the feeling and I could live together without my having to cry about it, if that makes any sense. What I mean is this: As an example, take a woman who has to feel the feeling of having to lose one breast because of cancer; she cries and cries and cries about it, feels the deep sorrow of it, then loses the breast but can live with the pain of the loss once she knows ⎫ the pain. I think that makes some sort of sense.
feels ⎭

The big lousy thing today was that I had to cop to the fact that I had been lying to Janov. I had a pain in the back of my head and in the mastoid area. Janov said it was an 'unfelt thought'. Damn fucking right it was: The thought was the knowledge that I had lied and I was keeping it a secret, and the pain was from the unfeeling of that feeling; in short, I was diseased. I got it out (that I stayed at home last night and not in a motel) and almost immediately the pain went away – I would guess two or three minutes after I said the truth. Of course, I've gone and impeded my therapy by doing what I did. I did it because of the money – not wanting to spend it – like my father. But really if it turns out that after all my desperate attempts to not be like my father, that I am like him in more ways than the ones I already know about, then I will be really pissed off at myself for having let myself become so sick. The really intriguing thing about Primal Therapy is that you cannot lie to the therapist, or rather you may lie to him, but you will plague yourself into having to tell him the truth. In the end, you won't want to lie. This will really be good for me because I've always been a crafty liar for most of my life, and I really want to stop.

Today, from 1.45–5.30 alone; 6–midnight alone. It hasn't been so bad; it's getting easier, but then maybe I'm not really working at this thing because it seems like it should be filled with more pain and suffering. But then maybe that's what's wrong with me; maybe I feel like I have to punish myself for something.

March 1st

I was rather edgy or prickly or something Saturday morning at group. The first guy to do his thing brought up a lot of anxiety in me – my stomach tightened; my throat became dry; my body simply wanted to unbend. When Janov signalled to me, it was more with a sigh of relief than fear that it was my turn. I did my best for the moment, but how good it was I don't know. The whole thing was wild for me. I mean it was the first time in my entire life ever that I heard so much lamentation, crying, screaming and none of it terrified me. I seemed to be in it, of it, and that was that. One screaming person would touch off somebody else and just as soon as things were quieting down, somebody else would start up, and then the whole thing would start in all over again. Finally, it subsided without any signal; it seemed to come to its own *natural* conclusion. This, too, is unique in Primal Therapy: The therapist doesn't go to pieces at the slightest scream or groan of the patient. In fact, he encourages it. So here's Janov, gingerly stepping over and around prostrate bodies, gently talking to first this person and next someone else, throwing private signals to his wife, and all around him people are screaming and crying out their pain. And he's drinking coffee through the whole bizarre mess. I don't know what the hell kept me from bursting out in uproarious laughter at the whole thing – it was just too unreal. And that's when it dawned on me that my life – my brainwashed life – was what had made me think that this kind of thing was unreal. Nothing could be more real than this for stark, really real human suffering. It was just that my whole stupid education said, 'No, people do not cry when they are hurting. They hide their hurts like good little jerks.' So it was real. Afterwards I felt purged, clean, weary. I hadn't spilled as much tears as others, but more than some – but even that is unimportant.

Spent time at the beach, and wanted to do something nice for myself, so I bought some clams and scallops. When I was buying the stuff, the guy who was selling it kept talking a mile a minute and wouldn't quit. It seemed like he was going on and on and on, but maybe it was no more than a few minutes. Anyway, I felt myself growing impatient, nervous; I felt helpless, and my throat seemed to tighten up, and my belly began to get upset. I just wanted to get the fuck away from the guy and get back to the sand and the water and have the smell of the tide in my nose, and the water lapping at my toes. I even considered walking away from the corner leaving him in mid-sentence with my unpaid-for fish all wrapped up and sitting on the counter. But I didn't. I wanted – really – to treat myself and my wife, Susan, to something nice for a change. After dinner, I went to the room and stayed there for a few hours; not much happened. I felt pretty relaxed, though. Watched *Wild Strawberries* and cried. I wasn't ready for that – it just sort of came on me. I guess the man's relationship with his father (the doctor) touched something in me, and the doctor himself, unable to feel and stifling it in his son, also brought up feelings in me. Went to bed at two after sitting in the living-room by myself for a while.

March 3rd

Beginning of the second week of individual therapy. For about the past five nights I have been sleeping (with the exception of Friday night) very undisturbed. However, there is a difference. Right before I began going to therapy, and for a very long time before that (like years), my sleep was 'drugged' – that is, I not only slept like a log, but also was about as difficult as a log to wake up. I think that I was using sleep to get away from my pains and problems. Particularly over the past half year I have used sleep as an escape. But now I sleep soundly and restfully, but I am also able to wake up promptly and get out of bed without finding it agonising and tortuous.

ITEM: If I live say another thirty years and go on smoking at my present rate ($1\frac{1}{2}$ packs a day), I will spend about $6,000. Even if the therapy costs me $2,000–$2,500, I will be ahead money and health because it will help me to learn to give up smoking. In fact, I've already given it up. I may even get to live longer than thirty years.

Today's therapy session was pretty good. I almost say 'enjoyable', but what I really mean is that I know that I'm doing something to help myself get mentally healthy. Strange about my folks: I keep changing from hatred to sadness to pity to outrage to scorn to defence to hatred etc. about them. This was/is very confusing. I know now that they were and are what they are. There's nothing that can ever change that. There is nothing that can ever change the hurt and the pain that they caused me. And here's something new to me: I too hurt them, maybe not as severely, maybe not as crippling, but I did hurt back. But mine started as defensive, then turned to offensive. So they initiated the hurt, the squelching, the loneliness. And now what comes out of all that is simply this: sadness, a big waste, a tragedy. I now feel the terribly sad human tragedy of people living together in close quarters and deeply hurting one another and leaving emotional scars. Now I feel how very very sad it all is. I mean it just makes me cry really heavy, not bitter, tears, but very genuine sad tears. I don't cry for the lost youth nor for how-it-could-have-been or should-have-been like I used to last week. Now I simply cry because I feel the terribly tragic human waste and loss and hurt.

I called my parents today. At first when my father answered the phone, I couldn't find my voice. Finally, I got into it, and I'm kind of surprised that I found it so easy to talk to the guy. With my mother it was a little different. I told her during the course of the conversation that I had had a 'breakdown'. She didn't hear me – that is, she had learned to not hear me, and she didn't want to hear this. I don't know what it is with her; it's like her 'little baby' can never break down or something. I then made it very plain and clear to her that it was a mental and physical breakdown, at which point she expressed what I could call concern or interest, but not alarm. She responded with her worn-out homegrown expressions like 'Well, you just can't go on doing more than your body can stand'; 'Well, I always say that whatever will be will be'; 'You've got to take care of yourself.' It was just rather generally unsatisfactory.

For the rest of the afternoon, I relaxed by myself. Susan didn't feel too good in the morning, so I decided to make the dinner tonight. I made curried rice, salad and fried clams. The clams were great; I started them just when she got home so we could both watch how they open up in the steam. Well, I just plain had a lot of giddy silly fun, pretending that the opening clams were creatures, that they were ugly, etc. I giggled a lot, and for the first time in a long time, I felt carefree and really giddy-light. For the rest of the evening I was alone.

March 4th

In today's session I became very confused about how I really feel about my parents. I feel the pain of hurts, the pain of pain, the pain of sadness. And now I can feel how painfully sad – really sad – the whole human waste and tragedy is. I guess I wanted my mother to respond with some interest and real concern yesterday. I know that if my son had called and told me that he had a mental breakdown, I would have been prompted to action, anything he would have wanted from me. It was at that point that I began to have a feeling for my mother, a feeling that said she no longer knew how to feel and that she didn't know how to respond. I blamed myself for some of this, saying that I had usually resisted her affection in the past and that her advice never seemed to have much substance to it, that it sounded ridiculous mostly. I became confused, not knowing any more what to say to, and about, whom. All I could feel was the tragic sadness of the whole mess.

I forgot to mention that I also called my brother Ted yesterday right after speaking to my mother. With him the conversation sounded crazy for a minute or two. I told Ted what I was up to with therapy and the whole thing, and he was surprised. He asked, specifically: Why was I going? I told him about how I was unhappy and felt like an all-around fuck-up. He couldn't see this. Then I asked him to remember me as I was in Brooklyn beating him up, persecuting him and Bill and others, bitchy, wilful, cruel, nasty. His reply astounded me: He said, 'All brothers do that – it's part of growing up.' He just couldn't catch the larger issue – the meaning of having to live with all the unfelt Pain of that kind of life, what it does to your insides and to the inside of your head. I mentioned that to him. He responded by telling me that whenever he gets to feeling shitty, he just thinks how lucky he is that he's not in a worse predicament. I imagine that by doing so, he thinks he makes his troubles disappear but I doubt it very strenuously. He probably swallows down the Pain like so many others do and goes on living with it unfelt. He went on to tell me that he and I and our family really are lucky or fortunate that things aren't any worse; he told me that we are lucky we didn't lose our parents in a fire or in an automobile crash. For a moment, he actually had me thinking that I was pitying myself. But then I saw it: What's real is real, and the Pain from being hurt is real, and the process of mentally defending yourself or insulating yourself from more Pain by not feeling at all is also real. And that's the real reality of what I was now struggling with. So it does me no good to think of myself as fortunate by comparing my misfortune to a theoretical and abstract misfortune. It makes for no feeling. It only provides you with a cerebral experience – the thought, not the feeling – that things could be worse. So really what my brother does, or says he does, is to anaesthetise himself against feeling pain by thinking up something to think about. It really would be fantastic for everybody who is hurting to imagine that things could be worse and thereby ease their Pain, but it just doesn't work out that way at all. You've got to feel or relive or actually live for the first time that Pain so that you can get it out of your system.

Anyway, in the session I also told Janov about this conversation with my brother. Now at this point I'm still having this terrible confusion in my head. That pain started in, that very same pain that I have felt thousands of times before. The pain is more like a throbbing, nagging kind of thing. When I get that pain, I am usually in a state of perturbation or irritability or peevishness or indecision. In other words, something is bugging me, and a decision or resolution is waiting, and I can't seem to do what is necessary. I then get the pain in the head, and not the pain but the knowledge that I've worked myself up into having a pain makes me become extremely agitated. Like agitated to the point of yelling, or forcing my point to be heard, or banging something, etc. Usually I get rid of the pain by blowing up or off and then lying down to relax or recuperate. Now at this point I had the pain, and I became very twitchy, itchy, peevish; my body became agitated, too – it trembled in spasms. I felt like I was entrapped in an elastic cocoon, let's say, and my arms, fists, whole body was struggling to get out. I wanted to resolve or come to some decision about this confusion with my parents. I then became more agitated, and when Janov asked me to say the feeling, I said, 'Nervousness,' which was the word I thought/felt best communicated peevishness-irritability-mild-panic-frustrations-hurt-pain. He said, 'Torture.' Yes, torture was certainly the word, the only fucking word really. I was being tortured by myself and by thoughts and by feelings and pain. And in about a minute or less the pain left my head completely.

I went out to see Ted in the afternoon. He's out of a job, feeling lost. He is lost. That's about all I can say. I like him very much, but there's barely anything I can do to help him right now. What he could use is a subsidy for his family, and I am no subsidiser. Mostly, I sat and listened and let him do most of the talking. He just sounded so screwed up, didn't know how to do anything, looking for a gas station job 'cuz that's the only thin' I know how to do'. I mean I don't know what's the matter with him that he can have his sights aimed so low on the horizon. Doesn't he want anything big out of life? I guess he's fucked up and over. There's nothing to feel but sorrow.

In the evening I thought about how I thought I wasn't getting better. I mean I had stopped the berserk screaming stuff, and now I didn't seem to be going fast enough. Janov told me again that it was my sickness – this idea that I have to be good at the thing, always trying to excel, to be good at whatever it is I'm doing. Like what the hell do I have to prove anyway?

March 5th

Today was just too harrowing, too terrifying. It started off with talking about homosexual fantasies, my visit to my brother yesterday. What the hell is wrong with me? I'm not his father, and I have no business acting like his father – that's sick. Anyway, I wanted to get into this homosexual thing because I suspected (or knew/felt) that I was a victim of that kind of crazy thing, like so many other males in the country. I just wanted to get it straight in my guts once and for all. It's simply an intellectual bullshit game to say that man is born of both woman and man and that, of course, he has some 'femininity' in him through genetic transference or heredity. That 'of course' phrase is the bullshit because it's not getting to where it's at. I know that.

Terrifying. Really. If asked how I felt about my first day in Primal Therapy, I would have said, 'Terrified.' Now today, after today's thing, I would say that the first day was barely scary, because today I saw and felt the terror. Okay, so I got started on the theme, got worked up into an agitated state, and then Janov said, 'Say that feeling.' I said, 'It says fear.' That's right; I mean I didn't say the word 'fear'. FEAR said, 'Fear.' Does that sound nuts? It isn't. In Primal Therapy, the real feeling seems to say itself; all you have to do is shape your mouth and let the word travel up from the gut through the voice box and out the mouth. It says itself, is what I'm saying. The word which is the feeling itself leaps from your guts (if you allow it to) and says itself. This is real. In other words, you cannot lie in Primal Therapy without knowing it. Yes, you can lie if you want to, but you will feel that you have lied, and it will have to surface. Yesterday I had the same experience with the word-thing-Pain 'hate'. HATE leaped out of my mouth.

All right, I went on. And after a while I said, 'Fear I'm a queer.' This was unbelievable because those are the words only, but I wasn't sure what I was saying. It could have been: (1) Fear? I'm a queer, as if I were talking to fear itself. Or it could have been: (2) [I] Fear I'm a queer, wherein I was omitting the very important 'I'.

Then Janov forced me to start telling Daddy that I was a queer. But somewhere around this time I lost the whole thing. I'll bet that it was so fucking terrifying that I ran away from whatever it was that I was going to feel in my guts. For about the next half hour I tortured myself. I went through the motions of pain and crying, and indeed, they were real. But here's the thing that's amazing: Each time that I would finish a Primal I was left with a hangover, a 'hanging-over' lingering knowledge-feeling that what I had done was not what I should have done. This was really fantastic. My self was telling me that I hadn't had a real Primal, that the big thing I had to face was still there for me to face. Once, maybe, I got close, so close that I gagged and thought I was about to vomit. I think I went through three make-believe Primals before I got the message loud and clear from my body that I was only jiving, that I wasn't getting down to the real thing where it really was happening. I became terrified at that point. I thought, or at least said, that I was going nuts. But now I know why I said that: It was because I couldn't fight my self who kept telling me that there was still something waiting for me to face. In other words, I couldn't evade what my self was telling me, and I was becoming very agitated. Janov kept saying, 'Give up the struggle.' I guess he meant give up fighting against what you know you must allow yourself to feel. But I didn't want to or couldn't give up the fight. Really, I was truly terrified.

What was terrifying me – or as close as I can come to saying it – was the lurking picture of me as a homoerotic person. There was a picture of me in my mind's eye being held by Father and liking it, and then I looked up and saw that it was a man's face and I became disgusted. The words 'shame', 'revulsion' and 'disgust' came to my lips. I'm not sure what got me bent all out of shape. It could have been that I knew I was enjoying the physical contact of a male; it could have been that I liked it, I guess. It could have been the feeling in my guts that approximated the urgency of wanting to ejaculate because I still had the feeling in my cock of wanting to take a desperate leak. Janov says that I can't because it's a pissing away of feelings, and because I want to trust the guy, I hold back the piss and become very agitated by it. It could have been a feeling – the beginning of a feeling – that felt like I was a helpless female-like sex object. That comes pretty close to my feeling, I think: that I was beginning to get the feeling that I was enjoying feeling like a female sex object hating feeling like that because of disgust shame hate and not liking the outrage of me at being so used. Now I just re-read that last sentence because I was going through a kind of revulsion as I was typing it and at one point couldn't even remember what I was typing. And now I see that I was agitated when I was typing.

Well, at least I know what I have to face. That's where we're going, Janov said. Into the really terrifying.

Now here's something fantastic. At one point today, when I was under great anxiety or fear or dread or something, I began to feel the inner workings of my body – particularly the heart area, the breadbasket, the lower and upper intestinal areas. Really fantastic. I felt juices being secreted; I felt the thumpings of some hammer-like machine; I felt the up-and-down motion of something else; I could feel rhythm, motion, placidity. But the really unique thing is that I felt these things as though they were operating on different planes inside my body; I told Janov 'layers', but now I see that I was feeling the working of one piece of apparatus, say, above another one which was doing something else underneath. I can't name any of the organs I felt, but I definitely felt movement and rhythm and a kind of harmonious working together inside me. The planes or layers I'm talking about would be roughly like this: Say, one is parallel to the back and close to it; another is parallel to it and somewhere in the centre of me; and the third is parallel to those two and closer to my skin or is the first layer. Fantastic.

The other thing today is that I really got bent out of shape and kept screaming about turning into a girl, a 'namby-pamby'. I felt lethargic and seemed to have all my 'fight' taken out of me lately.

March 6th

Last night I stayed up through the night, setting the alarm clock for every half hour, so that if I fell asleep, I would not sleep more than a half hour. It must have been about six thirty or so when I fell off to sleep. I dreamed that I was flirting or somehow engaged in amorous conduct with a female who was more of a slut or trollop than anything else.

She had a gigantic cunt which I was holding in both my hands and squeezing or manipulating. It was like holding a big sponge; then I held it to the tip of my cock and probably rubbed it against myself. It was at that point that I came awake or half-awake, ejaculating in my pants and feeling, as always, screwed up.

I told Janov about that dream today, and he asked me if my attitude towards women was one of that they are all a bunch of cunts. I said no, but then later in conversation referred to my mother as a stupid cunt, and then remembered that that was my favourite name for Susan and her mother and that I had written the very same thing a night before in my diary. That's not without significance. Today's session was nowhere near the terror I thought it would be. I just couldn't seem to get to anything deep down today, couldn't seem to cry out anything today. Just a few squeezed-out tears. This disturbed me because I thought it meant I wasn't getting anywhere. I have told Janov that I no longer smoke and in fact no longer have the urge (maybe a little urge occasionally); I no longer have that churning-stomach feeling when my wife is doing something that used to irritate or distress me; I no longer feel overwilling to get in there and start mixing it up verbally about some trivial bullshit with Susan; I'm now aware of our relationship in a different light; I can now sit down and listen to my folks and not get that impatient, intolerant feeling about them; I feel very much like not fighting with anyone; in fact, my limbs just don't seem to be able to tighten up, get belligerent. Of course, it's ridiculous to say that I'm not making any self-improvement. Here I am ceasing to do things I have done for years and stopping them in only nine sessions of therapy. Plus there are all the other minor changes and re-evaluations and the beginning of change in me in a dozen different areas. So I must be crazy to have doubts about my growth towards health. This leads me to speculate that the 'sick' person, even when he is moving towards becoming 'real' and 'healthy', wants not to believe it, wants to continue thinking he's sick.

March 7th

Today's session was great, just great. I can't remember how

I got into the real thing, but it must have been after spending nearly an hour on things that didn't seem to bring up anything in me. Finally, what I started getting was the feeling of loneliness, aloneness. It occurred me that the philosophers, the existentialists, and all the others didn't know what they were talking about when they tried to describe aloneness. There's no need for all these multisyllabic terms they use. They are, in the final analysis, full of shit. So I started working with this feeling. My eyes were closed, and then something really great happened.

I saw myself as a little boy or five or six or so, standing next to mother's bureau, looking up at her while she stood in front of the bureau's mirror in a bra, stuffed with her boobs, and adjusting the strings of her corset. I watched and watched. Then I grew up. This 'growing-up' process was very similar to the technique Walt Disney employed to show how a flower blooms – time-lapse photography. In other words, I saw myself 'grow up' physically – that is, become taller like a teenager, in a flash. Then I put my right hand on my hip, and I seemed to be sassing my mother for a minute. Then I started going at her tits. Not sucking them so much as I was rubbing my face into them, rubbing them all over my face, but particularly over my eyes, of all places. This was astounding. Janov told me to ask the kid what he was doing. I did, but he didn't reply. I yelled at him, 'What are you *doing*?' in a tone of incredulity. Imagine, rubbing tits all over his eyes. He didn't answer but continued for a while. I talked about other things but kept glancing over every now and then to watch the young boy and what he was doing. In other words, for all practical purposes, he 'existed' in the corner of the room doing what he was doing. But to me, he was very far away, and I would squint from behind closed eyelids to see what he was doing (of course, he was in my mind's eye). Then the boy 'shrunk down' to little boy size again. He was sitting on his legs which were bent under him, his back was bent over, and he held his little hands to his face while rivers or streams of tears shot out or flowed out. He was crying quite literally rivers and years of tears.

At this point I told Janov about something that had happened in my life hundreds of times. When I was drowsy, I could see senseless words appear in my mind's eye, and in my mind's voice I could read them. But because they were so unintelligible and difficult to say, they were unutterable. I tried to write about this once, and how pleasant it was, in 'The Bald Muckybullyfoo'. Some of the words might be *smlplgh, oxwyong, hmply*. Now Janov asked me to tell him what words I saw. I told him that they were behind a screen or curtain, like the kind of curtain hanging in a theatre. He told me to part the curtains and tell him what I saw. I remember having some dread and difficulty doing this. Finally, I saw a couple of 'words', tried to pronounce them. Then I saw a statement hanging over the little bent-over boy, much the same as in old-time theatre where a scroll-type apparatus would be turned by a female to announce to the audience what scene was taking place, etc. The thing for the boy said: 'I get g' got nuh nothing . . .' In other words, that is what he answered when I asked him what was wrong, why he was crying so many tears and so hard. 'I get g' got nuh nothing . . .' is all he could stutter-say-cry. Stuttstuttersay. Stuttstuttersay. Stuttstuttercry. Stuttstuttercry.

All through this experience I seemed to be aware that I was in a state of 'highly imaginative seeing and experiencing'. What I mean is that I knew I was in Janov's office, but that I was seeing and hearing everything that was going on in my closed-eyes theatre of the mind. I was experiencing a play which was very symbolic, and I was truly digging it. Some more time passed in which I kept up my description of what was going on – the boy crying the rivers of tears. I, too, was crying 'completely' at that point. Then Janov asked, 'What else do you see?' And this was remarkable. I saw my old Nightingale Street crammed with people, but I saw them as a movie camera would from the waist up only. So it was like watching a movie of my street crammed with people, about a dozen or so abreast, walking by one another. All were silent, all emotionless, all were sombre, tired, none noticed any other. Then I knew why the little boy never got anything. The anything was love, of course – the feeling told me that. He never got any love because nobody – his mother, father – had any time. The world (all the people) were walking by one another, never paying attention to one another; the world was too fast, and the little boy never got anything. Janov told me to tell him that, to comfort him. I stretched out my right arm and patted him on the back, on the shoulders, on the head, and told him that what was simply was;

don't try to figure out why you didn't get any love – you didn't, and that was all there was to it. Now make something good out of your life. You love a girl, and live with love together. And so on in the same vein. For about a minute or two I talked about something else to Janov. Then suddenly the boy was on his feet and running furiously towards me. I mean that boy was really running. He seemed to run through years. I grew frantic – I don't know why. I began to scream: 'Stay away, stay from me, stay away.' I kicked out with both feet, put out my hands before me to ward him off. But on he came. I remember Janov saying, 'Give up the struggle, give up the struggle.' I kept saying no, No. I was really frantic now – on he came. Suddenly he was gone. He was practically on top of me, coming into me, and then he was gone. I opened my eyes and said in utter surprise, 'Where is he? He's disappeared.' Janov told me to look for him. I did – I looked all around the room, I told him where I last saw him. Janov told me the little boy was inside me. I knew that in my guts, but I didn't want to believe it. I closed my eyes and tried to re-sketch the picture and see the little boy all over again. I tried very hard to do this, but of course, I couldn't. I knew where the little boy was and who he was. Then I cried good and clean.

I had seen my life unfold in front of me, maybe very symbolically, but nevertheless, it was my life, and there was no mistake about it. I lay there feeling very drained and even a little happy. I felt purged and happy. I accepted all that had happened – I had to – it was very real. I think that this Primal was a step in the direction where I should be going with all my Primals. It was harrowing, but that's where it's at. The after-feeling is one of relaxed lightness for me. It's like I've unloaded some awfully heavy, hurting burden, and now I'm a bit lighter, freer.

Still, today, I have a nagging doubt that I still haven't faced up to the terribly dreadful things I was bringing up on Wednesday and Thursday. The general theme is homosexual fears or something, and I think I've somehow evaded getting deep-deep down to where I am with that.

I spent some time at the beach for the rest of the day, did an errand or two, and came home. Susan wasn't talking to me, and I didn't mind. More and more, I can see her sickness. What particularly is disturbing me is her selfishness in bothering me when she should know how desperately important this whole Primal thing is. Yet she goes out of her way to antagonise me.

March 10th

Today has been a very important session. I had another of what Janov calls a 'conscious coma', which is a beautiful term. I referred to it on Friday as a 'state' or a 'trance' or a 'state of imaginative experiencing' or 'a theatre of the mind'. But 'conscious coma' is, of course, *the* term to use here. I started off trying to relate all that happened yesterday. I was having trouble bringing up real feeling. I began to get plagued with that cranky, peevish, irritated feeling. I couldn't express anything. I kept failing. I then had a long silent period. And then I began to feel sense out of what was happening.

First, I knew that below anger there is pain which I didn't want to feel. Anger and acting out are diversionary tactics we use so that real feeling of the deep pain or hurt doesn't have to occur. In other words, everybody gets so concerned with contending with a person's acting out or anger that the person escapes being forced to feel his Pain. In Primal Therapy, you know this because you have lived it on the couch, and if you want to get well, then you don't run from the Pain/feeling. So I knew I was having a feeling blocked. But I didn't know how or why. I lay there. Then I felt how and why.

I needed to take a piss. I then felt the truth which was saying that all I really felt was the NEED TO ESCAPE THE FEELING BY PISSING IT AWAY. An actual piss was not really necessary considering the amount of liquid I had taken in in the past twelve-hour period, and I had pissed about five times anyway. So what I was doing was creating the urge to piss as a way of escaping from feeling a certain unfelt Pain in my guts. I was pushing the Pain out through my cock; in other words, rather than bringing up the Pain, I was pushing it down and away. This was so simple to understand, I was amazed that I had never understood it before. Then other things began to make sense: the fact that many people throughout my life had inquired why I urinated so often, expressing an interest in my health; others complimented me for my well-functioning bladder. Bull, bull: I was pissing away my hurts and pains of my life.

At the same time another thing was happening. When I tried to breathe up the feeling through my wide-open mouth, I gagged; then I 'developed' a little bronchial cough. Now I knew damn well there was no reason to have a bronchial cough because I hadn't smoked one puff for two weeks. So the fucking cough, too, was a diversionary tactic my body had learned to perform so that I could have my attention drawn away from having to feel my painful hurts.

I was truly flabbergasted. Lying there calmly, it had all come to me, and now I was beginning to link up these significant things. (1) There is pain; (2) I wish to avoid feeling it; (3) because feeling means hurt, pain; (4) my body 'manufactures' the pissing urge as a diversionary tactic; (5) thus I concentrate my strength to feel on holding back the urine; (6) now I am unable to use my strength to help myself feel the feeling because I need my strength to hold back the urine that threatens to come out my penis if I release my holding strength, and after all, I can't leak on Janov's couch; (7) just to make sure all my power is being diverted, I 'manufacture' a little cough; (8) now I must concentrate on holding back pissing and coughing and I have no strength to feel the feeling because I would have to release my hold on my bladder and I can't do that. So I have protected myself from feeling by making a trap of my body. I simply lay there stunned at this knowledge.

I now remembered that about five minutes earlier I had had that cranky, peevish, irritated feeling. I now remember stretching my body as if to free myself from the clutch of the crankiness, but I was really settling into the embrace of the crankiness, establishing calmness for myself. I had been fooling myself like that for YEARS, YEARS! Naturally, I grew calmer when I did this. But now I knew that it wasn't calmness due to having felt the Pain, but that it was a form of anaesthetising myself against feeling Pain. I just lay there really amazed that I had learned this truth about myself. I lay there for a good long time – maybe twenty minutes – and gradually the real feeling began to emerge again, and this time I let myself go with it.

The feeling said loneliness. 'Tell Mommy,' Janov said. I did, and she didn't seem to be able to do anything about it.

She stood there with her head sadly bowed, arms hanging by her sides. I saw her in my conscious coma. This went on for a minute or two. Then she started to walk slowly away. I followed her wondering what would happen. I cried after her: 'Wait, don't go. Stop. Come back.' I was aware that my hands were outstretched and pleading. She kept walking and disappearing very slowly; then she was out of sight. Then, just as slowly, a new figure(s) began to come towards me, but painfully slowly. Finally, it began to look like Susan and her mother, then just like Susan alone. I became afraid, yelled, 'Stay away.' She came right up next to me, and my mother was right there. I was breathing very hard and kept it up for a minute until I could calm down from this fright of having seen my wife emerge from where my mother had disappeared.

Now I should point out here that as soon as the feeling began to come on about five minutes ago, I also broke out and cried out these words which seemed to float out of my insides: 'No(t) love – sick need – I married my mother.' I said these words a few times, and then of course the picture made a lot of sense to me. The theatre of my mind was acting out for me the fact that I had married my mother in another girl. This was, of course, a terrifying thing. But there would be no pissing away of this feeling. Besides once you're in the conscious coma, you want only to experience it; you know there is nothing to dread about it because you're already in it. GETTING in it is the tough part.

Okay, so here are my mother and my wife side by side, each telling me for my benefit or each other for their own benefit how marvellous each of them is, and how much they care for me.

March 14th

Today, Friday, has been simply unbelievable. I myself am not sure how much I believe what has happened, but I've got to get it down on paper at least. First off, I told Janov about my afternoon and evening yesterday. It was really a groove because I spent about seven hours listening to classical music – Bohemian and Rumanian and Hungarian rhapsodies, sonatas by Enesco, concertos, symphonies. I got completely lost in each piece I was listening to. Sometimes I got up and danced, or stalked about or marched around the room; sometimes I aped the sound of certain pieces – I became the orchestra. I was having an unbelievable time locked into the dimension of sound/music. I knew nothing else. A few times I cried; this was when I realised individual Primal Therapy would be over after Friday; when I began to feel really alone in that room with just the music; when I felt the desire to call somebody, but that there was absolutely nobody I wanted to talk to on the phone. I was feeling very light, rather ecstatic. Then Susan came home and brought an air of gloom and sullenness into the house with her. I wavered between many opposite feelings after that: anger, scorn, loneliness, irritability, lonesomeness, humour, self-interest, pissed-off feeling. I felt her as an invasion of my mood, my scene and then things just weren't the same with her there. After she went to bed I sat by myself in the dark, contemplated Century City, finally looked at some Joey Bishop and Johnny Carson and then part of a flick called *The Gangster* starring Barry Sullivan circa 1947. It was an unusual film in that it was showing you the deterioration of the human being – i.e., the human being being destroyed by crime (evil). Yes, very nice.

I then had a very tossing/turning night. I have had more and more symbolic comas and now symbolic dreams. This one was unbelievable. I was in a huge room, something like a ballroom where a party was going on. This room was a multi-dimension kind of thing; that is it must have had about five dimensions to it – maybe three or four different planes: People were within/without perpendicular/parallel to/with/at one another/many. It was that crazy. There are hardly adequate words to describe it, and the ones I've thus chosen seem to destroy the scene I had wanted to depict here. Now the creatures in this area were weird. There were a countless number of people/creatures dressed in weird costume. (Or maybe they simply *were* this way.) One person was a walking target – a black-and-white ringed bull's-eye; another was a bunny with a floppy tail; another was the Noxzema girl from TV; something else was a walking block of concrete (a 'square'); a skinny and pimply face pervert-looking type; a girl with a face that was distorted by having acid thrown in it. And more and more. What I was seeing was a crazy world. I had thought about this on Thursday night. I had thought about how difficult it was going to be going back into a world of nonsense and sickness and people's antics. I could see myself, not them, as a misfit because I was more real. Also, this gigantic room was peopled with the craziness of TV and movies, commercials people like an announcer girl (who was wearing her little short dress with a hole cut in it for her pussy and men were walking up to her and sticking straws in her pussy and drinking from it).

Okay, so there I am in the midst of all this craziness – which is more than symbolic. I find myself in/on/within a strange kind of bed and a guy who is dressed as an Indian nabob or prince is beside me. He's all decked out in a turban studded with glaring jewels and jewel-studded exquisite clothing. Something rolls onto me – it's a shape. I turn to the guy and say, 'Who's that?' He says 'It's ──.' I can't remember if he said a specific name, but the indication was that it was female. To test this, I reached for where the breasts should have been and found a firm, fleshy tit in my hand. I then attacked this creature which reminded me of a heavyset Brueghel woman who was covered in a flannel yellow kind of pyjamas. She/It was like a big soft girly/teddy bear. I grabbed its cunt in both hands and began to rub it against my penis and then lurched awake still ejaculating. I scrambled out of bed, thinking I had overslept and missed my appointment with Janov, but it was only 6.20 a.m.!!

After I related this whole thing to Janov, he tried to get me to do some feeling, to return to this general theme of loneliness and aloneness. I tried and tried to enunciate any feeling I could feel within me, but I couldn't seem to get anywhere. From experience, I knew I was fighting myself; however, my defences are so refined and so subtle that it is very difficult for me to know. Then it hit me – I mean a glimmer of knowledge. I screamed out: 'STOP COUGHING, STOP COUGHING!' I kept this up, telling myself to cut out this fucking coughing routine as a way of evading feeling. It worked. I then began to get down to some reality. The loneliness stuff was still there. I seemed to be ruminating in my mind. I was beginning to get remote signals or cues from the very interior-most parts of my body that was telling me that there was something to be felt – something very big – and that once again I was using some kind of subterfuge to fight it. I kept this up for a while: squirming, struggling, whining peevishly. Then I finally allowed a feeling to sweep over me, or 'wash' over me as Janov suggested. I like that term in contrast to 'sink below it' because it is more graphic for me and allows me to really get my imagination functioning so that I can really let the thing 'wash' over me. I was getting sharp pain in my heart, in my head, in my left mastoid bone. These pains alternated for most of the session. I also had the bellynags. I tried to bring up a feeling, and it felt as if I would vomit all over the couch and floor. Now I knew that it was really a bad feeling in there.

I was talking about sex because clues and cues and words in front of my eyes seemed to indicate the sexual theme. I was talking about Sylvia and how good it had been then and then how shitty it turned out for me, and I was talking about my sexual history in general and saying that I simply was no good or not good enough. I was talking around and about delivering a natural experience for my wife, talking about sex . . . and then I saw the words 'adoring . . . me . . . adore . . .' or some such thing. I couldn't make connections. I knew I was getting into something big, and I really was beginning to get eager, but linking and connecting was very difficult, futile; I just seemed to be rambling. I began to reminisce about the married couples in my life, and I could see each one of them in my mind's eye, and I could see where in each case the woman was stronger, more domineering than her unlucky hubby. I said a few things about that general theme for a while, then moved over into my parents' marriage and said that in that marriage my old man was always the boss. I saw him in the role that many cynics cast themselves in – keeping a woman barefoot and pregnant. In other words, a woman is a piece of shit. I then talked about my own attitudes towards women. But still I was having terribly agonising trouble linking up things.

Then Janov got me to talk to Mommy because I was telling him about life with Mommy. I could see that she had in a way de-sexed me, or more accurately de-maled me by treating me as a little girl, saying that I was so 'beautiful' that I should have been a girl, taking me into the ladies' toilet when in a department store, etc. Janov said, 'Tell her.' I was talking to her, asking her why she had treated me like that when all of a sudden she told me she wanted her daddy (her answer). She sat down, legs crossed, head bowed, fists pounding her lap, and she kept crying, 'I want my daddy...' over and over. I became so agitated I yelled out, 'He's dead ...' and a few more choice tidbits. Then she began to walk away. I called out to her, 'Come back.' Then she 'met' my father quite a distance away. She was still crying out for her daddy, thinking he was her 'daddy', while my old man began to undress her; then he got her down and began to lay her. I got stomach-churning sensations at this point – I didn't want to watch; I imagined I could even hear the squirshch of their organs making it, like a piston slamming into soft wet oatmeal. Anyway this seemed to go on for a while, and I was reporting it to Janov. (In other words, my old man had been banging my old lady for a good long while – maybe years – before they got married. She was almost thirty before they married. It seems to suggest itself that maybe she was a 'dog' heading towards spinsterhood, and the only way she could get married was to get knocked up. My speculation.)

At this point an amazing thing happened. I saw myself being conceived in her belly. In other words, as I yelled to Janov, I was getting made. I recovered from this picture to see my mom and pop walking down Barbary Ave., and people were saying hello to them, men were tipping their hats to Mom. Next scene Mom is saying, 'I don't want it...' meaning the baby in her. Old man says they'll get married. I see them get married in a flat. I report this to Janov. Next scene she's in the hospital, having the baby. Only this fucking baby is ME. I am staggered, amazed! ! This is truly unbelievable. I am not sure even now if I was fantasising, hallucinating, or having a conscious coma. I hope that the last is true. She's screaming/crying. Doctor is holding me up. How do I know it is me? Well, it's my mother's cunt and fleshy thighs, and I just popped out of her. Number two, I am born strangled by the umbilical cord. Mommy is yelling, 'Die ... I don't want it ... Let it die ...' some kind of hysterical bs like that. The doctor yells, 'It's strangling. ... It's a blue baby ...' or some such shit. Actually, this is factual.

Now, at this point, I am stunned to realise that I actually got myself back to Day/ONE today. I cannot say with very much certainty how much of today was conscious coma, how much was an overactive imagination, or how much was

200 The Primal Scream

fantasising. This much I can say: From my other experiences with conscious comas I would say that my experience today was a conscious coma. Once, maybe twice, was I aware momentarily of the intrusion of 'another reality'. I say 'another reality' because the state of a conscious coma is a state of reality that I am at that moment. For all intents and purposes I am real in it. However, it takes merely a sharp commanding 'Okay, Gary' to bring me back into the other reality. The intrusion of this other reality I felt when I began to fight for my life on the couch, and I had a cue that this is a couch in Dr Janov's office I've digressed here because I am very confused about what I have been through today. If it is true that the mind is capable of remembering itself even before conscious life, then we are really onto something.

Anyway, I began to fight for life in a frantic way. I remember that my arms were outstretched towards the ceiling. I was making sounds like a newborn baby: *waa-aa-aa* ... *maaaa* ... *ghaa-h* ... Something like that. I was screaming out to Janov that I was strangling; the words I wanted to say to prove I was alive to the doctors were very hard to form on my lips. Finally, I was born! I was breathing. Oh, I also remember that I was being held around the ankles upside down. Then calmness came to me, and I laughed. 'I made it. . . . I made it. . . . I made it. . . . I'm alive.' I was breathing very hard and finally settled down into a calm state. I then tried to connect pieces. I clearly saw myself as an unwanted/wanted child, as my mother's son/daddy. I then saw pictures of myself growing up with her. I must say that these pictures of myself, as I recall at this very minute while typing, are actual photographs taken of me and my mother and which are in her possession to this very day. I 'grew' in a unique way. Once before, in a coma, I grew vertically; now I was growing – but horizontally – from a basinette to a little crib, to a little bed, to a Hollywood-size bed. Amazing! ! Anyway, in one scene my mother is playing with my cock, fingering it like it was a toy. I yelled out, asking, what the hell did she think I was, a toy? ? And then I came to the knowledge that this is how she thought of me, regarded me.

In another scene, I am in bed, and I can hear ladies talking and laughing in a card game in another room. I even

indicated this room with my index finger to myself while
talking. They are talking about their sons and how they treat
them, play with them. Somehow they get around to cracking
jokes about how they play with their sons' cocks; then they
connect this little joke to their husbands. They are really
enjoying being risqué. I hear snatches like: 'You too, Bella?
... My Sam. ... My Solly. ...' Someone, my mother I realise, cracks a joke about doing it, too, but it's too small or
something. This is in reference to me, but I can't remember
the specific statement right now. Something about she would
if she could find IT. ... Anyway, I then get a picture in my
eyes from *Night Games*, the film where a mother humiliates
her son by first tantalising him to the point that he gets a
hard-on and starts to play with himself under the sheets, and
then she pulls the covers off him, exposes him, calls him
names, slaps his hands and then leaves him. I then remember the same scene between my mother and me: she slapping
my wrists and saying, 'Don't do that, Gary,' in that Jewish-
woman's-tone-of-voice – shrewish and whining in the
throat. I can't recall if this ever happened in real life between
us; if it didn't, then I can't explain why it got into my conscious coma.

Somewhere around this point I came out of it a little and
lay there kind of bewildered by the whole experience, not to
mention thoroughly exhausted. There was still a lot of
pieces floating around. I gathered that I was going to have to
go even deeper and tell off Mommy before I could get to be
sexually potent. But I don't know – I'm guessing: It came to
me that there had been no men for me in my life to go to, to
emulate in a positive way; just my old man who certainly
taught me enough to fuck me up, and a lot of working stiffs
in the neighbourhood who provided no 'role model of
success' for me to emulate. I also remember now, though it's
out of context, that back in the near beginning of today's
session, I talked about my preoccupation with thoughts of
women and about those dreams I used to have of my aunt.
Dreams about her huge cunt swallowing me up by my head
first, while her huge rolling thighs kept me a pinned captive;
dreams of her cunt running after me on legs! ! Dreams of
running into her cunt which was covered by pink bloomers
and then rubbing my face in the cunt ... enough.

That was it. I was left with a stale, dry taste in my throat and mouth – like the whole thing was distasteful, that there was more of it where it came from.

RANDOM CONNECTIONS REGARDING PRIMAL THERAPY

May 15th

On the seventh and eighth of May somewhere around ten o'clock at night, I felt myself alive. I felt my entire existence. I felt it for too brief a time – perhaps five seconds. To say it was exhilarating, luscious, exhausting, electrifying – to say all that – comes close to what the actual experience was. I am not sure if the language even has the suitable vocabulary, for how could a society of truly unfeeling people (as we know feeling to be) develop a suitable vocabulary to express what they have never experienced? I felt, at the very moment I was describing my experience, that it could not be accurately worded. Some speculation arises within me about this: Is the problem that we don't yet have the language to express feeling, or is it not a problem at all since it is entirely possible that feeling is a realm of its own not to be translated into mere words, defying man-made words?

For me feeling myself has not been only an inward experience. It has been total, the total being. I was on the floor after having gone through some preliminary sinking-in sensations when I was aware that my backbone felt differently. I felt and felt and felt until I said that it felt erect or something. 'But what is it?' Janov asked me. 'I feel straight,' I said. Then I cried. I cried for the sheer beauty of having felt straight (together) for the second time in my whole life. For I began connecting, and it came to me that I actually had felt straight or together only once before and that was exactly at the moment I was born. No wonder that I didn't know the words to express the feeling – I had felt only once and that was nearly twenty-seven years before. What has taken a simple paragraph to write actually took two months of therapy leading to this level of feeling total awareness. It took agonising hours of self-confrontation, acting out antics, crying, pain in the guts.

Anyway, for me to feel total was to feel exactly where I was in the universe. I opened up all channels. For example, I became aware immediately that I could feel the solidity, the strength of my pelvic area. In other words, I could feel my body, my 'me'. Also, I then felt my backbone to be straight. That's what I mean about feeling being a total experience. I am convinced now that true and complete health means mental or emotional and physical togetherness. The feeling me will be feeling everything. Probably the all-feeling human could develop a seventh sense about himself. Think of the possibilities of this new species of life being able to have that sense and actually being able to diagnose its own illnesses. Totally healthy, I would no longer be afflicted with psychosomatic or psychoneurotic ailments. I would be able to feel the growth, let's say, of a tumour in my innards or on my brain. I could probably feel the deterioration of my stomach lining signalling a stomach ulcer. On the other hand, such afflictions might never happen to me were I to be totally healthy and together.

The speculation is endless. What is sorrowful is to feel how my parents bungled it for me to ever be members of that kind of species, how it was bungled for them by their own parents, and so on back into the past. Victimised ignorantly, we then victimise ignorantly in our turn. To feel the great tragedy of the human species is to first feel my own self, my own being's potential gone to pot; it is to feel the painful smallness of me and to experience what we could have been.

On this same evening I was then propelled by my entire existence into a kind of feeling state in which I had a fraction of a moment's view of what the species could be were I, and other humans, healthy. The electrification of this feeling was no less startling to my entire system than the feeling of feeling straight. I just glanced over this page and saw that the language seems to be rather glorifying or elaborate. I am not choosing words; in fact, I can't. What is happening to me even right now is that I am feeling the excited exhilaration of frenzied feeling mememe!

I saw the potential of the life-span, perhaps to one hundred and fifty. I saw the end to maladies, and I saw humankind concentrating its scientific efforts on obliterating the diseases in and from the environment. I saw myself freed of all the shit in my head, and my head then doing what it was intended for: without stress and strain caused by unfelt thoughts, without a cluttered head, cluttered with the past, my inside head was free to grow. The visions of this human greatness, the feeling of my own nothingness – my tragedy – made me cry. Intellectualism is human-kind's curse. I felt that my own crazy pursuit of 'knowledge' for so many years brought me, paradoxically, further from it. For now I know that there is only one kind of knowledge: self-knowledge: where I am at: together: straight. When I felt myself for those brief seconds, I felt my beautifulness, my majesty-almost, my being, my grandeur. That, I feel sure, is loving my me. That feeling is one of being full, very full, and then and only then can I love somebody else. Then I will have some love to give. At that point, once I have me, once I can love me full time, I can then love a wife and children. Love to me means giving and the graciousness of receiving, not $\begin{cases} \text{wanting.} \\ \text{taking.} \end{cases}$

To me, taking now means extending the arms in a gesture of taking. Receiving is simply the ability to receive without any neurotic wanting. Thus, to receive love would put an immediate end to conditional love or forcing children to entertain or perform for parents. Receiving is simply receiving from others just what they are able to give, without evaluating or judging or comparing. It means that there would be no disappointment in not getting enough – that would be over. It would be knowing where I am at, and letting others be where they are at, and eschewing those who could cause me harm. This is true: The healthy person must stay away from sick people because sick people can fuck him up with their sick wants. Out of disappointment that he isn't getting the adoration he wants from Daddy, a sick boss could fire a healthy worker; a sick relative could harm a healthy person were he to not go along with the sick man's sick games.

This isn't all. A very important connection for me has been the tying in of me with my parents, mucus, phlegm, breathing, life, peeing, coughing, suffocation, illness both physical and mental. Over the past two months my Primals had been involving these elements, sometimes isolated and sometimes more than one. But this night I put it all together. This infinitely complex, yet astoundingly simple connection came when I felt everything that the connection was about, and then it registered in me what the connection was all about. I was coughing up thick saliva which seemed to be choking me. Also, my nose felt like I should just blow the fucking thing off; in other words, it felt stuffed up. Actually my nose was clean and clear, and what I was feeling was my plugged-up nasal passage all the way back into my head, and it was my head which was all stuffed up. Only when I let myself fall deeply and entirely into a gagging and choking feeling which by this time was racking my whole chest was I able to say the feeling. 'Mommy' – that is what was coming out of my mouth. I was coughing up the choking chunks of shit which had suffocated me my whole life. I was coughing up shit. To me this word, 'shit', means all this: being rejected, being ignored, being brutalised, being yelled at and becoming confused, being hit, being cut up by my parents' tongues. All of that tastes and feels terrible. But my mother's shit was focused in my guts. I could now feel the significance of why I had always been a cougher. I spent my life choking on the shit that was trying to come up. When I came into the world needing love, I got shit (already defined), and this continued most of my life. I now felt this entire corpus of shit within me. I should mention, too, that the very first thing that I did this night was to let go. This is very important. Previously, I had held my body in check, in other words uptight, rigid – i.e., unfeeling. I let go of my body: I relaxed the hold on my cock, my bowels, my chest. I was never really aware of how much of a hold I had on myself. Once I was able to sink into the feeling, I let myself go into it. The prime reason I went around for my whole life rigid, uptight, was to not let anything escape or come out of any of my secret openings. That 'anything' was feelings converted into waste material. Now that I had let go, and nothing came out, I could simply feel the great mass of shit lying inside me. The little ahemming business I had carried on for many years was a choking down of the emerging shit up my throat. I then felt my entire system of control: ahemming, nose sniffing and the tightening up. This elaborate system for keeping myself rigid and impregnable was developed by me to keep from getting hurt and to keep from feeling. Now, for the first (second actually) time in my whole life, everything was unlocked, opened. So now that my energy and strength wasn't diverted in keeping myself rigid, I was free to feel my shit. Agonising, of course.

May 16th

It is increasingly clear to me each day that I live that the healthier I am capable of becoming, the more others begin to assume that something is wrong with me. The clothes, the colour and style, just aren't me, my wife says. 'That isn't the Gary I know', she says. The same thing happened to me after a particularly gigantic Primal; the tension and strain of not feeling left my face, and as the skin relaxed, I looked younger. The very next day, people began asking me if there was something wrong with me, was I sick? What I see as very obvious is an obsession in most people to always know exactly where others are at (or so they like to think). This makes interpersonal relationships (if they can be called that at all) smooth in this society. People seem to be able to deal with one another by piecing together information, traits and other facts about a person so that they can somehow get an image of that person. Then let that person do something which he isn't noted for doing, and the others accuse him of being different. Actually, all he may be doing is letting the inner him show through a little.

May 17th

Connections started happening to me. Agony in my gut was the first thing I felt. A cry wanted to be born inside me (baby Gary, the real Gary wanted to be born), but I couldn't seem to gather my every part of myself to bring up that earth-thundering cry. About all I seemed to get out was a strong squeak. Feeling the system operating with all my strength, and feeling the intensity of the scream that wanted to come up but which I couldn't find the colossal energy to bring up, I then felt the connection that my sickness was my choice. All it would take would be one great erupting cry of lung-sucking lifefulness, I could come alive, be born. I struggled with this for what seemed to be a very long time. Finally I got up and went into the next room to be alone. The wanting to be alone, to be private was one reason that led me to get up. The other reason was that I seemed to be hearing the conversation of the other people with a new crystal-clear clarity.

I was still bringing up just merely strands of thick saliva/mucus stuff. I was full of it – in my guts, head, nose. This was the familiar shit I had been feeling for about the last week. There seemed to be a connection that I would have to bring up that tremendous weight of shit before being able to be born. I had to feel the shit before I could expel it from my guts up my throat out my mouth. Feeling the shit means feeling wanting Mommy and Daddy. And wanting Mommy and Daddy is being sick. My sickness I now could experience was not only the sickness of being crazy, but also the physical feeling of being sick throughout my guts, and being able to taste at the bottom of my throat what tasted very revolting – sick.

Suddenly I began to feel my entire self summoning itself into one colossal scream that seemed to be gathering at my very centre of gravity, deep within the pit of my stomach. My body seemed to pull in gathering force, and as the scream shook me, my body jack-knifed. I continued like this for several screams, each one bringing up the sickness of wanting Mommy and Daddy, and its form was heavy, gluey saliva/mucus. The pain throughout my guts was so severe, and had been for a very long time. I kept calling Mommy and Daddy from the deepest part of me, and every time I could bring up one of those screams I felt the same sickening sickness: the sickening rejection, the sickening hopeless and useless wanting, the sickening being-not-seen-noticed-heard, the sickening despair. All of that I could never have felt or it would have driven me permanently crazy. Sometime after this, I then began to feel the stirring of another cry for me. It gathered force and power inside my guts, and when I let it shake me, it seemed that it didn't all come up – I couldn't get the cry for Gary up all the way. The same mucus was coming up, but it felt like a clear clean mucus to me. Then, at the very moment I was feeling the liquid in my hands, I could feel the cry drop down into my guts again. The cry felt like an egg, rather like a loose yolk thing. Desperately I tried to bring it up, because it shot into my head that this was life itself. Hopeless at this point because I was thoroughly drained.

I slept maybe three hours and then went to the group. I was very groggy, but the same cry was gathering at every few minutes to be cried. Each time I reached in, way in, down into my very centre and cried, I felt a speck of relief in my guts. Also, this tremendous force of screaming had completely blown open the constricted passages in my ears and nose. Anyway, that's where it's at for me for now: the struggle to go for myself, to be born, to fight for my own life. All I have been feeling since last night is how sick I am in my guts. Primals dislodge chunks of cemented sickness.

Friday night and Saturday morning made me really feel the depth of my stupidity and sickness. There I was only a scream's distance away from being a step closer to health, and I couldn't muster it up. The great sickness I cried over afterwards was my tragedy of having it within my power to get well, and instead preferring to stay sick. I'm going for myself now – in a big way, all the way. My instinct and urge to get well have sharpened since this experience. A healthy person would want to keep coming to those Tuesday and Saturday sessions. I want to get the hell out of there as soon as I can.

May 20th

Tuesday night group was good for me because it was so painful. It was a carry-over from what I.didn't finish Saturday morning and had been building in me since then. A cry for my mother erupted from my throat and kept on erupting for the session. In my gut I was feeling the bitter disappointment and the emptiness from never having felt Mommy fill me with what I needed. I know that I was born with total need, completely needing, and when I got rejected the very first time, I was zonked out of shape for the rest of these years.

My crying and my cries reached a new lower depth last night. I mean I could feel my cry coming from my agonised gut, my middle. It sounded different, too – like the cry of a young boy, of course! That feeling sent me into more uncontrollable crying, to realise that I am nothing but a boy, a child really. All of that hurts – really hurts, and there doesn't seem to be anything to do but feel it. But I am glad that I broke through to that lower-depth cry because I was able to really feel the agony of the sick wanting.

May 24th

Today has been an important day because I was able to go deeper with my cry. The cries today were uncontrollable, and came from the very centre of me, and shook me. I imagine this is the first time really that I let myself feel the great wanting and the great emptiness from not getting Daddy's love. On Tuesday I went that road with the wanting and the not ever getting of Mommy's love. The cries go deeper, deeper than ever before. Because Daddy's shit is concentrated in my head, my nose naturally empties out like a gusher. All the tears I was ever 'prohibited' from crying and all the tears I sniffed back into my head all these years were blown up, dislodged and allowed to flow. With my mother the sickness is focused in my gut, so to feel that then brings on a violent coughing up of all the mucus and bile I would always swallow down to not let the feeling come up.

But my crying today! It's as if I have never really cried like that in my whole life. Occasionally it would strike me that the way I cried today was the way I had cried many times before as a boy. I heard my real sorrow, my real depth of having been robbed and now feeling the despairing emptiness. It was the cry I had to cry for my father, the begging cry which admits that I want him. Finally, when some degree of quietness and calm came over me, I was able to just lie there and let all the pieces fall into place for myself.

Last Friday night really did push me into a new phase of feeling experience. Phase Two is a greater intensity, a deeper awareness, a keener pain and suffering, a heightened sense or instinct to want to get healthy, a finer sense of self-sickness, a more pervasive tiredness, a more vigilant eye on staying out of the craziness of others, a more enjoyable feeling of being alone. I guess Phase Two simply is everything that came before it, but with greater depth, dimension and height. Which all adds up to feeling worse rather than feeling just lousy.

June 1st

The business of wanting a cigarette is so beautiful because I don't need any other clue to let me know that I want to suppress the feelings. Now I grow peevish, wanting to throw something – another antic devised for not feeling. Really, at this moment what is really there is a colossal scream. It's as large as my body and as loud as my being can make it. The scream is me, and the tears that want to flow are the tears of years, the tears that have been stored up. Exactly why I want to scream–cry right now, I am not sure. But I have a feeling or a sensation of smallness, helplessness, fallibility.

In my dreaming, some strange things have been happening over the past couple of weeks. My dreams are not only difficult to remember or even to construct, but also I'm not sure if anything at all occurs in them. In fact, my whole sleeping experience over the past couple of weeks has been weird. It is as if I were awake and aware that I was sleeping while asleep and knowing that I was asleep. It is that crazy. Once or twice I have awoken (I think) and asked, 'Am I awake?' It is in that 'dimension' of experience that I have slept. I am crying now because I feel even more crazy putting this down on paper. But really it seems that sleep is for me a dimensional thing in which a new sense – perhaps an undefinable seventh sense as it were – were operating. Strange things occur within that sense. Nothing is recollectable.

Twice now I have had the experience that I *know* I am asleep. In other words, I believe that something within the mind – perhaps that undefinable seventh sense again – is operable in the sleep experience. I wasn't dreaming that I was asleep. I *was* asleep, and it was as if I were awake within myself while my outside me was sleeping in the bed.

June 2nd

Today I could feel myself being enveloped by movement, the movement and rhythm of some feeling that I couldn't give a name to. Finally – it must have been about a half hour to forty minutes – the feeling came up. It had to do with wanting, not anything in particular, just wanting. It seemed to be concentrated entirely in my mouth. Finally, this wanting gave way to asking out loud. Suddenly I felt the urgency to call out to my parents, and call and call and call. The calling was a powerful thing, *as if my very life depended on being heard*. I could feel my screams come screaming up from my very deepest insides – and yet nothing, no satisfaction. In that split second of nothing, living that very feeling, I felt the total recognition that I *was* heard. Actually, in that split second it seemed that my body had already felt the emptiness but that my mind had to run through three alternatives to make a connection: (1) I couldn't be heard; (2) I was not heard; (3) I was heard. Number 3 was the instantaneous connection: I *was heard*, but they didn't let themselves hear me – they simply did not care that much. I say 'they' because this wanting, at this point in the Primal experience, didn't seem to be focused on any parent in particular. The full impact of that total recognition – total gut feeling and mind connection – sent me into a despairing fit of tears. The tears simply flowed, and with it my nose opened right up and I could breathe. I heard myself howling at that point. For me, that's the only kind of real crying there is – the crying that is my whole being's cry.

My lips, my mouth actually, seemed to start working on their own. I felt the urgency to suck, really suck. This was very hard for me to do. Hard, because there seemed to be an intervening or interfering consciousness that spelled doubt: 'Was this sucking really what I felt?' With Janov prodding me, I started the sucking, let myself do what my mouth felt like doing. I was feeling in my gut a degree of uncomfortableness. What I was wanting was simply Mommy, or Mommy's tit, that's all. The pain in my gut was the familiar pain I always get when I let myself feel my need/want for her – emptiness. That made me cry. Then my mouth started forming a question. 'Why didn't you take care of me?' I had already felt the staggering rejection of not being taken care of – i.e., given her breast, picked up, and held next to her breast often enough. (That's the crucial part and the main meaning of this experience: *often enough*. I am sure my mother did take care of me according to her temperament, but not according to my total infant needs.) And now tonight I let myself feel another phase of that rejection – the not caring, the not wanting to hear my cries. So there I was forming this silent question with my mouth, stretching my mouth as wide as I could. I couldn't see that, understand that. I was silently screaming out, 'Why didn't you take care of me?', realising that the unfocused wanting from an hour before was now really focused on my mother. It was simply her succulent breast's nipple that I wanted jammed in between my chomping lips and bare gums. And now tonight, for probably only the second time in my life, I was feeling that totally hungry want. (The first time I felt that was before I turned off twenty-six years ago, and the second time was tonight.) Somehow, all the elements of a perfect recognition of 'where I was at' at that precise moment were coming together. The meaning of my Primal hit me from behind. It was as if the meaning came swooping up from my guts and swept in from the very back of my head and jumped out my mouth: 'I can't speak', I screamed. Obviously, my wanting went silent because it was before I could put it into words; I hadn't learned to speak yet. Then later when I could speak, I was so turned-off and confused about love, that I couldn't ask for it. I had to feel the total stunning feeling of screaming silently as an infant for love before I could make sense out of my own wanting. That blew the top off everything. I felt tonight what I couldn't allow myself to feel as an infant: the horribly devastating emptiness that rewarded my pleading, and wailing and crying and genuine infant's sorrow. And additionally, feeling the knowledge that they did hear me but didn't care enough to offer that love, particularly my mother, whose love – or absence of it – I felt most keenly tonight.

It came to me soon after as I lay there that really my whole life could have been so vastly different had my needs been fulfilled as an infant. If only I had been held to her breast, and held in his arms those times when my body needed them. . . .

June 8th

I let my whole body summon itself from every remote part of me into one thunderous shout or scream or cry. I had done this before again and again – but, of course, I was never heard. The reason I was doing it again on Saturday was to not leave a drop of doubt that *I had* screamed out enough to be heard. That's why my screaming is so deep, so long. For me to have to believe that I was heard and that they didn't care would make me have to feel ALONE, and that feeling was what I was trying to avoid. Also, to feel that I could give up the struggle to get, simply stop the struggling, would mean that I would have to feel the devastating knowledge that I was always very much alone and that there never was anything to get. To give up the struggle of wanting them would be to feel alone, would be to know totally that there just wasn't anything to get, that there never had been anything to get, that I had been tricked into knocking myself out my whole life to get something from my parents which they simply didn't have – love.

But I tried anyway. First, in an agonisingly begging way with my mother, and then with my father. Both, nothing. With my mother, there was a moment when I thought I was going to dribble out piss. Then it dawned on me that maybe it would have been sperm, and that made perfect sense. Again, all I had been feeling was the wanting her with the body of my twenty-six-year-old self, and the wanting had grown right along with my sex instinct. That's why I can't be sexually potent – because my cock is enslaved to Mommy: In my insane wanting of her love, I've thrown everything into the struggle of trying to get her, my cock included.

For the past couple of hours I have been experiencing something very strange. I know that my body is ill with a cold, but I do not *feel* the sickness. In other words I feel zesty, perky and not weakened. It's as though some other me has the cold and the real me is here enjoying listening to music and typing out this story. This has never happened to me but for the brief experience yesterday. It's as though there's no reason to overplay my illness any more because no mommy is going to pay any attention to me. So I may as well let myself be sick only to the degree that my body has to feel debilitated. My spirit, my living me as it were, doesn't have to be sick just because the body has been slightly affected by a cold. I am, of course, still sick. But I want to say that both times I had the Primals my temperature dropped dramatically (Saturday, 101·5 to 98·6; Sunday, 99·8 to 98·6) and I felt better. I am convinced that all these minor colds and viruses and grippes and flus my whole life needn't have been so devastating and severe had I been loved at birth. . . .

I realise that there's no such thing as 'half-well'. One is either well or still tainted with some part of his neurosis. As for defences, I too thought I should have some. Now it simply doesn't matter. Nobody can hurt me except physically. So I don't need defences. It seems that some of the people find people generally to be oppressive. This isn't exactly my feeling. I do find a lot of things that people do are intolerable, but also very sad. Maybe these few people who talk this way are far and away much healthier than I am, and that when I reach the stage that they are at, I too may feel the same way. But for now, I can make out okay on the streets. I've withdrawn from socialising dramatically. My social life since I began therapy has been limited to maybe six nights at the movies, one play, one restaurant, three visits to old friends, three visits to parents. Then there are infrequent contacts. Our phone bill is now less than half of what it used to be, perhaps a third.

What's happened to me is that I no longer have such a great need or want for anybody. At the same time I find it remarkably easy to be just plain relaxed and nice. This I never was in my whole life. Outwardly I was Mr Tough, the guy who was hard, etc. But now I find it extremely easy to smile at people I know, to say things like good morning. I've felt some of the tragedy of life, of my own family living so physically close to one another, yet miles away from one another in our emotions, closed off from each other with our non-feelings. This profound sadness has, in me, somehow become translated into being soft. I like being tender.

Anyway, as I look at me now, today, there's no going back for me. People can say what they will about the passion for total health being as nuts as total craziness, but I'm going to find out for myself. I gave myself my own ulcers being totally crazy, and if ulcers accompany total health, then I want my own ulcers. There is no turning back for me, back to that brooding, moody, fluctuating, unstable, sombre, false, hostile, malingering, manipulating, afraid, superficial, empty phony that I was. And with that my smoking, psychoneurotic ills, oversleeping, overweight. To hell with being crazy. To hell with stopping. *To hell with 'defences'.*

June 14th

Today marks the end of my sixteenth week of Primal Therapy. I'm not sure what the actual significance of that is, but what I'm thinking about is how relaxed I feel and how unusual a feeling that has been throughout my entire life.

On Tuesday night I didn't get to anything, and when I reflect back on it after today's experience, I think I was trying to re-live an old Primal that night – any old Primal just to have a Primal. My week was a very good one despite the physical illness of having a cold. My mental/emotional me doesn't acknowledge the cold; only my sick and unreal me is suffering with the cold. So this week and most of last week have been good.

June 15th

Like Mother's Day last month, Father's Day today has made me feel the same agonising pain of the tragedy of me and my family. I simply paid no attention to Mother's Day as I'm doing today with Father's Day. There's just nothing in it. If I were still the revenge seeker, I could believe that my conduct was poetic justice: They screwed me from my earliest moments, and now I'm getting back at them. But that is entirely crazy – there's no such thing as 'getting back at them', or 'paying them'. There is simply nothing, and that's what I'm feeling, and it hurts very much.

What makes the tragedy even more acute for me is seeing how my folks have increased their effort to hold onto me. Since I have been married, they have increasingly lavished stuff on me to get me to remain fixed, like a butterfly fixed on a board with pins. First it was my mother's statement, 'Remember, you'll always have a home here.' Then it was actually forcing themselves to write once a week when I was in the Peace Corps, when they had never written me anything all my life when I had gone away to camp, out of the state, Europe. From that they resort to $10 gifts for my birthday, for Susan's birthday, for our anniversary, and 50 bucks as a housewarming present. Shit. All of this, to their way of thinking, is simply showing me the love and concern they think they've always shown me their whole lives. So they can't understand why in the past three months I don't visit, nor call them on the phone. They would like to make me feel guilty, I suppose.

But it's too late for that and for a lot of other things. I can't possibly ever feel guilt, not now after struggling with that hang-up for hours in Art's office and struggling with it for many more agonising hours in the privacy of my own crazy mind. What I feel – what I have had to feel to get well – is the emptiness that was my reward for all my desperate wanting of my parents' love. I've come far enough along to understand me and my feelings today. Understanding is simply feeling and connecting.

So when it comes to something like today, when children young and old are 'honouring thy parents' it is entirely devoid of meaning. For me it would be a senseless exercise in continuing my neurotic wanting for Mommy and Daddy's love. It would be starting in the struggle to get. It is futile. My parents cannot be honoured, nor can they be respected by me. I accept them for exactly what they have always been: unloving, uncaring. But I also understand that they were just as much victimised by their own early life's events as they victimised me. They were unaware; they were stupid, had no insight. So I can't put them down for any of that. I can't hate them. After all, I can't blame them for anything that has happened since the day that true insight came to me for on that day the responsibility of being well became mine. So days like these are sad because they remind me of the great lie that has been perpetrated on me, on my brothers and my sister, and on humankind. There is quite simply nothing, nothing at all. I'm happy that I have the freedom to feel the nothing. For were I still so extremely sick, I would be struggling to feel meaning, struggling to get approval for my gift-bearing childishness, struggle to get the love that was never there for me, struggle to stay sick. Nothing isn't very pleasant. Nothing is. That's about it.

July 12th

Today concludes twenty weeks of therapy. I'm not in any mood to write conclusions about myself nor even to write something that may sound like a self-serving testimonial, but there are some important things I want to say about myself. Twenty weeks ago I was at a point in my life where I was a mess. I've written before in this diary just what my hang-ups and craziness(es) were. Today, when I look at me and feel where I am at, I come up with this.

1. I am almost completely free of compulsive behaviour. I

no longer smoke, have severely curtailed overeating, never eat between meals. I have never bitten my nails or drunk alcoholic beverages to excess, so that hasn't been a problem. I have, however, cut out wine from my meals, and now that I am free to have wine, I don't. I used to like to think that I was 'urbane' or something by drinking wine at mealtime.

2. I am rarely hostile. Before this I was hostile to everybody with whom I came into contact. This means traffic officers, teachers, doctor, parking-lot attendants, gas jockies, waitresses and on it goes. Fistfights through my nineteenth year were a matter of course and continued infrequently for a year or two afterwards. I groomed myself in giving dirty looks, and filthy rotten language which I could heap on anyone at any time for the slightest provocation. Today – and this began to happen after only two weeks of therapy – I am practically meek. I am not even ashamed to use that word to describe myself. I'm just a plain kind person. The kind of work I do brings me into contact with adults who still fight and with others who like to use abusive or goading language, and I remain untouchable. This, for me, is beautiful. I am completely uninvolved with arguments.

3. I am only sometimes moody when I deny feelings. Actually, my moodiness comes so rarely I can't remember when the last time was. *But* – I used to be moody all the time. I would wake up gloomy and pissed-off, and I would stay generally morose, most days all day. Occasionally, I would have a buoyant day. Now all I have are mostly stable and generally buoyant days. This is not manufactured or contrived – this simply happens. I wake up in the morning usually without the alarm clock, and I actually *smile* at my wife. I actually say good morning to people I know, and I actually smile at some of them. To others this may be natural, but to me and my wife this is new and marvellous.

4. I am extremely proficient (in contrast to efficient, which is what machines are) or productive in my everyday life activities. In other words, because I don't have a lot of craziness in my head and in my guts forcing me to be crazy, I can go to work and do an eight-hour day's work in anywhere from five and a half to six and a half. I wake up later if I choose, come home earlier if I choose. I am holding down an important job and am the only person in my field who can do what I do in the entire country. The curious thing is

that practically nobody understands what I do, yet I have completely lost the neurotic zeal to run around all over the place explaining to people (parents) what I do so that I can win approval. Either they understand or they don't – it's entirely their thing. My proficiency also extends into other areas, such as being more adept at making minor repairs around this place, at giving concise advice when asked, at 'fixing up' things as it were.

5. My life is well ordered, stable (in contrast to well organised). This may sound anti-life, but on the contrary, 'well ordered' insures that I am going to have a life to enjoy and time in which to enjoy it. I used to conduct my affairs with an inordinate amount of bungling; my activities were blunders; I used to not care about taking care of things – paying bills, parking tickets, etc. Now, I expend *less* energy and time simply taking care of what needs to be taken care of and that's it. This is really a form of self-preservation. Because I am worth something to me, because I am alive and like it, then I like taking care of me, and that can mean making sure that as many things that need to be done get done with a minimum of effort and sweat.

6. I am 'naturally' more intelligent quite often. This may sound like conceit; however, whereas I used to 'think' I was smart, today and for the last couple of months or so, I *am* my intelligence. Thus, I don't need to stuff my head with information about a particular topic unless I am interested in knowing about it – which usually I am not. I am talking about intelligence in the sense of knowing what's going on with me, where I am at. When I feel that, then I have a kind of natural smartness. In fact my reading has diminished to three books in the last twenty weeks – three very enjoyable novels. Before this, I used to be known for my voracious reading appetite. It was common for me to polish off three to four books a week. I have a natural or groomed ability to read well and quickly and fully understand what I read. Now there's no reading.

7. I am socially inactive and like being with just plain me, alone. I used to make sure I always had something to do and considered being alone the mark of a jerk. That has been completely reversed. Alone is what I am, always have been, always will be, and to feel the freedom to be alone is luxurious. The more I continue through the therapy, the more

refined my aloneness becomes. By this I mean that 'alone' two months ago included reading a book alone, lying on a couch alone, walking around alone. From that it has moved to simply being alone; in other words, doing absolutely nothing alone. That means being able to lie on a couch alone, but not to have the record player going. Alone means alone, and it's exquisite.

8. I enjoy total physical health because I am relatively tension-free. Physical maladies and sicknesses were always a part of me. I would expect – and get – four or five very bad colds and bronchitis every year. I have had one cold since January. For years, headaches would strike four and five times a week. Now, since therapy began, I have had maybe a headache once every three weeks or so, and then I simply have to lie down and feel what it is, and it disappears without a trace immediately. Also gastric hyperacidity was a constant – I mean constant – source of pain. I am almost completely free of that, with the exception of occasional burning sensations after orange juice or tomatoes, etc. I don't suck on Tums or Rolaids any more, whereas I used to go through half a roll a day.

9. I am generally alert, have a new sense of clarity. This might be an outgrowth of Number 6. What I mean is that I am generally aware acutely and keenly of what's going on around me. I can sense danger, other people's conversations. Because when I feel me, I can then anticipate almost like a clairvoyant. This doesn't mean that I go around scheming and figuring things like: 'Aha, I know what he's going to say, so I'll say this and that'. It simply means knowing – feeling – what's going on.

10. I am a delicate person (in contrast to previous show of 'toughness') and enjoy delicate things. I was never like this – nothing seemed delicate to me. Now I actually like to tend the flowers, to watch them grow; I like to listen to the laughter of children in the streets. I like to pet dogs. I had next to nothing in the way of reverence for life other than human. I didn't hold a kitten until I was twenty-five years old, for example. I've lost much of the unreal me things which had been brutalised, and am allowing the real me to emerge.

11. Life is not struggling. I was never able to feel the knowledge of this before. For me, life or living isn't winning

a struggle or a battle; it's giving up the struggle, the battle. Whenever I begin to struggle (not to want to be the baby or try to be unreal) then I begin to get into difficulties. All I need do is simply be, and life could be forever beautiful despite the ups and downs.

That's about all I want to get down on paper. There may be some things I've written here that seem to require further elaboration. All I know is that I understand it all. I have allowed myself to be unselfconscious about the way I write; I just let myself take off my clothes and walk across the page: If I stink, I stink; if I look bad, I look bad. Walking naked, though, has been my first step, and if I'm looking still a bit unreal, that's because I probably am. But whatever unrealness I still retain, there's a new sense of inevitability in my life, the inevitability that the end of all unreality will be reached. There is no way of disproving my statement that Primal Therapy has saved my life and no way for me to prove it to anyone else. The entire question of proof is extraneous anyway. It is enough that I know that my life has been altered for the best because it's a more real life and becomes more real every day – slowly but assuredly. And I know it's more real because the more I feel the bad and the rotten and ugliness and the despair, the more I feel good, pure, self-loving, handsome and loving. The dialectic was never any more appropriate than in this therapy.

13

The Relationship of Primal Theory to Other Therapeutic Approaches

Primal theory is a conceptual structure formulated to explain a phenomenon that occurred in my office. I believe it is a unique theory and not a simple extension or modification of an already existing one. However, aspects of Primal Theory can be found in other psychological approaches. The purpose of this chapter is briefly to compare Primal Theory with some of these other techniques. It is not my intent to present these other theories comprehensively, but to discuss certain aspects of theory or specific techniques that tend to have wide use or acceptance. The concepts of insight and transference will be given special treatment because they play a part in a number of therapies.

THE FREUDIAN OR PSYCHOANALYTIC SCHOOLS

In some respects, Primal Therapy has returned full circle to early Freud. It was Freud who stressed the importance of early childhood experience in neurosis and he who understood the relationship of repressed feeling to mental aberration. It was Freud who focused on introspection systematically and who emphasised internal processes as they affect current overt behaviour. His explanation of defence systems stands as a towering contribution to the field of psychology. Unfortunately, improvements on Freud by the neo-Freudians have shifted the emphasis from early childhood to the here-and-now functions of the ego. What has thus been considered progressive by the neo-Freudians would be viewed as retrogressive in Primal terms.

Freud stressed throughout his expositions that analysis dealt with derivatives of the unconscious – which included free association and the analysis of dreams. I believe that we may proceed directly to the unconscious without having to examine any derivative material. Indeed, the examination of derivative matter seems to prolong therapy needlessly. It is the directness of the Primal approach which enables us to shorten the therapeutic period considerably. When analytic psychologists engage the patient in the analysis of dreams or of his mental associations while lying on the couch, they are doing the very thing that will keep the patient from confronting his feelings. For example, a dream might indicate that a patient has unconscious hostility towards his mother or fear of his father. This is pointed out by the therapist. What the therapist does *not* do, in my opinion, is allow the patient to become overwhelmed by his rage and to scream it out without any control. In the Freudian matrix this would be considered disintegrative conduct. I believe the opposite, that it is integrative – integrating the person's unconscious feelings back into his conscious system.

I believe that analysis of *any* kind is invalid. 'To be "analysed," ' one patient explained, 'is to be done to.' He went on, 'I have been "done to" all my life; what I need is to *experience*.'

I want to make clear exactly what I mean by the Freudian analysis of derivative material. Let us think again of the Primal paradigm. There is a need or feeling which cannot or dare not be felt. It is blocked and what emerges is something symbolic – a substitute thought or act. Analysis of derivative material is an analysis of that symbolic realm and is bound to become detoured into a never-ending entanglement of symbols, such as dreams, hallucinations, false values, illusions, or whatever. Graphically, it would look like this:

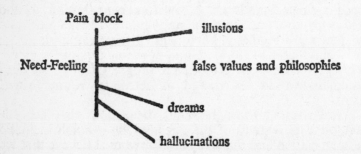

Let us think of this in the simplest terms. We have a hunger pang, and the symbol which emerges into consciousness is a thought of food – something which will satisfy that need. The mind automatically presents correct symbols to the body so that needs can be satisfied directly and survival assured. But suppose it becomes forbidden to think 'food'. Then the person, out of fear or pain, must substitute another thought – a symbolic thought. He must substitute something *unreal* into consciousness because his real need is still there but blocked.

So with the need for love. The child has a need to be held, to be talked to, but he soon learns that he is not going to be loved. The need is there and must be fulfilled somehow. So the child substitutes. Now any substitute, since it is not real, must be symbolic. The need which is blocked will be symbolised in dreams, illusions, delusions, in power drives, and so on. All these symbols derive from the need-feeling. Sometimes, when there are no more avenues of satisfaction open, the person may try to kill that feeling with liquor or drugs. Drugs and liquor, however, are still symbolic acts resulting from the need. To deal with drinking or drugs apart from that need is exactly the same as dealing with dreams apart from need in the body.

I am suggesting that to deal with *any* symbolic derivatives is useless, and this is what has made psychoanalysis such an agonising, drawn-out affair. It is time to plunge through the symbols, get to the need, shorten therapy by possibly years and get people well.

One of the central implications of the above is that projective testing (the Rorschach, Thematic Apperception Test, Draw-a-Person Test, etc.) should be unnecessary except in rare cases. Projective tests are tests of symbolic projections. How a psychologist decides on what is being projected depends on his theoretical outlook. If he is Jungian, he will see one thing; Freudian, another; Adlerian, still something else. It is all guesswork, no matter how many years we try to validate our tests, because we are inferring a feeling of another human being; only *he* (the patient) knows what it is.

One major difference between the Freudian and the Primal outlooks revolves around the concept of the defence system. The analytic view indicates that a defence system is necessary and healthy. One would, therefore, be unlikely to find a Freudian therapist forcing a penetration and explosion of this defence structure in order to liberate unconscious feelings *totally*. Instead, what feelings did arise would be incorporated, explained and finally understood within a Freudian theoretical framework. The *meaning* of the feeling would, in this way, be extracted from something completely personal and abstracted into something conceptual. That is why there is no interpretation in Primal Therapy. The ascending feeling contains its own meaning.

The Primal view is that there is no such thing as a healthy defence system. Defence systems are the sickness. This is not to say that feelings are not sought after in psychoanalysis. But these feelings are generally not the Primal ones which can convulse patients. For a patient to exhibit this kind of 'hysteria' in psychoanalysis would generally be considered a breakdown of the defences, and measures would be immediately taken to repair the system, rather than take the person deeper into his 'hysteria'. Freudians believe that there are certain destructive or aggressive instincts in us which require checks and balances in order to keep the person functioning in a social way. Working within this structure, it would be unthinkable for a Freudian therapist to unleash these 'destructive' forces. Yet the Primal therapist evokes these feelings *just so* the controlled defence system will be shattered. In this respect, Freudian theory and Primal Theory are antithetical. Freudians help the patient maintain some control in order to preserve the (unreal) defensive self, while the Primal therapist wants to destroy that unreal self in order to release the real, defenceless self.

Michaels summarises the psychoanalytic view: 'Medicine is gradually abandoning the myth of the normal person ... we are all relatively neurotic. The basic tenets of psychoanalysis affirm that conflict is the essence of life and that instinctual renunciation is the price of being a civilised human being.'[1]

Michaels goes on to paraphrase Alexander Pope: 'To be neurotic is to be human.' Levine also believes this: 'Normality ... is non-existent,[2]' he states. The Primal view is that normality is very much in the order of things and that abnormality is a perversion and distortion of this natural

[1] Joseph J. Michaels, 'Character Structure and Character Disorders', in Silvano Arieti, ed., *American Handbook of Psychiatry* (New York, Basic Books, 1959).

[2] Maurice Levine, *Psychotherapy in Medical Practice* (New York, Macmillan, 1942).

tensionless, anxiety-free state. This is the core of the difference. Psychoanalysis requires a defence system because it posits a basic anxiety which must be defended against. Because there is no basic anxiety (or destructive emotions which need to be renounced) in Primal Theory, there is no need for defences.

WILHELM REICH

In 1942 Reich wrote 'The neurosis is by no means only the expression of a disturbed psychic equilibrium, it is the expression of a chronic disturbance of the vegetative equilibrium and of natural mobility.'[3]

Reich explains that muscular rigidity is not simply a result of repression, but represents the most essential part of the process of repression: 'Without exception, patients relate that they went through periods in their childhood when they learned to suppress their hatred, anxiety or love by way of certain practices (such as holding their breath, tensing their abdominal muscles, etc.) which influenced their vegetative functions.' Reich is pointing out that neurosis is not simply a psychic event but that each psychic event is also a biophysical one.

What was important about his approach is that he believed that this biophysical structure could be approached physically: '[It is possible] to avoid the devious approach via the psychic manifestations and to break through to the affects directly, from the bodily attitude. If this is done, the repressed affect appears before the corresponding memory.' Thus, many current Reichian therapists are engaged mainly in certain physical manipulations which will ease bodily tension. And one patient who had been to a Reichian said that these exercises did often relieve tension. But because they were not accompanied with a mental connection, they did not seem to have a lasting effect.

Nevertheless, Reichian theory had some important things to say about the physical aspects of neurosis. Later Reich tied much of his theory into an exotic sexual concept which left him discredited in the eyes of part of the scientific community. But if we make allowances for this sexual bent, we see that Reich comes close to the Primal view: 'One is re-

[3] Reich, *op. cit.*, pp. 266–67.

minded of the loss of spontaneity in children, the first and most important sign of final sexual suppression at the age of four or five. This loss of spontaneity is at first always experienced as a "going dead" or "being walled in". Later on, this feeling of "being dead" may partly be covered up by compensating psychic behaviour, such as superficial hilarity or contactless sociability.' I believe that Reich is talking about the beginnings of neurosis. The 'going dead', the covering over with a defence etc., is what I ascribe to the Primal Scene. Even the age of onset is similar.

The main focus for Reich became abdominal tension: 'So important has the treatment of abdominal tension become in our work that today it seems incomprehensible to me how it was possible to bring about even partial cures in neurosis without knowing the symptomatology of the solar plexus.' He goes on to discuss how tightening of the abdomen produces shallow breathing and how in fright one holds the breath with the help of this abdominal vice.

What Reich believed was that the reduction in breathing reduced oxygen intake, permitted less energy in the organism, and thus, he reasoned, produced less tension. While I am not at all sure that this is so, I think that we should not negate Reich's important insights into the relationship between breathing and neurosis. When I first see a patient I find myself automatically trying to pinpoint where his voice comes from and how the person breathes.

I have quoted Reich because as time has passed I believe that psychotherapy has tended to neglect the body and its contribution to neurosis. Because neurosis often is a disembodied phenomenon (a split away from the body), we have treated it as if it actually were *only* something disembodied and mental. Thus, we find the focus on association of *ideas* in the conditioning therapies or the substitution of ideas in rational therapy. I think, however, that the modern-day Reichians may have erred in the opposite direction – that is, there is a tendency to neglect cerebral processes in the quest to ease *physical* tension. The Primal view is that the organism is a *psycho*physical unit. Any approach, to be lasting and thoroughly effective, must take into consideration that unity.

Thus, my objection to the various techniques such as touch therapy, body movement, or swim therapy – therapies designed to 'free' the body – would be the same as to those encountered in Reichian therapy. I would suggest that any physical approach implicitly carries on the neurotic process by a 'disembodied' technique where mental connections are neglected or at least not stressed, where the body is dealt with as an entity apart from the mind. I do not believe that one can truly free the body except temporarily so long as there are deeply hidden Primal Pains which produce continuous *physical* (as well as mental) tension. I would consider the physical attempt to do so symbolic. An example, quoted elsewhere, in which a person is placed in a circle surrounded by individuals locked arm in arm and is instructed to 'break free' is an example of what I mean by this symbolism.

I am suggesting that the mind cannot be cleared of painful memories which innervate the entire system by doing exercises designed to make the body more fluid and integrated. These memories, operating on a level below consciousness, continue to send impulses to the rest of the organism warning of danger; that danger will continue, in my opinion, until it is felt and resolved. At this point true relaxation will set in and body exercises may indeed be helpful and lasting. I would have the same objection to those approaches that hope to clear the mind by directing the person into 'healthy' thoughts. One may ignore Primal memories and substitute 'happy' thoughts, but this does not eradicate the Pain. Connection is not only desirable but essential in the Primal scheme of things.

When approaching neurosis, we must keep in mind etiology: What makes someone tense year after year, decade after decade without surcease? Habit? A conditioned response to the world? Perhaps, but I think it is more complicated than simple learning. Tension is a sign of a system at work trying to solve the body's needs. The system is inefficient, to say the least, since it goes on trying in inappropriate ways, never understanding fully that its way is never going to fulfil what is needed. It is with that interlocking network we must deal and not parts of it alone, such as the arms and legs in dance therapy or speech in speech therapy or a stuffy nose in allergic desensitisation therapy. We must understand that a stuffy head, for example, is often the pressure of the body focused in a certain area. It is with the pressure we must deal, or else the person will be forced to relieve his head pressure by blowing his nose constantly for the rest of his life.

BEHAVIOURIST OR CONDITIONING SCHOOLS

Conditioning techniques are growing in popularity among therapists, particularly in mental hospitals and universities. Without any attempt to explore the vast literature in this area, I shall discuss some general assumptions underlying the conditioning approach. The major one is that emotional problems are the result of adverse learning conditions. Neurosis, it is suggested, stems from miseducation. Thus, for reasons of reward or punishment, the neurotic has *learned* certain maladaptive or inappropriate responses or habits. These habits persist and tend to strengthen in time. Andrew Salter, in his book *Condition Reflex Therapy*, states:

> Maladjustment is malconditioning and psychotherapy is reconditioning. The individual's problems are the result of his social experiences, and by changing his techniques of social relations, we change his personality. We are not concerned with giving the individual stratified knowledge of his past – called 'probing'. What concerns us is giving him reflex knowledge of his future – called 'habits'.

This discussion by Salter seems to represent the general outlook of a number of conditioning schools, although they do differ on many points as well. Essentially, it seems to be that one learns to be happy by learning emotional habits, just as one has *learned* to be unhappy. This approach deals with how people function, by and large. Functioning in adaptive, efficient and productive ways would be an index of emotional health. I have discussed functioning elsewhere and would reiterate that functioning says little about how a person feels or *if* he feels while he is functioning. Patients who have functioned quite well in terms of position, status and income have said that they felt 'dead' and everything they did was meaningless, just going through the motions. Thus, while they may have been mechanised early in life by two very adept conditioning machines (the parents), who rewarded neurotic behaviour and punished 'well' behaviour, the Pain which was produced, I believe, cannot be dismantled by altering the route of the symptom or the surface behaviour. It will not disappear, in my opinion, by redirecting the outlet.

There are many examples of conditioning therapy to be found in the literature. For example, in a local mental hospital the following approach has been undertaken with alcoholics: A bar is set up, and each time the patient takes a sip of an alcoholic drink he receives a harmless but painful electric shock. The current increases until the patient spits out the liquor into a bowl before him, at which point the current is turned off. This is called operant conditioning. The idea is to pair a certain 'bad' behaviour, which is to be conditioned 'out', with an unpleasant stimulus, driving out the undesirable habit by making it feel unpleasant.

Another variation of negative conditioning is to show a series of cards to a group of homosexual men. On some of these cards there are pictures of nude males. Each time these cards are turned up the subject is given a shock. It is hoped that the sight of nude men will become painful and unpleasant enough to discourage homosexuality. A positive conditioning approach has been tried in England with male homosexuals. They are asked to masturbate to the point of ejaculation, at which time a button is pushed showing the picture of a nude woman. Again, the hoped-for result was to associate sexual pleasure with women, thus driving out the previous homosexual tendencies.

These experiments are based on the assumption that one will learn new habits by associations – pleasant and unpleasant. While it seems reasonable enough to assume that people will practise those behaviours which are rewarded and cease those which are not, this approach omits the dynamism behind a neurotic habit. In the case of the homosexual, for example, the tremendous deprivation of love and the great need to be held and caressed seem ignored; instead, the patient is more or less 'beaten' or punished out of his need. That is, the *expression* of his need is beaten back so that it is driven even further underground, thus deepening the neurosis. One cannot condition out a need for that is what is real. It is that need, I believe, which will always find new outlets when the old ones are dammed up. I believe conditioning techniques will result in heightening tension and assure the later adoption of other, perhaps more serious symptoms.

I do not think that one treats the illness by dealing with the symptoms. To treat neurosis, one must deal with needs; tension as such is usually not dealt with in these conditioning approaches.

The Primal approach is as different from conditioning methods as from almost any other approach. Rather than view a person's fears as entities, Primal Therapy believes that it is the *person* who is fearful.

Primal Therapy is involved with internal process while the conditioning methods concern themselves with overt behaviour. Thus, a present fear is not dealt with in itself in Primal Therapy but is viewed as emanating from something historic. So when dealing with a phobia, Primal Theory would indicate that the feeling (fear, in this case) is always real, but the context is symbolic. The person is fearful not really of heights, say, but of something else he doesn't understand. Conditioning theory would, by and large, deal with the presented symptom, the fear of heights, and would attempt to get the person more relaxed in such situations. Primal Therapy attempts to produce the correct connection to the fear. It is the connection, I believe, which eliminates generalised fear and the need to focus on substitutes.

Implicit in some of the conditioning methods is an assumption that man is more or less a machine whose behaviour is either stamped in or out by external manipulation without the intervention of consciousness. Drilling techniques in education or in military life would seem to be an extension of this philosophy. The assumption is that neurosis can be altered permanently even though a person has no idea about what gave rise to his irrational behaviour or what conditions stopped it. Aside from disagreeing on psychological grounds, I am concerned about the proliferation and acceptance of present conditioning techniques. This view of humans as units to be manoeuvred in this way or that is part of an overall *Zeitgeist*, part of the de-humanisation of man, in which feelings, purpose and intellect are but secondary considerations in the push to produce and achieve results. I think that the mechanical treatment of human beings is part of the current disease and is what helped produce neurosis originally. My fear is that psychology may become absorbed or co-opted into the general social mechanisation in which symptomatic effects, both social (college protests, for example) and personal, are stamped out by punishing techniques without anyone asking the critical question: 'Why?'

To understand symptoms, we must probe causes. We must keep in mind that humans have a life history.

Perhaps part of the problem has been that conditioning techniques have worked on animals and that extrapolations have been made to humans. But humans are not animals.

I believe that conditioning theory has had an important function in the history of education and psychology – namely, in the area of learning and education. Certainly, there are peculiar conditions which enhance or inhibit learning, and a learning theory can be helpful; how people learn, under what conditions, at what age, are all valid areas of investigation. But I do not think that the learning paradigm can do justice to the complexity that is the neurotic process. Needs are physical, as well as mental, and I cannot see how needs can be neglected and still allow someone to feel he is really doing something about neurosis. I see the neurotic process as totally psychophysical while the learning process is primarily mental. Thus, manipulations of the mental system alone cannot qualitatively alter the psychophysical system.

THE RATIONAL SCHOOL

The rational approach is the late creation of Albert Ellis. Rational therapy is often not classified as a behaviourist approach, but some of its techniques are similar. For example, a rational therapist might encourage a homosexual to try out heterosexual behaviour while telling himself certain sentences such as 'I like women; I am not afraid. I like sex.' It is behaviour that counts, and the hope is that by pairing 'desirable' behaviour with the proper mental associations, habits will change. Basically, the rational school believes that the neurotic is telling himself wrong things. That is, he is unconsciously repeating sentences to himself which produce maladaptive or irrational behaviour. When the patient becomes aware of these sentences and changes them to something more rational it is believed that his behaviour will follow suit. In a recent brochure, Albert Ellis had this to say:

> The approach of the [Rational] Institute is based on the belief that individuals can learn to live rationally by consciously seeing that their self-destructive emotions and behaviour arise from their own illogical philosophies. They biosocially acquire these ideas, then internalise and keep repeating them. The therapist helps the patient to challenge these self-defeating beliefs, employing behaviour modification techniques.[4]

In my view people do not live irrationally because of illogical philosophies. They behave irrationally because they were not allowed to act rationally and in accord with their own feelings early in life. I view humans as essentially rational. Irrational philosophies, in my estimation, arise to explain or 'rationalise' neurotic behaviour. When one denies his own truth, he is forced to construct a network of 'untruth'. Acting on one's own true feelings, it seems, is an inherently rational endeavour, and when Post-Primal patients finally feel the truth, they are able to become rational about many things in life without any belaboured, intellectual discussion. Why didn't they understand before? Because to deny feelings means to deny perception and understanding as well. Denials make substitute (hence, false) beliefs necessary.

Ellis mentions '*self*-destructive' emotions. The notion of self-destructive emotions is found in many theories. I do not think that there are emotions which destroy the self. Rather, it is *denying* those feelings of the self which destroy. Feelings cannot be destructive of the self; they belong to the self. What is often considered a destructive emotion – anger – is the result of a hurt self denied. Lack of feeling is what destroys the self, and it is lack of feeling which permits destruction of other selves.

If it is true that the neurotic acts irrationally because he is saying the wrong sentences to himself, then why is it that many of us can say the right sentences and still not change? The smoker can say that 70 per cent of all smokers will die of lung cancer and still smoke his pack a day. The alcoholic

[4] Institute for Rational Therapy; Brochure, 1968 (Spring).

can swear each day that alcohol rots the liver and still guzzle his fifth. The homosexual can tell himself that he really loves women and continue to have sex with men. If he hates women, he hates them. His hate is nothing rational. It is a generalisation out of an old, buried Primal feeling which cannot change, in my estimation, until that historic feeling is felt and resolved. Homosexual hatred of women may have derived from years of a terrible relationship with the mother. Placed in its proper context, hatred might be rational. To have a homosexual with a basic hatred of his mother tell himself that he likes women would, in my opinion, help along his pretence and hence his neurosis.

One Primal patient who had undergone rational therapy explained her previous treatment: 'I remember once I told the doctor that I was terribly upset because my boyfriend left me. He told me that my behaviour was irrational and that I needed to tell myself that I really could live without him and that I didn't need love to survive. Somehow it felt like Christian Science. I had to pretend to feel like how I didn't feel. No matter what I said to myself, I couldn't really convince myself that I could live without my boyfriend. Now I understand why. I have felt what I tried to get out of that boyfriend – a caring father.'

I think that the basic difference between the Primal and the rational view is the role one's philosophy plays in neurosis. Ellis believes that people act in accordance with a profound but unconscious philosophy which needs to be made conscious. The Primal view is that philosophies are adopted in terms of how one deals with his Pain – that is, a person who is straight with himself will tend to have straight ideas and attitudes and philosophies.

REALITY THERAPY

What I find essentially wrong about any presently oriented, now-confrontation therapy is that it neglects the patient's history or that there even is a history behind neurotic behaviour. Reality therapy has a wide acceptance today for two reasons. The first is that it is simplistic and therefore appealing to those who do not want to bother with probing depths. Second, and more important, it fits perfectly into the cultural mode – the very cultural *Zeitgeist* which produces neurosis, in my opinion – namely, the concepts of action and responsibility. It is a 'Let's get ourselves together and do something' approach – never mind how you feel about doing it. To act 'responsibly' is heavily emphasised. That responsibility seems always to be to someone or something else, not to the self. Reality therapy, in my opinion, avoids reality – the patient's reality. It wants the patient to face up to a world that he often is not in and cannot be in – until he feels what is making him do what he does.

The following report from a patient clearly indicates the differences between Primal Therapy and reality therapy:

'Three and a half years ago, on the verge of an emotional-nervous breakdown, I entered reality therapy. I had read *Reality Therapy* and understood from it that neurosis sets in when basic human needs are not fulfilled. According to the author, these needs are: to love and to be loved, and to feel that we are worthwhile to ourselves and to others. To be worthwhile, it is stated, we must maintain a satisfactory standard of behaviour. This we accomplish by doing what is realistic, responsible and right. This concept was a compatible and convenient one for me, and I thought I could easily get well since my entire life had been guided by what was "realistic, responsible and right". At twenty-two, I was a high school English teacher, and what anyone would consider "socially acceptable". But where had I gone wrong – why was I "falling apart"? Reality therapy, I thought, would help me uncover my mistakes.

'During my therapy sessions, I spoke of my distressing relationships with both my boyfriend and my parents, and of my general disenchantment with life. I found my therapist to be attentive as he sat behind the imposing desk between us, in his massive leather chair, continuously smoking cigarettes. The solution to my problems appeared very simple: I needed to find someone who really cared about me and who would make me feel worthwhile. The implicit assumption in all this is that I needed outside signals, and not myself, to know that I was valued.

'As each session was about to conclude, the therapist would ask: "Well, what steps are you going to take now to make your situation better?" I meekly gave the answers I thought were the right ones: I would try not to see my boyfriend; I would be nicer to my parents; I would get more involved in my work. In retrospect, I realise that I was strengthening the same "socially acceptable" veneer I had carried throughout my life and was masking a very unhappy me beneath it. I knew what I was supposed to say, and I played the therapist-client game with a straight and impassive face. I had always been an excellent student, and therapy was just one more thing I would "learn" to do well.

'Despite the good grades I was achieving in therapy (earning the therapist's approval), I found that deciding to change was far easier than actually being able to change. Unable to accomplish my weekly "New Year's Resolutions", and interpreting this as making no progress, I terminated my therapy. Two months later I married my boyfriend, and six months later, after bitter disappointment for us both, we separated. I was back in the therapist's office, believing that my current disaster was due to not following his advice at the outset. Now we decided that I would leave my husband permanently, find a new job, and begin life anew in search of someone who could really love me. I did get a new job, and temporarily my mind was taken off my problems. Yet in three weeks I was back with my husband. Now I began dragging him to therapy (as a "condition" of our reunion), and we would spend the therapy hour screaming at each other. This mutual tension reduction activity served to convince the therapist that we should come for individual treatment. We began to follow the therapist's advice, and after a short time we succeeded in establishing an atmosphere similar to the calm before, or after, a storm.

'As for the estrangement from my parents, I finally convinced my mother to come to therapy with me. That was our only session together; for the entire hour she ranted and raved about how unappreciative a daughter I was, what a "good little girl" I once was, and how hurt and "rejected" *she* felt. The therapist's suggested course of action was to forget about the past and to improve upon the present. Although my parents continued to misunderstand me, remained aloof, and still criticised me, we established the "socially acceptable" façade of the parents-daughter relationship. I told my therapist that I was seeing my parents: mission accomplished.

'At that point, within the reality therapy matrix, my basic needs were being fulfilled. I convinced myself that I was loved by both my husband and my parents, even though I felt agonisingly empty and unhappy inside. I thought, or rather now "knew", that I was worthwhile because I had a job and my husband, too, now had an important job. We were both doing what was "realistic, responsible and right". Yet there was no real happiness, no genuine contentment, no peace. We had succeeded in merely clamping down a tight lid on the embroilment raging within each one of us. We concluded therapy able to "cope" and "function".

'One year later, I followed my husband into Primal Therapy. It had been a year of violent skirmishes, bitterness and despair, and I had contemplated suicide several times. Reality therapy had merely "taught" me to alter my behaviour, but in no way had I relieved myself of the source of this misery. Clearly, all that therapy had simply postponed the inevitable confrontation between me and my deeper sickness. Today I am feeling my old pains, and am on my way towards health, not towards attaining just temporary relief.

'The differences between these two therapies are very clear to me. Whereas in reality therapy I would intellectualise and verbalise – in short, bullshit – for the therapy hour, now I spend as much time as I need feeling my Pain. The more Pain I feel, the less Pain I have. I now realise that it is not outside advice I need, but feeling my Pain that will help. Outside advice merely compels me to conform to a standard behaviour superimposed upon me irrespective of who I am and how I feel. It is the standard of a neurotic society, and unfortunately, in reality therapy terms, performing to society's standard is the goal; in short, do what is "realistic, responsible and right". Therefore reality therapy, ironically, was keeping me unreal because I was abetting the process of keeping myself unreal. In Primal Therapy, on the other hand, I am violently shedding the layers of the unreal me, the façade, the smooth mask. There is no building up to be able to "cope" or "function"; there is just a tearing down of the unreal me until I become a completely feeling human being.

'Reality therapy contends that the basic human needs can be fulfilled by any one person or number of people. This would have kept me forever neurotic by encouraging me to search for that which cannot be found, because it was my parents' love I needed. Primal Therapy goes to the heart of the matter: Only my parents could have fulfilled those infantile needs. I no longer expect my husband to fill the early needs my father left void. When I am well, I will be free to let my husband be himself, and I will be able to love him for himself and not as a surrogate daddy.

'In reality therapy my neurosis was reinforced because the therapist became my surrogate daddy He was kind, gentle, attentive and listened to me in a way that my own father had never done. This resulted in a dependence on the therapist and not on myself. In this manner, therapy would have continued endlessly with no progress ever being possible. I did not find to be true the reality therapy premise that the patient who can believe that he is worthwhile to the therapist will be able to duplicate this model of worth in other relationships. In Primal Therapy I have felt aloof from my therapist. I feel only me, my aloneness, and the truth that there is nobody to care for me but myself.

'Primal Therapy makes me confront what made me sick and is not concerned with teaching me to re-channel my neurotic behaviour. Reality therapy would have me dismiss my past and consider it inconsequential to the present. But Primal Therapy recognises that the past cannot be "forgotten" away cerebrally. The past must be evoked, remembered and, most crucially and central to the therapy, the past must be felt so that I can be free to have a present. For the first time in my life, I have the hope that the emptiness inside me will be filled and that the heavy blanket of Pain on the outside will be shed.'

TRANSCENDENTAL MEDITATION

A recent craze among college students, musicians and artists, transcendental meditation is promulgated by Indian yogis such as Maharishi Mahesh Yogi. Meditation involves repeating a mantram (a Sanskrit saying that is something personal between a man and his God, such as 'May God have mercy on me'), while concentrating only on the image of the God to the exclusion of any other internal or external distraction. Breathing exercises are involved, so that generally just before one hits the peak of 'transcendence', breathing is barely perceptible. All this is done amid flowers, flowing robes and incense. The aim is to achieve a oneness with God, to find supreme relaxation that feels like bliss. Meditation is aimed at transcending the worldly self, reaching the spiritual self with the goal of self-realisation.

The founder of the Ramakrishna order, Vivekananda, describes the purposes of meditation:

> The greatest help to spiritual life is meditation. In meditation we divest ourselves of all material conditions and feel our divine nature. The less the thought of the body, the better. For it is the body that drags us down. It is attachment, identification, which makes us miserable. That is the secret: 'to think that I am the Spirit and not the body, and that the whole of this universe with all its relations, with all its good and all its evil, is but a series of paintings, scenes on a canvas, of which I am the witness.'[5]

The only way I can describe meditation is to call it an anti-Primal. It involves detachment instead of connection, abnegation of self rather than feeling the self, and it believes in the necessity of mind-body split. It seems to be solipsistic in nature since nothing really exists except as a painting on a canvas.

This is not to say that people cannot use meditation for relaxation. One patient who was a senior Vedanta monk for many years states that he repeated his mantram and practised transcendental meditation for twelve years and that he often found himself in a state of bliss. But the final result of all this bliss was a complete breakdown and the need for therapy. Perhaps this deserves some explanation. I think that the state of bliss comes from a complete suppression of self, giving oneself over to a fantasy (deity) of one's own creation, a merging with this product of one's imagination, and a loss of reality. It is a state of total unreality, a socially institutionalised psychosis, as it were. If, for instance, a patient were to tell us that he had merged with God, that he and God were one, we would suspect his rationality. But when this process is sanctioned by a specific theology, we tend to overlook its inherent irrationality.

We must remember that one can meditate daily and still not reduce the need to meditate. Somehow the demon tension arises anew each day to be meditated away. The rituals,

[5] Swami Vivekananda, *Works* (Advaita Ahsrama, 1946), Vol. 27, p. 37.

flowers and robes would seem to be an elaborate going through the motions of relaxation, for rituals are not necessary in order to relax. Indeed, they are often an indication of a person who has made a struggle of relaxation, when relaxation is no more than being oneself. I do not think that you can go through the motions of being yourself. You just *are.*

Existentialism

Another stream in psychology today is existentialism. This approach is aimed at undoing some of the Freudians' emphasis on early childhood experiences while offering a more dynamic structure than the conditioning therapies. Existentialists stress the here and now. Existentialism is concerned with man's being. One cannot really say that existentialism is a systematic therapeutic system since there are few testable hypotheses generated, nor is there a methodical attempt to develop an ordered approach. Rather, existentialism is heavily philosophical, drawing its strength from the writings of Sartre, Binswanger and Heidegger.

A current existentialist leader is Abraham Maslow. Both he and Carl Rogers have had a significant impact on current psychological thought.[6] They believe that there is a drive towards psychologic health, which they call self-actualisation. Maslow believes that this drive is not definable, can only be inferred from the observations of people.

Maslow sees neurosis in terms of a deficiency disease; the neurotic is deficient in what he needs to actualise himself:

> Every human has both sets of forces within him. One set clings to safety and defensiveness out of fear, tending to regress backwards, afraid to grow, afraid of independence . . . of freedom and separateness. The other set of forces impels him towards a wholeness of self, towards confidence in the face of the external world at the same time that he can accept his deepest, real unconscious self.[7]

[6] C. R. Rogers, *A Therapist's View of Personal Gifts* (Wallingford, Pa., Pendle Hill, 1960); *On Becoming a Person* (Boston, Houghton Mifflin, 1961).

[7] Abraham Maslow, *Toward a Psychology of Being* (Princeton, Van Nostrand, 1962), pp. 150–67.

I view wholeness as something we are born with but would agree with Maslow that there is a need to be real or whole – that is, to be what we are. I do not believe, on the other hand, that there is anything like a basic neurotic, regressive force inside us – it results only when we are not allowed to be ourselves. I do not think fear, especially the fear of growing, is basic to human functioning.

Neurosis, for Maslow, is the basic conflict between defensive forces and growth trends. The growth trends he sees as, 'Existential, embedded in the deepest nature of the human being'. Because of the need to view man in struggle terms, many theories posit man's behaviour as a constant dialectic between something negative and positive. Thus, Maslow sees the need for safety as a 'prepotent need, more primarily necessary than self-actualisation'. Before someone will take risks and express himself, he must conquer or satisfy his more powerful safety needs. Conflict becomes the basic paradigm for growth. I would not view conflict as something basic and internal. Rather, I think that neurosis results from the pressure against natural growth and development tendencies of the organism. There seems to be no real evidence for anything like a safety need or a basic fear of independence and freedom. These seem to be descriptive of some behaviour among neurotics, but I think we must hesitate before imputing to these behaviours some constitutional or genetic factor.

What Maslow is saying is in some respects similar to the Freudian position – namely, that there is a basic anxiety which must be overcome. He calls the need to quell anxiety a safety need. But labels cannot seem to get Maslow away from a demonological view of man. Perhaps this is because we build psychological theories out of the observation of neurotics who are usually not in short supply of demons to slay.

It is not deficiency needs which keep us immature and neurotic. The lack of fulfilment of real needs does that. In any case, I cannot see how there are special needs which occupy only part of us. Each need is total. When needs are not met, *we* are deficient.

Maslow's self-actualiser is one who is capable of peak experiences – those out-of-time, out-of-space events where the self is transcended and the person reaches an almost Nirvana-like state. Existential literature abounds with discussions of peak experiences: Having a peak experience is something quite tempting. Many of us would like to transcend the misery and bleakness of our everyday existences. But exactly how one does this and exactly what a peak experience is are not made clear by Maslow. It is, rather, a mystical event. Because precise examples are lacking in Maslow's work, I shall rely on the descriptions of peak experiences by two patients who formerly were in existential group therapy. The first was a man who found himself depressed for days. At the end of a week of this depression a friend came over and asked him to go mountain climbing. They climbed a steep mountain, and the person felt absolutely exhilarated. He called it – no pun intended – a peak experience. What had he done? He had shaken off his depression. He made a defence work. Did he transcend the real feelings involved in the depression? I doubt it. Those feelings had only been laid aside for a time.

The second peak experience occurred during a nude marathon. The man was being passed around from one group member to another. Each person fondled and caressed him. He suddenly felt warm all over. He called it 'an instant of a oneness with humanity'. What was it really? He was getting what he thought he needed, finally: some warmth and human caresses. But it was only a momentary experience unconnected to the great Pain of what he needed all his life. The touching in group quelled his painful tensions and allowed him, therefore, to transcend what was real. His Nirvana was unreal. In my view, transcendence is what all neurotics do all the time – transcending a real feeling self. Whatever Nirvana they imagine they have reached must be an unreal state, for what they need is a *descending* experience into the real feeling self.

The search for a peak experience often seems to be one more struggle to find something unique in an otherwise humdrum, dull existence. It is part of unreal hope.

If a real self is allowed to flourish, if it has been accepted all along by parents, I can see no reason why anyone would want to transcend it. Persons who finish Primal Therapy never report peak experiences of which Maslow speaks. All the peaks have been ironed out because they are driven neither to euphoria nor to the depths of despair by their neurosis. To be totally oneself is a spectacular feeling.

The existentialists attempt to depart from basic anxiety drives and instinctual forces and to concentrate on self-actualisation processes – those drives which lead us to health. Rollo May and his associates explain part of the existential position:[8] 'The characteristic of the neurotic is that his existence is darkened . . . clouded over and gives no sanction to his acts. The aim of Existentialism is that the patient experience his existence as real.' This is similar to the aim of Primal Therapy. But the very language of existentialism clouds the reality we are dealing with. What exactly is existence? What does it mean to have one's existence clouded?

Commitment is a major focus in existentialism. The aim is to help the patient wrest himself out of the existential void and make a commitment to something positive and forward-moving. Existentialists reason that one gets a sense of self out of commitment. But in order to commit one's self to something, there must be a self to commit. The neurotic is split away from most of his acts and therefore, by definition, cannot commit all of himself to anything. A businessman totally committed to his business is usually trying to make his unreal self work and, if he felt what he was doing, in all likelihood would not be so totally committed to his business.

In clinical terms, the existential position is similar to the rational school. A homosexual would get a sense of his heterosexuality through commitment to heterosexual acts. But I believe that neurosis is not just a matter of what one does; it lies in what one is. A person can have dozens of heterosexual acts and still be homosexual because the feeling and the need are for love for someone of the same sex. An *act* will not wash away that need. This is the misbelief of the 'latent' homosexual who tries to drive away his homosexual tendencies (to deny even his want of parental love) by one heterosexual act after another – all to no avail. One may never practise homosexuality and feel quite homosexual (see section on homosexuality for discussion). A new *act* is

[8] Rollo May, Ernest Angel and Henri Ellenberger, *Existence* (New York, Basic Books, 1960).

always possible for the neurotic, but that scarcely will change his neurosis.

Existentialists, by and large, discuss the person's commitments, his here-and-now behaviour, and his philosophy. I do not believe that discussion can change his 'being'. 'Being' to me means feeling. Discussion is often (in the neurotic) something which rides above feeling. It keeps the person 'mental' so that he cannot possibly feel his true 'being'.

In the social sciences, 'rapprochement' refers to the attempt on the part of some theories to merge with other theories and so to strengthen their position. Thus, we find Freudian theorists casting their concepts within a learning theory context in order to make their theory more viable. Or we may find the opposite; learning theorists attempting to make their approach more 'dynamic' by placing the more dynamic concepts of Freud in a learning matrix. But this reconciliation of differences among various theories is often more apparent than real and leads to more 'statistical' than biologic truths. That is, by explaining Freud in other terms or in explaining learning theory in dynamic terms, we have found only a more palatable way to say the same old thing. I don't think that it is helpful to talk of castration anxiety in approach-avoidance terms if castration anxiety doesn't exist in the first place.

When we look at the history of psychological thought since the turn of the century, we find first a stress on early childhood and a focus on introspection. To counter this, the behaviourists or learning theorists eschewed introspection and early childhood and concentrated on behaviour. Then there were attempts by neo-Freudians to update Freudian therapy with ego analysis – a focus on the present defensive manoeuvres of the patient.

Of all the modifications on Freud which seem so progressive, it would seem that the early Freud, by concentrating in the past and elucidating current problems through an exploration of early childhood, was closest to the Primal position.

Primal Theory is quite distant from behaviourist conceptions. What behaviourism seems to do is abstract the symptom and attempt to condition or de-condition unreal behaviour. It works with unreal manifestations, rather than causes, and cannot therefore make real changes.

The Primal contention is that man is neither a compilation of habit patterns nor a mass of defences against inner demons or instincts. When a person can experience his Primal wants and needs without the fear of losing love, he is experiencing his 'being'. When he cannot, he is, to use the existential concept, a 'non-being'. I do not believe that any kind of special effort, sublimation, or compensation can transform a neurotic non-being into a feeling person. In order to be what he is, the neurotic must go back and feel what he was before he stopped 'being'. As one patient put it, 'In order to be what you are, you have to be what you weren't.'

Contentment or happiness, often the goal of psychotherapy, is not the result of accumulated insights, in my opinion, nor is it chants one sings, mantrams to be repeated, nor is it derived from the acquisition of 'positive' habits. I believe if a therapeutic goal is to help the patient feel contented, such a feeling can be reached only when the patient can finally uncover his real self. Happiness achieved by the unreal self will be just that – unreal. Real happiness, then, means that old unhappiness is resolved and out of the way.

A number of therapists have told me that they have seen a Primal on occasion, particularly in marathon (all-night) group therapy. Usually, it has been treated as hysteria, and people rush in to comfort and quell the feeling rather than help expand it. If they had Primal Theory to guide them, perhaps those hysterias would turn out to be something significant. The aim of the marathon therapies is generally constructive and, oddly enough, many therapists 'forget' their theories when they take part in a marathon. Generally they are trying to fatigue the defence system of patients during a marathon, and sometimes they succeed. But without some concept of what is happening, a marathon often becomes an exercise in exhaustion, in which patients blow up, break down and cry, become close and intimate, yet do not make those key Primal connections which could make the marathon a lasting experience.

A fast-rising variation of marathon therapy is the nude marathon. Professional societies often now include an expert in these techniques when workshops are given. The nude marathon is regular group therapy done without clothes. It stresses the sensual and is often conducted part of the time in swimming pools, where a great deal of fondling and caressing takes place so that members may get the 'feel' of another person. The general aim of the nude marathon is to help people strip those artificialities which separate them, to eliminate shame about the body, and to bring people closer together. This approach is part of the overall concept that people can learn to feel, to become sensitive and sensual and learn to accept their bodies by going through certain motions. While these motions may offer an interesting interlude to what may be a humdrum life, I do not think that they make anyone more feeling. The fact that it seems to be a sensual experience does not make it therapy.

I would stress again that we do not get a *feel* of someone else. We learn to feel ourselves first, and then we feel ourselves feeling others. So if a person has blocked feelings, he could conceivably touch and feel someone else all day long and not have a feeling experience. Being sensual, then, means being open to one's own sensorium. If this were not the case, then frigid women who act out a sexual promiscuity, touching and caressing and feeling constantly, might finally be satiated. But too often they report a continuous hunger for touch and a constant inability to feel anything. We must clearly differentiate going through the motions from having an inner experience; for people to be brought closer together, they must be first brought closer to themselves, to their feeling selves. Smashing the inner feeling barrier is what seems to tear down the barriers between people.

There is the notion that to strip one of one's clothes somehow makes people less defensive with others. To reiterate: Defensiveness with others is primarily a defence against the self, so that clothes, on or off, have little to do with it. I do not see how lifelong historic internal processes can be altered by the external alteration of clothing. It seems to be a magical idea held by some that when one goes through certain motions with one's pants or dress, inner barriers which have persisted for years will fall away.

I have taken some time with this discussion in order to differentiate an inner from an outer experience. If this distinction were not made, one might imagine people lying on the floor thrashing and screaming, deluded into believing that they were undergoing a Primal. We must keep in mind that activities which will make basic changes in individuals must flow from their feelings. The flow must occur from inside out. Otherwise, one may engage in all sorts of activities, struggle mightily, yet not change the feeling base one iota. One may show the body and feel unexposed or clothe the body and be totally exposed. Once the feeling barrier is removed, outer stimuli will penetrate the entire system. Then such sensitivity exercises as having persons stand on fresh grass to expand their sensual experience will have meaning. It will have a *real* meaning: that it feels good to stand on fresh grass – not some mystical super-meaning.

PSYCHODRAMA

A technique used widely in group therapy by a variety of therapists is psychodrama. I would term psychodrama the 'as if' game. The patient takes a role designated by the therapist and acts 'as if' he were someone else or himself in a special role such as talking back to his boss. The patient may take the role of his mother, father, brother, or teacher. But of course, he is not any of those people, so he must put on an act and try to feel like someone else when often he doesn't even feel like himself yet.

Psychodrama does have some limited use, as, for example, in loosening up a group in conventional therapy, but essentially, it seems to offer one more unreal role for a person to portray when he has been acting the role of himself for many years. The play is choreographed, in this case, by the therapist. I think that too often the neurotic was forced to act and submerge his real feelings in what was often a horror play written, directed and badly produced by his parents.

The magical and vicarious idea about psychodrama is that if one can speak out against a mother figure in a psychodrama play, he will be able to do so in real life. The act will carry over and the person may be permanently more aggressive, expressive, etc. But the person who takes a role is not being real, and how else can he make real changes in his personality and his life? All he can do is to learn how to be more neurotic by honing his acting ability so that he acts on cue instead of feeling.

There are times when a person is caught up in his psycho-drama role and really begins to lose control. Often this is stopped so that the feeling experience is aborted. I have never seen someone in psychodrama put on the floor and allowed to lose all control in his 'role'. More often, the person is aware that he is acting out a role. He is still that grown-up acting 'as if'. Primal patients are not acting. They *are* the little children totally out of control.

What all this means is that a person is his neurosis. Manipulating the front, rearranging the symptoms, offering symbolic physical and mental trips, teaching him contrived roles in contrived situations do not deal with sources of the problems. The reshuffling of the defences can go on forever and will not stop until the patient can feel himself. Until the Pain is felt, any one thing will be as ineffective as another – whether it be psychodrama, dream analysis, sensitivity training, meditation, or psychoanalysis.

It is not possible to discuss all other schools of psychology, just as it is impossible to answer all the questions raised by Primal Therapy. For example, is it a form of hypnosis? Quite the opposite, as a matter of fact, although some of the conditions are the same. Neuroses are born when parents require a child to give up his feeling self and become the person the parents need. In hypnosis, too, a strong and reassuring authority will lull the real, feeling self away while inculcating another 'identity' into the subject. The hypnotic subject gives his self over to the authority, just as the neurotic child gives that self to his parents and becomes what they expect. Hypnosis is the manipulation of the unreal front. Thus, an unfeeling person who is playing the role of professor in his life can be made into Liberace on the stage. The hypnosis can be brought about because the subject is split in the first place. Once a person does not feel, he can be made into almost anything. Conversely, once a person is totally himself, I do not believe that he can be made into anything else; he could not be brainwashed or hypnotised.

It is not accidental that as one progresses into deeper stages of hypnosis, one can be pricked with a pin and not feel anything. The pin prick test is often an index of whether the person is hypnotised. I view this as corroborative of the Primal view that the real, feeling self both in neurosis and hypnosis has been narcotised or dulled. Neurosis, then, is a more long-term, universal form of hypnosis. If this were not so, how could we account for the fact that the neurotic is ravaged with Pains of which he is unaware? It may be that in some cases hypnosis produces a quasi-psychotic state. When someone becomes Liberace, doesn't even know he is Liberace, and has no other consciousness, how different is it from the person who has become Napoleon in a mental hospital? In neurosis, psychosis and hypnosis, we are dealing with the split away from feeling and the imposition of unreal identities. Neurotic parents impose these identities or roles onto their children unconsciously, while the hypnotist does it deliberately. He can do it because some individuals are willing, indeed anxious, to give themselves over to another in order to be the good boy or 'subject'. The need to be a loyal subject is what helped produce Nazis – people willing to kill others for the fatherland.

Primal Therapy is the opposite of hypnosis because it has to do with grounding a person into his own feelings and away from what others expect him to be. Being totally involved in the present makes it unlikely that someone can lull part of you away and take the rest of you on an 'identity' trip. A real person could not be made into a Nazi. Nor could he become Napoleon or Liberace. He can be only himself.

Many neurotics who have finished their therapy explain that their lives previously were like being in a trance. Because they were dominated by the past, they were scarcely aware of what was going on in their lives. One patient described it as being in a perpetual daze. She would be whatever she thought others wanted her to be just to get along. Isn't this what the hypnotic subject is doing? 'I'll be what you want me to be (Daddy).'

Laura

The difference between Primal Therapy and other therapies is provided by Laura, who had experienced many of them first-hand. Laura, whose case is referred to briefly elsewhere in the book, has written an excellent, graphic description of a Primal, showing how it engages the entire psychophysiologic system.

I began Primal Therapy four weeks before my thirtieth

birthday, and have now been in it for ten weeks. There are no doubts in my mind as to its validity.

I am a typical example of the failure of 'insight' therapies, since after seven years (on and off) of basic techniques and three different therapists, I came to Primal Therapy not even feeling. In other words, seven years of therapy had not even broken down the first barrier towards 'making me well' (e.g., real and feeling). It would be a waste of time here to dwell on my anger at the waste of time (doctors' and mine) and money (mine) spent during those seven years. In this last year and with my last therapist (an existential therapist) I came to the only conclusion of any worth in my seven years of therapy: that I was on the verge of something very big, but that I could not feel it. I thought that I was going crazy, and I thought that I was going to find out something terrible about myself. I now see that what I was on the verge of feeling was, in fact, feeling!

I cannot begin to list all the differences between this therapy and my therapy of the past. Primal therapy works. Primal Therapy is not supportive in the sense of making me 'feel better' and function better. It is very easy to function well, but functioning is not necessarily an indication of feeling or of being well. I realise that most people disagree with this evaluation. Speaking for myself and others whom I know to function beautifully, I can honestly say that functioning does not indicate health. In my own case, it indicated only that: (1) I had learned at an early age that I was supposed to perform in order to get love; (2) I believed it (if I could only perform correctly, I would get love); (3) I needed that love badly enough that I would continue to perform in spite of the fact that I was exhausted from performing and really did not want to perform; and (4) I had learned a very good way to fool myself (e.g., 'if I can function this well, then I must not be very sick'). About three years ago I took ninety sleeping pills in order to kill myself. Before I took the pills, I cleaned my house, changed the linens on the bed, took a shower, and washed my hair. Right up to the moment when I was most ill, the moment when my mind and feelings separated completely, I had performed beautifully on my job and was a model housekeeper.

There is something else which has always bothered me and others about today's therapy which helps one feel and function better. If my parents didn't love me, as in fact they did not; if I am truly alone, as in fact I am; if the world is hungry and in turmoil, which it obviously is – why *should* I feel better? Take rational therapy. I saw Dr K (a rational therapist) once for a private session. At the time I thought he was very bright, mostly because he was hard on me. I recall part of the conversation. I said, 'I just can't stand it. I wish my boyfriend would come to see me, and I wish that I would not have to ask him to do so.' Dr K said, 'Now, isn't that a ridiculous and irrational feeling? Who are you to think he should have to call you? If you want to see him, why don't you call him?' On the surface there seems nothing illogical about what he said. Dr K's view, though, that changing one's thoughts will change one's feelings is most certainly *unreal*.

I have learned in Primal Therapy, *only* by way of feeling (and not by any figuring out), that at the bottom of everything is my unsatisfied need for my mother and then for my father to have loved me. It is basic need, the need for their love. If they had loved me, they would have let me be and they would have given me what I needed. As they were both babies and sick themselves, they could only give me what they wanted to give, not what I needed. Further, not being whole themselves, they required that I perform for them – rather than just be who I was. At the age of about five, I ceased to be a real feeling person. It became clear that I could not get what I needed – just being me – so I stopped feeling and started acting. This was the beginning of my sickness. Everything I did from that time on was more and more removed from who I really was and what I really needed. The more I separated from my real feelings, the sicker I became. I learned to act in order to survive, in order not to feel the pain of not getting what I needed – their love.

To change the symptoms, or the manifestations of that need, is not to cure the sickness. Dr K would like me to act real and to act well, but he does not seem to understand that this will not make me real, nor will it make me well. Therefore, in denying me my feelings of the moment, he denied me any chance of getting well. Dr K may well ask then how I would rid myself of this 'irrational' desire to have my boyfriend call me. Once I have felt the *real* need, not just once but as fully and as often as I can until that need is no longer there, the neurotic behaviour disappears – since it was only a cover-up for the real need. This may sound miraculous, and it even feels so to me, but it has been very real indeed. Little by little, as I feel more and more, I act out less and less. The more I allow myself (in therapy) to feel the baby me with my real need for my mother and father's love, the more I am free of that need – free to be an adult, alone, separate, free to enjoy the company of others and free to let them be, and free to know that I will never get what I needed from my parents, and that no one can fill that gap for me.

There are other differences between Primal Therapy and most therapies of today. There are, of course, the differences in technique. Another major difference, one which has obviously had a great effect on me, is the difference in the therapist. The transference we make from therapist to Mommy and/or Daddy will happen of its own accord, in the same way it does in life, since the need for Mommy and Daddy has never been fulfilled. Therefore, a therapist does not have to act like a mommy or daddy to get one to feel those feelings. In fact, acting like a good or bad mommy or daddy (instead of being a real person) is only inflicting the same phoniness on a patient that he has always received from his parents. Therefore, a therapist must be real with his patient. Only then will he not accept phoniness and lies from the patient.

My first therapist was a woman, a very nice lady, very understanding. She tried to help me understand my 'bad' behaviour. She tried to help me make sense out of a senseless home life. There I was, sixteen years old, attending school only half the time, my parents divorced, my father trying to make me put his marriage back together, my mother living with a woman, and my sister and I living with my mother. Now this made no sense to me, and I am now pleased to say that I was correct in that belief. The greatest relief is knowing that my struggle against the insanity around me is the only thing that kept me sane (it was the only thing that kept me partially in touch with my real feelings). Yet these therapists would have led me to the slaughter – like a meek lamb – and each one of them, as with my family, reinforced my lack of trust in my own true feelings (the only thing that could have saved me), reinforced my total confusion. I felt that everything was crazy around me, but the world said that *I* was crazy. They said I was a bad girl and that as I was a child I should lie down and take this phoniness they dished out to me, that this should be my reality. It was the actuality, but it was not reality. Fortunately, the kernel of reality inside me, my real feelings and needs, didn't go away. The little baby girl before the age of five (a real little girl who knows her own truth and yearns for truth and real feelings around her) had not been killed. This therapist had no idea that if she had once reached that real little girl inside me, she would have gotten somewhere.

My second therapist allowed me to spend more than two years talking about my husband. He often tried to get me to talk about myself, but without success. I never really cried in front of any of my therapists. I was often late to therapy. All three therapists knew that this was my way of acting out something deeper, but acting like the substitute parents they thought they were, all they did was scold me and discuss it, and for seven years I was periodically late to therapy. I was late only once to Primal Therapy. I was informed by Art Janov that I would receive no more therapy if I were ever late again. In doing this, he was not being a good daddy to me, though I wish my daddy had done something like that. He was not just using a good technique, though it was a good technique – since it worked. He was being real with me. Most important, he didn't give me what I wanted (which was his approval), he gave me something much more important: He gave me what I needed.

It's a shame that none of my previous therapists knew about this simple need. Instead, right in their office, they allowed me to continue to act out, to perform and to do and say all the things that covered up my real needs. They answered my wants. They let me ramble on and on about nothing, when I needed them to let me be quiet, real, without performance. They helped me cover up my feelings, to hide my feelings in my performance for them – my mommies and daddies.

I am dwelling on this therapy as opposed to other therapies because that is the thing that has most impressed me as a patient in Primal Therapy. It is amazing to me that after so much confusion, things could become so simple after a few weeks of Primal Therapy. Today more therapists seem to be realising that their patients are not getting well, and there is a flood of new ideas and approaches. In the new and popular existential therapy, the marathon groups and encounter groups, people are allowed and encouraged to express themselves more freely than ever before, providing them with a great sense of relief for the time being. The patients cry in public, perhaps for the first time. They express hidden thoughts for the first time. They act out fear, anger, hurt, pain, joy, etc. I am speaking from personal experience here, as I participated in a weekend-long marathon, which included two therapists and about sixteen people. At the time I was with my third therapist and it was during that period when I knew that I was close to something big. Therefore, I experienced a great sense of relief at this marathon and thought it a very worthwhile experience. There was no one there, though, who knew how to direct us to the core of our feelings, no one to direct us to the need from which spring all the fears, angers, pains and joy we were experiencing.

There is another big danger in these new approaches, and that is the emphasis on affection between members of the group, interaction, interdependence, and the comforting of one another. All the comforting that takes place only aids in covering up the real need, and as long as one can substitute comfort from others for the real need, one will not feel that need. These marathons often hand out approval for the most flagrant acting out (in marriages and friendships, in jobs, and with one's parents, etc.), instead of feeling. Once I felt my first Primal experience in Primal Therapy, I knew that it was the truth, and that I was alone, that there was nothing I could get from anyone else that would satisfy that basic need. Once I felt the real need, no substitute would do.

The Primal experience is a deep feeling and expressing of the deepest needs we have. I have never felt anything like it before, except perhaps an orgasm. After orgasm many women cry. I often did. I now see that this is because – at the time of orgasm – I came closest to feeling that real need. After a Primal (although I do not feel any contractions in my vagina during a Primal) I find that my vagina has secreted heavily. In fact, so far, my entire body secretes liquids during my Primals. It is as if all the pain were running out of me. My eyes weep, my nose runs heavily, my mouth is open and saliva runs out, my pores sweat, and my vagina secretes. Some Primals are freer than others. My body seems to know

how much I can take, and it lets a little out at a time. If I'm
not ready to feel it, I struggle against the feeling, only a little
comes out, I may cry, and I usually cry out what I think I
feel. But the greatest relief is when all the controls go, and at
that moment there are no thoughts. It is still amazing to me
how it happens, since I do not make it happen. And afterwards I can't figure out how it did happen, but I'm always
glad it did. I feel no more struggle of any kind; it is the
greatest relief I've ever felt; the words and sobs and noises
come rushing out of me – and they are no longer controlled
at all. There is no thinking, only feeling. Whatever comes
out is a surprise to me, in the sense that I don't have any
control over what direction the Primal is going to take, yet it
is not a surprise in the sense that I feel it to be the truth, the
real need, the real answer to all the confusion I have heaped
on top of that need.

It is sad that I have spent so much of my life struggling
against feeling, when the struggle is the agony, and the feeling is the relief. It is also pain. It is a relief to let go of the
struggle – twenty-five years of it. It is pain to feel, to know
that the need can never be answered – only felt. The struggle
has kept me from feeling that pain, the pain that I am alone
and that I can't make my mommy and daddy real or make
them love me – I can only feel my need.

My Primals have been of varying intensity, as I have said.
The freest ones have all been very simple and quite direct.
The first one occurred in private therapy during the first
three-week intensive period. It started from my being cold. I
have always been very cold. My hands and feet have always
been freezing, and I have always been unable to keep warm
while others around me seemed quite content. Lying on the
couch, I was freezing, my teeth were chattering, and I was
holding myself. Art told me to really feel the cold in me, and
before I knew it (or how it happened), I was curled up on my
side like a baby, sobbing 'I want my mommy'. I don't know
how long it lasted. I had no control over it. I have spent a
good part of my life crying, but there was never any relief.
These sobs were in a voice new to me, and I felt them as
more real than anything I had known before. The pain was
the sweetest pain I'd ever known. I have always acted the
little girl; my right foot always turned inward (like a little
girl), like it was protecting me. As soon as I began to feel

being a little baby, my right foot, which had been turned inward, snapped upright. Art saw it when it first occurred, and afterwards I looked down at my feet and saw that they both pointed straight up in the air. After the Primal I lay there for a while. It is quite a draining experience, and I couldn't do or say anything for a while. My hands were warm for the first time I can remember and they have been warm most of the time since.

14

Insight and Transference in Psychotherapy

THE NATURE OF INSIGHT

In 1961 Nicholas Hobbs presented his presidential address on the sources of improvement in psychotherapy to the American Psychological Association. Hobbs' questions about the role of insight are important because insight usually plays the major part in what I call standard therapy. Irrespective of theoretical persuasion, most therapists, other than the behaviourists, who use the tool of insight believe that if a patient can understand why he does something, he will almost inevitably tend to abandon neurotic, irrational behaviour.

Hobbs expressed concern because often very insightful patients do not progress. Many of us would agree with him. Hobbs began to question the efficacy of insight as a significant technique. He cited instances where change takes place without insight – play therapy with children, body-movement therapy and psychodrama. He noted that therapists of different theroretical schools seemed to promote different but equally effective insights with the same reported rate of improvement. He wondered if in their insight therapies, the patients simply had caught on to the therapist's personal system of interpretation. It seems, he said, 'The therapist doesn't have to be right; he has to be convincing.'[1]

The question Hobbs raises is: How can all these varying interpretations be right? Or is there a 'right'?

Hobbs defines insight: 'When a client makes a statement about himself which agrees with the therapist's notion of what is the matter with him.' At this point of despair, Hobbs leaves insight behind as a rather fruitless exercise and discusses what he believes really causes therapeutic gain in patients. He cites warmth, understanding and attentive listening as major factors in improvement – the relationship

---

[1] Nicholas Hobbs, 'Sources of Gain in Psychotherapy', *American Psychologist* (November, 1962), p. 741.

of patient to therapist, in other words. Hobbs ends his address by stating: 'There are no true insights, only more or less useful ones.'

What is therapeutic insight? I believe it is the explanation of unreal behaviour. True insight is no more than Pain turned inside out. Insight is the nucleus of Pain. It is what must be hidden so that the person does not have to face the truth. Thus, to liberate Pain is to liberate the truth. The implications of this are that not only are there simply 'useful' insights as Hobbs believes, but there are single, precise truths about each person.

Let us take an example. A Primal patient is discussing her father who she believes was essentially a loving man. She is talking about how abused he was by her mother, how weak he seemed. After more talk around this point, in which she says with disgust, 'I wish he could have stood up to her,' I urged her to call out, 'Daddy, be strong for me!' She has a moving Primal about how her father gave up on the family and retreated into himself, defeated and broken. He was the baby who could never help his daughter, who needed protection from her vitriolic, 'bitchy' mother. Once she faces that her father really didn't love her and couldn't help her because *he* himself needed help, she begins a stream of insights: 'That's why I married such a weak guy; I was trying to make him into my strong father. That's why I cry when my son hugs me. That's why I loathe men who let their wives deride them. That's why, that's why . . .'

Those 'that's whys' are her insights. They are the explanations of the myriad ways she sought to cover her Pain. The denied feelings drove each of those behaviours. Feeling the feeling made them understandable.

These insights are not simply discussed. They erupt out of a connected system so that they are end points of a total feeling experience. Patients call it a 'rush of insights', almost involuntary in nature. They are insights that are 'felt to the toes', as one patient put it. This woman's denied Pain – that there was no one to protect her from a vicious mother – was the *reason* for her unreal behaviour later. To liberate Pain is to make reasons clear. Reasons are the insights. Once the Pain is felt, it is almost impossible not to be flooded with insights because that single repressed feeling has caused so much neurotic behaviour.

Another example: A patient is discussing his irrational anger at his wife and children: 'They won't leave me alone, for chrissakes! There's just one demand after another, and I have never had time to myself.' He speaks exasperatedly about how there is no peace in his life. I ask if he felt that way at home with his parents. 'Oh, yeah,' he answers. 'Goddamn, I remember my father coming into my room when I was relaxing or listening to music, eyeing me suspiciously because I wasn't busy doing chores. Jesus! I get furious when I think about his prodding. Not once did he ever sit down and talk to me. He just shouted his list of orders.' 'Feel that', I say. 'Let that feeling build and overtake you.' In a few moments the feeling emerges, and then I ask, 'What did you want to say to him?' 'Oh, man,' he will say, 'I would have told that bastard to—' 'Tell him now!' I say. Now the patient begins a stream of epithets about what a no-good his father is, but soon that gives way to a much deeper feeling: 'Daddy, please. Just sit down with me. Be nice to me for once. Say something kind, please. I don't want to be mad at you. I want to love you. Oh, Daddy!' Here the patient sobs and is wracked by Pain. Now begin his insights: 'That's why I was always borrowing money from him or anyone else. I wanted someone to take care of me. That's why I never want to help out my wife. I was reacting to *his* demands. That's why I got angry when the kids wanted help with something.' More crying and more shouting to Father: 'Dad, if only you knew how alone I felt waiting for you to do just one warm thing. Just to come home and put your arm around me once – that's why when my boss says one nice thing, I melt. That's why my stomach gets tied up in knots when my boss looks critical.'

Here we see how interwoven Pain and insights are. Insights are actually the mental component of the Pain. This man felt his real needs which lay below all his anger and was able to understand all his so-called irrational actions which resulted from those needs.

Primal patients don't know they are being insightful. It is not something apart. When a patient is telling his feelings to his parents, he is in the situation. He is not looking at his feelings from a distance. It isn't 'I used to hate them for that.' It is 'I hate you for doing what you're doing to me'. There is no split self, in short, talking about another self.

Primal process is a single, unified experience. It is the real, little child speaking his truths in my office, not the grown-up explaining how it was as a child. The difference between talking *about* feelings to a doctor and talking *to* parents during Primal Therapy is all the difference, in my opinion. 'Talking to' means that there is no bifurcated self – only a self totally engulfed by the past.

When a patient says, 'Doctor, I think I did that because I felt like a little kid,' there is the separation of the 'I' who is explaining and the 'me' being explained about. Thus, the *act of explanation in standard therapy helps keep the neurosis going by continuing the split*. No matter how correct the insight offered, then, the neurosis will deepen.

The Primal approach does not deal in explanations by the therapist. Explanations often tend to *be* the disease, especially in middle-class homes where the children must explain their every move. Middle-class parents have elaborate rationales for everything they do, including why they are punishing the children, and they force their children into this mould. Sometimes the working-class child has it better. Father comes home after a few beers, beats the children for 'openers', and life goes on. Everything is up front. No elaborate rationales to confuse the children. It is no accident that Primal Therapy for working-class patients goes faster. They aren't too involved with analysing Father. They just need to scream at him for all the senseless beatings they received.

I think, therefore, that the explanatory process of conventional psychotherapy may make the patient *more* neurotic. What it seems to do is help him schematise his irrational behaviour in terms of one theory or another, lull him into thinking he is better because he 'understands', while producing what I call a 'psychologically integrated neurotic'. 'Understand' in conventional therapy is but one more cover for the Pain. Next to mental illness, one of the major afflictions of humanity today is the treatment for it. Patients do not need to explain feelings and talk them to death; they need to feel them.

Once we depart from the patient's feelings and enter the realm of therapeutic interpretation, almost anything can be made true. A patient who cannot feel is up for grabs. He must accept others' interpretations of his actions because he cannot experience his own truth. Moreover, the theoretical interpretation by a therapist may well be the expression of *his* denied feelings elaborately symbolised in theoretical terms. So he may find sexual or aggressive connotations in what the patient is saying which are more the therapist's problems than the patient's. It may also be true that the interpretation by a therapist has nothing to do with anyone's feelings and simply derives from a theory found in a book worked out by someone decades before. That theory may have appealed to the therapist because of his repressed feelings and so was adopted for use on others.

So long as the feeling barrier exists, both the patient and therapist are guessing what lies below. The therapist's guess is called a theory. When the patient learns this theory as applied to his own behaviour, he may be pronounced 'well'. Because I think that insights must never precede the Pain, I see the job of a therapist as helping remove the dam between thought and feeling so that the patient can make his own connections. Otherwise, the therapist must explain things to the patient for years, and the patient often has little else to say but 'Oh, yes. I see, Doctor.' What he usually is seeing is how brilliant the doctor is.

Perhaps we have looked at insight from the wrong end of the lens. Indeed, insight may not cause change but result from it. This becomes clear when we consider that insight is the result of the connection between feeling and thought as applied to specific behaviour. 'Connection' is again the key term, for it is possible to be pseudo-insightful – to know things mentally without making a connection and therefore not to make change. Without Pain, there could be no real insight for the neurotic. We might say that insight is the mental result of felt Pain.

Pain is integrally related to insight. So long as the insight process takes place within a neurotic system where Pain blocks the insight from pervading (thus changing) the entire system, I doubt if we can expect significant and lasting changes in behaviour. When the Pain block is there, the insight can only constitute one more disconnected and fragmented experience. The Pain barrier would keep the insight sealed off mentally, hence unable to do the entire organism much good.

I would liken the conventional therapy insight process to

a departmental report submitted to the government analysing the economic system. The report, like the insight, is incorporated into the system. It is gobbled up and stored away so that it can have no impact on the entire system. This is why I believe that when one is going to overthrow an unreal and unworkable system, one does not engage that system in a dialogue. We should generally, expect that no matter how precise the insight, or how analytical the report, the system will continue to react in irrational ways. It will grind up and absorb the truth until something happens to remove the unreal system.

Patients really don't want explanations from outside anyway. One patient said, 'My neurosis is my invention. How could anyone explain my invention better than I could?'

The shift away from trying to tell the patient the truth about himself seems to be much more relaxing for everyone, to say nothing of being more honest. The premise of most insight therapy is that the doctor is going to help the patient find out the truth about himself. But if the neurotic weren't forced to spend his life lying to himself, specialists in psychological truths would be largely unnecessary. It seems to me to be more efficacious to strip away the lie the person is living and thus permit the truth to out.

There are some critical differences between insight in standard therapy and insight in Primal Therapy. In standard therapy, the therapist usually takes some piece of neurotic behaviour of the patient and infers what the real reason (what is unconscious) behind it is. His focus is unreal behaviour. In Primal Therapy, unreal behaviour is discussed by the patient *after* he feels what is unconscious. In standard therapy, insight becomes an end in itself, the accumulation of which is eventually supposed to produce change. In addition, the insight is one-dimensional. It deals with one piece of behaviour, as a rule, and the single motivation implied behind it. In Primal Therapy, one major Pain can lead to *several hours* of straight insights. Most important, Primal insights often convulse the entire system. They are organismic, producing total change. Primal insights are convulsive because a connected person (whose mind is connected to the body) cannot think painful thoughts without having painful bodily reactions. Nor can he feel pain physically during a Primal and not have it connected to conscious awareness. Indeed, as a patient in Primal Therapy progresses, he may retell the same story towards the end of his therapy and experience a much greater physical reaction than when he told it earlier in treatment.

Standard therapy usually deals with known facts of behaviour. In Primal Therapy, everything is unknown until felt. One patient described the difference in this way: 'There seemed to be a large tumorous Pain inside of me. Attached to this tumour were tangled strands which were strangling the life out of me. My previous therapy seemed to centre on untangling the strands to get at the core of the disease, but we never got there. Here we seemed to have taken out the whole tumour, and everything fell into place.'

The statement 'Everything fell into place' is a common feeling among patients. It is not only ideas which fall into place, however, but the body as well. One patient put it this way: 'My brain kept my body apart. I think that if all of my body worked harmoniously, I would have totally felt my horrible Pain. I gave my brain to them and then my body.'

Thus, when I indicate that mental insights are part of organismic change in Primal Therapy, the results are keener perceptions *and* enhanced physical co-ordination. A mildly stoop-shouldered patient described this totality as follows:

'When there isn't any connection, the body and mind aren't straight with each other, and I believe that this lack of straightness always shows up both mentally and physically. In my case, it drew my chest in, I guess to tighten up against the Pain coming from below, and it drew my shoulders around my chest for even more protection. It drew my mouth into a straight line and made my eyes squint. When I made the connection during the Primal, not only did I figure it all out but my posture straightened out automatically. I wasn't even aware of my change in posture until my wife remarked on it. The odd thing about it is that it's all involuntary; I mean, I don't try to stand straight – it's just that I am straight with myself and the body just follows along.'

To return to Hobbs for a moment. Hobbs stresses the warmth of a therapist rather than his insightfulness. I would say that warmth has little to do with insight because Primal Therapy is *not* a therapy of relationships. Everything the

patient will come to know already lies inside, not between
his therapist and himself. There is no re-education, nothing
the patient has to learn from a therapist. I do not believe
that insightfulness can be taught any more than one can
teach feeling. Feeling is the teacher. Without deep feeling,
warmth by a therapist must be an act at best. But even if that
act were to 'work', I still do not see how being nice and kind
can undo years of severe neurotic repression.

DISCUSSION

The very person who might have gained a little something
from standard insight therapy usually was the one it did not
help – namely, the inarticulate, non-verbal, working-class
person. He was the one who needed most to learn to articulate what he thought and felt, but alas, he was untouched.
But because the middle-class individual could better afford
therapy and could latch onto a verbal insight system, it was
he who got most of the therapy. Yet the insight badinage
between that patient and the therapist has largely been an
engagement with the defence system, an intellectual meeting
of the *minds*. The non-verbal person could never enter that
realm and play that game. So he got action when he broke
down mentally. What he got, and still gets, is described in a
book called *Social Class and Mental Illness*.[2] It consists of
more action and less talk: shock therapy, pills, occupational
therapy, and so on. One wonders how scientific a therapy
can be when it applies only to certain social strata. It would
seem that any science of *human* behaviour ought not to
neglect the majority of the human race.

There has been such a mélange of insight techniques, each
with a different approach, that one comes to feel that behaviour can be discussed within almost any frame of reference. I believe that there is one reality, a single, precise set of
truths about each of us that is not open to interpretation.

THE TRANSFERENCE

The process of transference plays a major role in many ther-

[2] A. B. Hollingshead and F. C. Redlich, *Social Class and Mental Illness* (New York, Wiley, 1958).

apies; in particular, the analytic approaches. Transference is one of the key Freudian concepts to denote those irrational attitudes and behaviours of the patient towards his therapist. It is believed that the patient projects onto the therapist most of the old irrational feelings he had towards his parents. The aim of the day-to-day therapy is to 'work through' the transference – that is, to help the patient understand how the basic parent-child relationship has been carried forward and displaced onto others, particularly the doctor. Hopefully, an understanding of the patient's irrational processes will transfer to his life in general and enable him to be rational in all his relationships.

I do not believe that transference exists as a separate phenomenon apart from general neurotic behaviour. The patient who is acting symbolically with himself will be expected to do so with his therapist. Because the therapist-patient relationship is such an intense and continuing one, it is handy to analyse the patient's neurosis as it plays against the therapist. In addition, the neurosis may be intensified because the therapist is an authority like the parents.

What the therapist does with the patient's neurotic behaviour (transference) is the question. If he gives insight into the way that the patient acts inside the office, I believe that there are going to be the same problems as attend any insight process. That is, the patient will absorb the insight and continue to be neurotic, through *acting* a bit more maturely, less impulsively, or with less fear or hostility towards the therapist. The Primal Therapist does not deal with the transference. He is busily engaged in having the patient feel his wants towards his parents. In fact, the patient-therapist relationship is ignored entirely. To spend any time analysing the transference would seem to me to be engaging in a discussion of derivative, displaced and symbolic behaviour rather than getting at basic need.

Primal Therapy shuts off any transference and does not permit neurotic behaviour of any kind because that means the patient isn't feeling; he is acting out. We force the patient to be direct. Instead of allowing him to be obsequious or intellectual, we tell him to fall on the floor, screaming, 'Love me, love me!' directly to his *parents*. This usually makes all discussion of how the patient might feel towards his therapist superfluous. It seems such a simple notion that if the patient is carrying forward feelings about his parents and projecting them onto the doctor, the projected and displaced feelings are really unimportant. What is crucial are those early feelings towards the parents. Feeling them will eliminate neurosis and transference.

When a person suffers from Primal Pains, he expects relief from his therapist. He wants the doctor to be a good father or mother. He will usually act in such a way as to try to make the doctor into the good parent, just as he did with his unloving parents. But now the doctor may be that good, caring, listening and attentive parent that the patient always wanted. In this way, the neurosis 'works'. It keeps the patient from feeling what he didn't get from his parents. We must remember that the patient usually comes for help because his act is not getting him what he needs on the outside. But inside the therapist's office it may be doing better. When the therapist is helpful and warm and offers a bit of advice, he is encouraging the 'positive' transference. Since I believe that the transference *is* the neurosis, I think that doing anything else with the patient other than helping him feel his Pain is to render him a disservice.

Patients often 'fall in love' with their therapist because the therapist is supplying some of what the patient has been unconsciously searching for with his neurotic behaviour. It doesn't really matter what the doctor looks like; he is an authority who is kind and who listens. It isn't any wonder that a patient who has had nothing for most of his life will stay in therapy for years once this 'good parent' has been found. Patients are willing to play the therapy game and go through years of insights and explanations just to be with that sensitive, all-interested, warm therapist. In my opinion, the last thing a patient wants is a discussion of the transference. He wants to nestle in the analyst-analysand relationship. He may discuss transference as a kind of 'dues', but I believe underlying that is the desire just to want to lie there and not have to say a single word, not explain one piece of behaviour – just be bathed in appreciation and understanding.

What the Primal Therapist does is to get down to those underlying feelings. This means stopping every sign of the transference, positive or negative, because it is all symbolic behaviour. One might ask: 'What if in reality there is something actually to like or dislike about the therapist?' I would reply that the therapist is not there to discuss their relationship, nor is he there to be liked or disliked. He is the dealer of Pain, no more, no less. If the therapist has certain 'counter-transference' behaviours (irrational conduct projected onto the patient), and these behaviours intrude into his relationship with his patient, then I would suggest that the therapist has not felt his own Pain and should not be doing Primal Therapy. Counter-transference is not tolerated in Primal Therapists because that means they are still neurotic. A neurotic cannot do this therapy.

It cannot be emphasised strongly enough that *the result of any symbolic behaviour is to shut off feeling*. Counter-transference is the same symbolic behaviour aimed at being loved that the therapist is acting out with his patient. This, obviously, is going to worsen the patient's condition because it imposes certain expectancies onto the patient. He must act in such a way as to quell the therapists's Pain and must therefore be unreal and untrue to himself.

Let us take the example of a therapist who thinks of himself as kind and warm and especially sensitive. He embraces his sad and crying patient, comforting him with a 'There, there. It's all right. I'm here. Things will get better, you'll see.' I think that such an *in loco parentis* results in shutting off feeling, preventing the patient from feeling all the hurt he must feel in order to finally get over it. It may keep the patient from feeling totally alone and having no one to comfort him; that is the usual reality of many neurotic patients. The therapeutic comforting produces, then, a more shallow experience; in this way, the 'warm' therapist becomes part of the patient's struggle. Instead of making him feel alone and isolated, he helps the patient run from feeling. It is that feeling which produces the struggle and it is that feeling, when felt, which will end the struggle.

Hugging the patient may indicate that the therapist has his role confused. He may unwittingly try to be the good parent instead of being what he (the therapist) is. The aim, I reiterate, is to deprive the patient of his struggle, *not* to take part in it.

If a Primal Therapist should hold the hand or head of his patient, it would generally mean he wanted the patient to feel something towards his *parents* more intensely. The holding is done when the patient is feeling what he *didn't* get from his parents, and the contrast of the warm therapist at that point *increases* the Pain.

In the Primal view, the reason that the analysis of transference cannot work is that the patient is transferring unreal hope onto the doctor instead of feeling his hopelessness. When, in fact, the patient actually gets what he thinks he needs from the therapist, the situation, vis-à-vis his neurosis, may be truly hopeless. By shifting his real wants for a good parent into wanting the love and respect of the therapist, the patient has followed his customary path – has found a substitute struggle.

The very experience of standard psychotherapy alone often helps keep the patient sick, in my opinion. The patient comes for help and finds it in the form of an understanding and compassionate therapist. Even while the patient is discussing how dependent he is, how much he has always needed guidance, that feeling is being vitiated by the fact that someone is there listening and helping. In this sense, the patient is again acting out in the therapeutic situation the substitute need for help when he must be feeling how much he was never helped by his parents. New hope of help becomes neurotically invested in the therapy.

It is the attempt to satisfy need that forces the neurotic to make people, including his therapist, into what they are not. The neurotic cannot let people be what they are until *he* is what he is. Once that happens, there will be no more transference of past needs onto the present.

Phillip

This is the autobiography of a man who was severely deprived, who grew up in various institutions. Like many of my patients, prior to therapy he experienced physical manifestations of his inner cramping in the form of a mild hunchback. He was constantly delinquent, labelled a 'bad boy', and punished day after day. Later in life he had numerous sexual affairs, culminating in incest. His pathology was severe from any standpoint. Even after having been sent for psychotherapy to a woman doctor, he managed to manoeuvre the situation into a sexual conquest. In standard diagnostic parlance, he was a 'psychopath'. This case serves to illustrate that an almost unsalvageable human being can be rehabilitated, given the proper therapy.

I am Phillip. I am now thirty-six years old. I was three years old when my father and mother separated and later divorced. I remember my mother and sister going away, and me not knowing why or what it meant. My father re-married, almost immediately. My stepmother said I cried a lot, was a sullen, difficult child who didn't want to be touched or held. Only candy or other sweet foods pacified me. I re-treated inside myself and resented intruders.

My older brother and I were placed in a private boarding school when I was five. My father attended law school nights, and he and my stepmother worked days. I was constantly in trouble, never adjusting to the regimen peculiar to the boarding school. I isolated myself at the school, living like a distant outsider, withdrawn and resentful during holiday parties, visits and social events. My brother used to try to cheer me up and to get me to enjoy the events and treats as he seemed to do. But I would only cry.

One Christmas some older boys asked me if I wanted some candies and cookies from a package they had. I didn't usually get asked, and I ate all I could. We were called down to the principal's office before we were through with the package, and I remember being the last one called in. I was scared and didn't know why the red-haired Lutheran minister was so angry. The package belonged to another boy and had been stolen. I put my hand in back to protect myself from the hairbrush, peed in my pants and all over the minister, as the hairbrush fell up and down. My thumb was black and blue when I looked later.

My father's first job as a corporation lawyer was for a rayon and silk manufacturer in the South. He bought a house, and we all lived together year round, for the first time. My brother had a part-time job, working after school. Sometimes he would give me some of his candy or some money. Mostly I stole money and gum from my stepmother's purse and said nothing, or lied, when she missed it. One night she found some change in my pants pocket, woke me up, and asked me where I got it. I couldn't answer her. My father came in, lectured me, and sent me back to bed. I was ten and my brother twelve at the time. I began to steal candy and gum from stores.

My brother bought a pump-shot BB rifle with his earnings, and we would shoot it out in back. There were high telephone wires, and we would try to sail flat-edge stones over the top wires. I threw like a girl and never could clear the top wire. My brother almost always cleared it, and he could hit most anything he threw at. One time he was throwing rocks at me, and I told him to stop. He didn't. I took the BB gun, pumped it as high as I could, and shot him in the stomach. My father had to dig the BB out and whipped me with a belt. He wanted me to tell my brother I was sorry, and I kept telling him my brother started it.

I always walked with my head down, shoulders hunched, kicking rocks as I walked. I was crossing the street when a car hit me. I regained consciousness, and the man put me in his car and drove me home. My stepmother was upset and said if I'd have remembered to go to the store for bread like I'd been told, it wouldn't have happened.

I was eleven years old when we moved to Charlotte. It was customary for my brother and me to leave Cokes for Santa and his helper. I told my parents I didn't believe in Santa any more and that I knew they left the presents. I drank the Coke myself. Next morning, when I got up, my brother had been given all the toys and candy. He offered to share them with me and handed me the black rubber racer car I had wanted for Christmas. I threw it against the wall and got sent to my room.

My father and mother were out for the evening, and there were some cigarette butts in the ashtray. I lit one up, put it out and dumped the ashtray into the trash can. The curtains caught fire from the trash can, and my brother tried to put it out. The fire chief wanted to know how the fire started. I told him my father must have left a cigarette burning in the ashtray. My brother told what really happened. My father and stepmother wanted to know why I couldn't be good, like my brother. We would get into arguments, and I would bite my brother, stick him with pencils and dinner forks. My stepmother noticed the bite marks on him and bit me so I would know how it felt. My half brother was born.

I was twelve when we moved back up North, outside New

York City. I got to run my brother's paper route that summer, while he was a counsellor at summer camp. I sold the undelivered papers on the street corner and bought ice cream and candy with the money. My father had to settle the account at the end of summer. One-third of the customers quit subscribing. My father asked if I could do anything right.

My stepmother made me sit in front of her, on the floor, and do my school homework. Her legs were spread open, and she didn't have any panties on. She wasn't looking when I poked her cunt with my finger, and I had my head back in my book when she jerked her head around. My father and brother held me while my stepmother kissed me. I didn't like to be kissed. I spat in her face and got slapped. We had an argument, and I called my stepmother a son of a bitch. She threw a paring knife at me. I ran away from home, and my father had a six-state alarm sent out. That brought me home.

It was summer, and we had to go to bed by eight. My stepmother would lock me in my room, so that my brother and I wouldn't carry on while she was downstairs. My brother's room wasn't kept locked, and we could see each other through the glass panes in the door to my room. I could hear the other kids from my window, shouting and playing outside. My brother would hold up a candy bar and motion for me to come and get it. I would crawl out my window, over the tile roof, and into my brother's room. I got my brother to crawl with me, over into my room, that night. Crawling back across to his room was scary for him, as the room dropped at a straight slant, and you could see all the way to the ground. It was about a forty-foot drop. My brother froze and wouldn't go any farther than the roof ledge, starting down to his window. I crawled in his window and began eating his candy, while he sat up on the roof ledge, angry and scared. He threatened to beat on me and tell on me, between pleas for help. I promised I'd help him get down if he wouldn't hit me or tell on me and would pay me fifty cents. He eventually agreed.

We moved farther out in the suburbs of New York when I was thirteen. I was supposed to take care of my half brother after school. I would drink half the orange juice from his bottle, fill it with water, and then give him the bottle. I re-

ceived a pin for perfect Sunday school attendance that year,
and my half sister was born.

My father and stepmother decided to place me in a pre-
paratory school in New Jersey. I learned how to milk cows,
play chess and speak German. I joined the school choir,
played football, basketball and learned how to box.

We cut classes that day and took our swim trunks to the
river. It was about a fifteen-foot dive from the bank to the
water below. He was bigger than I was, and he teased me
because I was afraid to dive. I hit him in the mouth, and he
came after me. I dived, and my head hit the rocks along the
edge of the water. I got expelled from school, and my father
took me, by ambulance, to a hospital back in New York.

My stepmother said if I stayed in the home, she would
leave. My father had promised he would sign the papers if I
passed the entrance exam for the Navy. I passed, and he said
he couldn't sign because I was under age and that he never
thought I'd pass. I called him a liar and said I hated him. He
kept knocking me down, and each time, when I got up, I told
him he couldn't hurt me any more because I hated him. I
was fourteen, and he gave me the train fare to go live with
my mother, in Pennsylvania.

My mother, my sister and I all slept in the same bed, and I
held and kissed my sister all that first night. I skipped school
often and stayed out all hours of the day and night. My
mother locked me out of the house, and I broke in, after
spending all night in the basement. She got her boyfriend,
who was a policeman, to come over to discipline me. I
pulled a kitchen knife on him and threatened to stab him if
he touched me. The truant officer picked me up and put me
in the Boys' Shelter. I was labelled 'incorrigible' by the juv-
enile court and placed in a state reformatory school for delinquent boys.

I joined the armed forces and left reform school at
seventeen. My father died from an overdose of sleeping
pills, and I went to the funeral. I looked down into the coffin
at his face and felt nothing. After the funeral service, I told
my uncle I had been promoted to a corporal in the para-
medics. He got angry because I didn't show proper respect
for my father's death.

I was twenty, she was eighteen, and we met at a skating
rink outside the Army base. I had my first sexual affair, and

we were married in two weeks' time. My son was six months old, and I couldn't stop him from crying. I spanked him, leaving the imprint of my hand in black and blue, on his buttocks. My wife was pregnant when I volunteered for overseas duty, and our daughter was two weeks old when I shipped out. While overseas, I maintained my earlier religious teachings, went to church every Sunday, sent all but three dollars a month home to my wife, and practised strict fidelity the two years there. I returned home and within the year had sex with my two-and-a-half-year-old daughter.

From her letters I had concluded that my wife was running around. I began to drink, smoke and have sex with other women within that year. When another GI confronted me about my wife's infidelity, I attacked him with an entrenching tool. A general court-martial was set up. I took an overdose of pills before it convened and ended up in the psychiatric ward. I was discharged from military service and released from the hospital. My second daughter was born, and I questioned that she was mine.

I was twenty-five years old when I left for Texas, informing my wife I would send for them when I got established. I didn't plan to send for them, and in Texas I worked, drank and had several affairs. My wife joined me on her own, and in six months' time we separated and later divorced. I was bitter and disillusioned.

I was twenty-six, and I moved to California with the intention of obtaining a college education. When I first saw Gloria, she was selling magazine subscriptions, and I told her I wanted to help her. We lived common law my first year of college, and I left her after I started work at a school for mentally retarded children. I began to have sexual affairs with several women working there, and one woman told the director I had gotten her pregnant. I was fired and thought about suicide as a solution. I continued to have numerous sexual affairs, drank a lot, smoked heavily, and slept infrequently.

Fay was a young college student on probationary status when I met her. I offered to help her with her schoolwork, and I was unemployed at the time. I had a week to go on my rent when we were married and she went to work. I applied for employment with a county agency and took a job working with an aphasic child in the interim. I was to prepare him for a live-in placement, as his parents didn't want him committed to a mental institution. I was hired by the county and turned the job of working with the aphasic child over to my wife. I continually berated her for her inability to control and work with the child and became extremely critical of her. We were divorced around the same time the aphasic child was ready for school placement. I became preoccupied with thoughts of suicide and, for the first time, admitted to myself that I was sick and needed help. I contacted the college counselling service and entered group therapy.

I soon learned to master the techniques employed in the group setting. During this period my sister and I had an intellectual discussion about incest, then had a sexual affair and lived together for a brief period. The group with my psychiatrist ended without any discussion of my affair with my sister, and I entered private and group therapy with a woman psychologist. I talked with her about my numerous affairs, my past life, and my progress in therapy. Over a three-month period of time we reached a discussion on counter-transference, had sex, and I quit my job and moved into her Hollywood Hills home. She was in her late forties, and I was in my early thirties. I met my present wife while in that group and moved out to North Hollywood. I obtained employment with a psychiatric hospital. I applied for employment with a federal agency and began working with people in the community.

I entered my third marriage, and my drinking increased as my standard of living improved. The many therapies and therapy sessions had failed to cure the sickness in me. I had always outwitted, out-manoeuvred, or out-manipulated my therapists, my groups, myself. I had become skilled at verbal intrigue, intellectual rationalisation, theoretical explanation, problem solving, physical touch and many other learned techniques. And always I remained sick, and I knew it. I had progressed from an 'irresponsible, uneducated, incorrigible' psychopath through my education and therapy to a 'responsible, educated, middle-class' psychopath.

Janov was standing behind the desk and looked up at me as I entered his office for the first time. I had a fixed smile on my face when he spoke. 'Don't stand there looking at me; there are no answers out here. Have a couch.' This was the beginning.

The phony smile left my face, and I lay down on the couch. Janov asked, 'What's your feeling?' My responses were fragmented and irregular. I began to cry. Janov spoke. 'What's the matter? Let's talk about it. You look bad.' I began to cry more. Janov waited and then said, 'Say what you're feeling. Don't cry it away.' I stopped crying eventually and grew quiet. Janov said, 'All right, what's your feeling?' I replied, 'Anxiety; kind of a free floating, too.' Janov: 'All right, now sink straight into it; put your legs out. Now sink straight down inside, and don't have any controls whatsoever. Let go! Let go!' I began to breathe rapidly. Janov: 'Now breathe from the belly, deep; open your mouth and pull from the belly; say *ah* – deep – *ah* – deep *ah*. Sink!' I let go some. Janov: 'What is it?' Me: 'My head starts turning; I won't let go. I keep thinking back to my fear of criticism. My push, my drive, my whole thing – it really isn't what's happening with me. I don't want to fail. I don't want to be criticised.' Janov: 'By whom?' Me: 'I think by my family. I go back even more. I think I don't remember before three. I remember after three. I know I have resentment, I can't forgive—' Janov: 'Say it.' Me: 'I can't forgive my mother. She left me at three. I never accepted my stepmother. Criticism comes. Why aren't I as good as my brother? He conforms. I rebel. And I really don't; I really don't want to be good like him. He's not good.'

Janov: 'What would you say to your mother, if you could talk to her right now, your real mother?' Me: 'My real mother?' Janov: 'What would you say?' Me: 'I would ask her to love me.'

Janov: 'All right; ask her. Talk to her. Mommy – come on; say what you want to say.' I began to breathe heavy and felt the lump stuck in my throat. I pulled hard. I felt like I was being pulled apart, like I was split down the middle, and the two halves were pulling against each other. I was being pulled apart physically and every way. I tried to fight it. The two parts of me were locked. I couldn't stop it. I opened and screamed, 'Mommy; Mommy!' Janov: 'Call.' Me: 'I want her to come back.' I began to cry hard. It hurt. I choked and I gagged on my feelings. I screamed, 'I want to die.' Janov: 'Tell her.' I couldn't let go. 'Mommy, don't go.' I shut off. I couldn't stop the crying, the choking, the pain. It was pulling me apart. I opened, 'I hate – leave me alone. Mommy. I hate you all, you fuckers.' I choked and gagged, trying to keep my feelings down, to control. They kept coming up anyway. My body hurt. The lump in my throat wouldn't go away. I opened up and screamed out, 'Love me.' I shut off. I struggled. It came out anyway: 'Love me.' I was quiet, and I felt fear. But I still wasn't sure what feeling was. I saw I had done a lot of things, not because I had wanted to, but because I wanted my parents' love. I was afraid again. I was afraid I wasn't loved and that I wasn't capable of loving. I felt worthless. My mother had left me, and I asked, 'Why me?' I didn't know if she wanted me, and I resented her. I wanted to kill – to kill me. I felt unlike other people. I screamed out. I screamed some more, but I kept blocking. I was afraid to let go. Afraid I'd flail around, out of control. Afraid if I let go I'd want to hit. I hit the couch and screamed; out came 'I hate me'. I opened up to scream, fought it, and distorted the sound of a word I was afraid to say. I was beginning to feel my hurt for the first time, and when Janov said, 'Tell them; tell Mommy and Daddy. You've got to tell them you're suffering,' I could only choke, gag and hold on. The Pain was too great. Janov: 'Don't be silent anymore. Don't suffer in silence anymore. Get it out; call for help. Daddy, Mommy.' I screamed out the Pain and screamed it out again. Then there was quiet. I began to talk. 'I know why I hate me now.' Janov: 'Why?' Me: 'Because really underneath it all, I would sell any part of me for their love, and yet I hate them too. I hate them because I have to be what they want me to be for them to love me. They're all fucked up; they're more fucked up than I am.' Janov: 'What did you always want, what did you want from them?' Me: 'I wanted them to love me for me and to let me be what I had to be without their rigid "this is good, this is bad; you have to succeed; you can't say what you really feel, you have to say what's right, to say what's nice, to build them up and tell them what they want to hear". I did a lot of things because I never said, "Love me." I couldn't say, "Love me." That's why I was always in trouble. The scene of my mother leaving me flashed across my eyes, and I couldn't call out, "Mommy, stay." I felt helpless and alone, and I knew that it was back there when I shut off all feeling. I wouldn't call Mommy because it meant going back and feeling that hurt, which I'd never allowed myself to feel. I also knew why I wanted to be punished and why I was destructive and didn't fit in the family setting. I kept trying to go back to that initial scene and feel what had happened. I wondered, "Why am I the only one that really cared? Why did the rest of the family adjust?" I kept wondering what was wrong with me, and I lashed out at them, and at everything in life. I had to go back and feel that moment, and I couldn't if they closed it out. All my acting out began when I shut off and couldn't feel my helplessness, my aloneness, at that point.'

This was my Primal Scene and the first connection I made. The rest is a result from this origin of my conflict. My body felt the split, the pulling apart. My past, the past I had never felt, was coming up fast on me. I was afraid again. I shut off. I would go back to my room exhausted and fall asleep for hours. When I woke, the fear was still there, and I felt the lump in my throat. I tried to deny and run from what I had felt before. I vacillated between running to Janov's office for relief, like the scared and hurt little boy I really was, and running from the Pain that came from the struggle with myself on the couch. I had three lumps now. One in my throat, one in my diaphragm, and one in my lower chest. I screamed, 'Mommy, Mommy,' and I could see her hand reach down and pull my balls out and up through me. They became stuck, and when I pulled, they didn't work right. I pulled more, and after a while they became connected. The lump in my throat became cylindrical and moved up and down. All three lumps were attached now. I panicked, but I knew it was my cock and my balls. My cock went up and down in my throat as I breathed, and it was masturbating. The phlegm became semen in my mouth, and I gagged. I screamed out, still distorting and disguising the word 'cock' that I was so afraid of. 'Cock, cock, cock.' What did it mean? Maybe I was homosexual. I panicked. Eventually I knew that 'cock' was the symbol of all my destructive, sexual acting out. Feelings began to come up, sometimes in physical, sometimes in symbolic, form. But they were disconnected, and I would have to keep going back until they were all connected together. I began to feel the whole unfelt sequence of my life. First, the denial that I was left unloved and helpless at the age of three. Then the word 'cock', and my angry, destructive acting out through sex, to cover the fear that came from being alone.

I was alone in my bedroom, and I panicked. I wanted to check Janov out. Does he know what he's doing? How dangerous is it to open Pandora's box? I got scared and wanted to run from me. I phoned Janov and threatened to have him investigated. He asked me why I really called, and I told him I was afraid. Afraid of my feelings. I wanted to be well. I wanted to cough up and spit out the penis, testicles, semen.

Maybe well means real. Maybe real means a homosexual. I don't know, Janov had told me that his office was my room, and I could be anything I wanted to there. I wanted to run to my room, be safe there, be me there.

On the way to Janov's I had my throat choke up, and I wanted to cry. I felt I was a little boy going to my room, where it was all right to be a little boy. I lay on the couch, and the feeling came up. I opened, and 'Daddy' came out. I began to cry, and call, 'Daddy, Daddy, love me!' I choked off on the word 'love' and felt ashamed. Janov said, 'Beg.' I called and begged for the love I needed; gagged and felt contemptuous. It meant being weak, to need love, and it hurt because I had denied needing my Daddy's love for so long. I had to deny it, because he would never allow me to ask. It caused too much pain in him, so I had shut off rather than feel the rejection I always got. I sank into my feeling, and a picture flashed before my eyes. I was standing in the middle of a circle of people, who were staring at me, with my middle finger giving the 'fuck you' sign to them all, and laughing. All of a sudden the picture changed, and I was stripped naked, and the faces were staring at me. Mocking faces, leering, ugly. The ugly reflection of me. I became scared, and all alone, trying to cover myself with my hands. I couldn't see who the faces were. Janov said, 'See it, stay with it.' I looked close. My head wanted to turn. I wanted to run. Janov said, 'Look at it.' I looked hard and screamed in anguish. It was my family. My family, leering and staring at me, and I felt vulnerable and alone, and I wanted my Daddy to protect me. I saw he was a scared little boy, too, just like me. Where was he? I called, and I could see him, dead, in his coffin, but he heard me. I begged him not to go. I told him I needed him, and for the first time, I talked to him. I wanted him all to myself, and I told him so. He was there whenever I called, and I could see the early scenes in my life with him and say and feel all the unsaid, unfelt things we never had when he lived. I had numerous Primals where I wanted my daddy's cock, got angry, sad, harsh and gentle with him. Eventually the time came to tell him good-bye, close the lid to his coffin, and the process of letting him die and letting go took place.

My Primals took on more symbolisation, and I felt encased and constrained. I tried to force myself to feel what it was, but it didn't work. It was as if my body would only move at a certain pace, and I could neither speed up nor slow down the process. If I tried to smoke, my body became rigid with tension, and I was in pain. It was like a battle being waged inside me, and I was unable to control what was going on. Sometimes I wanted it over, and sometimes I was afraid it would be over. I had to feel what was encasing me. I sank into the feeling and saw a picture of me, with a leaden mould, like a mummy's tomb, on my back. I was walking through life, bent over with the weight of the mould pressing me in, controlling everything I did. It was the mould my family had impressed upon me, and I was going insane inside it. How to get out? I had to get out! I screamed and my back began to arch, my chest muscles and back muscles stretched, and I cried and screamed from the pain. Then the connecting, both physical and feeling, took place. I had been hunchbacked for years, bent to the will of my parents, but my body had never accepted fully the imposition of the foreign cast. With each successive Primal, my back straightened, and my muscles stretched into form. A whole new system was taking over inside me, and I could feel the physical connections. I was exhausted after each Primal and impatiently awaited the next step, the next phase. I couldn't believe it would ever end. Some days were sheer misery; some were quiet and peaceful; some were alert and graphically clear. I never knew what to expect.

During the time in between Primal phases, my body seemed to rest, to check out the newly formed features, and to prepare for the next phase. I became aware that my body was taking over as my brain was losing its control over my body. I was sitting in group, and the sensation that had been with me for several sessions was present. It was a pulling and tightening sensation that encompassed my scalp and head region, with a constricting sensation deeper in the bones and muscles of my head, neck and face. I lay down in the group, thinking I would be done in a few minutes, when I felt afraid and could feel my body wanting to flail and twist free. I yelled, 'I'm afraid,' Janov said, 'Let it happen'. My body began to move in various uncanny positions that defied any control on my part and brought screams of pain as the untwisting of both physical and emotional neurotic defences occurred. Sweat poured from me, as I was overcome by the power of my body, and my brain was powerless to dictate how it thought I should be. I knew then that my brain dictated what my parents wanted me to think and to be, but my body rebelled, and would no longer 'act' or 'perform' according to any dictates other than what was correct for it. For the first time in my life I was free and knew what freedom was. I no longer had any choice about whether I could be sick or not and act out. My body would not allow it. My head could no longer lie or deceive my body into submission. I tried to make a deal, so my body would stop twisting and unravelling me, but it didn't work.

My body had decided, and I had no choice. My body is a tabernacle and will no longer tolerate irreverence. I know that the great majority of rules, regulations, dogmas and controls imposed by parents and society are unnecessary when the child is allowed to be real and respond to his body and brain as it commands him.

15

Sleep, Dreams, and Symbols

When the young child denies catastrophic reality at the
Primal Scene, he stops being completely real and sets himself on a course towards becoming increasingly unreal. This
process is shaped each and every day by parents who won't
let the child be himself and demand that he project an invented image in accordance with what they expect. He may be
the 'good boy', the 'clown', or the 'helpless fool'.

Being a symbolic self is a full-time job. The necessity to
guard against the real self goes on day and night. During the
day there is the symbolic acting out; during the night symbolic dreams protect against real feelings, even in one's
sleep. If, for example, a person grew up trying to please a
bitchy mother, he would be helpful, smile when she looked
at him, speak tentatively to her, act ingratiatingly, apologise
for almost anything – in short, he would be engaging in
many behaviours which emanate from the unconscious feeling 'Be nice to me, Mommy; I'll do anything if you'll be
kind.' Each of these behaviours is a symbolic referent from
that central feeling.

Because the need does not change or disappear at night, it
is acted out in the dream, again in symbolic form. The
dream may be trying to placate a monster or trying to do
something impossible and never quite making it. That
impossible symbolic task is really trying to make Mother
nice.

The first point, then, about dreams is that *they are extensions of waking behaviour and not a different phenomenon.*
They are the night-time symbolic struggle – the night-time
neurosis. It seems reasonable that a neurotic doesn't go to
sleep neurotic, get well at night, and wake up neurotic the
next morning. Real people, on the other hand, do not have
unreal dreams any more than they would act in unreal ways
during the day.

The second point is that *symbolic dreams are only the
function of symbolic people.* Many months of Primal Therapy had gone by before I noticed that as therapy progressed,

dreams became more real. At the end of the patients' therapies, people became what they were – not only during the day but at night in dreams as well: Mother was mother, children were children, and New York was New York. Furthermore, their dreams were in the present and not in the past, as are so many neurotic dreams. This is logical since symbols arise to mask *old* feelings from childhood. They are an attempt to deal with the past. The normal has his past out of the way. He lives in the present day and night.

A person who feels unimportant cannot make important deals at night to cover that feeling. His dreams will take care of that. He may dream of being honoured at a gathering for his achievements. The dream and actually putting over important deals during the day are aspects of the same unfelt feeling. In Primal Therapy, when the patient brings in such a dream, he is made to sink into the feeling at its nucleus. What he will feel will be the painful feeling which gives rise to important symbolic behaviour in the dream *and* during the day.

The third – and major – point in regard to symbolic dreams is that *they serve to protect the sanity of the dreamer*. This is in contrast with the Freudian hypothesis that dreams serve to protect sleep and allow us to rest. If we can understand that the unreal self (the self that converts dangerous feelings into symbols) keeps us sane and neurotic, we can see that symbolic dreams are essential. Otherwise, there would be shattering Primals during sleep.

Sometimes real feelings do get close even during sleep. The usual dream symbols no longer bind the feeling, and a nightmare results. A nightmare is the Primal feeling breaking through the neurotic defence. The dreamer symbolises on a new level – a psychotic one. His dragons and monsters are what I would call psychotic symbolisation. Nightmares, then, are night-time insanity. That is why it is such a relief to wake up from them into the real world. The feeling of the nightmare wakes us into consciousness so that we can remain *unconscious* of the feeling in the same way that some neurotics make some of their feelings and thoughts unconscious while awake during the day with the use of defence mechanisms. If we think of this on a purely physical level, we find that some of us will faint (become unconscious) under intense physical pain.

A Primal is the logical extension and conclusion of a nightmare. It is that nightmare feeling, that terror, *without* the symbolic cover. If a person has nightmares, he is close to his Primal. He is actually feeling most of the terror even after he wakes up. His heart is pounding; his muscles are taut; all he has not done is make the actual connection and fall into a Primal. Pain prevents that. If a Primal Therapist were there at that moment, the person would be well into his Primals and well on his way to becoming real.

A recurring nightmare or bad dream is a Primal feeling which persists and has to be symbolised in almost the same way for years. Being attacked by an enemy, having one's guns jam, and scarcely being able to escape, for example, may be one recurring dream. The feeling in that dream is that there is no one to help. Often the person is not aware that anyone should help. He is all alone in his dream, just as he has been all alone in the world trying to handle himself against insurmountable odds. He needs to scream 'Help!'

Some dreamers do try to scream 'Help', but nothing comes out. There is a good reason for this. That scream is the Primal Scream, and the fact that it doesn't come out is protection. An example: During a therapy session a woman was describing her dream of the night before: 'I was being attacked and something had me backed into the corner of my room. I tried to escape and ran to my neighbour's house, where I planned to call the police for help. I kept dialling the wrong number, and I just couldn't get the police.' I made her sink back into the dream and re-tell it. She kept refusing. It was too frightening for some reason. I persisted. As she told of running to her neighbour's house, I interjected, 'Call the right number!' She yelled that she couldn't. I kept after her. Finally, she dialled the right number, and out came a horrifying Primal Scream: 'Help!' She screamed for ten minutes, writhing and thrashing on the floor. In every one of her actions she was screaming 'Help!' for twenty years because she could never get it from her parents. She had been so busy struggling to help them that she couldn't feel her own need for help.

Why hadn't she screamed out in the dream? Because of hope. If she had screamed and no one had come, all would have been lost – she would have had to feel her utter helplessness and the fact that no one in her life was ever going to

help her. Not screaming protected her against this realisation. When she screamed in my office, she felt all those
horrible feelings of helplessness and hopelessness. Thus, not
screaming kept her struggling (and hoping). It also kept her
feelings covered. Screaming broke through the unreal cover
and helped put her on the road to reality.

Many neurotics are so well covered that they never approach screaming in a dream. Indeed, they hardly remember
their dreams because the feelings and their symbols are so
deeply buried. But neurotics are a walking scream. (The
'screaming fag' is but one example.) We scream in sophisticated ways. Being obsequious is the scream to be treated
with gentleness; constant talking, the scream for attention.

As seen from the foregoing, neurosis is not simply social
maladjustment. We cannot judge neurosis or its absence by
how a person gets on in his job. A well-functioning person
during the day may have nightmares which testify most elo-
quently to his neurosis. For this reason, social adjustment
scales purporting to graph one's neurosis seem irrelevant,
since all they reflect are *daytime* behaviours.

The depth of the Pain, the density of the defence system,
the closeness to one's feelings – all can usually be measured
in terms of the dream symbols. The more Pain, the more
likely that the symbols will be complex. Also, the more Pain,
the more struggle in the dreams: crawling under fences, digging one's way out of a tunnel, climbing steep mountains,
etc. If the feelings come up during the dream despite the
symbols, we can suspect that the person has a flimsy defence
structure and is close to his feelings; this is an easy Primal
case, as a rule, and the person has a good chance of getting
real (well) soon. Pleasant dreams in the neurotic, on the
other hand, are suspect. For example, the recurrent dream
of flying and feeling free. The Pain below his pleasant,
floating feeling may be one of great constriction. Instead of
dreaming he is Prometheus Bound, which would be more
real, indicating closeness to constricting feelings, his dreams
of freedom indicate a breach, the split, from his real tied-
down self. A dream of trying to untie the binding ropes
would indicate a greater closeness to one's real feelings.

How exactly does a symbol refer to a feeling? Let us look
at a few examples. If a child denies his babyish needs and
tries to act grown-up to please his babyish parents with their

284 The Primal Scream

infantile needs, he may dream of being waited on by an army of servants. If a child has to listen to his parents' arguments each day over the bills, if he is made to earn his spending money and given jobs to keep him occupied constantly, he may dream of fainting so that an ambulance can come to take him to a hospital where he is totally taken care of. He dreams it not even knowing that he feels 'Stop, let me rest and take it easy'. His system is trying to tell him what he needs with its mental symbols. We must heed those symbols carefully.

Symbolic dreams (just as symbolic drug trips or any other symbolic behaviour) continue as long as Pain continues. They are an important index not only of the degree of neurosis but the extent of therapeutic improvement. Symbolism of dreams is something that cannot usually be faked because patients do not know that symbols mean anything. Even if they did, they would usually not know how to scale the complexity of the symbol and correlate it with degree of neurosis. A person who claims to feel better and to function well and who then brings in a highly symbolic dream may not be as well as he thought.

The feelings inside a dream are the most real part of the person. It is tempting to dismiss those feelings as something alien because they occur in a dream context which is so unreal. Obviously, there are no Nazis chasing us or guns firing at us, but the fear that made those night-time stories necessary is absolutely real. Otherwise it would not be there and most certainly would not wake us up.

It is the real fear that makes a dreamer dress up his terror in Nazi uniforms, just as it is real fright that makes a paranoid imagine that people on a street corner are conspiring against him. Not able to feel the real feeling, both the dreamer and the paranoid must project their fears onto something apparent. The paranoid delusion and the symbolic dream both attempt to make rational (to restore reason to) an inexplicable feeling: 'The reason I am afraid is that the Nazis are after me.'

The difference between the delusion and the neurotic dream is that the paranoid lives his dream during the day. He believes his symbols to be real. The neurotic knows his symbols (Nazis) are unreal. If someone were to walk into a therapist's office and tell the doctor that the Nazis were after him, his sanity would be suspect. If one adds, 'That was a dream,' the diagnosis is changed.

Many neurotics suffer from frequent nightmares. It has occurred to me that in a sense they go to sleep at night and, with their defensive guard lowered, border on insanity time after time. It is no wonder that they are afraid to go to sleep. These nightmares, however, seem to drain off enough tension so as to prevent them from being insane during the day. The person with inordinate Pain often is unable to confine his insanity to the night-time hours.

Let us look at one nightmare to see how sleep and waking behaviours are extensions of one another: 'Yesterday, when I thought things were going well, the principal of my school called me in about some complaint from the parents of one of my students. Even though I knew she was a chronic complainer and that her complaint was not justified, I was upset. I continued to be upset all day and could not shake it. I didn't know what the matter was, but I went to bed all tense. Here is my dream: I am driving my car down a narrow and winding road. Suddenly a car hits me from the side just when I thought I was safe. I manage to keep on going, but now I'm in a narrow tunnel with one hairpin turn after another. With each turn, I collide with the wall. This feels like a tunnel of terror; I can't stop banging into the wall. I look out the window and see a woman motor-cycle cop watching and waiting to cite me. I can't escape. She stays behind watching me scrape the walls one time after another. I am really terrified. Suddenly I wake up with a great relief that I'm out of that tunnel. What a relief to know it's not true.'

It is true. The *feeling* part of any nightmare is true. What is not true is the context, the mental model she invented out of the feeling. I put her back into the nightmare and have her re-tell it with a mask over her eyes just as though she were re-living it. The same terror starts to creep in. I have her sink into that terror and let it overwhelm her. Soon she is all upset and thrashing about on the couch. She begins to talk about her childhood. 'I could be so good for so long when I was young, but one wrong move was inevitable and brought disaster from my mother.' Here she begins to talk about an incident in her childhood when she did everything perfectly, cleaned the house, washed the dishes but accidentally spilled a few drops of perfume on a piece of furniture. Her mother was furious and sent her to her room. She became depressed because she had tried so hard. She moves again to the dream. 'Oh, I know now. Hitting those walls with the car was just like things continuously going wrong at home no matter how hard I tried. That 'mother'' cop has always been waiting, unrelenting, for me to make that one fatal mistake. No matter how good I was, something was always around the corner (just as in the dream) waiting to spoil things.' Then she ties this to the events at school when just as she thought she was doing so well as a teacher, someone had to smash it all. 'It's all the same,' she said. 'School, the dream – my life!' Here she feels that lifetime of hurt and screams, 'Don't be mad, mother, I'm not bad; don't spoil my life!' She is re-living the school, the dream, and her life all in one terrible feeling – the terror of her mother and how that made her cramp her life until she squeezed all the living out of it.

The situation at school triggered the dream. The feeling in both cases was unconscious. It is rather astounding to think that even in sleep our systems keep us unconscious of threatening feelings, but the human organism is a wonder. The nightmare is an exact allegory of the daytime school situation where things are going well and then things go bad and all is spoiled. How does the body know to produce such a perfect dream allegory when the mind (or part of it) is completely unconscious of the feeling behind it? I believe that symbolic processes of the unreal system are the unconscious, automatic and necessary devices to protect the organism.

This woman's nightmare was an extension of the terror, felt as tension, which she experienced at school. The feeling produced a dream in order to deal with that terror, and, it was hoped, resolve it. Maybe she could get away from the cop in the dream? No. Neurotics never can. Why is this? Why can't this woman get away from the cop in the dream? Because the real feelings of a lifetime keep the cop there. The cop was symbolic of my patient's fear. She used to have nightmares about a lady ticket taker at a movie catching her as she was sneaking in. The ticket taker always caught her no matter how adept she was because she could not get away from her until she actually resolved (felt) that terror.

I think that this explains why in our nightmares we cannot escape, why our feet and legs are like lead when we try to run from an enemy, why we are pursued without end – because we are pursued with unending primal feelings until they are ended in reality with a Primal. We are condemned to having nightmares so long as those feelings are not resolved. Any therapy which releases a patient who then still has nightmares has not resolved those feelings and therefore has not touched the basis of symbolic, neurotic behaviour.

In the case of the schoolteacher, we note that she woke up *automatically* when the feeling in the dream was too much to continue to bear. This is what I mean by saying she sought to remain unconscious of an unbearable feeling. Shutting off consciousness – and subsequent neurotic behaviour – seems reflexive. She woke up to reconstitute her defences. She never knew before that she had such fear of her mother. She did not know it because she was so busy being Mother's 'good girl'. Being perfect and sweet was the way she avoided the fear (the *conscious* fear) of her mother. That same defence worked well at school ordinarily because she was a meticulous teacher with clean blackboards, books in place, and students in 'control'. Her defences began to crumble with an outsider's complaint.

So a nightmare is a not a fear of the object in a dream; in this case, not a fear of 'cops'. My patient's reaction even during the dream was all out of proportion to simply having a cop waiting to give her a ticket. She was responding to something true – a lifetime of horror and fear. She overreacted to the mother's complaint at school in the same way. That complaint and the dream were symbolic of childhood feelings. After her Primal she said, 'Feeling the terror of the night helped me understand the terror of each day.' Her nightmare, day and night, was over.

Feeling terror or Primal Pains of any kind makes them go away forever just because they are felt. Once felt, once connected, it is over.

It is logical that neurotics will have disturbed sleep – disturbed by real feelings. The same Pain that drives them during the day forces them to produce dream characters to keep them occupied at night. No wonder the neurotic often wakes up more tired in the morning than when he went to sleep! He has spent a busy night warding off his feelings. The actions of his dream characters – say, of climbing – produce muscle reactions during sleep so that in some respects he really has been climbing for half the night. The poor neurotic simply doesn't rest. He wakes up tired and less able to cope during the day; this in turn produces more anxiety and more problems, which again find their way into his sleep, upsetting him all over again.

Let us look at a few dreams now in order to examine their symbolism:

'I am living in my present house, and my father comes to visit. We're on the second floor. He kisses me on the forehead, and I fall down and split my knee open. The split is getting worse, and Mother is there scolding Father for being so clumsy.'

In this dream we find that the people are real but the situation isn't. What is symbolic is the meaning of the situation. The patient's feeling inside this dream was: 'I guess I always knew somewhere that to accept Daddy's affection would split me in two. Mother and I seemed to have a pact in which we both put Daddy down. I guess I also put him down so that she would love me. I suppose loving Daddy meant giving up the hope for Mother's love.'

Dream number two took place one month after the first Primal:

'I am cleaning something with Janov. I have cuts or scars on my hand, but they are covered with a layer of wax. I tell Janov that I can't move my hands because they are swollen. He says I can. I attempt to coat the cuts with Mercurochrome but it doesn't work. The wax repels it. I realise that the cuts are symbolic of old hurts that still hold me back from being totally myself. I know I can't avoid it any more. I strip off the wax and use my hands.'

Here we see still lessened use of symbolism and a knowledge of the meaning of the symbol during the dream. There seems to be a blend of consciousness and unconsciousness. The patient sees the struggle is unreal even while asleep and corrects it. Shortly, perhaps in a few months, we may expect any remnants of struggle to disappear. The dreams will then be expected to be as straight and direct as his waking behaviour.

One final dream:

'I am in the backyard working with my father. My mother angrily calls us for dinner. The dinner is sombre. Everything is muted, quiet and dead. My father tries to tell a joke and my grandmother laughs a horrible laugh showing her false teeth. My mother looks at Grandmother with hope. I see that Mother's mother can't love either. Suddenly it hits me. I see the family for the empty shell it is. It's all so lifeless and dull. I start crying and excuse myself and go into the kitchen. The food for dinner is ready, but no one makes an effort to serve it. It makes me cry more. They're all too dead to make the effort.

'Mother says, "Was he crying?" Father says, "No!" I run upstairs and lock my door and look for a piece of paper to write down the dream; I know that it is important. Downstairs, I hear my father playing "Down Upon the Swanee River", I cry, thinking there's no home for me anywhere.'

There is very little symbolism in this dream. The situation is direct, and the feelings in the situation mirror his exact feelings about himself and his life. He understands even during the dream what it is revealing, and the dream explains itself. There appears to be no labyrinth of symbols to wade through. The dreamer seems to have felt the emptiness, the pretence of his own life, and how his father tried to cover over his real feelings, too.

DISCUSSION

If a person does not have a pained self, if he has a direct relationship with his feelings, I can see no reason for symbolising them. Graduate Primal patients do not have symbolic dreams for the same reason that they do not have symbolic LSD trips – there is no Pain and no need for a symbolic cover. Current upsets do not trigger old hurts which find their way into the dreams of the normal person because there are no *unresolved* hurts to become mixed with the present.

It must be obvious that there are no universal symbols just as there is no symptom with universal meaning. Symbols are referents from specific feelings inside an individual. Two people could have the same dream, and that dream would have very different meanings.

Post-Primal patients need less sleep, and report more restful sleep. They also report dreaming less. One patient commented, 'I go to bed and sleep now instead of spending the night dreaming.'

Here briefly is what some of my post-Primal patients say about their sleep and dreams. They independently maintain that very deep sleep is mostly neurotic sleep, in which 'sleeping like a log' is a defence even against the symbols in neurotics' dreams. They believe that very deep sleep means total repression and an encased defence system. One patient put it this way: 'I used to sleep like I wrapped a thick blanket over my consciousness. Now I sleep like under a light film of gauze.' He believed that his deep sleep, from which he often woke more tired than from lighter sleep, was analogous to his deeply unconscious (of himself and the world) waking state. He reported that he used to believe that sleep was unconsciousness, whereas now he sees sleep as rest. Most patients describe this state as 'superawareness'. In short, nothing is unconscious any more.

'It may be,' said one patient, 'that we have been split in our thinking about sleep as something separate from wakefulness.' One wonders whether the polarity of sleep versus wakefulness has kept us from seeing that they are simply different aspects of the same state of being, not two distinct entitities with only some mystical connection.

Americans, with all their daily struggles, still find their sleep disturbed. The Louis Harris poll[1] showed that more than one-third of the population is concerned because it does not sleep well at night. Twenty-five per cent of these people feel too exhausted to get up in the morning. The same poll indicated that more than half the population feels lonely and depressed some of the time, and twenty-three per cent confessed to feeling 'emotionally disturbed'. Hard work takes care of some feelings, yelling at the children helps a little more, cigarettes and alcohol drain off even more, yet there is still a need for tranquillisers and sleeping pills.

In an interesting study reported by a member of a UCLA research team[2] to a conference on brain physiology, it was noted that those who stop smoking dream more – and more

[1] Los Angeles *Times*, 19 November 1968.
[2] Los Angeles *Times*, 16 September 1969.

intensely. Here we see evidence for the Primal hypothesis concerning dreams and the release of tension. When ordinary tension relievers are removed, dreams take on a double burden. Conversely, sleep research indicates that those who take sleeping pills in order to sleep deeply, dream less than they would without pills. *But* the after-effects of not being allowed a dream release is that the person is more irritable and depressed and requires more tension relievers, such as increased smoking. The neurotic system, in short, is going to find a way.

When the person who has not had sufficient dreaming owing to the ingestion of sleeping pills goes off his medication, he tends to dream much more than he would normally. And these dreams are more upsetting. One cannot drive away neurosis with drugs. It can be allayed for a short time, but then the neurotic must pay his price. This means that tranquillisers during the day only postpone and ensure the inevitable serious depression and possible breakdown which will occur when the drug is removed.

The implications of what I am saying go beyond dream and sleep phenomena. I am indicating that pills, heralded as they have been, do not seriously affect mental illness in the long run. They only help suppress the real self, producing *more* internal pressure, *more* serious neurosis. Pills are in the same position as conditioning techniques which help through mild electric shock to suppress 'bad' behaviour. Is not this what parents do in their own unsophisticated, nontheoretical way, and isn't the result a deeper neurosis? There are studies, for example, which indicate that more heart attacks occur in sleep than in waking states. Perhaps there are sound physiologic reasons for this. But one must wonder if the use of daytime tranquillisers builds so much pressure which must be relieved in sleep dreams that the vulnerable cardiac cannot withstand it.

Neurotics have trouble sleeping because they are constantly being activated by Primal Pain, and that activation is the opposite of sleep. The use of tranquillisers and sleeping pills is like keeping a tight lid on a pot over a high fire. Eventually, some part of the system, if not the entire organism, must give.

16

The Nature of Love

The concept of love has been around a long time; it may help to view it in Primal terms.

At its foundations, love means being open and free to feel and permitting others that freedom. It means to allow them to grow naturally and to express themselves naturally. To be oneself and let others be natural is essential.

The primal definition of love is *letting someone be what they are*. This can happen only when needs are fulfilled.

Implicit in the definition of love is the existence of a real relationship between loving people. After all, you can let someone be himself by ignoring him, but response to another is an integral part of love. We must remember that to let someone really be himself means filling his needs. This is the job of loving parents. Later there will be few needs to fill, and love then can be a true giving to one another. Unfortunately, love for the neurotic means fulfilling his unreal needs (in the form of wants). It means gifts or many phone calls or other 'proof' of one's undying devotion. The neurotic feels unloved when his sick needs are not being catered to. What better example of this than the suffering of a homosexual man when his lover has left?

Love is feeling. It goes on when two people talk, drink coffee together, or have sex. When there is no feeling (that is, when feeling is blocked and hidden), neurotics may indulge in all these activities without there being a shred of love. Instead it is a 'suck (as my patients put it), trying to get something from someone to fill up the emptiness inside.

Love early in life means meeting Primal needs. In the first months and years this means a great deal of holding and fondling. The child has no name such as 'love' for the holding, but he hurts when it is missing. Physical contact is a *sine qua non* for children. Love cannot be shown without it. It is not enough for a child to 'know' that he is loved somehow by an undemonstrative parent; he must *feel* it. Not to fill that need is not to love, no matter how many verbal protestations of love one makes. The parents who works so hard that he scarcely ever sees his children may rationalise that he is working for them, but when he has no contact with them, when he does not give himself to them, we must assume that he is working to relieve himself. If a child needs a parent around and that parent is away at work most of the time, his needs are not being met.

Infants brought up in institutions where there is little affection or personal attention develop flattened or dulled personalities. There is an apathy or deadness about them which continues into adulthood. These children automatically do what will protect them against no love – they dull themselves against further hurt. They close in and close up.

Studies with dogs raised in isolation without physical contact with other dogs or with humans were found to be everlastingly unstable and immature. They became 'cold' and 'hard' when adults, were largely asexual, and could not learn to respond to affection. No amount of later affection seemed to alter their state.

The same conclusions were made with monkeys bred in isolation. In the now-famous experiments carried out by Harlow, monkeys were segregated into three groups; one group was raised in complete isolation, another group was raised with cloth-doll mothers, and the third group had 'mothers' made out of wire and spikes.[1] Harlow found that the isolated monkeys suffered most. They seemed to be unable to give and receive affection. Those with cloth-doll mothers seemed to do as well as those with real mothers. They ate as much, showed as few fears, were more social and were more willing to explore a strange environment. Harlow stressed the importance of bodily contact. When a monkey was allowed to hold and cling to a cloth mother, the bonds of affection between them were as strong as the bonds between an infant monkey and a real mother. We might conclude from these experiments that what is called love in the earliest months of life centres on touching and warm physical contact. An 'unloved' infant may be the one with insufficient touching.

Early caressing is important, especially when we consider that for decades many of our children have been brought up

[1] Harry F. Harlow, 'Love in Infant Monkeys', *Scientific American*, Vol. 200, No. 6 (June 1959), pp. 68–74.

by the 'book'. Parents have responded to their children according to a schedule of rules rather than acted on their feelings. They have fed the infants by a timetable instead of when the infant screamed out his hunger, and they have not held the child when he cried, for fear of 'spoiling' him. Pediatric guides over the last several decades have been influenced by the writings of the early behaviourist psychologists who seemed to feel that to prepare a child for a cold, hard world, he should not be pampered and 'loved' whenever he cried. We now see that the best treatment for living in the world is all the holding, touching and caressing parents can give children. But we must be concerned not merely with the act; the feeling matters, too. When a parent is tense and jumpy and handles the infant abruptly and jerkily, the infant is going to suffer; but with some kind of handling, even 'bad' handling, damage to the infant is not irrevocable and total.

A young child knows when he's wet, hungry, tired – and when he is in pain. When he is made comfortable, we could say that he is experiencing love. Love is what takes the pain away. When he is allowed to explore, to yell, to suck his thumb, to grab Mother, we can call it love. When he is kept from all that, when he isn't held or talked to, he may become uncomfortable and tense. We might say that love and Pain are polar opposites. Love is what enhances the self; Pain suppresses it.

Touching and holding are not all of love. If a child is denied expression of feeling and has to board up part of himself, it is likely that all the caressing and holding by his parents will still leave him feeling unloved. I cannot stress enough the importance of free expression, for it may determine the child's fate for the rest of his life. A few hugs or 'You know how much we love you' cannot make up for that denial.

Because feeling is unified, I do not think it possible to prohibit certain feelings and expect total expression of others; whatever the neurotic child will feel later will tend to be blunted and subdued. Deny a child anger, for example, and it is bound to affect how happy or loved he can feel.

No later affection – a new station in life, numbers of 'loving' people around – will reverse the early deprivation, I feel – unless it is re-lived with the original feeling that was denied. The neurotic spends much of his adult life trying to cover his Pain with new lovers, affairs and flirtations. The more lovers and affairs he has, the less he is likely to feel, paradoxically; the chase seems endless because for him to feel loved means first that the old Pain of being unloved must be felt in all its intensity.

Because love involves feeling the self, we cannot transfer it to someone else. When someone says, 'You make me feel like a woman' or 'With you, I feel loved', it usually means they cannot feel and need acts and symbols from outside in order to convince themselves they are 'loved'. Love is not a matter of giving something to someone so that his tank can register 'full'. Nor can we be emptied of love any more than we can be emptied of feeling. It is not something divisible to be doled out in bits and pieces, nor can it be broken into specialities such as 'mature love' and 'immature love'.

The older neurotic may assert his undying love verbally, but when feeling is impacted, protestations of love tend to be meaningless. Moreover, these verbal affirmations of love usually are transmogrified pleadings to have one's desperate needs fulfilled. Feeling people rarely need verbal reassurance. Unfeeling people seem to need it constantly.

What the neurotic is looking for in love is the self that was never allowed to be. He wants a special somebody who can make him feel. He will tend to define as love whatever he missed and whatever keeps him from being whole. Sometimes it is physical touching he needs, and he may try to manufacture love out of sex – that is, to 'make love'. Sometimes the quest is the search for protection; in other cases, it is the need to be understood and talked to.

The dilemma of the neurotic is that while love is no more than the free expression of the self, he had to give up his feeling self in order to feel loved by his parents as a child. The neurotic, by definition, must believe either that he is loved or that he will be loved; otherwise he would not continue the neurotic struggle. In short, like Harlow's third group of monkeys, the neurotic child maintains the illusion of love through his struggle so that he doesn't have to see that there are only wire and spikes.

Thus, if a child at six years were to face the truth and the hopelessness, it is doubtful that he would struggle. The *promise* of love, both implicit and explicit, seems to keep the child hoping rather than facing the reality of his young life. He may spend a lifetime looking forward to something that not only doesn't exist, but never did – his parents' love. He may play the comic to entertain his parents, the scholar to impress them, or the invalid to evoke some caring. The very *act* prevents love because he is covering how he really would act and feel.

From what I have observed, the neurotic re-creates his early unloving situation later in life in order to play out the same drama with a hopefully loving ending. He doesn't marry a mother figure simply because he wants his mother. He wants a *loving* mother, but he does not take his love straight. First, he must set up his ritual. He may find a cold person like his mother and try to extract some warmth from her. Or she will find someone rough and crude like Father and try to make something gentle and kind out of him. This is symbolic acting out. If the person were to become involved with a truly loving person, he would have to leave because there would still be that gnawing *old* unloved feeling inside. In short, finding a warm person would *prevent* the symbolic struggle to finally resolve the old feelings. In this sense, finding present love and warmth means to feel the Pain of not getting the old love.

Even in the neurotic's dreams he creates the same struggle. There are often obstacles in reaching a loved one. He may make himself crawl up mountains or go through a maze, and still he can never quite make it to the 'land of love'.

Because he has not been allowed his own feelings, the neurotic often believes that love must lie somewhere else with someone else. He seldom can understand that it lies inside himself. I think his frantic search is an attempt to reach himself. The problem usually is that he just doesn't know how. He has no lever to get at his feelings. In these terms, then, the quest for love is no more than the quest to 'be', to feel. The desperation, the pursuit, the travel to new places are often the attempt to find that special someone who is going to make him feel something. Alas, only Pain can do that job. And so, one sees endlessly repeated the same sad drama – a third-rate play with a monotonous script, inept actors, and no happy ending.

I believe that the struggle is set up so that the person can finally get, even in a substitute way, the *little boy or little girl love* he needed years before and never got. What he is *not* after is adult love in the present. Even when it is offered, it seems to be avoided in deference to the struggle. Thus, the Primal notion about love centres on the fact that it is the search for what was missing possibly decades before. The neurotic will tend to define as love whatever fills that need. Perhaps, this is why there are so many different definitions of love – there are so many kinds of needs.

Unfortunately, even if the neurotic's parents could suddenly metamorphose into loving, understanding people, nothing would be changed. The neurotic cannot use this love later in life because it, too, would only be a substitute for what really happened years before between the child and *unloving* parents. Feeling unloved has priority.

The young miserable child is trying with his neurotic behaviour, his aggression, his illnesses, his failures, to tell his parents, 'Love me, so I won't have to live my lie.' As we have seen, the lie is an unconscious pact between his parents and himself in which he has agreed to be untrue to himself in order to be what they expect. He agrees to meet their needs if later they will meet his and stop the necessity for his lies. But as long as he keeps up the lie, the politeness, the helplessness, the helpfulness, the independence, etc., both he and his parents are convinced that love is being exchanged. He does not end the lie out of the fear of being 'unloved'. Oddly enough, later in life, when something happens to challenge the lie, the person tends to feel unloved. The Primal therapist is rarely liked in the beginning, as other therapists might be, because he doesn't take part in the lie; he doesn't allow it so that the person has no recourse but to feel unloved.

The neurotic is confused as a rule. He comes to think that love is what the unloving parents gave him. If his parents were always 'concerned' about him, he may try to provoke concern, through illness or failure. By provoking reactions similar to his parents' behaviour the neurotic manages to keep up the myth of love. He is often so engaged in the struggle to maintain the myth that he doesn't feel his misery. He may, for example, come into therapy saying, 'My parents weren't perfect. Nobody is. But they loved me in their own special way.' I think that 'special way' kept the child a special way – neurotic. He may go on to say, 'Father was a stern disciplinarian, not much on open affection, but we knew he loved us kids.' Translated, this could mean, 'Father expects perfection, never says a praising word, shows no real warmth, but as long as we complied with his orders, we could tell ourselves we were loved.' But it doesn't seem to matter what we tell the self. The real self that is unloved feels it. When someone in therapy with the above rationale is forced to call out to be held and caressed by Father, he hurts. All the things that he *thought* were true seem to crumble before the Pain.

A proper young lady said: 'Mother was just a bit old fashioned about manners and etiquette, you know, but she loved us all the same.' When she cried out for freedom, she felt the suffering she always had had but never felt. We conclude, therefore, that only when individuals feel their own real needs do they come to know what love is and isn't, perhaps for the first time.

One patient insisted that she was loved by her parents, both of whom were openly demonstrative. She maintained that her husband was the source of her problem. In her second week of therapy she felt it: She went back and re-lived a scene when she was singled out over her sister for being so good and well behaved. All her life she never felt unloved because she became the good daughter. Help, presents and affection were lavished on her by her parents: all she had to do was be 'good'. Because she was good, and not herself, she never felt unloved. Nevertheless she suffered from Primal Pain. This Pain could surface only when I would not allow her to be the sweet person she had always been. This again is an example of the Primal notion that *love is letting someone be what they are.* This girl seemingly had everything – but herself. She was unloved.

One other example to make this point clear: A young woman had a mother who was with her constantly, played with her, held her, never hit her. Yet this mother was a little child who was not strong enough to let her daughter be the little girl. The daughter had to be grown-up, strong and protective of her weak mother. Despite everything this mother did for her daughter, she did not love her because she could not let the daughter be what she was – weak and little.

Children surrender and sacrifice in order to cover the feeling of being unloved. Parents may do the same thing to cover the fact that they cannot feel for their children. Though these parents may offer proof of love – 'Look at all I did for you' – it usually means, 'Why don't you do something for me?' Surrender of the self seems to be part of the Judeo-Christian ethic, in which we surrender ourselves to a deity in the name of love. (As a patient put it: 'I gave myself up to get love from my mother: when that didn't work, I tried my father; and when that failed, I tried God.') The neurotic seems to extend this process so that he may begin to measure love in terms of how much others give up for him.

It is not accidental that when a child is loved he is rarely concerned with love. He usually has no need to label things 'love', nor would he question his parents' love. He doesn't need the words because he has the feeling. I suggest that those who need to label things 'love' are those who are unloved. There don't seem to be enough assurances, proofs, or words to fill the childhood void.

If parents want to prevent the neurotic struggle for love in their children, I would suggest that they allow themselves full expression of their own feelings, tears, anger, joy – and allow the children to say what they want to say in the way they want to say it. This means allowing them to complain, to be loud and exuberant, to criticise, to sass. In short, permitting children the same rights as other humans able and uncomplaining children. Children should be allowed to express themselves because feelings belong to them; they may not break furniture or the dishes because those belong to the family. But a child isn't likely to be destructive in a physical way if he can be verbal about it.

When we specify what a child can feel and require that he examine his feelings, we have already dented his feeling ability. When the child is allowed total spontaneity of all feeling, chances are he will become the kind of child who will spontaneously run up and kiss and hug his parents. In this way, the parents will be loved as well. Too many of us have come to see children as order takers and do not expect them to be spontaneously affectionate. Love tends to be ritualised in the neurotic home. There is the *duty* of affection, the hello–good-bye kiss devoid of spontaneous feeling, the reprimand when the child fails his duty. What the neurotic usually gets from his child, therefore, is an *act* devoid of feeling, when the child has much more to give if allowed.

Why is the search for love so universal? Because it is the search for the self that could never be. More precisely, the search for that special someone who will let you be you. Since so many of us have had our feelings ignored or crushed, we end up doing what we don't feel. The early marriages, quick romances, I believe, derive from the inner frustration and desperation to feel *through* others. The search seems endless because few people really know what they are looking for.

Rarely should the loss of a lover in the present produce such catastrophic results as attempted suicide unless that loss reflected a deeper, older loss from one's youth.

When the neurotic finally *feels* unloved, he paves the way towards feeling loved. To feel the Pain is to discover the reality of the body and its feelings – and there can be no love without feeling.

17

Sexuality, Homosexuality, and Bisexuality

Primal theory differentiates sex as an *act* from sex as an experience. The sex act involves all the overt motions that individuals make during sex play and sexual intercourse. The sex experience is the meaning of these motions. In neurosis, the experience of the act can be quite different from the act itself. Thus, a heterosexual act can be experienced in a homosexual way, with homosexual fantasies. And a homosexual act between a 'butch' (masculine) male and a 'nellie' (feminine) male can be experienced as heterosexual. I would characterise the nature of the act in terms of its subjective experience – a distinction that will be important when it comes to discussing treatment of sexual malfunctions and perversion.

It is possible, for example, to find someone going through the motions of sex without experiencing any sexual feeling whatsoever, as any number of frigid wives can testify. What gives sex its meaning, then, is the full feeling of the total situation; what alters it is the neurotic effort to derive symbolic value from the act.

It is the Primal hypothesis that when needs are deprived and feelings are blocked early in life, they emerge in symbolic form. In sex this means that the act will be experienced (usually via the fantasy) as fulfilling the need.

Let us take several examples. A thirty-year-old male patient suffered from impotence. He lost his erection whenever he entered his wife. The man grew up with a cold, demanding, 'bitchy' mother who gave him no warmth, only orders. Since it was beyond his realm of understanding that he deserved warmth from anyone, he denied or did not recognise any need for warmth. He married a woman who was very aggressive and demanding like his mother, but someone who also took charge of his life and allowed him to be passive. When it came time to enter her, it was no longer a matter of having sex with a woman: It was the little boy being loved symbolically by Mother. The symbolic aspect of the act (incest) prevented him from functioning as an adult.

This man had denied (did not recognise) his early needs for warmth and sought this motherly affection from other women. Women were symbols of mother love, and the sex act with them was symbolic; functioning was thus impaired. Clearly, if women were only adult females, we would not expect sexual malfunctions; the problems arose because they became mother symbols.

Sex organs, like any organ system, function in a real way when the person is real and in an unreal way when the person is unreal.

In each act of the neurotic there is a dual system operating: the real system with its deprivations and needs and the unreal system which tries to fulfil these usually unconscious needs symbolically. So the unreal self seems to be having mature sex while the inner child is trying to be loved. Because he is trying for childhood love, the neurotic must unconsciously make his partners into parent figures (somebody unreal). It would not be surprising, then, if the person were impotent or betrayed by his body in other ways.

Another example: A man could not become aroused with his beautiful wife until she told him about other men she wanted to sleep with. Elaborate descriptions of other men's penises stimulated him – he was sexually excited by the thought of men's sexual organs. The relationship with his wife, in Primal terms, was essentially homosexual. He was not relating to her; he was relating to his *need*, which was denied in early life and which emerged in the symbolic preoccupation with sex organs. This man had a weak and ineffective father who never talked to him, much less hugged or held him. If he wanted anything, he had to go to his mother, who then asked his father. That is, he had to go through Mother to get to Father, which is essentially what he was doing in sex. The need for his father was always there but, denied, came to be symbolised in the form of a penis. So what he was relating to in sex was the symbol of father love, not his wife. He had to get his need for his father out of the way before he could be truly heterosexual.

One final example: During sex, a woman fantasised being dominated, ordered about, and held against her will. The experience of the act was that of the helpless child, a victim of sex rather than an equal partner. This woman had a brutal and sadistic father who called her a 'whore' when she was a young teenager. He refused to allow her to date and derided her use of makeup. She denied her want for Father's love but during sex re-created herself as a helpless victim (of her father) in order to allow herself to feel anything.

In each of these cases, the sex act is symbolic, an attempt to solve old needs. The person does not feel the situation he is in, because he is relating to a fantasy. Thus, to some women the act may mean love. To some men it could mean virility, power, or revenge. The function of the fantasy during sex is the re-creation of the early parent-child struggle. The crucial difference, however, is that during sex the person is getting what he always imagined would lie at the end of his lifelong struggle; to be kissed, cuddled, caressed and loved, and allowed to feel. The neurotic symbolically makes his struggle 'come out right', by giving it a fantasied outcome that could never happen in reality. As one woman put it: 'My fantasies during sex are a good example of how I lived in my mind instead of my body. I couldn't even feel what was going on below my waist.'

When the person can feel his original need, the fantasy has no further function. When the impotent man in the first example felt his deep need for a decent, humane and caring mother, he had no need to seek substitutes. His wife was no longer a mother since he felt the reality of what his mother was. His sex problem vanished because it was built on a symbolic act that had no relation to what was going on with his wife. The same was true of the man who needed to be told stories about big penises. When he felt how terribly he had been deprived of a father, he no longer needed the tangible symbol of his father.

The above examples would indicate that neurotic sex is symbolic sex in which the person rarely 'sees' his partner. Indeed, holding it in the dark only increases its symbolic value. The fantasy may not even be conscious; the neurotic may relate to his partner as mother or father without realising he is 'living out' the fantasy.

One cannot be fully heterosexual with Primal Pain. If, for example, a girl wants her father's love, she may have a great deal of sex with men to try to get it symbolically, but she is likely to have problems of frigidity, because while the unreal system is having sex with men, the real system unconsciously is trying only to be held and to feel loved (by

Father). The experience is not sexual. It is infantile; the woman is trying to resolve her past deprivations. As one frigid woman stated, 'I think that instead of stuffing myself with food, I was stuffing myself with penises trying to feel filled up with love. I could never get enough to feel loved.' She then added, 'I think I know now why I could never really feel during sex; if I really let go and felt, I would have felt all the Pain of how unloved I was. I would have felt what I was trying to get out of sex. My illusions prevented that.'

Sexual problems become compounded when a young boy has great needs for both a mother and a father. In sex with women he may act like a little boy and let the sex partner (the mother symbol) take charge. While this is going on, he may have homosexual fantasies. The same is true of a woman who has been deprived of her mother's love. So long as that need has not been fulfilled, it is bound to get in the way of any heterosexual activity.

Needs from the past predominate over the present. One can scarcely wonder that a large number of women are frigid when one sees the small child that resides inside many of the women I have seen. They need a kind father and are angry and disappointed when a man wants adult sex instead of offering fatherly love first. If one understands that there is a frightened little girl inside, afraid of her father (and men), it becomes clear how difficult it will be later to have a wholehearted, easy and giving relationship in sex. Little girls don't have grown-up sex.

LOVE AND SEX

A number of women say, 'I can only go to bed with some-one I love.' What this can mean in neurotic women is: 'In order to enjoy the natural feelings of my body, I must con-vince my mind that it means something more than what it is. In order to be free to feel, I must be loved.' Here, again, is the unconscious expression of the need for love as a pre-requisite for feeling.

When a person has been loved early in life, he does not have to try to extract it from sex; sex can be what it is – an intimate relationship between two people who are attracted to each other. Does this mean that sex is something isolated from love? Not necessarily. A well person is not going to run around trying to get everyone in bed. He will want to share his self (and this includes his body) with a person he cares about. But he or she will not preface that relationship with some mystical concept of love. Sex will be a natural outgrowth of a relationship just like anything else. It does not have to be 'justified' by love.

When a neurotic woman has suppressed her feelings, no matter what she thinks is going on in terms of a loving relationship, she is not likely to enjoy sex fully. But if she is normal, she will not have to make something special out of sex. She won't be loyal to a concept such as love; she will not have to hear special words, 'I love you', in order to enjoy her physical self.

When a child has never got love from his parents, he may become terribly excited about the prospect of sex because he feels he is finally going to get what he needs. As a result, he or she may become quite impulsive, unable to stop to use contraception because of the urgency of all those old denied needs surging to the fore. The result may be an unwanted pregnancy – an unwanted consequence of a desperate impulse to fill desperate needs. However, when a person has felt his needs for parental love, all the desperation in sex seems to vanish. It becomes but one more pleasurable, feeling experience.

Being loved early in life by one's parents is the *only* protection against later promiscuity. Too many deprived girls are deluded into thinking they are loved when they have sex in their teens because they need to believe it. Tragically, this often is the first warmth and physical affection they have had in their lives.

True love is when a boy and girl like and accept each other for what they are – and that includes their bodies. Neurotics exploit the bodies of others to satisfy old needs. This precludes having an equal, give-and-take relationship. Too often, the neurotic boy relates to parts (the sexual parts) of a girl; he cannot treat her as a whole person. This split has been called the Madonna-prostitute complex – good girls are bodyless (non-sexual), and bad girls are only sexual.

Normal women do not need to be seduced by phrases. They will have sex when the *relationship* calls for it. Marriage counsellors see any number of women who profess to love their husbands, yet who feel nothing during sex. A frigid woman cannot be loving because she cannot give of herself totally. Only a fully sexual person can be loving.

One might cavil with the foregoing and point to a number of so-called neurotics who seem to enjoy sex very much. Yet these self-same neurotics have great tension which they may have eroticised *mentally* and labelled 'sex', investing it with little more content than a good sneeze As evidence for this, I cite the fact that the majority of patients who lose their tension in the first few weeks of therapy also lose their sex drive for a while. In some cases, it disappears completely for a period of weeks. Further, both men and women who believed that they were quite sexual before treatment state they had no idea what a real sexual feeling was until they learned to feel again after Primal Therapy. Women, particularly, who claimed not to be frigid report on the differences in the kinds of orgasms they enjoy after therapy – a fuller, more convulsive experience, as a rule. One man put it this way: 'My orgasm used to be like squirts out of my penis. Now it seems like my whole body is with it.'

One's whole body can be 'with it' when each portion of previous suppressions (each denial of self) has been re-lived and resolved. Those denials need not have been sexual; the body does not differentiate between its self-denials. To suppress part of the feeling self is to suppress sexuality.

FRIGIDITY AND IMPOTENCE

From my observations of patients over the past decade and a half, I have found the prevalence of frigidity and impotence extremely high. This is especially so with frigidity.

By frigidity, I mean the inability to obtain full sexual feeling. Most often this means an inability to achieve a climax. How women act as a result of frigidity varies with the personality. Some women become promiscuous based on the hope that they will find just the right man who can make them feel. If the problem has been with Mother, the frigid person may simply ignore sex. What she experiences through her action, then, may be the *hope* of retaining her dignity and honour and so keep Mother's love.

Many frigid women find that they can have a climax only

when they masturbate. This is a good example of relating to one's own needs instead of to a partner. Women who do this have often masturbated since the early teens, usually accompanied by the same kind of fantasy. The penis in these cases may be only symbolic of threat, dishonour, of invasion, etc. and is avoided because of its meaning (which is usually unconscious).

An example: A woman is reared by a prudish mother who fills her full of myths about sex, men and morality. She hears such things as 'Men are animals, only after one thing. They'll love you and leave you.' In addition to what she hears, there is proof in the form of a brutish father. The young girl comes to believe what Mother has said. She denies herself any sex experience until marriage, only to discover she is frigid. She complains to her doctor that her vagina seems to be anaesthetised. What I believe happens is that this woman no longer experiences sex in her vagina. She experiences *fear*, based on the *denial* of sexual feeling. It is not necessarily a conscious fear, but having no father to go to and having to rely on Mother for what crumbs of affection there were at home, she came to associate free sexuality with loss of hope for Mother's approval. What she did, then, was almost literally give up part of her feeling self for her mother.

Figuratively speaking, her vagina belonged to her mother. *Not feeling* became the girl's way of presenting the image to Mother of the 'nice girl' whom she could be proud of. Once she felt the hopelessness of parental love, however, an abundance of new vaginal sensations was produced, which is the case in many of my patients.

Why did feeling the hopelessness of ever getting her mother's love free this woman to feel her vagina? Because she was trying to find that love in each sexual contact – by being the 'good' (i.e., frigid and unsexual) little girl her mother wanted. The 'good' girl was the only one Mother would love. Giving up on *that* love freed her from the struggle of trying to get it symbolically through her frigid vagina. A previously frigid woman explained her frigidity in the light of her completed Primal Therapy: 'I grew up in a very religious household where sex was never mentioned, much less condemned. There was talk about "loose" women and promiscuity – enough to scare me about sex. Later in order to accept my own body's sexual feelings, I had to imagine I was someone else during the sex act. Often my mind just wouldn't recognise what my body was feeling so it often conjured up scenes of being held down and raped. Then, and only then, could I feel sexual.'

Another woman had to fantasy having cunnilingus by another woman. She married an effeminate man who preferred this mode of sexual relations, so the fantasy was made that much easier for her. Again, in the Primal view, the fantasy – that is, the *experience* during sex – is an attempt to fill the real needs to be loved and kissed by Mother. It is fulfilling the needs that produce the ability to *feel* (sexual) and (ultimately) heterosexual beings. But unreal fantasy can never fulfil real needs, so the symbolic behaviour becomes repetitious and compulsive. When this woman's husband attempted to penetrate her with his penis, she became completely frigid, and intercourse was extremely painful. In its inimitable 'language', the body was telling her that there was Pain inside.

We must not ascribe frigidity solely to faulty sex education or bad sexual experiences. Many young girls are so shut down that we can predict they will be frigid. If a young girl has deadened herself and can barely feel any sensation (such as the taste of food), in all likelihood she later will be deadened to sexual sensations. This means she will need quite intense stimulation to feel almost anything in what she learns is a forbidden area. This is the reason I believe frigidity is such a frequent problem. A repressed woman is bound to be frigid to some extent. Scarcely a woman who has had Primal Therapy doesn't feel completely different in sex, even though she may not have come for an overt sexual problem.

To give the reader an idea of the complexity of frigidity, here are the words of one previously frigid woman who had completed one month of Primal Therapy:

'One thing I learned from this therapy is how my body helped block my feelings. I had been frigid, so I thought to myself that my tight vagina must be the way I defended myself against some feeling connected with it. I got home from a group session, took off my panties, and physically opened my vagina with my hands so that it was wide open. Then I let myself feel whatever there was to feel. To my amazement, a memory came into my head at the same time that I began to feel a pain around my vagina. Suddenly I was on my bassinet; my mother was diapering me roughly and pinching my vagina. I remember that she always gave it a little pinch while she was diapering me. I felt my vagina close off to stop that hurt. The next day I had the first pain-free sex with my husband.'

This is the point Wilhelm Reich has made (that the body forms a defence). However, this woman could have spread apart her vagina manually for days with no appreciable result if she had not already felt many Pains which paved the way for her early memory on that bassinet. It was the connection, not the physical manipulation of her vagina, that was crucial. Opening her vagina manually did help unblock a specific defence in much the same way that loosening a tight abdomen through deep breathing will bring up feeling.

This situation reminds me of another event which occurred to an impotent man. During one of his Primals he was urged to go into his most fearful fantasy – that of incest with his mother. During the fantasy a memory came to him of being left alone by her at nursery school. He felt bad (and here began to re-live that painful scene). In order to make himself feel better, he began to play with his penis. In the Primal he connected feeling alone and wanting his mother with playing with his penis. He wanted her to return and make him feel better, not so alone. Later this turned into a fantasy of wanting sex with Mother. As he became older, these fantasies frightened him. For some reason unbeknown to him, they changed into homosexual fantasies, which continued into adulthood. During this Primal he finally felt what it all was: 'Don't worry, Mama, it isn't you I want. It is men.'

This man suffered from homosexual fantasies for years because of an event which occurred in nursery school. Obviously, that one event alone didn't turn the tide, but he was neglected and left alone enough early in his life to make that event crucial. His homosexual fantasies, painful and troublesome as they were, served to cover something even more intolerable – incestuous feelings towards his mother.

Many frigid women (and impotent men) find they can function better in sex after a few drinks. This is so because liquor dulls Primal Pains, thus easing the need of the unreal self to control the body. Remember that the need for the unreal system is to control Pains. With lessened or dulled Pains, the need for control is decreased. As control is minimised, the body can let go more. What does letting go mean? Less mental control over the feelings of the body. Unfortunately, alcohol also dulls sensations during sex so that the experience is not as rich as it might be.

Sex means feeling the body, not controlling it. If that body is holding back old feelings, letting go means to let go of those feelings. Thus, some women become 'tigresses' in bed, clawing, scratching and biting, mistakenly believing that they are sexually passionate. There is passion, true, but that passion is not sexual. It is repressed rage, which is brought up when the body starts to feel. Here again we see that feeling is an all-or-nothing proposition. To feel at all means to feel everything. It may be that sex for neurotics is half violence, and perhaps the juxtaposition of sex and violence in movie advertisements is not accidental. But it is not necessarily violence which is repressed. Some women who cry just after the height of their sexual experience are expressing repressed sadness. Whatever the repressed Pains, the person cannot feel full sexuality until all contaminating neurotic feelings are out of the way.

Sexual frigidity is not only a problem of sexual feelings; it is a problem of feeling. To be free to feel means to be free sexually. To be suppressed means to be suppressed sexually – even when there seems to be adequate sexual functioning. When a person comes for Primal treatment and says she has only a sexual problem, we soon learn about her other fears and suppressions. Conversely, when someone comes for other problems, we must suspect sexual problems. The problem is not with parts of us; those parts are connected and interdependent.

In conventional therapy I have helped women understand their puritanical attitudes about sex and often advised on sex technique, but it rarely did any good. Feeling Pains in Primal Therapy seems to undo sex problems without any discussion of technique. The way to the vagina does not seem to be through the head.

The neurotic has a storehouse of Pains which prevent new information from making the body feel. Sexual information will remain mental, then, until the body is liberated.

A physician's wife whom I had seen years ago used to sneak off into a CCC camp near her home and have sex with five or six men, one after another. She was looking for just the right man to turn her on. But no man could turn her on because she had effectively turned herself off. And only she could turn herself back on. Though this woman was intelligent and *knew* that her trips to the labour camp were fruitless and dangerous, though I had pointed out to her what she was really doing, it did not stop her. She had needs which drove her relentlessly. *Knowing* the dangers, *understanding* why she was doing it, did not stop her because her needs did not stop. She wanted to feel.

I believe that it is a mistake to think that one can receive a liberal sex education, thereby change his attitudes about sex, and, by fiat of this changed attitude, solve sexual problems. No matter how much education, no matter how liberated one becomes about sex, sexual dysfunctions will persist until those new attitudes grow out of the body and its feelings.

Cultural factors must be considered in sexual problems; the general subjugation of women – the belief that they are put on earth to make men happy – has bred special notions, such as a 'feminine' psychology. Implicit in the idea that women should make men happy is that men are superior and that women should live for their man. This again is pure neurosis. No one can live for anyone else or through them without being sick – which, unfortunately, is how many men want their woman. No one can make another person feel anything and that includes feeling 'happy'. It is the job of humans to live.

Neurotics think that women have to be romanced – soft lights, special phrases and drinks – to become aroused. So instead of getting down to sex, a struggle is played out in which a woman is seduced. A woman who does not require this seduction, who is open and free about her sexual wants, is too often considered immoral. Part of the reason for this is that men who feel quite unmanly seem to feel that to be aggressive with women – to conquer them sexually – will somehow make them real men. Dominating a woman won't make a man feel any more manly than dominating a child will make an adult feel important.

In a non-split, non-neurotic society there will not be this cleavage between men and women. They will be equals with the same needs and feelings. There will be no masculine or feminine psychology because that would be a split psychology.

PERVERSIONS

There are times when a person needs more than a mental fantasy during sex. A man may wear a dress, put on makeup, walk down the street, yet still know he is a man. But should he wear a dress and actually believe that he is a girl, he has taken a giant step along the symbolic path to unreality. Inner pressures may make a man not only fantasise being beaten during sex but may require him to be actually flagellated in order to achieve orgasm.

Perversion implies that the weight of past denials has mounted beyond the person's usual method of coping and, for the moment of the ritual, has engulfed him in almost total symbolic behaviour – perhaps a momentary quasi psychosis.

A man I had seen, needed to be tied down and beaten by a woman in order to achieve an erection. Although this ritual had a number of psychological facets, it seemed to stem mainly from the relationship with his sadistic mother who beat and abused him constantly. What he seems to have done is to have re-created his old mother-son relationship in an almost literal way with the same unconscious hope he held years before – to be beaten enough to find surcease, pleasure and kindness.

This masochistic ritual was a circumscribed drama that symbolised a whole host of past experiences which the person tried to resolve vicariously. At its nucleus lies hope – hope for someone to see his suffering and put an end to it. It seems to take real blood and bruises for some parents to have even an inkling that their children need help. Some children dramatise it by stealing cars, others by setting fires, and some by being beaten. The contrived ritual of the pervert can be considered an extension of the *unconscious* ritual that the neurotic plays out in all his experiences during the day. In the generalised ritual, for example, he may *act* beaten and defeated, as if to say, 'Don't hurt me any more, I'm down already.' The non-perverted neurotic seems to have a more generalised, rather than contrived, ritual.

One patient who was an exhibitionist tried to describe his perversion: 'It's like when you're too young to know better, somebody systematically sets out to blow your mind. My mother hated men. Maybe she was a dyke. I guess I tried to be a girl for her. Eventually, I had to show my penis to strange women on street corners to prove I wasn't a girl. I was pretty far gone to have to do something like that.' This man, married and with children, certainly had all the visible evidence he needed of his virility and manliness. It didn't seem to matter. He had to continue his ritual until he went back and re-lived the origins of his ritual, re-lived all the ways that he contorted himself in order to make his mother say one kind thing.

Though this man knew better, he was impelled into his act through an uncontrollable force. This impulsiveness can possibly offer us some insight into impulsivity in general. The real desires of this man – to be a male – pushed through, no matter how his horrid experiences had turned him around. This aim of his ritual, then, was to be what he was – real. It doesn't seem to matter what a person *tells* himself he should or should not do when that self has been denied over and over again and now presses for release. I view impulsivity as propelled by tension, by old feelings which make the current impulsive act irrational. The impulsive person is not acting on feelings; he is acting on *denied* feelings. This is the opposite of the spontaneous act which is based on feelings. Spontaneous behaviour is less likely to be irrational, no matter how quick the response, because it is a response of a real person to real conditions.

What seems to eradicate perversion is to feel and call out the implied message in the ritual. For example, if the exhibitionist wanted to say (by showing his penis), 'Let me be a boy, Mama,' then he will have to feel all the ways that he was not permitted to be that boy. Each scene remembered – that is, each new Primal – will remove one more piece of the exhibitionistic ritual until no more impulses are left. Each scene will re-live the ways his mother did not let him be a boy ('Don't touch your penis. Don't have sex with girls.' Keeping the young boy in curls. Not letting him engage in sports, and so on). Each of those incidents when his mother forced him away from being what he was (a boy) built the perversion until it was acted out. Each re-living of those scenes dismantles the perversion as methodically and surely as it was built. During one Primal, for example, an exhibitionist held his penis, shouting, 'Mommy, it's not dirty. It's all right. It's me I'm holding. Let me feel me!'

This man's exhibitionism, as with any perversion, really made sense. He was trying to be real by showing his penis – obviously, an unreal way to do it. But though his whole history had tried to make him into a girl, the need to be what he was persisted, albeit in a distorted way.

Perversions are easily treated by Primal Therapy because of their obvious symbolism. They are really 'packaged Primals.' They usually say directly what the need is without guesswork. By simply stopping the ritual, the tremendous force that impelled the ritual turns immediately into a Primal – and into its proper connections.

Lenny

Lenny is a twenty-six-year-old graduate psychologist. Though he had studied psychology and abnormal behaviour for years in college and put his background to practice in the agency where he worked, it helped not a bit in overcoming his own personal problems, as we can see – dramatic evidence that knowledge alone is not sufficient to change neurosis. When Lenny was into his ritual, he was in another world where everything he had learned about behaviour was forgotten. Lenny's case helps us understand perversion, in general, and impulsivity in specific terms.

I came to therapy after having been arrested for exposing my penis and masturbating in public. I had been a compulsive masturbator at home, but that did not seem to relieve all my tension. I took to doing it on street corners or in my car beside bus stops filled with women. Whenever I was alone for long at home, I'd be overcome by some impulse to go out and masturbate. I just could not control myself. I became a full-fledged exhibitionist.

Where other people might reach for a cigarette or a drink to ease their tension, I used my penis. All I ever knew was that when I was alone, I began to feel bad and I wanted to feel good. But in time my fantasies of women during masturbation at home were not enough, owing to the nature of my sickness. All of my pre-therapy symptoms were physical – asthma, ulcers, sinus trouble, post-nasal drip and chronic dandruff (all gone now). I was always body-oriented. I seemed to have to do something physical. I knew I was getting sicker when mental pictures during masturbation were not sufficient. But I didn't know what to do. I had to see the look on women's faces – real, live women. I would walk down a street searching for a woman whose face I could watch during my act. Sometimes I would drive in a car and park near her. During my orgasm, I would look into her face – I wanted to be sure she saw me. I was sort of living out my fantasy.

After my orgasm I would feel tremendously relieved like some great weight had been lifted. I would drive away feeling free and go to work trying to help other people, just like nothing happened. But it was only a matter of time until I had to do it again.

What started out as little forays on the street occasionally ended as a full-time occupation. I would spend four or five hours a day at it; nothing else was on my mind. I knew I was going crazy because one part of me knew how insane all this was while the rest of me just had to do it.

What happened was my mind just took off from my body. I mean, I was doing things with my body that my mind didn't even known about. During my exhibitionistic rituals I was in some kind of haze. I knew where I was dimly, but I was in a fog at the same time. My impulses seemed to come from something besides my conscious mind.

I tried to fight it; my profession and my job were at stake. When the impulse hit me, I would try to deny it, but it was impossible. My conscious mind seemed to be crumbling. The force inside me was increasing day by day, and I never knew why. Mental confusion took the place of rational thought, so that even at work I couldn't think straight. During all this I felt like two people. I was an actor and an observer. During my episodes there was no question of knowing right from wrong. It was like a fugue state where someone goes off and kills five people. I was just the other unconscious person doing my things.

I know now after therapy that soon I would have gone crazy. I was losing more and more control of my self. My mind was going. One day I'm sure I would have stayed in the fog, and that would have been that. I guess what this means is that my body would have been completely apart from my mind, each doing a separate thing.

As that neurotic person I was unable to experience what was making me impulsive. It was too painful. The pain was coming up whenever I was alone, and I just acted it out. During therapy when the pain came up, I just felt it. This is the difference between feeling and acting out that I learned so well during Primal Therapy.

During therapy I allowed the impulse to envelop me. Rather than split away from the feeling and masturbate, I finally allowed my mind to go where my body was – and that was to some pretty horrible truths. I remember my first Primal: I came in feeling my impulse. I almost drove down a street looking for a woman on my way to the office. The therapist said to let the impulse happen to me. I got a hard-on and felt terribly sexual. I thought I was going to come, for sure. At the height of the feeling, I began screaming, 'No! No! No!' Then I saw a woman's face. Jesus, it was my mother's face. I yelled, 'Mommy, I hurt, I hurt!' I began screaming, 'Don't leave me alone; Daddy will kill me.' I could never tell her how frightened of my father I was. I understood instantly that when I exhibited my penis. I wanted a strange woman to see my face twisted in orgasm (in fear and pain) and recognise that I needed protection. But it was my mother who needed to know my fear. Somehow because of the way she was, I never dared tell her. She was too sick herself for me to dare say I needed her help. So I said it in a pretty crazy way in front of bus stops.

The pressure that drove me to do all that was fear of my father and need for protection from my mother. When I connected all that vague pressure to what it was, I didn't have to act it out any more. In fact, there was no more pressure – just pain.

Before therapy, my mind was never with my body. I'll never know how I got through school. I still can hardly spell or read. But I was a good athlete, and I could fix anything with my hands – plumbing, electrical stuff, anything. I had to be stupid because when I got smart and made the mental connections with all that pressure which drove me into the streets, I found myself flopping all over Dr Janov's office like a fish. Those feelings were a powerhouse. I know now that if I could not have kept up the acting out, if I didn't get out on bail after I was arrested and had to stay in prison, I would certainly have gone crazy. I exhibited myself because it was the only way I instinctively knew to keep the feelings away. To stand still and do nothing would have exploded my mind. Crazy as it sounds, even after being arrested, *knowing* what trouble I was in, I still went out and masturbated in front of women while awaiting trial! I had no choice.

Prior to therapy, I always thought of myself as highly sexed – a 'fuck freak' as I used to say. But now I've changed those orgasm convulsions into Primal ones, and my sex drive is far less. It's the reverse of what I did originally. Originally, I changed my Primals into sex convulsions because I couldn't feel the Pain. Perversion is very unsexual, in my opinion. I masturbated, but all I really wanted was help. It was my way of yelling 'Help!' What I did was not related to natural sex drive; it was a perversion of another feeling. Many of us are perverted in different ways. Businessmen pervert their need for love into making deals. I perverted my feelings into my penis. All I wanted was for my mother to see my hurt and finally give me what I lacked as a child.

Jim

I am twenty-two years old and was born in Alabama. I now live in Los Angeles, the one city that had always symbolised to me all that was impersonal, unresponding, crass, dirty, superficial, pretentious, tense and desperate. Thinking of or being in Los Angeles always threatened to make me *feel* how impersonal, insensitive, superficial my own life had been. It is now simply a dirty, tense city that doesn't make me feel anything.

My father is a career officer in the Air Force. He is also a Presbyterian minister and was from a small town in Indiana. My mother is from Mississippi.

I never had a home. My earliest memories are of Japan, where I once ran away from home at the age of four and where my father was stationed. We moved every one to two years after that, travelling in the family Oldsmobile which served as temporary arena for family fights, whether we were driving past cacti in Arizona or totem poles along the

Alcan Highway. The car also served as the place I couldn't get away from when my mother decided to beat me with a rubber hose when I misbehaved. I finally left the hose in a Denver motel's bathroom garbage can.

All the travelling could have been fun for a kid; sometimes it was, in spite of the fact that as a family we never knew a happy moment. Everything was a struggle, an argument. Whether it was which motel to stay at, what TV programme to watch or where to stop and eat, it was always a verbal hassle. The same thing applied to my very personal choices of what to wear, who to be friends with, when to be sleepy, how to eat and so on. She was always there to tell me what *she* thought was best, and with the kind of inflection in her voice that said, 'Go ahead and do what you want – if you don't care about me.' AAGH! This was a devastatingly effective method for her to use to get me to do and *be* what she wanted. You see, I did care about my mom (and my dad) – more than any other two people in the world, naturally. So when she says she doesn't believe I love her, she is also saying, 'There's no point in our continuing this relationship.' – i.e., she won't love me any more 'either' UNLESS I do and be what she wants. It's a lousy choice, but a youngster is in no position to bargain. So first of all, any and all decisions I make must be corroborated by Mommy. If she doesn't like what I like, I simply have to find out HOW TO HIDE MY FEELINGS and HOW TO DO AND BE WHAT SHE LIKES.

My mom does not like men, that is, ballsy men. So. First I can't be a man, even though, as all males are, I was born with a cock, tiny though it was. (And it never did get fully grown. Not yet.) By her constant daily and verbally opinionated ballsiness, my mom efficiently raised me as a transvestite. I got the message early. 'Mommy doesn't like me (to be me). She likes me when I'm what she likes.' There's not much to change when you are four, five, or seven except your sexuality; you don't have world opinions and theories to alter – just yourself. So . . .

With that as a starting and continuing factor in my upbringing, I also had the terrifying spectre of my parents' divorce looming in front and back of me for twenty-two years. (They are now finally getting divorced as I am about to finish therapy. They've struggled for a long time.) When I was seven, living in Texas, my father came home slightly drunk one night. According to my mom, he was more than slightly drunk, and she proceeded to get angry, shout and finally beat on my dad until *she* slumped to the floor, crying that she wouldn't be *hit* like that and sobbing she was going to get a divorce. I stood terrified beneath and beside them the whole time. The two of them hardly noticed I was there. I even tried to get between them, reaching up to their waists and pleading for them to stop and kiss and make up. I was old enough to have a notion of what 'divorce' meant: separation. It scared hell out of me. I said, 'Mom, what's going to happen to me, what about me?' Mom said, 'I don't know,' and proceeded to pack her trunk. Neither she nor my dad cared one hell of a lot about me then. I padded around the house with my stuffed horse, muttering, 'What's going to happen to me? What's going—' etc. I'd been padding and muttering ever since until Primal Therapy.

When I got home from school the next day, after having fretted all day about who I would 'go' with (Mom, of course), I found that all was well. (Good and sick.) Dad would 'never do it again' (poor guy), and Mom would not leave. For the next fifteen years it was the same scene over and over for me, always anticipating with dread the separation that never came, but that was always there anyway.

I haven't mentioned Dad much because Dad wasn't there very much. I've hated him because he wouldn't protect me from destruction by Mom. And I loved him deeply the few moments we had together. Daddy and I wanted to love each other but were afraid to let our feelings out because we would hurt so much.

With a neurosis and a family like mine, I had to be careful not to get too close to my feelings. Stay cool when with the family. On the outside, *act* strong and independent. Transvestites aren't even as 'in' as plain homosexuals. There is a difference. So I was a very active and lonely kid. I was so afraid of girls that I didn't kiss my first girl good night until I was a sophomore in high school on my thirteenth date. And she was older than me, besides, which figures.

I beat off a lot and that kept my tension down some, but I had to be careful because Mom was always about to catch me. She didn't like me feeling my cock.

I discovered at the end of my sophomore year that not only was I good with words and ideas from repeated verbal struggles with Mom, but I could also run very fast. By the end of my junior year I was all-state in the sprints and beginning to take out girls. By the end of my senior year I was all-state again, graduation speaker, state oratory champion, journalist and on my way to college as a general red-hot. I was miserable. For a long time, when my mom was out of the house, I had taken to putting on her clothes – bra, nylons, panties, etc. – acting out my fantasy that if I was like what Mommy wanted, she would finally want and love me. It was a shitty deal, to say the least, and a difficult way to get to feeling good about feeling my prick.

I repressed such activities in college. I kept the fantasy in my mind and simply beat off like everyone else. The work load and the atmosphere were so overpowering that pretty soon even beating off wasn't helping much. I hardly dated. Also, running track was so dead serious, sick, and difficult with studies that it didn't help get much tension off. But my track affiliation was good enough to get me into a good fraternity, so the next year had something in it to look forward to. Grades did not help, C+ and B−. No prestige, no attention, no relief from feeling alone and insignificant.

The end of my sophomore year I became an activist. The track coach turned out to be a bigot. He kicked a foreign student off the team because he had a long Beatle haircut. Another disillusionment. I was mediator. I got tense, sorry and sick of track and all the other irrelevant bullshit the college was trying to feed me.

That summer I had a girlfriend for the first time in my life. She was the first person I ever let myself feel with. But I could never let myself even bring up the subject of fucking even when my cock was right in her hands and we were in bed. I wanted a girl to let me feel my prick, but I wanted to feel it safely and she let me. But it was stormy. For six months she and I struggled like hell to give some permanency and stability to our mutual tension-relieving. But alas, she dumped all over me. I had nothing to fall back on and almost went crazy. I was scared badly enough to drop out of school and began writing my Kierkegaardian-type notebooks, *à la* Bob Dylan, Ken Kesey, *et al.* I was so tense that writing about myth, existential awareness and tragic heroic common little people seemed the only way to stay sane. I was trying to keep the Pain down; and I did.

At that point I made the remarkable discovery that no one had the right to tell me when to kill someone else. Very simple. But simplicity, like feeling, had simply escaped me since I started worrying about what was going to happen to me. I was so elated by the simple notion that I turned it into sort of an anti-dogma. I did some resistance work in Arizona and tried to figure out how to synthesise politics and art. To go to jail over the draft, or to expatriate and write my great books to the world and die at thirty-nine? How to do both? Big questions. Big feelings underneath. About Mom and Dad. Needing to feel worthwhile (Mom); needing to help people stop fighting (Mom and Dad); needing to find a home of peace and simplicity and permanence (all of us together); needing to be strong and effective (Dad); and so on. I turned in my draft card, but in a very unantagonising manner. I would write and study until they came and put me into jail. Very passive.

The first day in therapy I was telling Art about how I wanted to tell my dad to fuck off when Dad refused to give me the money for therapy. Art said, 'Really?'

I said, 'Well, I'd also like him to have helped me.'

'Ask him.'

'On the phone?'

'Just ask him, right here.'

I started, but my throat clogged. 'I don't want to do this, and you know I don't.'

'Ask him!'

I did, and the next thing I knew I had been writhing all over the couch screaming for Dad to help me and FEELING the anger in my body and mind that I had repressed for so long. As I ran out of energy and began to relax, my hands began to tingle as when the circulation has been cut off and they begin to 'wake up'. Colours in the office were brighter, like on grass, only with no surrealistic separation of time and space. I could feel my gut. And it was only the beginning.

It was enough for the day. I walked out feeling great. By that afternoon I felt shitty. Other feelings were starting to come out now that the tension was cracking. WATCH OUT. WHAT'S GOING TO HAPPEN?

The next day I was anticipating the Primal and was trying to make things happen. Which has been my way of not feeling. For five days I fucked around until finally, in the group,

I was so tense it finally exploded naturally with my dad again. Wanting him to help. The next day it was tears, deep tears. I had been so lost – all my life – never really listened to, and most of all I had tried so hard to achieve something that would make Mom and Daddy happy so they could love me. Unhappy parents don't have the time to let their kids be themselves. Love requires unselfish attention.

Since that time I have gone through one feeling after another. Some are anger, some aloneness, some are sad and some are very subtle sensations of warmth, smell, cold, taste and touch that must be linked to the memory in mind that they belong to. It's a process of putting your head completely back in touch with your body. It's feeling all the repressed feelings so there is no longer anything to be afraid of feeling. It's hell and it's wonderful.

Sometimes the feelings have come out easy; sometimes they require days to build until the tension cracks. I went through one three-week period of feeling very crazy, as when my girl had left me. It was a total separation from feeling effected by THINKING every second about what might happen next. It got to where I could almost SEE the invisible shield between my body and the world around me. It got thicker. I figured a big feeling was on the way. Okay. I'd help it get here. BULLSHIT. It was a very sophisticated way of not feeling. To control, to anticipate and to guide. One morning I went into Art's office and talked to Mom and Dad at that Primal Scene where I first asked, 'What's going to happen to me? Don't get divorced.' I said it feeling the fear, like a seven-year-old kid. I finished, and the shield was going away. I relaxed. I would just let things happen. Later on I was to go deeper into that feeling, and more of the shield disappeared. Now every time I have a Primal feeling I can let myself feel a little more of the present. The shield has been destroyed.

What I'm beginning to experience as a result of Primal Therapy is simply MYSELF. At first I felt stronger in a neurotic way. I was getting a little freedom of feeling for the first time in my life and it really charged up my hopes and dreams. But hopes and dreams are the symptoms of repressed feelings. They are the abstract words we use to refer to and cover up our NEED. When all the NEED has been felt, there is no more HOPE to fill it. There is just being alive. No more need for political utopia or artistic success. There is no such thing as success or failure. Just YOU. ME. There is no more need for me to be a chronic tragic failure so someone can pick me up like Mom and Dad never picked me up. Or hugged me or listened to me.

It's not completely over for me yet. I still need my mom and dad a little. There is still more NEED left to feel. But I'm all but through with my dad, and Mom is only left in part. I still have an occasional dream where I'm caught naked in the ladies' supermarket with a hard-on and no place to hide it and wanting to have it if only some kind lady or my mom would be nice enough to let me feel it. That is acting out in my head, while asleep, what I want to feel for real.

Still, I've changed incredibly. My voice is almost an octave lower because I'm no longer disconnected from my stomach. I hear people the *first* time they say something instead of making them repeat. I no longer (need to) rap for hours with my sick friends about what is happening in the world. I have lost about twenty pounds without thinking about it because I no longer eat to avoid feeling my stomach being empty and lonely like the rest of me was. I don't smoke the pack of Camels a day that I had begun to smoke after quitting track. They now taste awful. Alcohol no longer uninhibits me but simply makes me clumsy. FOOD TASTES. Real objects are no longer symbols that set off trains of thought and piles of tension. Cops are just cops, not my father. (I don't like them better; I simply don't feel angry towards them any more.) The ocean is just the ocean, not the MOTHER AND FATHER OF LIFE; a cracked mirror is no longer the symbol of Irish art; etc.

Tits are *almost* just tits. A cunt is almost just a cunt. They are nothing like the symbols they used to be, and they won't be at all much longer.

I am well enough and FEELING ENOUGH TO know what REAL is and it's like nothing I *expected* and everything that has always been ME.

As a result of the therapy, everything is becoming literal. Money strikes me funny because it is simply little bits of metal that we carry around and trade for things. It's like all that unreal stuff hasn't any relevance any more to my life. It's as though words don't mean anything any more, just feeling. I feel like that world I live in is like a whole pop art scene – all a put-on. I think that everyone is in the wrong ball game, and they don't know it because they're so busy playing the game. It's even boring me to write about it, like, who cares? At last I've turned completely around. Transvestism is a thing of the past. All my life I was told that my sanity was insane, and I came to believe it. Now, I understand that they are insane and I'm the sane one.

HOMOSEXUALITY

The homosexual act is not a sexual one. It is based on the *denial* of real sexuality and the acting out symbolically through sex of a need for love. A truly sexual person is heterosexual. The homosexual has usually eroticised his need so that he appears to be highly sexed. Bereft of his sexual fix, his lover, he is like an addict without his connection; without his lover, he is in the Pain that is always there but which is drained off sexually. But sex is not the goal – love is.

The homosexual is usually the tensest of all neurotics because of how far he has been made to go from his real self. The tension can drive him to liquor, drugs and compulsive sex, and these outlets are still not enough. Many homosexuals I have seen report psychosomatic complaints. The violence we see in homosexuals is the result of self-denial. When a person cannot be what he is, he is angry.

I would define homosexuality as any act between two people which is experienced as though it were occurring between members of the same sex. If a man makes love to a woman but is totally involved during it with a fantasy about men, I would call the experience homosexual. The motions one goes through are less critical than the internal situation. When a person actually makes love to a member of his own sex, it means that he is more totally involved in the symbolic behaviour. There is no split or fragmented part of him that drives him to hold onto heterosexuality; he has given up the battle and become more completely what he is not.

There are men and women who have homosexual marriages but do not recognise the fact. An effeminate man selects a masculine woman for a mate – he may, as one patient reported, prefer to be on the bottom in sex, rationalising that he is more comfortable that way – without once recognising he is essentially having sex with a man. There is some kind of special radar that drives these people to find each other. The man with an unconscious need for a loving father, yet too fearful of admitting to homosexual impulses, will become involved with a mannish woman instead. He will relate to those masculine aspects of her so that she will be the mechanic around the house, handle the finances, drive the car, and so on. The point is that when you are neurotic, you can make anyone into something he is not. Thus, a man can make a woman into a man in his mind in the same way that he makes a policeman into his father or a teacher into his mother. It is the need which is uppermost.

Someone who must fantasise during sex is closer to his feelings than someone who lives out his fantasy. Fantasy at least connotes a mental recognition of a need – more correctly, a recognition of a symbol of the need. Living it out means total suppression of the need and its symbols.

It has been my experience that homosexuality may derive from any number of permutations of family interaction. A homosexual boy can have a weak father, tyrannical father, no father. What matters is that the boy has a need for a *loving* father. There is no reason to work through the specific relationships the boy had. What must be reached is the need. It is the need that is being acted out in homosexuality.

Much depends on the child himself. If the child is naturally athletic, he may become the kind of rugged person the father wants. If he is weak and unco-ordinated, he may be completely rejected because he didn't fit in with his father's needs. If his mother is a bit warmer, this child may become closer to her; if his mother is cold, the child may try desperately to be like his father. No one family constellation produces homosexuality.

A young boy with a brutal, drunken father may well turn against things masculine. Another boy with the same father may decide to be the kind of decent man his father wasn't. If a mother hates men, it may turn her daughter against men. If a mother is a hateful human being, it may turn her daughter against women. There is no formula which accounts for a specific neurosis. The child's inner reaction to what happened is what must be understood.

The child's resultant behaviour usually isn't a consciously thought-out decision; a slow accretion of experiences warp him into an image to fulfil the parent's repressed needs. What this means in practical terms is that he must be what his parents need him to be so as to make them (and thus himself) temporarily comfortable. If his mother cannot tolerate aggressiveness and she believes men to be sexual beasts, her attitude and behaviour will soon let the child know that it is not safe to be either aggressive or sexual.

Because the young child cannot understand that his father is a sadist or that his mother is a lesbian with a hatred for things male, he comes to believe that whatever he does naturally is wrong. He may deny more and more of his natural inclinations until one day he is totally inverted.

Many homosexuals do not seem to realise what appears so obvious – they are in pursuit of substitutes. Many apotheosise homosexual love as the only true love and may cite the Greeks to prove it. But it is unreal love made by unreal people. What gives the sexual search of the homosexual such intensity is the need to feel loved at last and so to find an end to nagging tension.

'Each new sexual contact left me slightly dissatisfied, and I never knew why,' a former homosexual told me. 'I thought it was a penis I wanted, the bigger, the better – until I got it. Then I needed more and more. After I felt how much I wanted my father, I knew that it wasn't a penis I wanted. I guess I became a *screaming fag* because I could never scream for that bastard.' This patient said that his effeminate behaviour early in his teens was a constant scream for what never came – his parents' help.

Another patient, whose parents were 'dead' inside and completely unfeeling, said, 'I know now why I used to be so hung up on blowing guys. I think I was literally trying to suck some life from someone.' What homosexuals, both male and female, seem to agree upon after Primal treatment is that each of their previous homosexual contacts seem to mean 'Mommy (or Daddy), love me!' If we can agree that homosexuality in most cases is this need for parental love, we can then say that the aim of homosexuality is heterosexuality. I do not think that this statement is simply semantics. It means that the aim of all neurosis is to have one's Pain taken away so as to be a real, feeling person. When the Pain is gone, we would expect the homosexuality to be gone also, and this does happen.

What the above indicates as well is that no amount of heterosexual acts can alter the homosexual state until that Pain is felt. Having sex with dozens of women cannot, I believe, take away the desperate need of a man for his father. This means that no amount of hugging, kissing and fondling from either men or women *in the present* will alter sexual deviation.

What the homosexual may experience when he is kissed by a woman is something symbolic – father's love. Those kisses do not fulfil the real need; nor do the kisses of a man fulfil that need, for that matter. Women's kisses and caresses may even deepen the homosexuality in the male homosexual by temporarily covering the need for a father. Women's warmth, then, prevents him from feeling his Pain, which is the very thing he must do in order to become heterosexual.

Would the homosexual man need male love if he were fully loved by his mother early in life? I think not. He needs male love because he was deprived of love by both parents, each in his own way. He seeks after male love because for a variety of reasons he was put in the struggle by a father who did not love him.

Even if a wonderfully loving father were suddenly to appear in the home when a boy reaches his teens I do not think it would make a significant difference. If that boy's past history made it necessary to deny himself and his needs in order to survive with a sadistic father, for example, then a loving stepfather who arrives later will not be able to undo that early history. This means that the boy, now in a loving home, still must experience his early Pains. This point is corroborated in areas other than homosexuality. Patients whose parents have 'mellowed' over the years still cannot undo the tension and the neurosis brought on by earlier hurts. The past is always in the way of the present. If a person could fully feel the love in the present, it means he could fully feel. But to feel fully, for the neurotic, means to feel all his Pain *first*, for that is what arises when he feels. After feeling the Pain, he can accept all the present love.

So long as old denials exist, they will impel distorted and

perverted symbolic behaviour. Homosexual marriages, for example, may go on for years. Both partners seem satisfied and loved, yet there exists a high tension level *and* homosexuality (neurosis). Why? Because homosexual lovers are satisfying themselves symbolically and not actually. They are usually trying to get Father's love out of each other. When they feel this real need, the symbolic quest drops away.[1] Homosexuality is not a special disease; it is only a different route for the satisfaction of deprived and often denied need.

As for going 'straight' without solving the neurosis, that only deepens the lie; it means to pretend to give up the need for the father's love, and no one can do that so long as that need is there and real. The only way to get rid of that need is to feel it.

IDENTITY AND HOMOSEXUALITY

If a person cannot be what he is, he will have to search for his identity. He will be foredoomed never to find it, since it is no more than the real, feeling self which was not allowed expression. Thus the search for identity is a neurotic enterprise, carried on by unfeeling people who generally need to find something or someone outside themselves to tell them what or who they are inside. The post-Primal patient, for example, would not suffer from an identity crisis. Because he *feels*, he would have no reason to wonder who he really is.

It is the Primal contention that only when a child is not allowed to be himself does he need to copy, consciously or not, the behaviours, ideals, attitudes and mannerisms of others. A child brought up by normal parents will not identify with them. They will not want him to do so. Rather, he will have attributes that are his own.

To clarify the above, we can ask the question 'Would a boy born into a world composed only of females become feminine?' I think not. If he were loved and allowed to be himself, I believe he would be quite masculine. If, however, this same boy were brought up by women who were neurotic there would be all the likelihood of his becoming feminine.

[1] Homosexual marriages tend to be unstable *just because* they are symbolic arrangements which cannot lastingly satisfy the partners.

People who struggle with the question 'Who am I?' do so because they had to be somebody else in order to get what looked like love from the parents. All the ways they were forced to *act* instead of *be* tend to confuse their so-called identity. The only person you can identify with is yourself. If you are not yourself, you will have to search for yourself. One woman told me, 'I went to Europe last year to find myself, but I wasn't there.'

One implication of the Primal view of identity would be that a single parent who is a loving human being can successfully raise either a male or a female child. A woman can rear a young boy who will grow up to be a real boy, without needing male models or father surrogates to pattern himself after. Some mothers will keep a child with a cold or brutal father because somehow they think the boy needs a father and might suffer sexually without one. It is more likely that a boy would turn out effeminate by staying with such a father than if he had no father at all.

I do not think that there is a major difference, in terms of pathology, between a boy who tries to identify with the 'he-man' and the one who identifies with women. The difference between a butch homosexual and a nellie seems only a difference in the direction of the flight from the Pain, rather than in levels of Pain. When a butch adopts tattoos and motorcycles, grows a beard, or takes up weight lifting, it can indicate that he still may not feel himself and must identify with what he *thinks* is masculine. He may still be after Father's love and attempts in various ways to be like the real man Father wanted. The nellie may have given up on Father and tried to copy Mother's interests and ways. Because the butch may have been unloved by a father, he still could be seduced by men, prefers the company of men, and in many ways seems similar to the effeminate homosexual. He may not feel any more manly than the nellie and may be worse off because his pretence must be so great.

In less obvious ways many men and women who cannot feel themselves adopt the trappings or the image of what they want to be. The man may sport a large moustache, boots, or rugged clothes, while a woman, in an attempt to appear feminine, may wear low-cut dresses or tight slacks. The very need to project an 'image' can be a clue to very opposite feelings inside, and with these buried feelings one often finds sexual dysfunctions as well. It has been my clinical experience that though a man may put up a good masculine front, the attempt to be a 'he-man' is often betrayed by impotence or homosexual fantasies or fears. 'The struggle', as one formerly bearded patient put it, 'was to keep my beard on long enough to feel like a man so I wouldn't need it any more. I didn't understand it then, but I do now.'

BISEXUALITY AND LATENT HOMOSEXUALITY

Since Freud, a number of schools of psychology have posited a basic bisexuality in man. They state that each of us is part heterosexual and part homosexual. The aim of a good defence system then would be to suppress the latent homosexual tendencies and work out a proper relationship with the opposite sex. Thus these theories believe that adolescent homosexuality may be normal until the youngster grows into what is called the genital stage of development. Homosexual dreams are also to be considered as part of normal functioning, according to some theories. *I do not think we are dealing with bisexuality so much as with neurosis.* So many of us have been deprived of love from *both* parents that there is often a lingering need for love from either sex. This need seems so universal it might be tempting to consider bisexuality a general phenomenon.

I do not believe that there is a basic genetic homosexual tendency in man. If this were true, the cured patient would still have his homosexual needs, which he does not. Post-Primal patients who have been latent and overt homosexuals before report no homosexual leanings, fantasies, or dreams. Judging by the way male and female parts fit together, it seems to make sense that given a healthy body, there is only heterosexuality. When we consider that sex between man and woman is the very essence of life, it is hard to find a logical rationale for the basic bisexuality theme.

One male patient told me this experience: 'At work I used to get aroused by the guys on the job. When a guy bent over, it was everything I could do to keep from looking at his ass. Standing close to my boss, I could hardly hear what he was saying because I was staring at his lips and thinking how it would feel to kiss him. I thought everyone was a little homosexual, so I pushed all these thoughts away and concentrated on thoughts about girls.' This man had great needs to be held and kissed by his father. He was not aware of these needs, however, since he hated his father, who had abandoned the family when he was ten. We might say that his latent homosexual needs were the most real part of him at the time and his heterosexual behaviour the least real, since it was only going through motions of pretending he didn't want men. What is latent in the neurotic, then, are the unresolved needs. When they are fully felt, they would no longer exist, latently or otherwise.

For example, if a young girl were deprived early in her life of warmth and cuddling from a mother, we would say that she had latent needs for female love. If she were later seduced by another woman who was kind and caressing, the latent tendencies become translated into overt behaviour. The difference between the latent and the overt homosexual, then, would only be the *act*, not the need. What prevents the act in many latent homosexuals may be fear, social disapproval, religious beliefs, etc. It may be that no one comes along at a critical time to seduce the latent homosexual girl; in that case the tendencies remain latent. Sometimes these latent tendencies are recognised, and at other times they are completely unknown to the person who may be busy acting out his latency instead of feeling it. If the person's social milieu militates against the acceptance of homosexuality, such as in a deeply religious home, it is likely that the latent tendency will not be recognised. The need remains underground, creating tension.

This concept of latency may be important to an understanding of behaviour such as addiction and alcoholism, where the rate of latent homosexual leanings is inordinately high among both men and women. The craving for some kind of physical relief, such as alcohol, seems almost inevitable in those who deny these leanings. The overt homosexual has at least given in to *apparent* wants and does find what he calls love from time to time. In this sense, he takes his unreality straight. The drunk and the addict pay a high price, evidently, for refusing to recognise any wants at all. The need for some kind of love by someone of the same sex may be equally as strong in the latent person as in the straight homosexual. Pretending that it isn't there changes it not at all. The person, such as the woman in the above example with a need for her mother, may find herself in women's clubs, or riding clubs, having special women pals, and drinking heavily, yet still not recognise her need.

The paradox of the male alcoholic is that often he uses his drinking as a measure of his masculinity. The drinking further masks his need until possibly he reaches the point of 'feeling no pain'. It may be then, when the fear cannot be felt any longer, that he can finally do what he's possibly wanted to do for years – put his arms around a man and hug him.

We may say that the essential difference between the latent and overt homosexual is that the latent has been brainwashed into *acting* like a man (or woman as the case may be). His ideas have been changed around so that they are no longer even close to how he really feels inside. He comes to believe the lie he lives. But there doesn't seem to be any way to wash away those latent feelings as one does with ideas. Though he thinks he needs no warmth and cuddling, the alcoholic finds it necessary to suck warmth out of a bottle until he can finally ease the knot in his gut and feel warm inside for a few moments. He may leave his house night after night to go to an anti-Pain station (a bar) and never recognise that he is in Pain. But to deprive him of even this symbolic behaviour might exacerbate his neurosis.

I think that if we all could recognise the latent tendencies in many of us for what they are – a need for parental love and not as some kind of strange perversion – we might be able to make headway into some of the critical social problems that plague us.

DISCUSSION

I think that it is essential for us to see sexually deviate behaviour as part of a total neurosis and not as some special, bizarre act disconnected from what the person is as a whole. but I do not think that it requires a specialist in homosexuality to treat him, any more than it requires a specialist to treat any other flight from Pain. The treatment of homosexuality does not mean producing either masculine or feminine behaviour. It means, to me, producing *real* behaviour.

Perhaps we have attempted to use categories and abstractions and have not seen that we have only been treating people who have found different ways to protect themselves against hurt.

Many homosexuals have not come for psychotherapy partly because we professionals have tended to consider it largely untreatable, as though it were some special disease that required special knowledge. I do not consider it any different from any other kind of neurosis except in degree of pathology. What this means is that if we can cure one neurosis, we should be able to cure any neurosis.

Psychotherapy has taken a number of approaches to the treatment of sexual deviation. Because of the failure of insight therapy, we often have only tried to help the homosexual accept this affliction and live more comfortably with it. One of the current treatment methods that seems to be finding favour among professionals is the use of conditioning methods. One of those already described involves presenting male homosexuals with pictures of nude males while administering a mild shock to their bodies. The aim, presumably, is to decondition (called aversion) the habit of homosexuality. Another method is to encourage the homosexual into heterosexual acts while having him tell himself that he isn't afraid of the opposite sex. Or he or she may simply be asked to imagine heterosexual relationships while being given relaxing suggestions.

Because conditioning methods do alter a number of sexually deviate behaviours, there is the appearance of cure in some cases. This helps complicate our understanding of cure – that is, if we look only at overt behaviour. If we look below the behaviour and measure the continuing high tension level, we may find that we have only modified the sex habit to bring it more into accord with the therapist's value system.

It is better to treat the latent homosexual *before* he has received overt homosexual pleasure. Once he has found this substitute satisfaction, he is more likely to believe that he has found what he really wants and less likely to come for help. Nevertheless, even if he should become homosexual for a period of years, I believe he can still be treated. The time he is most likely to come in for treatment is when he has lost his lover – his sexual fix. Without his lover, he hurts.

He may drink, cruise, travel to another city – all in flight from his terrible hurt that shadows him everywhere. When the homosexual stops his flight and actually feels his Pain, I think that he can be treated successfully. I have found that homosexual habits that have persisted for years have faded away in the face of reality. The homosexual is symbolic self without basic foundation. It evaporates with the Pain because it was only a fantasy in the first place.

I do not think that young children differentiate between male and female love. It is *human* warmth they need, not the special caresses of a woman or the hugs of a man. What produces neurosis, I submit, is the presence of someone who should be loving and who is not. It is the struggle to make them loving that I believe sets in motion deviation of any kind. If a child could always be spontaneous in his hugs and kisses, in his general relationship to his parents, I doubt if detours would be necessary.

Elizabeth

When I first met Elizabeth she was a lesbian. She looked, even walked, like a man. She was addicted to Methedrine (speed). She has now made a complete about-face and is a narcotic parole agent, helping those whose fate she knew so well. Her solution of the problem of frigidity has application to many other people who suffer from this widespread problem.

My name is Elizabeth. I was born in the South, with a twin brother, twenty-six years ago. I have a sister a year and a half younger. My father is a professor of engineering. My mother has worked at odd jobs to make ends meet.

My earliest memory of something wrong with me was when I was four and a half. I was allergic to what seemed like everything: dust, feathers, flowers, furs and starchy foods. We moved to California when I was six. About that time I started stealing change off the top of my father's dresser to go buy candy at the corner store. Sometimes I would swindle my sister out of her allowance. Then I'd really gorge on sweets.

I spent most of my early school days gazing out of the window, obliviating the world around me, where nothing ever happened to me. Taking flight into a fantasy world I could make things happen to me – like creating a prince who would take after me through the forest, and finally catching me, he would hold me in his strong, warm arms.

For a brief time, when I was seven, my parents sent me to a psychiatrist. At the time my mother said it was because I was always telling her, 'Mommy, you don't love me.' Years later she told me it was also because I stole nickels and dimes from my girlfriend's home. The doctor's diagnosis was that I was a child in need of and capable of a great deal of love.

In the fifth grade my teacher encouraged me in my art-work. I loved to paint pictures of the Hopi Indians. I used vivid oranges and turquoises and purples. Most all the pictures were of Hopi women holding their babies in their arms. I never could give the faces any expression. Painting is the only thing I really enjoyed doing when I was little. After I won a few awards, my parents sent me to art school. I was overwhelmed. They tried to teach me form and line. My only freedom was being taken from me. My parents thought I was creative. 'Everything she touches turns to gold,' they would say. It was no longer fun. It was a chore. My hands became tense. They wouldn't do what I wanted them to do. I felt I had to be perfect for them to pay attention to me.

My parents spent most of their free time building onto the house. We kids had to 'assume responsibilities' at a very early age. There was always so much goddamn work that had to be done. Some friends of the family used to call our home 'the work farm'. We were placed on a quota system. We were always scheming how to get out of working. When I did get to go out and play, I always felt so 'guilty' because there would always be that something I had left undone that would have to be finished when I got home. I never cleaned my bedroom. It was so cold and such a mess, a screaming mess. It did my screaming for me.

During my teens I had the average amount of girl- and boyfriends. Actually I spent more time with girls than with guys. I always had crushes on the most popular girls in school. My 'best' girlfriend, Roberta, was gorgeous and cold as ice. We were in intense competition with each other. We played at being 'women'. We sewed ourselves cute and sexy clothes. We wore padded bras. We were always trying some new miracle method to make our breasts grow. Our small boobs were a shared humiliation. We double-dated, partied, got drunk, did everything together. We loved each other, yet hated each other. In school we were known as the Gold Dust Twins. My parents thought my association with Roberta was making me wild.

When I was fifteen, I went East for a year because my mother couldn't 'cope' with me. A popular schoolgirl, Stacy, took me under her wing. We became fast high school chums. Our chummy relationship later, through correspondence and brief cross-country visits, became a gay one.

When I'd returned from the East, my parents had placed me in a different high school, hoping my friendship with Roberta would fade away. It did. However, I picked up with Janet. We spent most of the time rapping intellectual bullshit. We each thought the other was brilliant. We had all the answers. She called me her 'alter ego'.

I usually pursued the hard-to-get guy, got him, then dropped him. When I was seventeen, I gave up my virginity because it was the thing to do. I didn't feel a thing. However, after *I* had been pursued and screwed, *he* dropped *me*. I really felt I had been used. I did my best to hide the hurt.

By eighteen I was really confused, lost and miserable. I was never really satisfied with anything. There seemed to be something I wanted, but I didn't know what it was or where to find it. Things came to a head one night and I ran into my parents' bedroom and asked please if I could see a psychiatrist. So for about six months I had weekly visits with a shrink. The other day I came across a list I had made up one night of things I wanted to talk to him about:

> my interest in semantics
> feeling like an amoeba
> happiness?
> screaming feeling
> teachers don't like me
> want to devour – apathy
> analysing people
> older boys – men
> I'm egocentric
> hate for society.

Nothing really changed except that I had found someone who listened to me. My father was also seeing a pysch. This resulted in my parents getting a divorce. That really shattered me. I just couldn't quite believe it. My father remarried. Then I went to college where my father was going to teach in the Midwest for a year. I had another 'best' friend there. Bonnie and I were inseparable. She was so soft and ethereal and like poetry to me. We adored each other.

This time, when I came back to California, things really went from bad to worse. I really slid downhill. My mother had remarried, and they didn't want me to live with them. My sister, who had married and started a family, let me live with her. By this time I had stopped seeing guys altogether. When I'd sleep with them, I never felt a thing, and besides, I had a growing interest in dykes. So by day I would dress conservatively and work in a bank. By night I would let my hair down and join the gay crowd at the local gay bar. Still, I could never let myself go completely with women either. I was seeing this dyke, Mary, who had the exact colouring of my mother. We'd do a lot of necking, but I never let anything happen below the waist. I really couldn't make it with girls or guys. I told my stepmother. She was really the only woman friend I had. She told my father, and they took me out of town to where Dr Janov was living. I remember our initial interview. All I'd say in answering his questions was 'I don't know'. It was decided I'd move to his town and start intensive therapy.

It worked out quite well. I was able to hold down a job. I stopped dating girls and started dating guys: only the guys were mostly older men. One was a fifty-year-old professor of philosophy and an ex-minister. I was screwing him and dating his twenty-year-old son at the same time. Well, I thought I could function pretty well, so I moved back up to Los Angeles. I lived with my mother and stepfather briefly and found work and moved into my own apartment. Almost every Sunday night I would have these crying fits. I always felt so unprepared for Monday. It seems I never could get my work done on the weekend. Instead, I was out gallivanting around visiting my sister or friends. One of my best friends was Hildie, a girl I had known since I was six. She was my period shot of stability. I also had a 'platonic boyfriend', Raymond. We did a lot of hiking, driving around, eating out, seeing movies together. Sex was off limits as far as I was concerned. He just didn't appeal to me that way. For about six months I was seeing a psych. Only *he* did the talking and preaching. I barely got to open my mouth. Things just weren't working out. When I heard that Dr Janov was moving back to Los Angeles, I decided to see him again. So I attended group.

I had a pill habit. My doctor had prescribed them for weight reduction when I was seventeen. I'd take one amp a day about five days out of the week and binge on food during the weekend. I told Dr Janov: 'I take pills to keep from feeling life ... I feel less with pills ... I'm so sensitive to life I can't stand it. I need pills to dull life. The pill makes me feel dead. Music sound brassy. I'm like in a shell.' Each morning it was like saying, 'I won't live this day, but I'll get through it.' With the pill I was able to maintain my weight, binge on food whenever I wanted, and keep from feeling what was happening to me. This went on for about seven years. One morning I realised that I couldn't get through the day *without* the pill. I was hooked. I was addicted. Well, I knew that Art was working on this new idea about Primals. I really felt he could help me, so I quit the pills. A few weeks later I quit cigarettes. I saw Art a few times in individual, and he seemed to be priming me for something.

On the afternoon of 17 September 1967, I wrote: 'HELP ME FEEL THE PAIN ... I'M SO SICK OF NOT FEELING AT ALL ... I'M SURE THAT AT LEAST THE PAIN WILL LET ME KNOW THAT I AM ALIVE ... 'CAUSE I REALLY FEEL DEAD.'

In group that evening, I was relating a situation that happened to me a few evenings previous; Raymond had been massaging my neck and shoulders when I recalled how much I had missed being held by either of my parents. The doctor asked me to engage in a little psychodrama with Steve, one of the group members. I lay on my stomach on the floor. Steve began telling me a bedtime story while rubbing my shoulders. I wanted to relax and enjoy it, but I tensed up. When he caressed my hair and the back of my neck, I got excited but scared, so I squirmed away. As he gently continued to stroke my hair and neck, the tension mounted. Then I focused on Steve's hands, and all of a sudden they became my father's hands. I said, 'My God, they're my father's hands . . . I'm in a bed with wrinkled sheets.' I was there and I became so small I felt six months old, and my father was the one caressing me . . . I was so excited that I thought I was going to have an orgasm . . . Then his hands left me, and I lost control – I started to fall inside myself . . . I was being sucked inside myself . . . I fell and I fell . . . I thought I'd fall forever . . . There were flashes of red and white lights and rushing and roaring sounds . . . I was exploding into a million pieces . . . I knew I was going to die . . . This was the end of me . . . I felt that I was being electrocuted . . . Then from the core of my being I found the strength to scream . . . As I was screaming, I was vaguely aware that I was convulsing and rolling around on the floor . . . I knocked something over . . . Then I stopped rolling and said that I wanted an orgasm . . . Once again I fell inside myself and felt my body being electrocuted and screamed and rolled around the floor . . . Then I turned over on my back, and a cool breeze swept over me. I opened my eyes and looked around . . . Then I very calmly said, 'I was the pain.' I was alive. I had survived. I had shattered the brittle shell and was now inside myself.

I later realised that this was my Primal Scene. I was barely held at all as a baby or ever for that matter. However, my father says he used to 'fondle and caress' me when I was a baby. Exactly, that was when I turned off. I was never held except when my father 'fondled and caressed' me as though I were a woman. I was touched enough to know 'they' were there but not held enough to know *I* was there. The excruciating Pain was *needing* to be held in order to survive. Instead, I was tantalised by my father and brought to the point of excitation and left. As a baby you have to be held a tremendous amount so that you will know where you begin and the world lets off. I turned off because if I lay there any longer and felt, I would have exploded into bits. Instead, I split. From that day on I was tense. I had turned off so tightly that I couldn't even feel my tension. I became the symbol of what I was too small to feel – fragmented.

The next morning I was supersensitive to everything. My legs were still tense, and I had a hard time holding myself up. I was very aware of my surroundings. I wanted to talk slower and to walk slower. The big rush was over. There was nothing to say and no place to go. At moments I felt dazed by it all – and then tremendous sorrow at the loss of the struggle. My whole life had been a struggle for my parents' love acted out through my friends. It was all such a big sham.

My job at the hospital, answering phones and making appointments for shrieking old ladies, became unbearable. I quit.

The first Primal that began to make sense to me was when I tried to go back and feel that first Pain but found the pain of *nothing*. Yes, my life was empty – I had had nothing. I had been the great pretender. To keep from feeling the deadness, I had become dramatic. Now my face could no longer go through those sucking – notice how alive I am – contortions. I felt alive for the first time in my life. I started writing down the changes that were taking place. Everything was becoming real to me. Colours were vivid. Landscapes looked like paintings. I no longer saw the world through a telescope. My ears were very sensitive, and I could not stand a lot of noise. My hands hung loose, for there was nothing for them to hold onto any more. Such liberation! I was really free. I wrote, 'I'm starting to flower. Today I'm starting to come out of my cocoon! ! I like being born. There is so much to learn ... mostly that *now* is *now*. Yesterday is gone. Tomorrow isn't here yet – now is now.' I felt five years old. So very new. I wrote: 'I can swallow now because I have a throat that connects me.'

Other Primals started happening. I felt the coldness of my body. The coldness came from waiting for warmth from my mother and father. After this Primal my circulation increased. My hands and feet were pink and warm for the first time in my life. There were many Primals of wanting my mother and father. Art would have me call for Mommy or Daddy, and as I called, the feeling would fill me – of how much I wanted them and then that they weren't coming. In fact, that feeling of wanting them lasted until the end of treatment. Each time I felt the want it was on a deeper level, more encompassing and more real. When I felt what I really wanted, I no longer had to stuff myself with food to fill the emptiness of not getting what I wanted. That's why I had to eat so much of it on a binge – I was never satisfied. This was because food was not what I really wanted. Also, I never felt my stomach, so I never felt when I was full. There are some 'dreams come true' in this therapy. While I was a glutton, I used to dream of being able to maintain a slim figure effortlessly. I never thought I could get out of that vicious binge-diet cycle. Now I eat what I want when I want, and I have a very lovely figure.

I was frigid. I loved kissing and hugging and petting, but I never felt anything in my vagina. For a while during this therapy I was dating a really warm guy, but my lifelong pattern with men continued. When we'd screw, I just couldn't let go, and I wanted to feel an orgasm so badly. Art said, 'You think sex is love; you don't want sex; you still want your daddy.' It was true. The feeling came up from the tip of my toes – this longing for my father. I was saving myself for Daddy; I'd put myself in deep freeze for him. Then there was this warm rush from my vagina. Two days later I had another dream come true – I experienced a total orgasm. It was beautiful. I felt every cell in my body totally. It was delicious. When it was over, I felt equal inside and outside. There was such serenity. I know now that if I hadn't felt that key feeling which unlocked my vagina, I would have been frigid for the rest of my life. No amount of rationalising in standard therapy about why I was frigid could make me *feel* the reason. I would have continued acting out with sexless Raymond. My father and Raymond were very similar – intellectual and unphysical. Only Raymond I could understand; my father I couldn't. Raymond paid a lot of attention to me; my father didn't. Raymond even read to me the way my father used to when I was a child. Raymond was a giving father. He met *my* needs – I didn't have to meet *his*. All my life I lived in apprehension of my father. He was such a stranger to me as a child. He seemed to live in his study except when he was pounding nails into the house. I never knew what to expect from him, except that I shouldn't disturb him. The thing that made it so hard for me to give him up was that my father is a basically good man. He's very humane – in principle.

There were some violent Primals. One was the horrifying feeling that my parents had killed me. They were dead and couldn't let me live. Another was that I had been my parents' slave. These feelings would boil inside and with jolting screams erupt from my guts. Then I had feelings of terrible anger at my mother. She wouldn't let me want her.

She never played with me. I wanted her so bad. 'Please play with me. Please be real.' She never made sense. 'Please be a feeling person. Please, please love me. Please, please hold me.' Now I *felt* the reason I had chosen the girlfriends I had. I'd tried to make them love me because I had buried my feelings for my mother. I secretly felt so ugly I had to surround myself with beautiful girlfriends. Instead of admitting I felt inadequate with my mother, I entered in intense competition with Roberta, who was cold, beautiful and vain like my mother. Janet demanded I pay attention to her like my mother. She sucked off me like my mother did – ah, but she *did* at least talk to me. Hildie was the good mother, was bright and clever, and she was my favourite. She would listen to me for hours and be consoling and helpful when I was down. I was never satisfied, of course, because they weren't my mother.

Since I was still feeling unfeminine, I switched to women who were even more unfeminine than me. I tried to make it with dykes. With both Stacy and Mary, I could feel totally like a 'woman'. They were women who wanted me and let me feel 'female'. My mother was normally very cool with me except when she got a few drinks in her. Then she would hug and kiss me in such a sexual way that it would repulse me. It was still while I was in Primal Therapy that I received a phone call from her one morning at 2.30 a.m. I said hello; then my mother's voice said, 'I love you and miss you terribly.' I was stunned and hung up without saying a word. Later the next day I realised what lesbianism is all about. My mother was *taunting* me so that *I* would love *her*! The mother wants the daughter to love her – my mother never let me feel pretty or feminine or be a little girl; she tried to make me her mother – she couldn't love me, yet she demanded that I love her. So being gay is when the daughter rejects the mother's rejection by going to another female and saying I will love you if you will love me – and so a symbolic acting out begins. The difference between a 'fem' and a 'butch' is the degree of femininity denied. The fem is still fighting to feel like a woman. The dyke or butch in drag goes so far as to say I will even discard what's left of my femininity and become a man for you (Mother). A psychotic dyke friend of mine once wrote a prose poem called *The Brittle People*. Nothing expresses lesbianism better:

This is the well of cyanide.

This is the spring from which lost ones drink and seek to quench a thirst – and think that their search is ended ... and yet the nectar turns to acid in the foul mouth. The dew evaporates from the blossom and it withers on the stem – or the flower is plucked and discarded. The violet becomes a hothouse plant – a thing that lives in pottery – and, losing its forest shyness, it assumes a city glitter. ...

This is the well – this is the limbo of liquid – and the liquid is tears, and the well is dug in the chasm of shattered lives. ... Of love we sing, and we think of the first love. Ah, yes, we vision those eyes whose depth seemed bottomless and clear as a calm lake. We feel again the trembling, the clinging of those lips we were afraid to touch – and the thrill. And we search endlessly for the thrill of our first love. ...

Now we are hard – and bright – and brittle, ours is the shiny surface – the gay and tinkling laughter – the casual handshake and the tears which come after. The years flow swiftly – and we are the people who chatter – we have buried our youthful dreams. For some of us the well has dried – only the saline crystals remain. This we forget – until some deft stab re-opens an old wound and we feel the salt sting. ...

Yes, we are the gay ones – the clever and bright – and brittle!

Towards the end of therapy, I took acid. I started to feel a very deep feeling; then I flipped out. Flipping out is really cutting yourself off from the feeling and flipping into your mind. I went crazy. It was pure hell!

I felt like I was in Sartre's *No Exit* – I couldn't find the entrance back into reality. The next day I wanted to kill myself. It wasn't that I really wanted to kill myself, it was that for the first time in my life I felt terribly alone and afraid. I could no longer suck anything from the world. I was afraid to feel alone totally because it might destroy me, yet I was also afraid I might impulsively destroy myself if I decided I couldn't bear to feel it. So I felt alone bit by bit.

For weeks I would get the feeling of being crazy. I couldn't tell what was real and what was unreal. One night in group I found myself on the floor *wanting* with every cell in my body. From deep inside myself I could hear the wailing of an infant. I felt two days old. I had never felt anything so totally except an orgasm. Then I developed periods of

The Brittle People

This is the well of cyanide.
This is the spring from which lost
ones drink and seek to quench a thirst
— and think that their search is ended, that they have found themselves ——

OLD HANDWRITING

The Brittle
People

This is the well
of cyanide.
This is the
spring from
which lost
ones drink
and seek to
quench a
thirst —and
think that
their search
is ended, that
they have
found them-
selves — — — —

NEW HANDWRITING

vertigo. This imbalance continued until I went back and felt all of that want.

There have been some physical changes, which I hope are permanent, which have occurred throughout Primal Therapy. My allergies completely disappeared. My skin softened, and my mild case of acne cleared. My breasts grew, and my nipples matured. My muscles are finally relaxed.

Is it worth it? Do I really feel different having gone through this? Well, it is the difference between life and death. Only I never knew I was dead until I became alive. But now that I'm alive I have nothing to live for. I went into therapy to find a new self-image, and all I found was me. The one thing about reality is that it will never let you down.

18

The Basis of Fear and Anger

ANGER

One of the myths about humans is that underneath our placid exteriors we are a seething cauldron of fury and violence kept in check solely by society. When the checking system falters, man's innate violence erupts, resulting in wars, holocausts. However, I am continuously struck by how unaggressive and non-violent people are when their so-called civilised fronts are removed. Primal patients who are wide open and defenceless aren't angry. There is no rage. Perhaps the civilisation process itself makes human beings so uncivilised to one another, producing frustration and hostility. Being civilised too often means being in control of one's feelings, and this control may be the source of inner rage.

I believe that the angry man is the unloved man – the man who could not be what he was. He is usually angry at his parents for not letting him be and angry at himself for carrying on the this denial of self. But need is basic; anger is secondary – it is what happens when need is not fulfilled. When we look at the Primal process, we see a sequence that is almost mathematical in its lack of variation. The first Primals often deal with anger, the second group of Primals have to do with hurt, and the third with need for love. The need and its lack of fulfilment are usually the greatest hurt. The Primal sequence is like life in reverse. First, early in life was the need for love, then the hurt over not getting it, and finally, the anger to ease the hurt. What has often happened to the neurotic is that he has lost steps one and two and finds himself with inexplicable anger. But the anger, like depression, is a reaction to hurt, not a basic characteristic of man. Sometimes it is easier for a young child to feel anger than to tolerate the terrible feeling of aloneness and rejection which lies under it, so he pretends his feeling of being unloved and alone is something else: hate. But patients in Primal Therapy rarely are just hateful towards their parents. It is more a case of 'Love me, please. Why can't you love me? *Love me, you bastards!*' By the time the neurotic has grown up, he tends to think that his sole feeling is hate, but in therapy he finds out that hate is one more cover he has spread over the need. Once the need is felt, there is scarcely any anger left. In Primal groups, for example, there is almost never the hostile interchange among members one might find in conventional group therapies. Nor is there anger at the therapist. There is just a great deal of hurt.

The Primal view of rage is that it is a rage against someone trying to crush the life out of you. We have to remember that neurotic parents are unconsciously killing their children, in a sense; they are killing off the real selves of their offspring; psychophysical death is a real process where life is being squeezed out of them. The result is the anger: 'I hate you for not letting me live.' To be anything else but yourself is to be dead.

When the neurotic suppresses the need for love and just feels angry, he may attempt to discharge it on symbolic targets, such as the wife, children, or employees, each day of his life. Because he does not make the correct connection to the source of his anger, he may go on discharging it in unreal ways. For example, one patient, a usually respectful and moderate man, was horrified by what he had just done to his wife – he spat in her face. Why? Because she wouldn't believe him when he told her where he had gone one morning. Im Primal Therapy he felt his rage over never having been believed by his parents about anything. Unfortunately, years later it spilled over towards his wife.

Make anger real, and it will disappear. Until that happens, many angry outbursts against people in the present will be acts and, therefore, not real. Obviously, there is real anger, too, that does not emanate from the past. When someone botches the repair job on your car, there can be legitimate anger, but daily inordinate tantrums mean that the past predominates. This means that the neurotic is always on the verge of feeling now what he denied then. What was left unresolved in childhood will infiltrate almost anything a person does later in life until it is resolved.

I consider the differentiation between real anger and symbolic anger important. An example may clarify the point.

A young schoolteacher with a constant smile and ingratiating manner came for help because of a continuing state of tightness and tension in her muscles. During her second visit she was discussing how her father always criticised, gibed, poked fun and generally ridiculed her. She suddenly felt furious and began pounding the pillow for more than five minutes. Afterwards she felt relaxed and told me that she had no idea that she had that much anger in her.

The tension persisted, however. During her fifth visit she was again discussing past injustices, and the feelings began to well up once more. This time she wasn't allowed to pound the pillow; rather, she was urged to, 'Say what it is.' She began shaking violently and uncontrollably and at the same time began verbalising her hatred – how she was going to strangle them until they died, how she was going to pound her father to pieces for all the hurt he had caused her without once ever letting her defend herself, how she would drive a knife into her mother for allowing it to happen, etc. All this was screamed amid writhing, groans, clutching at the stomach, and complete loss of control. At the apex of this event she began shouting, 'Now I know, now I know – I've been tense in my muscles to keep myself from attacking them,' and then again more verbal violence.

Never once in this woman's life can she remember having raised her voice. She was always shushed in her very genteel home, where young ladies conducted themselves with decorum. She said after this last Primal that she felt loose and unpredictable for the first time in her life. She had been holding onto her (unreal) self all these years to keep her parents from totally rejecting her should she ever let go and become her (real) self.

There were necessary stages in this woman's therapy. First, she had a vague and diffuse tension throughout her lifetime which kept her tied in knots. The first Primal had to do with getting under that tension and feeling the physical part of the anger, to recognise that she was even angry. Later she pounded a pillow because she had not yet made the mental connection. The pillow punching was symbolic acting out. The anger was felt but not directed (which is why any persistent anger goes on). Obviously, she was not angry at the pillow; the pillow was a symbolic object for her fury in the same way that some children are the punching bags or whipping boys for angry parents. In the case of the defenceless and helpless child, unfortunately, the angry parents can usually find something wrong to justify their rages. As time goes on with this kind of treatment, the child soon gives the parents real reason to be angry as well.

Once this woman made the major connection, she no longer had the anger or, needless to say, the chronic tightness in her muscles that had left her sore and aching most of her life. She could have come in and pounded that pillow for days and years without changing that anger. Possibly she would have found temporary relief, but the anger would have returned after a time.

In her previous therapy this woman was encouraged to vent her hostility to group therapy members. She felt that she was making progress towards becoming an assertive person in her therapy, but the tightness and shoulder aches persisted. This was because her real, little-girl anger persisted. No matter how 'grown-up' one acts in therapy or in life, it must be an act which has little bearing on one's maturity until the 'little girl' is felt. All that happens, in my opinion, is that the real, helpless and passive self *pretends* to be assertive, especially in the safe atmosphere of group therapy. A 'good' girl in therapy *expresses* her anger just as a good girl at home suppresses it. Both behaviours are still the struggle for love. This might also explain why there was often so little carry-over from the aggressiveness shown in group and the ability to assert oneself in daily public life.

The difference between real and unreal or symbolic anger is important because I believe that failure to distinguish between them has led to a number of therapeutic distortions. Thus, a great deal of time is spent in child psychotherapy having the children punch bags. On the adult level, there are so-called fight clinics in which marital partners are placed in a room where they learn how to attack and defend themselves in arguments with each other. All this is symbolic and therefore cannot resolve anything in a real way, in my opinion. The woman whom I discussed above was angry towards her group therapy peers but not really angry at them. Things they did set off her old anger. When they ignored, criticised, interrupted, or suppressed her, the fury at her parents was unleashed, only she didn't know that it was an old feeling. The force of her anger towards group members, once verbalised, was really inordinate and irrational. It's analogous to reading in the papers about a wife who has murdered her husband because he wouldn't put out the garbage – something from the past triggered the violence. It also helps explain why some parents are afraid to spank their child over something minor. They rationalise that their philosophy of child rearing forswears spanking, whereas they are terrified – they don't admit it is fear – that some triviality on the part of a child will unlock all their latent violence.

Possibly one of the reasons fight clinics exist, together with the encouragement of hostile expression in group therapy, is that anger or violence is seen as something natural that must be drained off periodically – 'instinctual aggression' is the Freudian expression. It is particularly tempting for psychologists to believe in this so-called instinct, because we do, in fact, see so much hostility in our patients. We see this violence and little else because we have not taken the patient deeper into his feeling, into his need. What we see is what lies atop the need – that is, the frustration reaction to the need.

Because of the belief in an aggressive instinct, we have often spent time in our therapies helping people 'handle' their aggressions – meaning 'control' them. I think we must do the opposite. We must feel the anger fully in order to eradicate it. When a person can feel himself, instead of acting out his feelings symbolically, he will be unlikely to act either impulsively or aggressively. The dialectic of anger, as with Pain, is that when it is felt, it disappears; when it is not felt, it remains waiting to be felt.

The concept of handling oneself implies the neurotic split. It is the split which is dangerous because it means that denied feelings must be controlled. Thus, a free-swinging, spontaneous, uncontrolled person is the one who is apt to have least internal aggressions.

Again, I want to make clear that spontaneity means feeling, while impulsivity is the result of denial of feeling. Thus, an impulsive person is indeed apt to act out aggressively and would need control. Over the years we have perhaps looked at the impulsive individual as someone free and anarchic, forgetting that he is usually bound by precise old feelings which he is acting out in a circumscribed way, not at all the freedom or anarchy that it seems.

A person can blow up every day of his life and not realise

that he is an angry person. He is usually able to arrange things to justify present anger so that he does not have to feel its source. If the neurotic cannot find something to justify anger, we can be sure that he will arrange to misinterpret something innocuous in order to keep his overflowing anger released. Misinterpretation, in general, would seem to be slanted towards suppressed need and is not simply a matter of semantics.

What makes a neurotic angry will depend on the exact early situation which caused him to be hurt. For example, a woman patient became angry because her children wouldn't help her around the house. She beat them severely for not picking up after themselves. Her feeling, as it turned out, was 'I've worked so hard and no one seems to care or appreciate my efforts' – feelings she harboured towards her mother, who had had her cleaning house from the age of eight.

Another person became furious when he was kept waiting. Whenever he asked his father to play with him, his father would say, 'Later. I'm busy right now.' 'Later' never came, but rage did. The problem often is that the child is frustrated and made angry and then not allowed to even show this feeling, so he is forced into vicarious releases – fights at school, headaches, allergies, etc. Thus, a child is robbed of his wants and then robbed again of his feelings about his wants not being fulfilled; he loses twice. On top of that, if the angry child shows a sullen face, he is apt to be met with 'Smile! Why the long face?' So then he is thrice robbed and driven back further into himself to hide the feelings.

High blood pressure is one possible result of this deep repression of anger. When patients who have a tendency towards high blood pressure have finished their angry Primals, we often note a drop in their pressure. If one looks at it in terms of pumping increased amounts of pressure into an organism until that pressure exerts a force through the entire blood system, it is easy to see how violent that person can potentially become when restraints are removed. Conversely, elevation in pressure becomes understandable when restraints are continuously imposed.

The split in the American culture today between the family ethic and the societal ethic is particularly sharp. The 'good' boy in the home never sasses or shows anger towards his parents, while the 'good' boy in society kills for his country. One becomes a condition for the other; the same boy may repress himself and exterminate others in order to be 'good'.

Anger is often sown by parents who see their children as a denial of their own lives. Marrying early and having to sacrifice themselves for years to demanding infants and young children are not readily accepted by those parents who never really had a chance to be free and happy. So the child often suffers. He must pay for even being alive because the very fact of his existence constitutes a denial of his parents' freedom. The child is punished soon enough. He won't be allowed to show his wants (called 'making demands') or be permitted to whine, shout, or be heard. He'll be given a barrage of orders to carry out to earn his right to be alive. He is being groomed each day of his life to take care of himself, not to ask for help, and, eventually, to take over the parents' duties and responsibilities. He will sense, early in his life, that he is in the way and try desperately to atone for a crime he never committed. He'll grow up too fast, take on too much just to appease irritable parents who hate him for no reason. One patient, who was the cause of his parents' having had to get married in their late teens, said: 'I spent a lifetime trying to find reasons for my chaotic life. All those criticisms and harangues over the most trivial things I did. I finally studied philosophy in order to find a reason for life – I mean, in order to cover the fact that there was no rational reason for what went on in my home.'

There is so little post-Primal anger because, I believe, that anger is inverted hope. The hope in this kind of anger is that of converting parents into decent, feeling people. For example, the fantasy of some patients of mine who graduated from my conventional therapy was that they would see their parents and confront them with all the abuse they had taken from them. But implicit in this confrontation is the hope that the parents will see how horrible they have been and become new, loving individuals.

If anger is left in Primal patients, I take it as a sign of neurosis. First, because it implies unreal hope. Second, because anger implies the *little child* still wants and has not cut himself off from the parents. There is no *adult* anger, if indeed the patient is now a real adult, for the same reason that the patient would not be angry at the neurotic antics of any other person he meets. He would be an adult seeing the neurosis of his parents objectively. (Objectivity is the absence of unconscious feelings which make a person slant reality away from one's Pain and towards fulfilment of need). They would simply be two other adults with neuroses. There is only anger at parents when a person wants his parents to change and be what he needs. When the needs are felt and are gone, so is the anger.

What does exist in Primal patients is the great sense of tragedy over the waste of their childhood. There is at the same time a great relief that the lifetime struggle is over. These patients are not interested in revenge for the past; they are more interested in leading the lives they have now in the present.

JEALOUSY

Jealousy is another face of anger. It, too, is caused by feeling a lack of parental love. Because the child is not permitted direct hostility towards his parents, it tends to be diverted sideways towards his siblings. But the child usually isn't angry at his brothers or sisters; they are but the symbols, the focus of hate.

Why is a child so angry and jealous? Perhaps because early in life parents convey the notion to children that love is some kind of limited quantity that gets used up fast. So they will say, 'Look at your brother. He's finished everything on his plate [a virtue that constantly escapes me]. *He's* going to get the biggest piece of cake.' Or, 'Look at your sister. She cleaned up her whole room, so she is going to get to go to the movies.' Because a child soon sees that love is dispensed when you're 'good' and not when you're bad, he may think of it as a special gift. Jealousy implies that the child feels he is not getting his share. Under this feeling is the implicit assumption that there are shares. This assumption occurs in neurotic households, where parents do not give freely but tend to dole out everything on 'condition'. The children must then struggle for anything. They fight the way ladies fight in a department-store sale. The child may be angry at others because they seem to threaten his percentage.

To be wholly loved means not to be jealous. Children, in my opinion, are not naturally jealous, any more than they are naturally angry. They may take it out on their siblings, but it is the parents who most often demand, criticise and withhold what the child needs. It is the parents who tend to be impatient and irritable with childish ways and who may favour one child over another. What neurotic parents see when they look at their children is hope: an image of what they need (respect, adulation, attention). They are relating to a symbol, not the child. The child who gets what passes for love is the one who comes close to being that image, the one who becomes, therefore, symbolic neurotic instead of a person who can call all his feelings his own. It is that favoured child, by and large, who has been utterly destroyed and yet often the one who can function quite well in life. The rebel, the one who wouldn't conform and submit, may never have functioned well and yet may be much closer to being a human being than his functioning sibling.

The poor child who is the favourite is often beaten by the non-favoured child and must spend his youth paying for a crime committed by his parents. He must pay the price of being taunted and needled by his brother or sister for being what his parents need. In one sense, this jealousy is the way the non-favoured child tries to get his share: If only he can destroy and remove the favoured sibling, if only he can point out what he did wrong, maybe he can be liked a little more.

Childhood jealousy ('I want my share') continues in life. The jealous sibling, ignored by his parents, may grow up and have children of his own whom he will taunt and punish when they demand attention from *their* mother. His children will pay the price for diverting their mother's attention from the children's father. This jealous behaviour will continue, I submit, until the person finds the correct context of his anger and feels it fully. Then his own children will no longer have to suffer for their father's childhood neglect. It is often the jealous child who grows into that competitive adult who wants more than what anyone else has, who cannot see his child's defects because he must have 'the best'.

Not only is the young child angry for not being loved, but he is also frustrated because he couldn't give it to anyone. 'If only they knew how much I had to give them,' moaned one patient. 'I gave it all to the dog instead.' In addition, there is bitterness because of not even being allowed to *ask* for the love that was needed. 'Needing became a crime in my house,' said one patient. 'I sensed that if I were to say, "Hold me, Daddy," he would have ridiculed my need as sissy stuff.'

For those who believe that jealousy and hostility are natural instincts in humans, I can only report that post-Primal patients' dreams (as well as daily behaviour) are devoid of angry and jealous content. Thus, even if they were somehow able to control their anger during the day, we would expect it to show up at night when controls were loosened. Apparently, it doesn't. This suggests that the concept of an instinctual pool of aggression seems to be erroneous; if there is any 'instinct', it is to be loved – that is, to be oneself.

FEAR

When my son was ten years old, he suddenly developed night fears and I could not understand why. He was afraid of a man in the closet. This fear hung on for a month before I decided to try to get to the bottom of it. One night when he was going to bed and asked me to leave the radio and lights on, I put him into a Primal. I had him sink into that scary feeling and let it overtake him. He began to shake, and his voice got shrill and 'spooked'. He kept saying, 'I don't want to do it, Daddy, it's too scary!' I persisted. As he sank into that terror, I urged him to scream out the feeling. He kept saying, 'I can't, I can't.' I urged him to say it. Finally, he said, 'There's no words, Daddy. Mommy is holding me down by my diapers and trying to pin me or something.' He was terrified of being pinned down and feeling completely helpless. He said, 'You know, I never felt the man in the closet was going to kill me with a gun or anything; I felt that he was going to hold me down and strangle me.' What set it off? One afternoon, just before the fear began, I was wrestling with him and pinned his shoulders down. It didn't seem to be anything traumatic, and both of us forgot all about it – until his Primal. His memory during the Primal went straight back to when he was eight months old. He recalled the shape and colour of the bassinet. After the bath, he was scurrying around while my wife was trying to diaper him until, in exasperation, she held him down firmly and with anger. That experience scared him.

In Primal terms, a current, persistent, but seemingly irrational fear is generally a manifestation of an older and often deeper fear. It is fear of *then*, not now, so trying to talk someone out of an irrational phobia, such as my son's fear, would be tantamount to talking him out of a memory. My son's fear persisted, I believe, because there were feelings of helplessness associated with that memory which were overwhelming at the time.

The reason any phobia continues is that it draws on the Primal pool of fear. To harken back to an old theme: Neurotic fears are symbolic fears. The real fears cannot be reached without help and support, so the person must settle on substitutes. Thus, he can be afraid of elevators, caves, heights, dogs, electrical outlets, crowds, when in actuality his fears come from the past. We might say that current fears are like dreams – an attempt to make rational generalised lifelong feelings which are, in the present context, irrational.

It is more than a matter of making old feelings presently rational, however. It is a symbolic way of managing and controlling those fears. Somehow the neurotic must think that if he keeps things in control and 'cooled', he won't have to be afraid any more. So the neurotic avoids what he fears – or, what he thinks he fears. He stops flying and avoids heights.

These activities often do help control these fears by isolating and compartmentalising them. But should a person come close to the *apparent* object of his fear, such as a high balcony with a low railing, what arises is the real fear which is symbolised by the current situation. The neurotic caught on this balcony may really fear loss of control over self-destructive feelings, *not* a simple fear of heights.

Current fears – which often contain a kernel of reasonableness, such as in the fear of flying – often help the neurotic avoid the fact that he is simply a fearful being. Were he forced to feel his constant fear, life might become intolerable.

I believe that there are two key reasons for the choice of

an unreal fear (phobia). The first is the actual occurrence of a real trauma, such as an auto accident or a bad fall from a roof. For a neurotic who undergoes such an experience, the fear of driving or of heights might continue long beyond reason; it might last a lifetime.

What the neurotic often does is generalise from a single real experience to a broad class of experiences which are unrelated to the original fear. So a person who fell off a roof might thereafter avoid high balconies even though the two are not related. In this way, the neurotic is impelled to expand his fears because a single incident has opened up the Primal Pool of fear. This is the same as the neurotic who has a bad experience with his mother and generalises this to *all* women. Generalisation takes place because *original* feelings were not responded to (and resolved) for what they were.

The second reason for the adoption of a phobia would be the symbolic value of the present fear. If a person never fell off a roof or had an accident, his fearfulness still requires him to find a suitable focus for his fears. He will generally choose something symbolic of the real fear. Someone who felt crushed by parents might be afraid of getting trapped in small places such as a crowded elevator. Someone who felt totally neglected and undirected by parents might be afraid of broad, open expanses in which he might lose his way and *feel* lost (feel the original feeling of being lost, that is). This same person, by the way, may also be the one to marry a take-charge type who will direct and run his life so that he can continue to act out but not feel undirected and lost. This is significant, in my opinion, because a neurotic fear is part of the total neurotic system, not an isolated event. Thus, attempts to deal with the specific fear itself without relation to the entire system would only perpetuate the fragmented neurotic system and misdirect the patient's focus from the real thing.

Recently, a woman was referred for therapy because of an inordinate fear of bugs – not any bugs, just big black spiders. We did not take up the fear directly, but after several weeks of treatment she began to discuss her feelings towards her father. She discovered how frightened she was of him most of the time. She recalled one scene in particular where he suddenly turned on her for something trivial – he was quite unpredictable. As she re-lived the scene, she was enveloped by fear of him and shouted, 'Daddy, don't scare me any more.' This gave way to another feeling: 'Daddy, let me be afraid.' He had so derided her feelings that she became fearful of showing any fear. This led to another intense feeling about how his eyes and 'look' kept her terrified throughout her childhood. Later she felt confused and experienced two feelings almost at once. The first was 'Don't touch me, Daddy!' and the next was 'Hold me, touch me, so I don't have to feel all alone and in that blackness.' These deep feelings erupted amid rapid-fire discussion of memories about him. As soon as she could scream out her fear of her father, she began a stream of insights: 'I see it all now. I was always afraid, but it was so subtle and seemed so unjustified. One day I saw this big black spider in the bathroom, and I screamed and ran. *Finally, I could scream my fear.* I found my reason. My fear was always real. I just connected it to something that wasn't.'

A fortuitous event in her life allowed her to channel her latent fears and focus them on something specific. Primal Therapy re-channelled the fears to the source: 'I'm afraid of you, Daddy!'

Vague anxiety is what Primal patients experience as their defence systems are attacked. When I stopped a Marine captain from swearing during treatment, it threatened his pose as the 'big man'. It made him come closer to the fact that he was a little, hurting boy. He didn't know exactly what he feared except that he felt somehow afraid (defenceless) when he couldn't curse. Neurotic anxiety is the fear of lying defenceless against Primal hurt. Neurotic conduct serves to cover the hurts. But it was the real self which was rejected, abused and humiliated, so it is no wonder that there is fear when the real self is close. The man I just mentioned was part of a Marine family. His father and brothers were Marines. To get by in his family, it was necessary to be tough, independent, and unemotional. To be a little 'crybaby' needing to be held by Daddy was an intolerable feeling for him to face. The buried need kept him tense. When his cover was weakened, that tension became anxiety.

Conversely, another man became fearful when he had to assert himself aggressively. The fear was: 'I won't be Mama's sweet gentleman if I get mad.' So whenever he became angry, he shook from an unexplained fear.

Fear is an agent of survival. Fear not only allows us to jump out of the way of falling objects, but keeps the child alive by not allowing him to feel those catastrophic early feelings that might make him give up on life. Fear is what helps produce neurosis to protect us against catastrophe. People who can't continue to be neurotic often become fearful or anxious. When we stop therapy patients from acting out, they feel worse.

Just as every neurotic must be angry for not being loved, every neurotic must be fearful inside. Some deny the fear, others project the fear into phobias, and some act out the fear in counter-phobic ways. Fear signals when Primal Pains are close. One indication of this is that when Primal Pains ascend, after a defence has been weakened, fear also arises.

Neurotic fear is the fear of the loss of the lie the person has been living. Any challenge to the lie evokes fear because the lie contains hope. When a girl tries to be a boy for Daddy, when she tries to excel in athletics for him and fails, she may become anxious because the 'real her' is coming up. When a boy pretends to be Mama's 'gentleman', he may become anxious when she derides his boyish language as 'crude and common'. One patient explained it as follows: 'I've always had a fear that if I led my own life my way, if I did what I wanted and said what was on my mind, my parents would have nothing to do with me. I had to be what they expected. To stop leading their lives for them (living the lie) meant to be abandoned or totally rejected. That was terrifying for me. I became terrified of *me*.'

The Primal patient is most afraid when his whole neurotic game is about to be over. Our aim is to evoke those fears so that we can push him beyond and into his real feelings. He is afraid to be real; that is why he is neurotic.

The relationship of fear and pain is important. One puts up a front in order not to be hurt. If someone is exactly what he is, he cannot be hurt and has no need for anxiety. The function of fear, real and unreal, is to keep us from being hurt. The only way to conquer fear is to feel the hurts. As long as the hurts are unfelt, fear remains.

COUNTER-PHOBIA

Counter-phobia is plunging into the very thing that is most

feared. Thus, if a person were afraid of heights, he might take up skydiving to prove he wasn't.

Counter-phobic activity must be compulsive and continuing because the person is trying to deny a real fear with a symbolic activity. I consider counter-phobia a more serious form of neurosis because the real feelings are buried so deep they compel the person to act out totally. Counter-phobia, therefore, indicates a more total repressive state. A skydiver I saw in therapy had an inordinate fear of death. 'Each jump,' he said, 'was a "There I've had a brush with death and it wasn't so bad"² kind of thing.' Each of his jumps was an attempt to quell unconscious fear. What made his activity compulsive was that the *real* fears returned anew each day of his life and required new proof that they really didn't exist. After he broke his leg on a jump, he was greatly relieved that he didn't have to go on answering the question 'Am I afraid?'

Any action counter to a real fearful feeling can be considered counter-phobic. Sex is a good example. Many men fear sex, yet are drawn to it compulsively out of fear of not being 'real men'. This is particularly true of men with latent homosexual leanings. To prove to the world that these leanings do not exist, they may try to make every girl they see, talk about sex with women constantly, poke fun at 'queers' (which is our favourite counter-phobia), and fight other men. Or they may marry and have many children – the more boys, the better – to prove their virility.

Most compulsive sex and sex talk are counter-phobia in action. The fear may be: 'I'm not doing it as much as someone else' (and so I'll have to face that I am not à man).

Most neurotic anger is counter-phobia. It is in response to fear. A mother beats her child because he stepped in front of a moving car, terrifying the mother into anger. Anger, for the most part, is denial of fear. 'Men' do not show fear (that would be unmanly), they show anger – a more 'masculine' trait. How many men not only would say they are afraid but show it?

To indicate the causes of counter-phobia, let us take the example of a young boy of five who runs up the stairs to find his father. 'Daddy, Daddy, where are you?' he shouts as he reaches his father's bedroom. He opens the door to find his father packing a suitcase. 'I am going away for a while,' says his father. 'You're going to live with your mother alone.' The idea of not seeing his father ever again may be catastrophic. What does the young boy do with such a fearful feeling? Since there is no place to release it, no one to help him understand what he is going through, the fear becomes buried. Later, in order to be rid of the nagging, yet vague tension which the buried fear produced, he may contrive situations of fear. He may fight bulls or drive race cars – activities to legitimise latent fear. At last he has something to pin his fears on. He may admit to fear in these situations, which are substitutes for the real one – that he will never have a daddy.

One patient remembers falling into a pool and almost drowning. When he got out, he was immediately made to go back into the water to conquer his fear. His father made him act counter-phobically.

Counter-phobia is a general personality trait. To act against one kind of feeling often means to behave counter to different kinds of feelings. Society helps us become counter-phobic as well. Every day we are told how to *conquer* fear; how to *overcome* frustration, how to be *rid* of inadequacy. All we have to do is eliminate our feelings.

But those feelings constitute our lives. There is no way to conquer life and live. Eventually, that may take on a literal meaning, for I believe that counter-phobics, those who have suppressed the life feelings in themselves so deeply, may finally manage to snuff out their life in one way or another.

Counter-phobia is what keeps fear alive. To deny fear means to have to fight it for a lifetime symbolically. The phobic at least recognises that he is afraid. That is one step up the ladder to health.

CHILDHOOD FEARS

A large percentage of childhood fears occur when the child is alone in bed at night. Children can be brave enough to dive off a high diving board and still be terrified of the dark. Part of the reason is that the child is all alone with himself. The fear is the same kind of fear which occurs when we isolate pre-Primal patients in hotel rooms – it is the fear of the 'me'. The child often denies the fear by projecting it outside himself, saying that he is really afraid of robbers.

362 The Primal Scream

His mind focuses on apparent causes – the rustling of a leaf, the thump of a garage door, a shadow on the wall. Each noise or shadow helps justify a latent fear.

Parents must take care not to rob a child of his fears. It is easy to say, 'There is nothing to be afraid of. There is no one in the closet. Don't be a baby. I won't leave the lights on. Stop the foolishness.' All this does is to drive the fear underground, where it may show up as bed wetting or physical ailments. If a parent cannot understand the reason for his child's fear, it is better to pamper it in every way than suppress it.

Many of us suffered from night fears when we were children, and most of us never grew out of those fears. We are still afraid of the boogeyman, but instead of fearing a boogeyman in the closet, we may be afraid of some vague conspiracy of a nation or group against us. The content of the apparent fear changes, but that content is largely irrelevant. We will need the boogeyman in one form or another until we are well.

What is it about being alone in the dark that arouses such fear? There is the inchoate knowledge that sleep is close, and that means one's guard will be lowered, letting through all the demons which have been warded off during the day. There is nothing intrinsically fearful about feeling oneself alone. But the neurotic who is running from or defending against his self *is* fearful. He must have the radio and television going so that he will not feel alone. 'Alone' means something different to the neurotic from what it means to the normal. 'Alone' means feeling the lack of support and protection and love from one's parents, and it is this that must be defended against. Children's fears become exacerbated when parents leave for the evening, say; it is then that fears of death may arise and become associated with sleep because to be without protection in early childhood can mean death.

DISCUSSION

Since the meaning of any phobia is symbolic and therefore idiosyncratic to each person, there are no universal meanings for phobias. Two people with the same phobia may have entirely different reasons for it. A fear of heights may mean to one person not having his feet on the ground (not being supported), while to another it may refer to the fear of jumping. One could spend a lifetime trying to figure out meanings of phobias. The crucial focus must be on what is real – the real fears. To make fears real is to make phobias unnecessary.

What seems to validate the Primal hypothesis regarding fear is how phobias disappear, not to return in *any* form, once real fear has been felt. I wish to stress that any current irrational behaviour cannot be solved by dealing with the irrationality; no logic, no facts can dissuade irrational conduct. Current situations do not call forth irrational behaviour in normal people. The basis of phobias (Primal fears) is something real; only the current context makes the phobia irrational.

It is tempting to believe that someone can help dispel a current problem by one means or another. The whole idea of counselling neurotics and presenting them with brochures offering facts (Methedrine destroys liver tissue, for example) seems to me misguided. Information is of some value, but the great force behind irrational behaviour is the Primal force. A few facts sprinkled here and there are not going to turn back the Primal tide. Counselling someone to be nice to his wife or child is not going to mean much to someone who has decades of suppressed fury inside him waiting for release and resolution. We need to keep in mind that we are not dealing with fears or anger; we are dealing with *people* who have fears. The essence of Primal Therapy is to help people live through the great fears of their early experiences so that they can experience all there is to experience now without fear.

KIM

My early family life contains the seeds of my neurosis. The theme that runs consistently through these years is the failure of my parents to demonstrate their love for me in any way other than the bestowal of material gifts. I do not remember one instance of being picked up or held as a child. And yet I could never admit that my parents do not love me. I felt ugly and angry instead of feeling or even figuring out the implications and consequences of this absence of love.

But how do I know that my parents never have and never will love me? Not too long ago my mother related a scene to me (in much the same way as she might have described the ninth innings of a baseball game) in which my father saw me for the first time when he returned home from the Second World War. He made my mother wake me up, he saw that I looked like any other baby, and he left the room. When I heard that, I am told, I cried for hours. Of course, I do not remember this scene, but I do know that for about one year after that night I went through a nightly ritual of getting up on all fours and banging my head against the headboard of my crib. I think I was afraid of being abandoned. By means of the noise of my head crashing against my crib, I wanted to remind my parents, who slept in the next room, of my existence.

Another indication of this lack of love is that my father made it quite clear that he wanted a son. He used to tease my mother about not being able to have a boy. My hair was always cropped short. When I came home from school, I was told to change into jeans and a T-shirt. Later I drank beer while I watched football games with my father on weekends. If he wanted a son, I would be that son in order to have him love me.

Finally, there is one incident in which my father overtly told me that he could never love me the way I am – that is, that I would have to change into someone else to win his love. Following an argument with him over the telephone when I was away at college, my father wrote me a 'conciliatory letter' in which he told me not to worry about our disagreement. He asked me to return home for the summer so that together we could 'create a new Kim Storey' – presumably one both he and I could accept.

The love that I was given took the form of meaningless restrictions and rigid discipline levelled against me 'for my own good'. I used to have to beg to obtain consent to do the things most children ordinarily are allowed to do: to spend the night at a friend's house, to invite a friend over, to stay up past my bedtime. I used to wake up in the morning and trip over a list of ten things I had to do before I could leave the house. (I am convinced my mother lies awake nights composing these lists.) These restrictions made me a nervous, irritable child. Failure to comply brought on spankings when I was small and vicious slaps and/or grounding (restriction to quarters) for a month when I was a teenager. The 'administration of justice' was usually accompanied by a good deal of screaming. I can remember my father on various occasions when, after a battle, he came into my room and demanded to know why I was so miserable and nasty when I had everything anybody could possibly want. What could I possibly want? I could never answer. His question confused me. It did seem that I had everything. It never occurred to me to tell him that what I really wanted was for him to love me and to show it. It seems as though I stopped wanting out loud. To have asked him to love me would have been to risk his refusal. Then I would have to admit and feel how much I did want him and how much it hurt not to have him. Instead, I submerged my want beneath a vague, solitary, yet violent anger. In answer to my father's question I never once said anything.

The last thing to mention regarding my early life is the tone of life in my parents' house. There was constantly an argument, and I was constantly involved. The idea was to say the one thing that would cut the adversary (in my case usually my mother or sister) the most deeply and in the most vulnerable spot. With continual practice this art became almost a reflex – a reflex employed by all of us against each other. Such verbal exchanges usually exploded into violent swinging between my sister and me or a sound slap delivered to me by my father. I remember an argument between my mother and me when I was twelve in which she said to my father, 'Bob, either she goes or I go.' I volunteered. Being that this activity was not merely occasional, I learned to keep myself covered at all times and to behave aggressively or to speak sarcastically so that I would not have to show how hurt I was and therefore not be vulnerable to future attacks. Moreover, the aggressive or sarcastic defence often enabled me not to feel the hurt underneath at all.

The common denominator of what I have been describing is lack of love – a lack that I could never admit or even feel and that I had to cover with a variety of defences. I mean by defence the cutting off of all feeling by almost any means available in order not to have to feel the enormous pain of never having been loved. This cutting off is not a decision consciously made. Rather it seems to be a reflex employed by the body to protect its integrity way back when I began to bang my head against my crib. My life (until therapy) had been a recurring cycle from that point on. The motivating force in that cycle of defences is not being loved. There had been no progress; the only thing that changed was the degree of sophistication in my defences which covered my need and desire to be loved.

One defence – part of me since age four – is the acquisition of many chronic conditions. When I was four, my father punished me by throwing me (like a football) into the top bunk of my bed. I vividly remember my fear at finding myself flying through the air and landing partly on my bed and partly on the wall. Shortly thereafter I developed the inexplicable and untreatable eruption of my skin into huge boils. Arising for no 'apparent reason', this condition lasted for two years.

I believe that this infection, as well as others (acne since age ten, fungus infection on my feet, vaginal infections), were the result of unexpressed and only partially felt fear. On the occasion of my being hurled into my bunk I realised that my father could seriously injure or even kill me if he wanted to. I would have to change myself in order to please him and to appease his potential anger.

I can remember playing fantasy games with my sister. Both of us always wanted to be the guy (both of us were always males in our games) who was injured in the act of helping others. He was the one who received love and attention. This desire to be taken care of and, by extension, loved could be acted out in games but never expressed to my parents. To do so would be to risk their refusal.

Only when I was sick did my parents seem concerned about me in a positive way (as opposed to imposing restrictions for my 'benefit'). This explains why during my first year at college and away from home I was sick constantly. I think I was trying to tell my parents indirectly that I still needed them and that I wanted them to take care of me.

Another defence is that I became a very cold person. I rejected any warmth directed towards me as weak or limiting. For me love meant only restrictions. Moreover, if I had shown my love for my parents or, by extension, for anyone, I would have been vulnerable to their attacks. Even more important, to accept affection from anyone could only serve to remind me of all the years I had been denied that warmth by those from whom I needed it most. I would have to feel all of that pain.

Rejection by my parents and especially by my father drastically affected my relationship with males. Until the age of sixteen I competed with males on both an intellectual and a physical level. I looked like, talked like, and had the athletic ability of a boy. Later I made all males the reservoir out of which I tried to extract the love I never got from my father. A mind-body dualism was at work here. My men had to be very tall, athletic and muscle-bound. At the same time they had to be beneath my intelligence level. I had to be able to control them and my involvement with them in some way. I could have all of the physical love that I had been denied without getting involved mentally. I never had to take the risk of being rejected as I had been by my father. The result was promiscuity. At the time I could not understand the irresistible force that led me to sleep with anyone who resembled Charles Atlas.

This pattern of promiscuity broke down after a boyfriend with whom I did get involved, if only accidentally, rejected me. I fell to pieces. After that, the only males I felt comfortable around were gay, sexless, or old friends. I also began to spend more and more time with gay girls. Although I never acted out being a lesbian, I often felt like one. (I wore a dress to therapy for the first month in order to appear more feminine.) At the same time I developed a chronic vaginal infection which prevented me from sleeping with anyone. I had tried to be a boy and failed to win my father's love. Then I pretended I was a woman in order to get love from anybody. I ended up a neuter.

My primary defence against feeling unloved was school. This defence was intimately related to the hope that I could *make* my parents love me. My performance in school was perfect: high grades, school offices and a variety of honours. I hoped to get my parents' approval by showing them that others approved of me.

While intellectuality was the means by which I hoped to be special enough to earn my parents' love, it was also the means by which I could keep myself one step removed from my Pain. Whenever I felt badly as a child, I picked up the nearest book and lost myself in it. I might feel my Pain by crying when something very good or very bad happened to a character with whom I could identify. In college I studied (avidly) European intellectual history with an emphasis on German history. My parents had always hated Germany – somewhat blindly in my estimation. They seemed to dislike me for no apparent reason as well. I wanted to find out where Germany went wrong. Perhaps I could find out what I did to lose my parents. Germany, being confusion and anarchy inside, always sought power and influence outside her boundaries. I, being confusion and unfelt Pain inside, always sought to prove myself to anyone who would listen to me how smart I was.

By the time I entered graduate school the illusion that scholastic achievement would win my parents was gone. Moreover, school bored me, and I no longer had the discipline to do well. It was then I needed a new defence against the ascending Pain. I found it in drugs. I had smoked marijuana for a few years in college. I found that no matter how badly I felt, grass would make me feel better. I also enjoyed dropping acid. Aside from the moments when an unhappy scene from my childhood emerged without warning, my trips were pleasant. I hallucinated and at one point experienced complete ego loss. Ego loss is, after all, not knowing who you are. Having denied all my Pain, this loss of ego really was symptomatic of my condition. Both the hallucinations and the ego loss have stopped now that I have felt my Pain and have given up the struggle to win my parents' love.

When I went away to New York to attend graduate school, acid and grass were no longer adequate to keep the Pain inside. I frequently burst into fits of tears without warning. I had to find some way to kill the Pain and to mitigate the loneliness and desperation I felt in New York City. I turned to Methedrine to lift my spirits and to heroin to allow me to go to sleep. But even these drugs were not enough. The physical and mental breakdown came anyway.

I left New York and completely fell apart. I entered Primal Therapy two months later. I did so because all of my defences were breaking down and I was out of control. My brain was of no help. I could not understand why, when I had analysed myself so thoroughly, everything was not all right. Primal Therapy taught me that the feeling of not being loved by my parents had never been resolved, that the cycle of breakdown and recovery by means of the adoption of substitutes of new defences to cover my need could never have been broken because I always had run from my Pain instead of feeling it.

The first stage in therapy was the blasting away of what was left of my already crumbling defence system. The mere absence of drugs and cigarettes heightened my tension to the point where my body shook. Although I had lived alone in a city where I knew no one, it was not until the isolation required by the first three weeks of therapy that I really felt completely alone. I had always thought that I was alone because I chose to be, and if I did not want to be alone, I would not have to be. Now it became clear that I have been alone all my life and that during all these years the thing I had wanted was to be a part of something (the family) or, more specifically, of someone (my parents). I realised that when I was alone before, I could always feel somebody watching me move and penetrating my thoughts. I believe now that this undefined presence felt before was the hope that my parents cared about me. Now I feel as well as know that I am completely alone.

With the most obvious of my defences removed, my mind became flooded with memories of my past. All of them made me sad – even the happiest of them because these were so few. I began re-living scenes from my past. I re-lived them by placing myself back in a scene and re-experiencing it – this time without my defences – giving full expression to my feelings.

The greatest number of my Primals during the first few months of my therapy centred on my being cold. As soon as I lay flat, my body shook, my teeth chattered, and my hands and feet turned blue. I had Primals lasting up to two hours in which I just shivered. At first I regarded the cold as caused by something outside me: The weather or a distasteful person or experience 'turned me cold'. Then I realised that the cold (the neurosis) was inside – not just on the surface of my skin, but inside my entire body. These neurotic layers of ice which covered the Pain caused by my parents' not having loved me had to be discarded before I could re-live the painful experiences they covered.

When the shivering had almost subsided, I became completely defenceless. Often when I saw my parents, I would cry at the slightest sign of their disapproval. One night I went to see Chekhov's *The Sea Gull*. During the scene in which the son begs his mother not to leave him, I felt a wave of feeling rush up from my stomach. Knowing I could not have a Primal in the theatre, I tried to shake off the feeling. I blacked out and had to be carried from the theatre.

Once such deeply seated pains are released there is no stopping them. Not allowing these feelings to come out often results in complete and utter confusion. In my case this confusion often takes the form of incoherent speech and a kind of aphasia. One night I talked with five members of the therapy group. I could not understand anything anyone said. I could understand individual words, but put together in sentences, nothing made sense. I could hardly talk at all. I had the feeling I was not all there; part of my mind was somewhere else. When I did try to talk, I made no sense. The confusion resulting from the lack of communication cut me off from everyone in the room; it was symbolic of my aloneness. Once I realised this, I went right into a Primal in which I begged my parents not to leave me all alone. The confusion subsided.

Another time the confusion arising from not allowing an onrushing feeling to come up caused acute spatial disorientation. My boyfriend was angry with me, and although we had company over, he made a point of demonstrating it. I began to feel that complete rejection was coming very soon. I would be all all alone again. I cut off the feeling and tried to play good hostess. Then I turned around and walked into the wall of my own kitchen. I had an enormous bump on my head for quite a while. As soon as I allowed the feeling of being rejected by my boyfriend to burst through and connected it to the much larger Pain which was the rejection of my father, I regained coherence of speech and co-ordination. When the final break did come, it was relatively painless since I was being rejected only by a boyfriend and not by my father.

My big breakthrough came five months after I began therapy. While I was sitting in a group session, my eyes went out of focus and I felt as if I would black out. I often felt this way before an intense Primal. Then I was on the couch screaming louder than I ever have. First just shrieks, followed by: 'Mommy, Daddy, please take me home. Please, I want to go home. Mommy, Daddy, I love you,' followed by still louder screams. During this time I was not aware of my body. My entire being was concentrated in this screaming voice. I became my Pain. I was saying what I have wanted to say ever since I can remember. I could never have said this to my parents because of the fear that they would reject overtly my love and me. But with no defences, the words just burst out of my mouth. I was completely defenceless, completely out of control for the first time in my life. This was the turning point in my therapy.

For the next three months I begged my parents not to hurt me in my Primals. I had told them I loved them – I was wide open and therefore completely vulnerable to my Pain. In one Primal I screamed, 'Stop hurting me, Daddy,' at the top of my lungs. I must have sounded as though I was being murdered. I certainly felt like that was what was happening. This is in fact true. I did kill my real self and become an unreal person, first, so that I might have a chance to get my parents' love and, later, to cover up the pain of never having received the love I wanted and needed so badly. The Pain came up in huge waves several times daily. Often I had to leave my classroom on the verge of tears. Each night I dreamed scenes in which my parents rejected and even hated me. I awoke with a sob in my throat each morning. I found it hard to get out of bed at all and almost impossible to function as a teacher during the week. It seemed as though I would never be able to function in the face of the waves of Pain which I thought would go on forever.

It is now nine months since I entered Primal Therapy. I am a new person – or, better put, my own person, myself. My psychosomatic symptoms are beginning to disappear. The poor circulation in my hands and feet has improved significantly and I have rid myself of the tension which I thought would be part of me for the rest of my life.

Although I had been through a period of sexual promiscuity, I was frigid before, during, and after that time. I could never have allowed myself to feel anything, not even sexual pleasure. If I had felt anything at all, I would have had to feel all of the denied Pain inside of me. Now I find that when I try to delay the emergence of a feeling or to quell it in any way, I am sexually frigid. When I face the oncoming feeling – that is, when I can feel myself – I am no longer frigid.

I no longer require drugs to keep me as far away from the fact that I am all alone (and always have been) with nobody to love me or even to take care of me. I cannot feel and be on drugs at the same time. I learned that I must feel my Pain (as opposed to keeping it submerged with drugs) in order to be rid of it permanently. Once I could face my Pain instead of running from it, drugs no longer served any purpose. I stopped using. I *feel*, as well as realise, that my parents have not and will not love me as I am. I have chosen to be myself instead of trying (consciously and unconsciously) to figure out what they want in exchange for their love. I am free.

SUICIDE

Suicide is attempted, in my opinion, when all the ways an individual has tried to kill his Pain have come to naught. When neurosis fails to ease Pain, the person may be forced into more drastic measures. It may sound paradoxical, but suicide is the last refuge of hope for the neurotic determined to be unreal to the end.

A young woman of twenty-nine who went through Primal Therapy made an attempt on her life several months before treatment. Her lover left her for someone else. She begged, pleaded, and finally threatened him all to no avail. She then went home, cleaned the house, took a shower, got into a fresh nightgown, and took ninety sleeping pills. She counted out the pills methodically in half-dozen lots feeling totally separated from what she was doing. She said, 'I felt strangely detached from it all, as though it wasn't really happening to me. It was only when I began to feel my breathing slow down that I got scared, called my friend, and asked for a doctor.'

When this woman's lover left, he left her feeling unloved. While she may have convinced herself that she was trying to kill herself because of what was happening at the moment, the current loss seemed to have set off the feeling of the years of being unloved. When he left, she said she began to re-experience the emptiness she felt as a child. Rejected by her parents, she had come to feel ugly and unlovable; she was certain that something must have been very wrong with her to be so neglected. She used her lover to cover that ugly feeling. But when he left – he saw the impossibility of filling the void left by a lifetime of rejection – she was forced into those rejected and hopeless feelings all over again. She tried to kill herself before the full impact of those feelings set in.

The detachment often reported by attempted suicides reinforces the Primal hypothesis that suicide is a split act in which the aim rarely is to destroy oneself irrevocably. It is an attempt to *preserve* the *self* by obliterating the Pain that neurosis can no longer cover. This woman never thought she would die; witness the fact that when her death looked imminent, she called for help. Evidently, neurotics try to kill themselves symbolically, as they do everything else. Some are willing to go the whole way to keep the neurosis intact. As one patient put it, 'Suicide isn't so irrational if you consider that any neurosis is the struggle to keep what you don't want.'

Neurosis is psychological suicide. If one has given up part or all of one's life (one's feelings) for one's parents in order to be loved, it is not too big a step to killing that self off in a more literal way. When neurosis fails, suicide is considered.

Many neurotics seem to want to die rather than live the way they do. I do not believe a real urgency to die produces the suicidal act, so much as the feeling of not knowing what else to do to ease the Pain. The person is all out of struggles. Either he needs a new struggle which will offer temporary relief, or he needs to kill the struggle altogether in Primal Therapy.

Neurosis, it must be remembered, both saves and kills. It protects the real self from further disintegration, but in doing so, it buries the real self. The child then grows up clinging to an unreal self, which paradoxically is strangling the life out of him.

If we think of this as a progression, it may become more clear. The young child first tries to be loved for what he is. Failing that, he tries for love through being something else. But when that something else (the unreal self) fails to get anything like love, there are two choices left open. Early in life it may be psychosis. Later in life the choice may be suicide.

Suicide is hope; it is acting out in such a way as to kill the feeling of ascending hopelessness. It is often a desperate attempt to avoid the castastrophic feeling that not a single human on this earth really cares. At the very moment when the person through his attempt is saying, 'I give up,' he is also saying, 'I'll make you care even if it's the last desperate thing I do.'

Sometimes the attempt does produce the desired result. People begin calling; the family may come to help out; everyone seems sorry for not realising how desperate the person was. But when the friends stop their visits, when the family leaves, the would-be suicide is again left alone with the self he is willing to destroy rather than feel.

In general, the suicide attempt is an act of someone who has lived outside himself and through others (not having been allowed to live within his own wants and feelings). 'They' have become the meaning of his life, and their loss removes that meaning. The centre of suicide-prone individuals' existence often lies outside themselves. They are as strong as others' support, as presentable as the appraisal of others will permit.

A young man in Primal Therapy reported the increasing agitation of his mother with whom he lived. The more he improved, the more depressed she became. Most of this patient's life he had been caring for his mother, who was usually too sick to do much and was suffering from one vague complaint after another. As he grew independent, she became desperate. He planned to leave home and live on his own. At this point his mother tried bribing him with a new car, then pleading, threatening, becoming ill. When all failed, she made a half-hearted suicide attempt with sleeping pills. She called a friend almost the minute she took them, however, so that she was never in any real danger.

This patient's mother found it inconceivable to have to care for herself. She had been separated from her husband for many years and tried to make her son the new husband. Since the earliest years of marriage, she had manipulated everyone so that she could act out being the dependent child – precisely what her own mother had done to her. At the age of fifty she was still trying to be the baby she was never allowed to be. She was willing to kill herself to continue that act. It was the baby in her which evidently felt that it could not go on without someone to lean on.

There are, of course, quite serious attempts at suicide

which do succeed. In such instances, the person may have suffered such a serious mental disturbance that he can no longer distinguish between real or unreal. Even here, in the inner reaches of his sick mentality he may harbour hope that his death will finally make 'them' see and feel.

When we closely examine self-hate and the resultant attempts at self-destruction we find it is the unreal self that is truly disliked. Because suicide is, for the most part, an unreal act, we must assume that it is perpetrated by the unreal self. The point of suicide seems to come when *neither* the unreal nor the real self can be loved. What must be done with the pre-suicide, in my opinion, is to help him feel the self he wants to destroy, to feel 'if no one loves me, I'll die' to its full intensity. Once he feels that the unloved self isn't really a threat to his continued existence, he is not likely to want to destroy it.

What the pre-suicide and attempted suicide usually receive is help in covering the very feeling they were close to. Perhaps they will find their way to a crisis clinic, where efforts are made to patch things up, to reassure and keep patients functioning. Often drugs are prescribed to ease the patient, thus taking him still farther from his feelings. Yet it is those very feelings that must be felt in order to do away with the irrationally acting unreal self. The danger, I submit, comes from the unreal, acting-out self, and it is that unreal self that seems to be bolstered by the crisis approach. I suppose that as long as the person has a therapist to hold onto, the danger of suicide will be minimised. But when the patient leaves the therapist, what reason is there to believe he is not still self-destructive and still suicide-prone? If he has not felt the agony of that unloved, hopeless little child inside himself, he may unwittingly kill him.

Crisis clinics address themselves to temporarily bolstering the desperate person's coping techniques when the patient cannot handle his life in the accustomed manner. Yet isn't it just this 'accustomed manner' that needs overthrowing instead of reinforcing? To reinforce a defence system tends to be de-humanising, in my estimation, because it alienates the person from his deepest feelings. Of course, there are practical considerations: It can be reasoned that there isn't enough time to do what can otherwise be done quickly with a crisis approach. And what if the person doesn't *want* to change radically? I believe that anyone has a right to be unreal, but at least he should be informed that there is an alternative to trying to get by from one suicide attempt to the next.

We must also consider the societal effects of allowing a potential suicide to roam the streets. Behind the wheel of a car and wanting to end it all, he may also take someone else with him. A person who disregards his own life isn't too likely to consider the lives of others inherently precious.

In this conjunction, it may be significant to note that Primal patients do not consider suicide. They come to value themselves and wouldn't consider taking chances with their lives. They learn that the real self is a 'good' self and find no reason to want to harm it.

It seems incongruous to say that the aim of killing oneself is to live, but my experience with the attempted suicides makes it difficult to reach any other conclusion. There are exceptions – such as the chronically ill – but as a rule, the attempt at death is one more neurotic plea to be loved. In this sense, the attempt at death is a cry for life.

19

Drugs and Addictions

LYSERGIC ACID DIETHYLAMIDE (LSD-25)

For many young people, LSD (also known as acid) is a way
of life. The effects of LSD seem so profound, yet so mystical,
that it has become a cult, a *Weltanschauung*. Chronic users
often call it the 'big voyage into inner space'. Others term it
'the reality trip'.

I believe that LSD is a reality trip in the sense that it
stimulates intense real feelings. But the neurotic does with
this reality what he does with reality in general: changes it
into something symbolic.

There is little doubt that LSD stimulates feelings. We
have clinical evidence for this. Recently LSD was fed to a
group of monkeys, who were then destroyed and autopsied.
The greatest concentration of the drug was found in those
areas of the brain known to be related to feeling.

The problem with the use of LSD is that it artificially
opens up individuals to more reality than they can tolerate
within their neurotic systems, resulting in a daytime nightmare – psychosis. The defence is there for a reason – to
maintain integrity of the organism. LSD upsets the defence
system with the tragic result that LSD users are filling the
wards of neuropsychiatric wards across the country. Generally, when the drug wears off, the neurotic defence can be
recaptured. But in some cases where the original defence
system was weak, it cannot be.

The strength of the defence system plus the dose ingested
will largely determine how a person reacts under LSD. It can
and does happen that a person with a fortified defence
system can have no reaction whatsoever to the drug. To
remove artificially a weak defensive front when there is a
great storehouse of Primal Pains is to produce an overwhelming onrush of stimulation.

One of the reasons LSD has been called a mind-expand-
ing drug (psychedelic) is symbolic flight. The stimulation of
feelings produces an explosion of symbolic ideation, and
this is often mistaken for mind expansion. What we need to

understand is that this expansion is a defence. The manic psychotic with a wild flight of ideas is a perfect example of mind expansion in the race away from feeling. Manic patients I have seen, often with brilliant minds, have on occasion written reams of material during their manic phase. One wrote the equivalent of a book in a matter of three or four weeks.

What distinguishes psychosis from neurosis is the degree and complexity of the symbolisation. In neurosis there is still ample hold on reality. In psychosis that hold may be lost, and the person may be enveloped by symbolism, no longer being able to differentiate between symbols (voices in the walls) and reality. As the deterioration process continues, the person may no longer even know who he is, 'where he is at', or in what year he is living.

The results of the use of LSD would seem to bear out one of the key Primal hypotheses: that neurosis begins to keep us from the reality of our feelings and that those feelings, if fully felt early in life, could lead to insanity. To stimulate *all* the old Primal feelings suddenly and unnaturally with the use of a drug is to produce the same possibilities for insanity.

In the early days of LSD research, the drug was called a psychotomimetic (psychosis-imitating) agent. It was used to study psychosis. At first there was not too much concern because the drug itself was believed to produce the psychosis – when the drug was removed, the psychosis would disappear. But when in some cases psychosis remained after the drug was removed, enthusiasm waned. Consequently, LSD was outlawed for most research purposes, as well as for general use.

I believe that LSD not only mimes psychosis but produces a real, though often transient, insanity. Furthermore, I do not think that the intrinsic properties of the drug have anything to do with producing bizarre reactions except insofar as they stimulate more feeling than can be integrated.

Several months ago, a young woman of twenty-one, diagnosed at a local neuropsychiatric hospital as a 'post-LSD schizophrenic', was referred for Primal treatment. She had taken a large dose of acid after several marijuana cigarettes. During her acid trip, she went into a panic state. When the drug wore off, she found she was having 'spells'. At times she felt as though she were being lifted out of her chair and carried away. At other times she would stare desperately at a light bulb or a lamp, never sure if what she saw was really there.

She was sent to the neuropsychiatric hospital for observation, tranquillised, and returned home in a week. The spells of unreality continued, however, and after many weeks of this I began treating her. She was immediately put into a Primal, where she began to re-live the acid experience without any prompting or direction. She said, 'Everything smells like shit. There's shit on the walls. My God, it is everywhere. I can't get it off me.' (There she tried to brush it off, but I pushed her to feel what it was.) 'Ooh! Ooh! I'm going crazy. Who am I? Who am I!' (I made her stay with the feeling: 'Stay with it! Feel it!') 'Aah! It's me, I'm shit, I'm shit!' At this point she began weeping and poured out a trail of insights about how 'shitty' she had always felt (but never recognised). She talked about her impoverished family, which consisted of a drunken father and a beaten, abused mother. She discussed how 'lumpen' she felt. She had never aspired to or tried to do anything because she felt like 'a piece of shit, not worthy of anything from anybody'. She had covered her feelings and background with a pseudo-intellectuality and cultured veneer which the acid evidently blasted off. At the point where she would have felt the reality – 'I'm shit' – she flipped out (of her feelings) and hallucinated faeces on the wall. She made her ascending reality unreal in order to survive.

Another case of psychosis was not drug-induced at all. This patient at the age of seven was sent away to boarding school as a result of her parents' divorce. Her father moved to another city, and her mother had to work. The little girl was promised that she would be visited often by her mother. This did not happen. Her mother's visits became infrequent, she showed up drunk, with boyfriends, and then she stopped coming entirely. Her mother wrote letters explaining why she could not come but soon stopped writing altogether. The child began to feel the reality of her abandonment. She started to withdraw from social contact, and to quell the abandoned feeling, she devised an imaginary companion who was always with her. As time passed, this companion began talking to her and telling her strange things. It told her that certain people were against her and trying to isolate her from everyone. Slowly, she began sinking into a psychosis to ward off a shattering reality.

In both cases cited, I believe it was *reality* that produced the unreality; both persons went insane to keep from going sane and seeing the truth. They 'went to pieces', so to speak, as protection against comprehending a whole truth.

At the Primal Scene, faced with this truth, an alternating system came into being to help hide reality. Its function was to fragment and then symbolise the truth enabling the neurotic child to act out his feelings without being aware of them. He began his act. But when reality is overwhelming, either because an event is shattering or because a drug such as LSD doesn't allow for the usual act, psychosis looms. With LSD there is little room to act out in the usual way. The person cannot become involved in his paper work, for example; the feelings are too strong and immediate. They must be symbolised mentally (bizarre ideas-delusions) or physically (from the inability to lift one arm to a complete lack of physical co-ordination). In the case of bizarre bodily changes, we may say that such a person has 'physicalised' his psychosis. This would mean that the same split or dissociation is there as in psychosis.

This split was discussed by a formerly psychotic patient: 'It was terrifying to feel the body becoming mine – to see my little girl self trying to understand the movement of her legs and feet. My body had always acted on its own, like something that had nothing to do with me. Could it be that the reason the schizophrenic is so often obsessed with his body is that it is such a foreign thing? I guess that eventually the body must truly be separate from awareness in order to stay far away from the Pain. The secret twisting of meaning of what is going on around you, I suppose, is this automatic process of making the body and the feelings so separate.'

Another example of the physicalisation of feeling is provided by a patient who, in a one-year period prior to therapy, had taken LSD ten times. Among his other reactions he always felt a persistent buzzing in his mouth throughout each trip. During his Primals the buzzing sensation also occurred, and he inexplicably began to suck his thumb. The buzzing still went on, however, until he realised that it wasn't a thumb he wanted to suck, but his mother's breast. As soon as he felt this feeling, the buzzing ceased.

This man was weaned abruptly in the earliest months of his life according to some timetable his mother found in a child-rearing book. Though he smoked two packs of cigarettes a day and sucked on his cigarette with a vengeance, this man found it hard to believe that he still had an old need to suck his mother's breast. But he did recall having had something in his mouth from the time his memory began. He had covered his feelings so well that the only time he came close to feeling them was when he took a powerful drug, and even then he could not get to the feeling completely. But the point is made – symbolisation sets in to protect the organism when feelings are excessively painful.

About twenty Primal patients took LSD before their therapy, several repeatedly. In the early development of Primal Therapy, several patients took LSD during their treatment without my knowledge. These patients later told me that they believed that LSD would hurry their therapies along. (As previously pointed out, not only are all drugs, even aspirin, prohibited during Primal Therapy, but patients are now given written instructions to make certain that there will be no repetition of the LSD usage that occurred before our controls became so stringent.) Nevertheless, the LSD experience of some seven patients who took the drug during therapy was valuable in terms of understanding the psychological reactions to LSD. Those Primal patients with old Pains were bombarded directly by their remaining feelings and were able to connect them immediately to their origins. These feelings were not symbolised in any way but arose and were felt in successive order. In some cases, these Pains continued in free-association style for two to three hours.

Two patients who took LSD after their third and fourth months of therapy had momentary, symbolic reactions. In the first case, the patient began to hallucinate seeing people on the panelling of the walls doing strange things to one another. As he became intrigued by the drama staged in the panelling, it suddenly hit him: 'I was putting on a show for myself outside so that I wouldn't have to feel what was going on inside. That sideshow drama really did contain a lot of my feelings, especially anger. I guess I was trying to convince myself that all those battles were outside me and had nothing to do with me.' He added, 'As soon as I knew that those were *my* feelings, I let go and felt what it was all the way, and my little drama on the wall disappeared.' Prior to Primal Therapy, however, chances are that he would have remained in his hallucinations, possibly for hours or even weeks until all the affects of the drug had worn off. In any case, the symbolism was short-lived and did lead to feeling because there was no impacted defence to maintain the dissociative process.

The second patient took LSD in his fourth month of therapy. He had delusions that people were being unnecessarily hard on him, that no one in the room was kind, and that everyone wanted him to suffer for some reason. His hands became swollen and tender, he reported, and then he felt the feeling 'Be tender with me, Daddy.' The swelling and tenderness disappeared along with his delusions about people conspiring to be cruel to him. It is doubtful that he could have made that simple connection if he had still had much Pain to block his feelings.

Most of the seven patients who took LSD after several months of Primal Therapy had used it before; not surprisingly, they unanimously reported symbolic trips prior to therapy. One person found that his hands were paralysed during a previous trip, while another writhed on the floor with terrible stomach cramps for hours. A third person saw worms coming out of his nose and feet, and someone else saw his skeleton when he looked in the mirror. Later, as they looked back at those experiences, they were surprised by how automatically the body seems to symbolise Pain. The symbol in each case referred to a specific unfelt feeling. The person who saw worms was projecting how dirty, slimy and ugly he felt and, during the Primal, re-lived the ugly feelings in the context which produced them. The one with paralysed hands later felt his deep helplessness and immobility and felt what caused them. The person with stomach cramps (still a symbolic Pain) felt that he was giving birth under LSD. Even that feeling under the drug did not bring an end to his cramps. I suspect that *pains* do not cease until they are felt as *Pains*.

Those patients near the termination of therapy had no measurable affect from the drug. They did not report anything except minor sensation and perception changes. There were no delusions or hallucinations, none of the depersonalisation feelings. Their trips were neither mystical nor beautiful – only real feelings emerged. This is a significant finding because it adds evidence to the Primal hypothesis concerning mental illness and Primal Pain. In the absence of significant Primal Pain, there is no mental illness under intense stimulation (stress).

My observations indicate that LSD does *not* appear to be a hallucinogen in the normal person. Nor is it a psychotomimetic drug except for those with Primal Pain.

What LSD does not do is allow connections to be made solidly. And only connection accounts for lasting change. There are many reasons why connections cannot be made under LSD; the most important is that connection means experiencing Primal Pain. Under LSD, persons may have a feeling and several minutes later not be sure they even had it. The drug drives them from one fleeting feeling to another, no single feeling being anchored solidly into consciousness. Full consciousness is absolutely necessary for a full feeling experience; otherwise, it is a mass of sensations which some people think are feelings. One patient put it this way: 'Primals are surer than LSD. When you've had a feeling during a Primal, it can last an hour, and then you can hook it up to events in your life, why you did such and such, why you picked so and so for your friend, and so on. With LSD I was driven on and on. I couldn't concentrate long enough on anything. The drug produced so many impulses at once that one beginning feeling led to another in an endless chain until I thought I was going crazy.' What he was saying, in effect, is that drugs tend to cloud consciousness; even a drug such as LSD which is supposed to heighten consciousness still produces a drugged state. Another patient who had taken LSD remarked on this: 'Even though I knew I had a feeling under LSD, I would turn to my friend afterwards and say, "Did I just say that or was I imagining that I said it?" ' In short, he wasn't sure what was real even though what he was saying and feeling might have been very real. The drug mitigates the full impact of reality.

Not one of the people who had taken LSD before Primal Therapy said that they ever got to the basic Primal feelings with the drug. For example, the horrible aloneness feeling during a Primal, the aloneness coupled with a memory of being left alone in the crib, was never experienced with the drug. Too much was going on under LSD to allow oneself to be taken back step by step into painful early memories, and even with the drug, real traumatic Primal Pains will still be symbolised.

What LSD does not do, in short, is allow to take place the specific decoding process in which certain feelings are linked to special memories and then resolved. The man with the buzzing in his mouth had ten LSD trips and never felt its real meaning. It took a Primal to make the proper connection.

This is not to say that LSD does not produce many insights that would not be achieved under ordinary conditions. But those insights are still fragmented, taking place within a neurotic system. It is as though the terrible physical pains that many suffer under LSD and the insights they later have during the same drug trip never seem to link up. Primal Pain is the intermediary keeping them apart.

The statement that LSD is not necessarily psychotogenic (psychosis-producing) in normal people may need more clarification. I suppose if a person were given enough LSD, it might produce such a plethora of impulses in the brain as to bring about complete disorientation and a momentary psychosis. But the point is that this state would not last beyond the effect of the drug in a normal person, while it may have a permanent effect in the neurotic. I cannot overstress its danger to the neurotic. Even one trip, though not producing a psychosis, can leave the user's defence system sufficiently rattled to make him susceptible to situations at a later date that might not have ordinarily affected him.

There are LSD trips called bummers – scary experiences or very depressed ones or both. The person may be overwhelmed by fear of monsters, or he may see spiders crawling all over him. These people can be brought out of their bad trips with the use of tranquillisers such as chlorpromazine. Tranquillisers are also used extensively in mental hospitals to reduce hallucinations and delusions. I believe that what is being tranquillised in these situations is Primal Pain, thus reducing the need to symbolise. The tranquilliser seems to ease the patient's agitation and gives him a chance to recover – that is, to re-*cover* the Pain and, with that, to recover his neurosis. All things being equal, the bummer is a trip that comes dangerously close to the Pain.

It is possible that the first LSD trip may not be a bummer because there are defences at work. But several trips seem to constitute an assault of the defence system, and then trouble may begin, for when there is Pain, the trip must be painful. Not surprisingly, after a bum acid trip, the person is not likely to try the drug again, yet he is just the one who seems close to getting real. He stops before it happens, possibly because he senses that real and unreal are a package – the closer one gets, the farther one must flee. Primal Therapy patients at the *very end* of their treatment often feel they are going crazy when they are about to strip themselves of the last shred of defence against the total feeling of aloneness and hopelessness which has always been there. It is perhaps not accidental that we have had good results with people who reported several bad acid trips before therapy.

I am wary of those with continuously beautiful trips because it means that the split is so deep that not even a powerful drug can affect it. The person who is not close to his feelings will tend to take acid or marijuana (or both) time after time in some cases, unconsciously drawn by the implicit hope of feeling which they offer. Each time, however, he may be having neurotic trips in which he may find himself in a garden of paradise, in a green forest, in an Aztec palace. The substance of the symbolic trip is not crucial except as it may refer indirectly to the underlying Pain. What we need to remember is that the pretty trip for a neurotic *must be unreal* since to stimulate feelings in a neurotic with the use of drugs is to stimulate Pain. The person on a pretty or mystical drug trip is doing no more than the pesudo-happy, effervescent (bubbly with tension) neurotic does without drugs: painting pretty mind pictures to hide from what is going on in the body and in the recesses of the mind.

HEROIN

LSD is one of the few drugs that stimulate feelings. Many others deaden them. One of the most effective deadeners is heroin. Heroin is pressed into service when the neurosis cannot suppress Pain. Neurosis is the internal narcotic of the non-addict.

The heroin addict has usually run out of internal defences to stop his tension. He has to rely on something else to help – the needle. It is my experience that heroin addicts generally fall into two categories. The predominant number of them are lifeless and lethargic, completely zeroed out by tension. They have to dull every inch of themselves to quell their Pain. The other category is manic – the hyperactive person, constantly on the run. Both kinds of people have found different ways to deal with enormous hurt. Both have to use drugs when their defence no longer can drain off enough tension. Some neurotics can feel better with the use of marijuana (see page 392) but marijuana is far too mild for the Pain of the heroin addict. It may be that the heroin user started with marijuana but graduated to stronger drugs when marijuana couldn't do the job. Others with some defences still working for them may have tried marijuana and found it sufficient. In any case, it isn't marijuana which leads to the use of heroin; it is Pain.

Pain alone does not account for the use of drugs. The cultural milieu is certainly a factor. If an upset person grew up in Harlem, near the jazz scene where drugs were commonplace, he could easily gravitate to heroin. But someone who grew up on a farm in Montana might turn to alcohol and bar brawls to rid himself of tension. The internal dynamics for both kinds of individuals might be the same; only the outlet differs.

The high tension level of the drug user usually has kept him on the move – he never could stick to anything long enough to succeed, and this long history of failures has compounded his problems. One reason that standard therapy has not been successful with addicts may be that the average addict cannot sit still long enough for the slow, laborious insight process.

As we know, addicts for the most part are not terribly interested in sex. The reason is not hard to find. Those in pain, whether psychological or physical, are not terribly interested in sex. 'Pain-killers' suppress feeling, thus increase sexlessness. To feel Pain is to be able to to feel all other feelings; to kill Pain is to kill other feelings – and sex is a prime casualty.

The relationship of addiction to latent homosexuality can be seen from a trip to any narcotics hospital, particularly in the case of female addicts. Many of them are homosexual or have a history of suppressed homosexual tendencies. One woman addict explained it this way: 'I never really wanted a man, but I kept having sex with them to keep from feeling how "queer" I was. I know now that I needed and wanted a mother. The more sex I had with men, the more upset and revolted I became. I needed drugs to carry me through. Once I gave in to the dyke scene in prison, the less I needed drugs.'

This woman's early compulsive sexuality with men was the way she *denied* her feelings (her needs for her mother). As long as she denied all her needs, she evidently needed drugs. When she could give in to substitute outlets, her needs for drugs lessened. When put into a prison without drugs to kill off her feelings, she succumbed to overt homosexuality. Once she felt the need for her mother in a Primal, she needed neither drugs nor sex with other women.

Those who need the amphetamines (called speed by the users) and those who require 'downers' (narcotics, barbiturates) similarly reflect only a difference in the direction of tension. Those with deep tension seem to need something to break them out, while those already broken open, who have ascending tension, seem to need something to help them suppress it. There are times when the same person may use both in alternating cycles: Once he is 'tension out', he uses something to calm him down; the more suppressed he becomes, the more he needs stimulants again – and so the cycle goes.

The following is a quote from an addict's letter to me before his treatment:

As I read the word 'pain-killer' to describe heroin, I am reminded of the countless times that people have told me that heroin is a death trip . . . a slow suicide. Yet not until recently did I feel the *killer* aspect of the pain-killer. I've watched other junkies with no hope, job, interests, family, remain in a perpetual state of nodding, on the verge of death-life and I always felt that for me, dope was just a dangerous way of practising medicine without a licence. All I wanted to do was take the edge off an anxiety-filled existence . . . a short-cut to that perfect state of pain-free comfort. It was a way to bring myself up to snuff in order to do my number, to function with concentration and do those things that gotta be done.

All I ever wanted to do was get through life without suffering all those pains which man has lived through since long before I was born. I've lied all of my life to escape punishment and suffering. I scammed my way through school, never studying, ditching classes, never quite getting down to reality. The only thing I ever really accomplished as a kid was to be a magician and it looks like I've been looking for magic ever since. Since early in my life I've mastered the half-truth. This was easy to accomplish since nobody in my family was ever interested in what was really going on.

By the middle of my junior year in college, everything was catching up with me. I had coasted through school without ever exerting myself. I bullshitted, bluffed to make it that far. I left school and went into a business where I had big ideas but little knowledge. I borrowed a lot of money and needless to say, I blew the whole thing in short order. I took a job and got fired. Then it all started crashing in on me and there was no more place to scam. I tried cheating on my wife but ran out of money. Then I found junk ... the perfect cover-up again. With it I didn't have to face anything. The world was fine. I didn't have to admit defeat ... just built new and greater plans in my mind. I started making the Harlem jazz scene. I had known about heroin and knew it was dangerous so I just started snorting it. WOW! Too much. It cooled everything out; no grief, no fears, no disgust with the way I led my life, no nothing. It was the all-time assurance to comfort, grooviness, peace, you name it. H was for me. I didn't have to put it in my veins until the ninth month. My sex drive was gone, I pissed away all the remaining money we had, and things really got bad. I went to a shrink, and I did stop using for a while, even got a job. I said to myself then, Hey, you just walked away from a year and a half of heroin and I was really happy. I still smoked pot but I thought that was just a social thing. My job situation and things really were soaring. But the job ran out, and I hadn't prepared myself to do anything. I planned to write but I didn't. As weeks passed, I started to get scared again. A weekend guest turned out to be a junkie and had some stuff with him. I took my first shot in almost two years. It felt really good again. This time I started right in mainlining, thinking I could control it. I moved to California, hoping things would change, and now I'm strung out on good old California Smack(H). I've cleaned up at least thirty times in the last two years. I can't really stay off it any more except for rare instances when I get some dolophine and percodan. I find that the pain of withdrawal during the first few days is just like the pain that overtakes me even when I've been clean for weeks. It just envelops me and makes me feel that I can't go on without a fix. Until last month I didn't even think I wanted to quit ... I felt so rotten and in so much pain just waking up in the morning that for the first time I understood how some people could kill themselves. I don't want to die. I want to live. I've got to stop; I've got too much to live for. Junk is no answer. Junk stops my pain but brings its own pain. Junk is junk. There must be another way to live. Help.

Thirty minutes after he wrote this letter he went out and fixed.[1] It would seem that a knowledge of the dangers of heroin and a desperate desire to stop are still meaningless when a person is suffering.

When a person is withdrawn from heroin, he goes into what looks like a Primal. In fact, the letter writer was convinced that he was seeing drug withdrawal when he witnessed his first Primal: the stomach cramps, the perspiring, the shakes – and the Pain. I am sure that initially the symptoms that occur when heroin is withdrawn are physiologic. However, heroin addicts who have had Primals believe that most of their withdrawal syndrome *is* a Primal. What seems to give addiction such intensity is the Primal pool of Pain. When we view heroin as the defence, we can understand how a person will go into a Primal when that defence is removed.

Like heroin, Primal Therapy kills the Pain by having the addict *feel* it. In my experience, the addict is more treatable than many kinds of neurotics who have built up an elaborate network of defences which must be dismantled. Treatment of the addict is quick and to the point.

There is a very important difference with an addict in Primal Therapy. He must be guarded and watched constantly for the first month or two of his treatment. Other patients who have cracked the feeling barrier may, under stress, return to their symptoms – and they get headaches or asthma perhaps. But when the addict returns to *his* symptom, it is usually disastrous. Whatever promises he makes to

[1] It is interesting to note that some addicts use the term 'stoned' to describe their drugged state – indicating the person no longer wants to feel anything. Feeling seems intolerable for the addict.

stay off drugs or even report to you when he uses are totally meaningless. I had one well-motivated addict locked in his room for the first days of treatment because the usual sanitorium will not admit addicts. Even with a twenty-four hour guard, he still managed to take the hinges off the doors and attempt to slip out and fix. No one on earth is more ingenious than an addict out to score.

If we can get through the initial treatment period with the addict, we are fairly safe. But I still would recommend ten to fifteen weeks of incarceration during Primal Therapy.

DISCUSSION

Some of the current approaches to the treatment of drug addiction tend to take a hard line. The addict is shamed, called 'stupid', told to grow up and be a man. I tend to disagree with this approach because I think many addicts have had a hard enough life without added social pressure. Possibly the group pressure found in some of the retreats for the treatment of addiction does help condition out addictive behaviour, but this pressure certainly cannot touch the great needs for love in the addict. When the Pain exists, all the threats and punishment in the world won't help. When Primal Pain is gone, it will no longer be necessary to berate or plead with an addict to stop his behaviour.

I also do not believe that it helps the addict to make him behave 'like an adult'. Many an addict was forced to be adult before he was a child; what he needs to do is feel like that pained child instead of *acting* grown-up. Social pressure and threats, in my estimation, produce more self-protection, not less. Many addicts are prepared for a tough world. What they can't defend against is gentleness.

People don't put needles in their arms every day of their lives because they are weak or stupid. They are sick, with a deep sickness as real and as painful as most so-called physical sickness. The use of drugs is usually not a flippant choice; it is the inevitable result of the suffering body trying to make sense – to find relief from the sickness. Trying to moralise and talk someone out of this sickness would be like trying to talk him out of his Pain. Calling an addict 'stupid' without providing people who care and understand or an environment to offer its share of needed protection against the painful world would, in my opinion, just ensure the next fix.

Many private and state addict treatment centres can point to excellent results – high percentages of those off drugs for years, functioning well in jobs and in marriages – and they certainly have a better addiction remission rate than the federal treatment centres where the rate of return to drugs is between 80 and 90 per cent. I do think it is important that the addict not use dangerous drugs; any way that this can be accomplished is helpful. But I do not regard the absence of usage as cure. Though a heroin addict in an addiction retreat may have 'traded down' to a 'healthier' addiction to cigarettes and coffee (and they usually consume both in large quantities while off heroin), I would still consider him an addict: high levels of tension will be there waiting for him to weaken. So long as he can work hard, smoke away the Pain, and have the support of those around him, it is possible to stay away from drugs for years and perhaps forever. But any change in these outlets may again cause the Pain (which is still there) to rise, and addiction will result.

The length of time off drugs does not seem to be any indication of susceptibility to addiction. Given a supportive environment, someone with a high level of tension may stay off drugs permanently. Others who have a lesser degree of tension but who are thrown back onto the streets may again start doping immediately. Almost every day I get calls from men and women who have been in prisons for years and who have begun to use almost immediately. This, despite an intensive psychotherapy programme in the California narcotic prison system.

While the addiction retreats which are now flourishing around the country have served the highly useful purpose of getting people off physiologic addiction and helping them function in society, I would have to consider this approach still a missionary one. The addict is taken in by well-meaning people who have ideas about what is good and bad behaviour. Perhaps it is logical for them to consider the addict stupid rather than sick, but if addiction is a sickness, its causes must be probed – well beyond mere surface behaviour.

MARIJUANA

Marijuana has a different effect from heroin. The latter reduces or 'kills' Pain, narcotises against hurtful feelings. What happens to someone under the influence of marijuana depends on three factors: (1) the dose (how much is smoked); (2) the depth of his defence system; and (3) the amount of Primal Pain it shields. With large enough quantities of marijuana, it is possible to produce a quasi-LSD reaction complete with hallucinations and delusions. This would happen if there were great underlying Pain which required symbolic flight or if the person's defence system were particularly vulnerable.

It is not uncommon, for instance, for someone who has already taken LSD to be tripped off again into a momentary (and sometimes not so momentary) psychotic state with the subsequent use of marijuana. The original LSD trip would be the first major assault on the defence system, bringing the person close to his Pain; the subsequent use of marijuana might bring the whole neurotic system down. This is why both LSD and marijuana in continuous use are dangerous. One patient who had followed LSD with marijuana began to have an obsessive fear of being split in two by a razor. This gave way to continuous fear of being enveloped by the bed she was sleeping in. Those symbols became compulsive and obsessive because the defence system against fear had been weakened by drugs. Soon those fears would become so insistent that more symbolic reaction would be required and the person would break down completely.

Generally, marijuana trips are pleasant because the defence system only 'bends' under the drug and does not shatter as it may under heavy doses of LSD. So the person may experience euphoria or mystical journeys for his first few drug experiences. Eventually that is going to give way to something more serious and unpleasant. Primal patients whose defence systems are removed cannot tolerate smoking marijuana. I recall one college student who near the end of his therapy was offered a marijuana cigarette and reluctantly smoked four or five puffs. Within minutes he found himself in the bedroom having a Primal. He was surprised by what happened because before therapy he had been a chronic marijuana smoker and could easily smoke two cigarettes and feel only 'loose and giggly'. The absence of a solid defence system changed all that.

The 'average' neurotic, smoking marijuana for the first time, may be able to smoke a good deal and suffer only physiologic changes – palpitations, dizziness. Others develop uncomfortable anxiety reactions. But the answers to reactions to any drug cannot be found by looking only at the chemistry of drugs. In the case of marijuana, the well-defended person on his first 'trip' may be allaying his defences sufficiently to allow his Pain to rise but not sufficiently for the defence system to be threatened – only producing feelings of anxiety over strange new sensations.

The same thing is true of a much more familiar drug – caffeine, the stimulant found in coffee. We don't usually think of ourselves as addicted to caffeine, but there are many people who really find it difficult to function each morning without coffee. A heavily dulled person such as a heroin addict can easily drink ten cups of coffee without noticeable effect. But Primal graduates feel enormously agitated from one cup or two. Nearly all of them have gone off coffee; without a defence system to intervene, any chemical has a direct and potent effect on the body.

Thus, we see that the defence system can determine to a large degree how we react to drugs. That system filters, softens, or blocks external and internal stimuli. This internal-external reaction process is interdependent. Thus, one cannot defend the inner self and be straight in one's external life; nor can he be real psychologically and not experience a potent and direct effect from drugs such as caffeine or marijuana. To be unreal means to be systemically unreal; to be real means to be systemically real.

I believe that many users of marijuana are trying to be real but are going about it in an unreal way. In a sense, 'getting high' is symbolic. It means going through the motions of liberation and freedom. But real liberation means feeling that pained self, not temporarily freeing the self with drugs from oppression by the unreal system.

The difference between the real heroin addict and the marijuana user is that by and large, marijuana is not the key or sole defence of the 'pot person'. The marijuana user has other defences to help him get by, albeit with tension. But the heroin addict has run out of defences. Heroin is his defence, and he must have it to function. In general, the marijuana user is far less repressed (in less Pain) than the heroin addict. Marijuana helps lift the repression so that the person often feels an opening up of all the sensoria; he can hear nuances in a record or see exquisite colours in a painting. This lifting process also produces insights – not the case with heroin. One patient recalled a pre-Primal marijuana trip as follows: 'While high, I suddenly had a memory of my folks making fun of the way I said "sky" when I was little. They used to call me to perform in front of relatives. They made me repeat "Twinkle, twinkle, little star" over and over while they laughed and laughed. I realised while on grass that since that time I have been afraid to speak in front of people.'

This insight came out of a repressed memory which marijuana permitted into consciousness. The scene was painful and ordinarily would not have been remembered. Once it was conscious, it was possible to connect present behaviour with past Pain. That is insight. If that same memory were to occur during a Primal, the Pain might be excruciating and the insights more prolific and physically encompassing.

It is no secret that many young people today are attracted to marijuana. For some reason, society has decided that the way to solve that problem is to stamp out the drug instead of the causes for taking it. But taking marijuana most often feels good for the neurotic because feeling feels good. Marijuana seems to do on a minor scale what LSD does – stimulate feelings. Many young people honestly do not know any other way to get to their feelings except through the use of drugs. Because of their early experiences which helped turn them off, they have had to turn onto something – drugs. The question is not what turns them on. The problem is what turned them off.

What happens to many people with the use of marijuana and the rise of feelings is that defences become magnified. The person will begin to laugh uproariously (because he can feel, even if it is not the real feeling) or eat voraciously. What the drug does, essentially, is put the person back into his body. That uncontrollable laughter, for example, is a much fuller body experience for many neurotics than laughter without the drug. But post-Primal patients who have their bodies no longer need marijuana or drugs, which strikes me as a much better solution to the drug problem.

Sally

When Sally first came to me she had been diagnosed at the local neuropsychiatric hospital as a 'post-LSD psychotic'. The final breakdown resulted from an acid trip, followed by heavy use of marijuana. Sally was a very rapid treatment case, as are many who are at the breaking point.

I am twenty-one years of age. My life at home as a child was a constant battle. My parents fought and argued and made me a nervous wreck. Plus my first four years of school were spent in a Catholic school which was absolutely disastrous to me. I can remember several incidents of pain because I wasn't well liked and I was constantly being punished by the nuns. My punishment would usually be a penance of writing my catechism lesson ten times during recess while the rest of the children played, which to me seemed like a removal from God rather than getting closer to God, and I never really understood why I was being punished. I gave signs of my misery such as wetting at my desk or picking my nose and eating it. No one saw or helped me. I remember vividly being terribly alone at this young age, a fear that was with me even into later life.

Since life at home was shit and school was shit, I resorted to my only way of not going out of my mind: my singing. In school, especially during junior high, it made me well liked. I had a good voice even in early grades at Catholic school. I was in choir at church on Sunday, and on St Patrick's Day I did a little song about Ireland for the school. When I was at home alone, I was in a world of drama. I would make movies for myself starring me with the most beautiful costumes in the world, and with every performance came an Academy Award. I would have gone insane if at this early age I realised exactly what my life was – SHIT – but my fantasy kept my life beautiful. I was happy entertaining myself and confident of the day that I would be a great singer and movie star. I remember twinges of pain every once in a while when I would be singing or putting on a play for myself, a pain of 'This is not real; it's a dream.' Sometimes I would collapse and cry and cry because I was just a little girl and I was anxious to make my dream come true, anxious to be a somebody, because in reality I was a nobody – but really nobody – my identity was in the future for the rest of my life. A future that would never be there because I would keep putting it off, not wanting to find out that if I ever reached that future, I would find out that the success didn't find me. Where would I go then to become somebody? Also, my whole life I never left the little girl in the plays and musicals, so I never came to reality. I still picked my nose and ate it, still kept crying out 'Help me', 'Help me grow up'. But nobody could help when I got older because my crying outs were done in secrecy. No one could help if they wanted to, and believe me, I didn't *really* want them to.

It's funny when you're neurotic. You grow up physically; you know more, understand a lot more, sometimes even act much older, because you're supposed to be. But inside is that little girl just waiting to be caressed, loved, helped and protected. There's a constant inner battle to have the things you desperately need, which is love, protection, etc., between what you are supposed to be (an adult) and want to be – because you want to grow like your body has grown and like your awareness has grown, but there is a section of you that is in suspended animation.

I started therapy in January. I took myself there because of events that had started about eight months before. I had been taking LSD. I had taken LSD a few times with no bad effects. It was the last time that I took the drug that triggered off what I term as insanity.

My boyfriend and I had each taken two capsules of acid. I was in a bad mood because that night I had wanted to go to a party with him where old friends of mine were with whom I used to work. He refused to go, so instead we took the acid.

We ended up by going to another kind of a party. There were people there who had taken the drug and some who hadn't. There was a boy there who made beautiful earrings, and I got my boyfriend to buy me some. I was feeling better until the LSD started to take effect. All of my senses became acute. I could smell the smell of myself. I could smell my own body odour. I looked around to see if anyone else could smell me, too. No one seemed to. I ran into the bathroom, grabbed a bar of soap, and started washing my armpits and arms, trying to drive the smell away. I felt so dirty, like shit. I couldn't get rid of the smell. When I left the bathroom, I told my boyfriend something was wrong. We went into the driveway to talk about it. Suddenly I had what I can best describe as an attack. It was like I was gone out of my head for a few minutes, and then, when I came down to a lesser high point, I knew I had been gone somewhere but didn't know where, and terror struck me because of the fear that it would happen again and maybe next time I wouldn't come back. It happened again and again over a period of about seven hours. Each time not knowing if I would ever come out of it. I discovered no realities. It was just a series of flipping out and then complete terror and being convinced that I was totally insane.

After the seven hours I started to come down a little bit. The attacks were gone, but I was still up and I still had so much fear.

I tried to sleep but kept opening my eyes from fear. It was like my head was so blown apart that it wouldn't fit back into place.

After a few days I was my old self again.

It was about two months later that I began having side effects from the acid. It started with a nightmare. I awoke screaming because I dreamed I went insane. That horrifying fear was total all through my body. I couldn't sleep and awoke my boyfriend, who was living with me, and he tried to comfort me. I didn't want to be comforted. I wanted to know what was wrong. I had to know.

That day, and for many months after, was *hell*. I was sure I was crazy. There were ideas in my mind which caused me to feel this way. First was the fact that I couldn't understand having fear of nothing. I hadn't taken any LSD in two months so why was I feeling like I was on acid twenty-four hours a day?

To try to explain all the little thoughts which contributed to making me crazy is practically impossible, except to say that all my defences were completely down. By this I mean there was no way I could rationalise anything. I couldn't take it for granted that the wall was a wall or a chair was a chair. I couldn't feel myself at all. My mind was so hung up that I had no body or feeling except the fear. I felt fear constantly. I felt that I was locked up in my mind like in a prison and the only way out was the gas chamber. I had no hope of surviving this crisis.

Through all of this, there were things happening all around me which really didn't bother me. My boyfriend, whom I was living with, was dealing in drugs. He had no job; I had no job; we had plenty of illegal money. There were flocks of our longhair friends constantly over at our apartment getting loaded, and there were large quantities of drugs in our place at all times. It was a doper's heaven. All of this didn't bother me because I really didn't care. I wasn't really aware of what was happening all around me. I took no drugs of any kind during this time and didn't want to. The only thing that I cared about was my mind and how it was flipping out and why I couldn't accept even a light bulb as being a light bulb. To myself I was crazy, and the terrible fear was the constant *knowing* that I was crazy and I was going to make sure that my end would be doom. I was going to go crazy rather than accept the simplest reality that a light bulb was a light bulb.

It was at this point that I would have been ready for a Primal experience, but unfortunately it hadn't been discovered yet. So when I first went to therapy, because I was so desperate, things did change but in a totally different way than now. It was then that I learned to build up my defences. I wasn't afraid all of the time any more, only most of the time. I built a defence in myself to slough off anything. When I felt the fear, I would rationalise that it really didn't exist, that I wasn't afraid at all, and that it was just an ordinary acid flash (whatever that is). I also had someone to lean on, someone whom I was sure had the right answers and that person was my therapist. If he told me that the moon was made out of green cheese, I accepted it because he knew everything about the mind and there was no reason to have fear. I had complete faith and trust in this man that I made in my mind a God, father and protector of my sanity.

When our group therapy started finding things out about the Primal Pain, something inside me so strong wanted to go through it (myself) because although I was 'adjusting' to life, I was miserable. I didn't know what I wanted to do or be. My first Primal experience was triggered by a decision. I had decided to get married to my boyfriend. Things had changed: He had a good job, was not connected at all with drugs, and I had a good job, too. We were starting to look like the average young couple.

After this decision, one night in group I was talking about some nonsense of how happy I was, when I stopped talking, took a deep look inside myself and knew that this wasn't it. That this wasn't going to make my life happy.

I lay down on the floor and started with deep breathing from my stomach. This was followed by screams of anger. I felt like shit. I felt I was the dirtiest shit. I sat up, and I remember people in the group asking me questions, and I would reply. I can't even remember what my responses were, but everyone seemed happy and was saying, 'You did it, you did it.' All that was going through my mind was that I was shit because I'd been lying to myself all of my life. That all my life was one big sick joke with no meaning. I was nothing.

This was my first breakthrough to reality.

After this Primal I had several more. Each Primal got rid of a major hurt that I had locked inside myself.

It was much easier to give up my father's hope for love than my mother's, because my father had always been more real. My father had a job, which he kept for thirty years, but drank alcohol excessively. Whenever they had a fight (my parents), which was practically every day, I always sided with my mother, as did my brother and sisters. Poor Mom was the one always being hurt. Poor Mom had to put up with being beaten up, called a whore, and had to have her kids go through hell, because she wanted to keep the family together.

Dad was easier to give up because all my life I knew what he was: a no-good bastard.

With my mother it was a different story. I was convinced she loved me deeply and she will always be convinced she does, which made it hard to give up a hope for love which I always believed was there but knew it wasn't.

One of the last Primals I went through was when I gave up hope for her love. I was on the floor screaming. I felt the pain in my stomach. My mother came out of me with the words 'Mom, Mom, why don't you love me?' Which I screamed out over and over. I really knew that this was the truth and knew that all my life I had been struggling for her love more than any love I ever struggled for because she was the promise of love. She told me in words she loved me. I knew that being a sweet little girl, maybe someday I would get real love. But being sweet wasn't me. I wanted to get mad at people sometimes and wanted to disagree with them, but I didn't because I felt I would lose their love.

After each Primal my voice dropped a little lower. At one time my voice had dropped to a bass. All of my life my voice had been so high and tiny and sweet. Right now it has evened itself out to a natural real voice.

My vision after the Primals seemed to broaden. I could see more because I wasn't afraid to see the light.

My thoughts were much clearer. I could talk to people and be understood. I had confidence in what I had to say because it was me myself saying it. Before I would have trouble getting a point across. There were two people inside me struggling with each other.

I would usually end up saying something and feeling that what I said was all wrong.

There is no struggle in my life now because whatever happens happens. Now I have some choice to what will happen, and whatever I want to do I can.

I've found happiness because I've come to the realisation that we live in an unreal world with most of its population filled with unreal people. It's just the realisation that people should have when they're well people and that is there is nothing we can do about other people's lives even though it may endanger ours, so why bother worrying what they do? If there is a way to protect yourselves and others, you do it; if not, you don't do it.

Unreal as the world may be, I've found my reality in it, and my own reality is what makes it real – because it's mine.

OVEREATING

I place overeating among the addictions because the person who must continuously eat is generally using food as a re-laxant, much like a constant injection of a tranquillising drug. The overeater often does not eat out of hunger. He eats out of some uncontrollable impulse – an impulse that usually strikes when he is alone and has to spend time with himself. The fat he develops from his overeating seems to form a literal layer of insulation against Pain. For this reason, obese individuals are sometimes difficult Primal patients.

I discussed earlier the difference between ascending and descending tension. This is particularly evident in the treatment of the obese or the overweight person. Many of the overweight people who first come to therapy are not particularly anxious. Their Pain has been kept dormant by whatever they could stuff into themselves – drugs, alcohol, or food. What they were stuffing back was the real self – the real feelings that are ready to erupt when unprotected by food. This is descended tension. It is largely unfelt as tension; rather, it is a gnawing or empty sensation that masquerades as hunger. One patient explained: 'I used food to eat away the tension which was eating me away. My whole life was planning for the next meal. There was so little else in my family that food had to do everything for me. It was the only thing my mother gave me that was pleasant.' She ate to keep from feeling that complete unpleasantness of her family life.

Ascending tension is what happens to the overeater when he has his food defence taken away for any length of time. For example, during the first week of therapy when the patient is not allowed much food, at the same time as his defences are weakened by the therapist, he is completely anxious. He begins dreaming as never before, cannot sit still, and soon could not eat if he wanted to. This is because his feelings are on the rise and are so powerful that they inhibit food ingestion. He will lose a good deal of weight during his first three weeks without any effort.

When one eats more than one should, clearly it is not food that is being eaten. It is something symbolic. Some patients call it stuffing the inner void so that the emptiness of one's whole life won't have to be felt. Others believe that the frustrated little child inside still has infantile oral needs which must be met. As one patient put it, 'I'm eating for that deprived little kid.'

Overeating is not just a satisfaction of vague psychological oral needs, however. Each 'fatty' has a particular constellation that has led to his condition. So one person can be eating too much now because he was deprived of the breast, another because mealtime was the *only* satisfaction of his childhood. There are many dynamics which go into making an overeater.

What is crucial to keep in mind is that eating (like compulsive sex) is the outlet for many kinds of needs. Food quells Pains that may be unrelated to early food deprivation, thus, to deal with such food problems is too often useless therapy. Food may be chosen to quell Pain instead of drugs or alcohol because of the subculture the person grew up in – which may place heavy emphasis on eating, while having strong prohibitions against alcohol. The neurotic has false wants. To deal with pseudo-wants therapeutically means not to treat the real ones.

For example, a woman in Primal Therapy reported that she suddenly began eating during the past week. She had a dream: 'My mother is floating in the sky with a butcher knife in her hand ready to pounce on me. I'm terrified and try to escape. I pretend I'm not me – just an ugly monster – but it's no use. She's about to attack when I wake up.' I have her sink into the feeling of the dream while telling it as though it is happening at the moment. She re-experiences the terror and then sees the whole picture: Her mother was very possessive of her father. The mother wanted to be the perky cute young thing who would be attractive and hold the father's attention. Somewhere early in her life, this patient began to feel that her mother didn't want her to be pretty and trim. In order to short-circuit her mother's jealousy, the young girl became fat and stayed that way throughout most of her life. She had sensed her mother's competitiveness, and her Primal shout was, 'Don't be angry, Mother, I won't take Daddy away!' – something she acted out with her obesity. Being fat and ugly was the way she denied her fears of her mother, and when this feeling threatened to surface during the previous week, she began overeating again to stave it off. A major threat to her existence, then, was being trim and shapely. Shapelessness was her defence, and no amount of previous therapy or diet plans could radically alter this overweight until the central feelings were felt.

After she went through this Primal experience, this patient was able to remember early in her life when she was active, peppy and even feisty. She realised that her mother really didn't want her to be alive and almost methodically began to push the life out of her. She acquiesced in this and soon pushed everything back and down, with the aid of food. After the Primal, she lost weight effortlessly.

This one Primal indicates how complex the overweight problem can be. Some women fear looking attractive because of the sexual activity it might lead to. Others eat because food is available and love is not. Some neurotics eat to keep from feeling that no one is ever going to fill them up. They stay 'filled up' so as not to feel unfulfilled. Not having what they needed early in life, they come to believe it is food they want. One patient explained her overeating in this way: 'I never lived in my body because there was too much Pain of unfulfilment there. So I lived in my head and fed my body food to quiet the gnawing hurt.'

According to the well-known axiom, there is a thin person inside every fat one. This is another way of saying that there is a real person inside every unreal one. The fat person is literally presenting an unreal front to the world – testimony to an unreal self trying to protect and insulate the real one. I have found that the more normal the body, the closer the neurotic is to his reality and his Pain. Therefore, the first order of business in the Primal treatment of the overeater is to starve him out and take away his unreal front. During this period he has to be watched almost as closely as a drug addict because that fat front was necessary in his psychophysical make-up. He is very likely to cheat on any diet, just as the addict is likely to shoot drugs when we begin breaking down his defences.

The overeater will be in danger until most of his real needs are felt. One patient told me, 'If I got thin and life was not any better than it was when I was fat, I'd really be out of hope. There was hope in being fat, hope of getting thin. More than that, I could feel that it was my fatness that caused my social rejection and not really me.' The hope involved in obesity varies with each person. One young woman was waiting for the day that she got so fat that her mother would finally recognise that something was wrong with her and offer her help. Another said that he had to have something to look forward to and food was it. His life was completely barren outside his meals.

A compulsive need for anything has little to do with the object (in this case food) itself. Getting rid of those old needs is the only way to stop a voracious appetite.

A book on obesity by a well-known physician states that the patient must be *educated* towards proper nutrition. It urges that he learn the calorie content of each food, and even then, it continues lugubriously, he may have to watch himself for the rest of his life. Many of my patients can quote chapter and verse about the calorie content of foods and race to the refrigerator every night with the statistics dancing in their heads. As a matter of fact, the alacrity with which they snap up each new diet that comes along – that special *painless* way to lose weight – is evidence of their unreal hope.

As long as the overeater can dwell on food and diets, he does not have to face what is really wrong. Which is why any split approach to the problem of obesity cannot succeed. Those who approach it from a dietary angle, with pills and shots and special techniques, are dealing only with the body. The purely psychological approach errs on the other side.

Any approach that is not psychophysiologic will not succeed in the long run. Indeed, a colleague who works with a team of diet doctors told me that the eventual return to obesity among their patients is about the same as the rate of recidivism among addicts.

20

Psychosis: Drug and Non-drug

My experience has led me to conclude that there is no such thing as a latent 'psychotic process', no arcane bizarreness tucked away in what Aldous Huxley has called the 'Antipodes of the Mind'. Deep down in each neurotic is a painful reality – a sanity (when felt). Insanity, in these terms, is a defence against this crushing reality. People go crazy to keep from feeling their truth. This is a turnabout from many theories in psychology which view man as inherently irrational, controlled only by society. All irrationality, dreams, hallucinations, delusions and illusions seem to me only shields to keep us safe and functioning.

As for the severity of psychosis, if the self has not had six or seven years, say, to solidify before the split occurs, we can expect a weak self or ego, as it is known to the Freudians. If the child continues to be denied support and love and is not given outlets for the Painful wounds, these added assaults on an already-weakened self would result in a strong, unreal self to protect the defenceless child. The unreal self then predominates, protecting the child but driving him towards psychosis. This predominance of the unreal self (the non-feeling self) accounts for the deadness we see in the very repressed neurotics and psychotics, the so-called flattened affect. They are almost literally more dead than alive.

Psychosis, therefore, is a deepening of the neurotic split, producing a new quality of existence. Graphic evidence of the split is paranoia, in which the person can no longer contain the dissociation inside himself and is unable to continue to use the body as a defence. So he projects his feelings outside himself, putting his thoughts into the heads of others or imagining that they are conspiring against him or controlling his thoughts.

Though the content of the paranoia will differ with each individual, the process is the same – to protect the person against intolerable Pain. For example, the person who cannot bear to feel his terrible aloneness may conjure up someone who is always watching him. What the imaginary person is thinking is symbolic of his feelings. For example, the paranoid may believe that a waitress is thinking something bad about him. This person may have had a childhood where his parents constantly thought he was bad, so he learned to be wary in order to ward off their psychological blows. This wariness may have continued until he expects hurt even where it doesn't exist; thus, memory from the past superimposed on the present gives his present reactions a bizarre quality. This bizarre quality is the inability to distinguish past from present, inner from outer.

It is not terribly illogical to expect hurt if you were constantly abused in your early life. The paranoid doesn't know that it is *memory* that he is responding to. His delusions are real. They are repressed memories projected onto the world, the Pain made real. Will he see worms crawling out of a wall? Only if that has internal meaning.

Whatever the paranoid content, it usually involves seeing or hearing things outside that will ease the hurt inside. The hurt must be very intense to force a person to put such a great distance between himself and his feelings. Often paranoid delusions will involve explosive power – he will imagine someone has a switch which, when thrown, can literally blow his mind. But that power may be the power of his feelings safely placed *outside* himself so as to protect him from *internal* danger.

The paranoid is still somewhat connected to his feelings. At least his delusions have some organization to them in contrast with the more disintegrated kinds of psychotics who seem to speak gibberish and talk only in 'word salad'.

The paranoid can, by and large, still make contact. He can talk to you about the price of tomatoes or quote the scores in the World Series. The only time his bizarreness may show itself is when the area of the covered self is touched. In Primal terms, when the real feelings are set off, the unreal system must rush in to change them into symbols. Though the paranoid is acute to the scores in a ball game, he can be made anxious by a simple transaction with a concessionaire, imagining that the man selling him ice cream is secretly conspiring to hurt him. The reason the paranoid often sees secret conspiracies rather than something out in the open is, I believe, that it is a parable of his own secret and unknown feelings. Having projected the secret 'outside', he can now focus on something to be wary of. This is similar to the neurotic except that his focus of fear – his phobia – is a bit more plausible.

In order to understand hallucinations and delusions fully, one must understand that depth of Primal terror – a terror we almost never see because we keep it controlled so much of the time. The way we control it, for the most part, is to wrap it in comforting ideation. Let us take a commonplace example: the belief in a hereafter to make death less final and irrevocable. Now we would not consider belief in a hereafter psychotic because it is a socially institutionalised idea. But if most or many people did not believe in a hereafter, what then? This irrational belief, 'irrational' because it is based on nothing that can be validated, may exist in a person who otherwise is eminently rational, but because of Primal terror, he is forced to spin a largely irrational web to keep the feeling at bay. To bridge the apparent incongruity of his rational and irrational ideas existing alongside each other, he may have to develop yet another irrational notion – namely, that there is a 'dark' or 'irrational' side to all of us that defies reason and explanation.

All this ideological superstructure just not to feel the real feeling!

The bizarreness of the ideation (delusion) or of the perception (hallucination) will depend on the depth of the terror. The greater the fright, the more strained the reasoning to cover it. As long as the feelings can be *thought* in some way, the mind can keep itself ordered and in control. When for one reason or another the person can no longer order or organise his feelings, he will be brought close to his terror.

The Pain of any psychotic is immense because his real self, as well as his unreal self, was not accepted. The person has had little recourse early in life except to withdraw from the world. If I were to characterise in a sentence the difference between the neurotic and psychotic, I would say that the neurotic has found a way to make himself comfortable in the world (his front gets him by); nothing can make the psychotic comfortable – nothing worked.

What happens when a person becomes paranoid is that for reasons of stress the unreal self cannot be held together any longer and 'goes to pieces'. It happens when the mind can no longer hold back the feelings of the body. At this point the person's psyche is reconstituted on a new psychotic level. As one patient put it, 'Crazy is when you can't keep your neurosis going any more.'

The fact that the paranoid often talks to himself and answers that self as well is an indication of the split I have been discussing, of one self talking to another. The neurotic is usually able to contain this dialogue inside his head. The psychotic is not so fortunate. An insight into this process is discussed by one formerly paranoid patient: 'Early in my life, I stopped listening to my parents' lies and began to hear only when I wanted to hear. My hearing for outside things began to close down literally, so much so that I thought I was going deaf. Pretty soon I began to hear only my own invention – voices. After the Primal, my hearing opened up again. I found out that I could no longer listen to the way things really were in my youth – only to the way I had to make things.'

The dialectic of paranoia, as with any unreal behaviour, is that the closer one comes to painful truth, the farther one must flee. So there are varying distances from reality. It ranges from misinterpreting what one sees to seeing what is not even there. The Primal view is that the closer one is to his feelings, the closer he will be to external reality, the more sharply he will see into others and into social phenomena. The more blocked the inner reality, the more askew the social perception. So the paranoid in desperate flight from his truth must alter his external reality in an often bizarre way.

True contact with reality is always an inner process; defences are set up against the inside world, *not* the outside one. It isn't others the schizophrenic is terrified of; it is others who set off the fears of his own feelings. Patient after patient after a Primal has touched his face or a piece of furniture, say, and remarked it is as though he has touched and felt reality (outside reality) for the first time.

Paranoid projections do give us clues to what lies in the Primal pool. But to analyse these symbolic projections, to get inside the delusional system, to pretend with the patient, or to try to cajole him out of his unreal paranoid ideation can serve no useful purpose, in my estimation. A paranoid, like all other sick humans, cannot be talked out of his Pain.

So long as diagnostic categories for psychotics (catatonic, schizophrenic, manic-depressive and paranoiac) do not *materially* affect the kind of treatment they get, that diagnosis is largely irrelevant. If the person can make interpersonal contact, he is probably treatable.

The concept of neurosis and psychosis as defences is pivotal. A critical point occurs when feelings are aroused – and a person can either feel them or deny them and become mentally ill in the process. The young child denies his feelings – his real self – and becomes someone else, someone his parents expect him to be. His neurosis is a defence. The adult who denies his Primal feelings may also break down and become someone else; only that someone else may be totally at odds with reality – Napoleon, Mussolini, the Pope. A nervous breakdown is analogous to a Primal without a Primal Therapist. It is beginning to feel the Primal feelings and fleeing in terror to an unreal mental enclave. A Primal is that same *breakdown of the defences into the feeling*.

If a young child had someone to turn to with his Primal feelings, someone to help him understand what he was feeling, someone who could support him, chances are he would not have become split into someone he was not. Similarly, when an adult has someone around to help him feel and understand his feelings and support him through the process, there is no way for a mental split into psychosis to occur. He can only break down into himself – which means health, not sickness.

This is the report of the treatment of a psychotic woman, thirty-five years of age, who was previously delusional and had hallucinations – hearing a voice talking to her and directing her life. Thus far she has had more than sixty Primals (convulsing, diving off the couch, hiding under the desk) over a period of twelve months, and from all indications there is no evidence of the return of her psychosis. Her dreams are real, and she no longer hears the voice she had heard for years.

This woman had a life that beggars description. She was raped savagely and nearly murdered by her drunken, sadistic father when she was three and a half. Her split seemed to have begun with that rape – memory of which did not recur until after some twenty Primals. Once memory began, she could re-live only aspects of that trauma with each succeeding Primal. It took some twenty more Primals to integrate that one shattering experience.

Two selves developed when the split occurred at the age of three and a half. With each succeeding year, she became more and more directed by a voice which told her how to act. It was the voice of the real self keeping her alive. 'It was she who pulled me through,' she later said. She discusses her split selves:

'Was I insane to hear my self separate singing like an Indian in a forest? Was I crazy to think that she told me how to act and what to see and not see? I guess the answer is yes. I could never see the real world around me because I lived in the Pain. I ran from any situation that was at all fearful for fear it would bring back all those early horrors. I think I lived in madness because I could not feel it. I never dared comprehend or even remember what happened. Out of fear of destroying myself, I had to project my feelings of fear out into the world – to other people.

'I think my madness was caused by too much Pain and under that craziness was the real Pain I couldn't stand. I know now that I repressed all feelings so that nothing would lead me to the Pain. Maybe the difference between me and other people was that I saw my feelings in everyone around me while they just acted out their feelings. Because all around me was madness when I was growing up, was I crazy to refuse to see anything as it was? Can wanting to survive in any way possible be called insanity when it means dying inside so that part of you can live? If I felt the horror I was living in, unshielded by some imagined world, realising there was no one to hear me if I spoke the truth, I doubt if I would have ever come out of it.'

Clearly, her insanity was a defence against sanity. Living with a mother who kept her with a sadistic, insane father, suspecting at a very young age that her mother didn't care about her, wouldn't take care of her when she was sick, perhaps even wished she were dead, was an overwhelming experience. There was no place to turn. She later told me:

'What is so impossible to take is knowing how absolutely despised I was for absolutely no reason other than that I was alive in their house. I tried to be nice and quiet and obedient, thinking all the time that there must be something wrong with me to be treated so despicably. I never knew that they were really insane when I was young. I kept trying to be good to make sense out of my mother's hatred for me. I thought that she kept me with Daddy because I was bad, maybe I caused him to do it.'

Feeling the reality of her unreality (her psychosis) was the beginning of the end of the Pain. She had suffered from a roaring in her head from the time she was a young girl, and during a late Primal she realised that the roar was all those screams bottled up since childhood.

Towards the end of her therapy she wrote: 'I think it is a miracle that I lived, and that I am living now. I am entering a degree of humanness that others probably have all of their lives. My wholeness is fragile, I can feel it. I am so afraid of being separate again.'

She talked about the separate self:

'I saw my self separate and heard her separate because she was never allowed expression. I was compelled to follow her, to listen to her, afraid to leave that world to enter one I thought insane. She told me about real beauty, real colour and sound. She said that the drabness and the search for illusions was because I did not follow her. She told me that I didn't hate anyone because the hatred was never real, only the fear of being hurt. It was the fear and the expectation of Pain.

'She told me that reality was love because only in reality is there true understanding and acceptance of the self and others. She told me that I am human and that is all I can ever be; I believe her now. Now it is the unreal people who frighten me because they tend to use each other to provoke, soothe, or reject the not feeling loved. Maybe conventional therapy would have tried to force me to see those feelings in a sort of contrived way. But it could not have worked because I know now *that the needs have to be felt before the lack of their fulfilment can be faced.*'

During this woman's Primals she felt 'crazy' and became delusional whenever she got close to the feeling that she never was and never would be loved by her mother, never would have an understanding father who would talk to her and listen to her problems, never would be cuddled and rocked *no matter what she did*. The aim was to help her feel what made her come apart, to enter that chamber of horrors she had fled years before and descend into the most excruciating agony one can imagine, so as to become whole again. It can be entered only in small steps that the body can accommodate; otherwise, the feeling will not be felt. Fear and Pain will join to hunt the feeling away and continue the split.

From this it can be seen that under Primal Therapy the process of reversing psychosis is similar to the Primal treatment of neurosis. The psychotic, however, differs from the neurotic because of the tremendous amount of underlying Pain and the fragility of the real self.

Because of his enormous Pain, the amount of time required to treat a psychotic may be double or triple that of the neurotic. In addition, we have to guard his environment during his treatment to make sure there are no external stresses. But our experience thus far would indicate a cautious optimism about eventual recovery, since the treatment of the neurotic and the psychotic is similar – feeling those feelings which caused the split so that the person no longer has to make reality unreal in order to function.

To quote once again from my previously psychotic patient:

'I am still ignorant in many ways, so moulded into bondage, yet my feelings wrote the truth. Beneath my psychosis is the emptiness of hope, the being unloved and the terrible aloneness. If another insane person can feel those feelings, it will take the screams from his body as it did mine. Tonight, feeling in the dark silence of aloneness, I felt that in every action, in every sound and in everything I see, I am becoming a unique human being. The world is becoming beautiful because I am becoming what people hope God is – love with no Pain, never changing.

'In the Psalms is the line "Though I should walk in the valley of the shadow of death, I will fear no evil", and I know that valley is where I began so long ago, where I believe someone loved me – God loved me, yet I sensed that He was in my mind. I feel a new reality dawning.'

21

Conclusions

> How astounding to me to find that the language of my
> feelings and the language of my intellect have been
> saying the same things in different ways. What an
> example of the division between mind and body, feel-
> ings and thought. ... The not being able to com-
> prehend because of not feeling, the not being able to
> feel because of not understanding – the fear of the
> unknown.   — BARBARA, a patient

Primal therapy is essentially a dialectical process in which
one matures as he feels his childish needs, in which a person
becomes warm when he feels his coldness, in which one
becomes strong through feeling weak, in which feeling the
past brings one wholly into the present, and in which feeling
the death of the unreal system brings one back into life. It is
the reverse of neurosis, in which one is afraid and acts brave,
feels little and acts big, and continually acts out the past in
the present.

I believe that Primal Therapy works because the patient
finally has a chance to feel what he has been acting out in a
myriad of ways throughout his life. He no longer has to act
grown-up and controlled; he can be what he never was allowed to be, to say what he never dared utter. The disease, I
submit, is the denial of feeling, and the remedy is to feel.

The unreal system was necessary early in life, but it
strangles and warps us later. It will not permit rest or sleep
without terror and tension. It is this unreal system that must
feed tranquillisers to the real system to prevent its scream in
an unguarded moment. It is the unreal system that stuffs the
real one with food it neither wants nor can digest. It is that
system that drags the real one around in a never-ending
cycle of work and projects. In a methodical way, it is literally killing the person off. In the meantime, it usually does
its job well. It keeps the Pain away, wrapping such a shield
around the feeling self that nothing can be felt. Life is just a
process of going through the motions until death – all with

the feeling of gnawing desperation that time is running out and one has not yet begun to live.

As long as any part of the unreal system is allowed to remain, it will stay vigorous and suppress the real system. It is total in every sense of the word, and I make such a point of this because so many serious therapies deal with fragments of neurosis in the belief that they are entities in themselves unrelated to a system. Thus, there are smoking and drinking clinics, special hospitals for drug users, diet farms, hypnosis of fears, conditioning of symptoms with the use of shock or reward, meditation and touch therapies.

Primal Theory states that the entire system must be uprooted. Unless this is done, we may find a father in a parent-guidance clinic swearing to do right by his delinquent son, to spend more time with him and stop criticising – and he does ... for about six months before he reverts to his neurosis. Or someone loses a great deal of weight at a diet farm, only to gain it back in several months. Neurotics can sometimes rearrange their front (literally, for the obese) for a time, but neurosis wins in the long run.

Feeling is what this therapy is all about. We are not simply involved with today's feelings, but those old feelings which keep us from feeling the present. We are after the *feeling of feeling* – something which the neurotic has left behind, yet which intrudes into his life each and every day; the feelings which say, 'Daddy, be nice. Mama, I need you.'

It is those Primal feelings which become superimposed onto daily living and produce lingering upset. Those are the feelings which make up bad dreams, impel people towards hasty marriages (we marry the struggle), or produce overpowering perverted impulses. Those are the feelings which are untouched by sixty or seventy years of life experience. The cure involves no more than feeling them.

It is a curious contradiction that the neurotic who is trapped in the past really has no past. He is cut off from it by Primal Pain. Thus, he must continuously act out his history day after day. For this reason, he does not change significantly throughout his life. He is much the same at forty as he was at twelve – weaving in and out of his struggle, performing his neurotic rituals, uttering his neurosis with every word, finding ever new sources to re-create with him that early family situation.

The normal has a history, a continuity of self, which has not been short-circuited by Pain. He has all of himself. Because the neurotic is being dragged by his past, his development – both mental and physical – often lags. The body and mind do not develop fluidly, so we may see retarded physical growth. Once the lag is out of the way, we find such things as beards for the first time in mature men, real sexual functioning and all the incontrovertible evidence I have described having seen of complete psychophysical change. A number of psychological theories discuss personal growth, but I wonder if they really mean growth of the *entire* person.

The dramatic downward shift of blood pressure, the changes in resting body temperature, and the lowering of pulse rates have left me convinced that Primal graduates not only will lead healthier lives but will enjoy greater longevity. Aside from all the other reasons for becoming real, I think that unreality kills. It literally seems to tear the body in two, suppressing certain hormones, over-stimulating others, racing the mind and keeping the body on a treadmill.

To be real means to be relaxed – no more depressions, phobias or anxieties. Gone is chronic tension, and with it go drugs, alcohol, overeating, smoking, overwork. To be real means no longer to have to act out symbolically.

To be real means to be able to produce without all the usual blocks that plague so many otherwise creative people. It means to have non-exploitative relationships so that finally the mould can be broken and we can produce new human beings on this earth who can truly be content. To be real is to have your needs satisfied, and to be able to satisfy the needs of others.

Need is what is basic. Children need. What they can relate to early in their lives is need. One can divert need, suppress it, ridicule it, ignore it, all to no avail because it will not change the need a scintilla. Thus, the frustrated basic need may later become transformed into a need to drink, to have sex or to eat, but the real need is always there making substitute needs so compulsive and importuning. This is what Primal Therapy is about – feeling the need.

One would think that a normal society in which real needs are recognised and fulfilled would have little irrational behaviour to contend with. There would be little need for so many rules (the shoulds) because normal people would understand the need to slow down or stop at intersections and have no need to drive dangerously. They would respect the rights of others and have no stake in suppressing the life of anyone else.

The suppression of feeling and need requires a good deal of control. When a real system is not trusted, each piece of behaviour must be checked out and examined and finally controlled. The control is needed to hold back the real system. But sickness demands its symptoms. So a control here or there means a different symptom elsewhere. Total control means building internal pressure until the system itself may break down or explode.

In an unreal society, those who show the least feeling may be held up as models, while those who show a good deal of feeling are often termed 'hysterics' and over-emotional. It seems so inverted. But in an unreal milieu, dispassion is safe and passion suspect. This has been extended so that the very healers in our society, the psychologists and psychiatrists, have been trained not to show any emotion. They have been made into the impassive reflectors of feeling, instead of its dynamic purveyors. A child brought up on a diet of unresponsive parents, laconic movie heroes, teachers and professors who are often the very essence of unemotionality finally must go to an impassive therapist for help.

The emphasis of Primal Therapy is that reformist measures of the conventional therapies only help re-channel the front but leave the neurosis intact. As I see it, the laborious and time-consuming insight therapies keep the person in the process (more precisely, the struggle) of getting well while never actually *being* well.

I suggest that conventional therapy has been acceptable to middle-class intellectuals because it has been, by and large, a genteel approach which may have pricked feelings without ruffling the basic structure. Too often, the intellectual sickness of explaining and understanding seems to have been unwittingly exacerbated by a therapeutic process which mainly dealt with explanation.

Implicit in the method of conventional psychotherapy is that we come to understand our unconscious feelings and needs and that we change by making them conscious. The Primal view is that consciousness is the *result* of feeling; simply making needs known solves nothing. This is because needs (and denied expressions – both verbal and physical – *become* needs until resolved) do not reside in a capsule in the brain. They must be felt organismically, because needs permeate the entire body. If this were not the case, then there would be no psychosomatic symptoms. If it is true that tension is the disconnected Primal need and that tension is found throughout the system, then it is clear that needs are systemic. Otherwise, we would have to conclude that needs reside in only a pocket of the brain and that simply making the unconscious conscious would do the job.

Moreover, the needs not only have to be experienced in a total body way but have to be re-lived *as they were*. The reason the adult Primal patient can finally rid himself of his needs is that they occurred in childhood and, once resolved, no longer are true needs in the adult. One patient was Mother's 'good boy' early in life by not wetting himself. He grew up seldom having to urinate. During therapy he began urinating almost every hour until he re-lived the earliest times he had had to urinate but had held it in so as to be loved. Once re-lived, that need was gone for good.

Though there is unspeakable tragedy in the world today, there seems to be an insufficient sense of horror. Perhaps neurosis is why we can permit such atrocities to go on, each of us being in a mad scramble away from our personal horror. That is why neurotic parents cannot see the horror of what they are doing to their children, why they cannot comprehend that they are slowly killing a human being. They never see that being. The societal result of this mass denial mechanism is similar to what happens within individuals – behaviour out of keeping with reality. It is what allows so many of us to be brainwashed: seeing and hearing only what eases our Pain, robbing our bodies of feelings.

When an unreal system cannot fulfil needs, it must offer hope and struggle in its place. In this way individuals will be willing to forgo real needs in order to pursue symbolic values – power, prestige, status and success. But symbolic fulfilment can never be enough because need remains.

A number of psychologists and psychiatrists have left the doctrinaire schools of psychotherapy and no longer classify themselves as Freudians or Jungians, preferring an eclectic approach. What seems insufficiently understood is that ecl-

ecticism can be an inverted solipsism, in which almost anything can be true because nothing is. Eclecticism, I would
suggest, is a defence against the belief in a single reality; it
feeds the delusion that we are open to all approaches. I think
that what has happened to psychology is that it has cut itself
away from the feeling of individual patients and has woven
hypotheses about certain behaviour, based on animal research or on theories set down decades before. These theoretical abstractions often have proved little better at
explaining and predicting psychological processes than a
patient's view of his own behaviour.

Perhaps we should not expect psychologists to be
different from anyone else. The theories they adopt are
simply sophisticated views of man and his world. These
ideas must fit in with the rest of the psychologist's ideas –
that is, they must help bolster the defence system and stay
the Pain (the truth). So unless the psychologist is fairly un-
defended, it is unlikely that he will adopt an approach based
on the absence of defences and opening people up to total
Pain. To try to get a well-defended psychologist to adopt a
new set of ideas about individuals would be somewhat like
trying to talk a patient out of his unreal ideas, talking him
out of his Pain.

Psychotherapy, by and large, has thus far dealt with interpretation. This suggests that psychologists are holders of
some special body of truths about human existence. Not
only do I think no such universal truths exist, but I do not
think there are special truths one person can *bestow* on
another. Psychological problems, in my estimation, can be
solved only from the inside out, not from the outside in. No
one can tell another what the meaning of his acts are. Thus,
confrontation and encounter therapies have to fail in this
respect.

And when a patient is able to feel, I am convinced that all
the charting, testing, diagramming and schematising we
have done in order to understand human behaviour will be
unnecessary, for these seem to be no more than symbolising
the symbolic actions of people. I propose that we avoid
analysing and treating what is unreal and *go straight to what
is real*.

I find it unfortunate that psychologists have spent so
much time refining their descriptions of human behaviour

(the games and ploys) in the belief that such refinement will lead to answers about human behaviour. But descriptions are not answers. They do not explain why; no matter how detailed the description, it brings us not one step closer to an answer.

Now that the reader has come this far, he may wonder who may properly do Primal Therapy. Our experience in training psychologists at the Primal Institute indicates that only someone who has been through the therapy can practise it. The reason is that going through the full process is the best way to understand the techniques and their impact. Second, and more important, the absence of significant blocked Pain is required if one hopes to do an effective job with a patient. Someone who is not psychologically healthy may be over-controlling and steer the patient away from the site of his Pain. Or if he is holding down his own Pain, he may hang back just when the patient needs a push to the brink of a Primal. A neurotic Primal Therapist who is playing 'the professional' may bomb the patient with insights or technical vocabulary. If he wants to be liked, he may be unable to assault the patient's defence system. Whatever he does, he must not rob the patient of his feelings. This is easy to do; I recall early in my own experience with Primals saying to a young man who was bemoaning what a tragedy his life was: 'Look, you're only twenty. You've got a whole life ahead of you.' I robbed him of his need to feel the tragedy of his past twenty years.

A Primal Therapist cannot have any defences. He is going to permit bone-chilling Pain to erupt in his patients and he cannot be defended (against Pain) and do that. When a therapist is defended, he may be automatically tempted to calm and reassure a patient when just the opposite may be called for. I do not think that patients really want reassurance, in any case. They need someone to let them be what they are – even when that means letting them be miserable!

An unreal therapist unwittingly may force his patient to accept his unreality. His prestige and position represent reality to the patient; even though he may scarcely speak to his patient month after month, his inscrutability is often accepted as standard practice. If the therapist is cold and aloof, the patient struggles to get warmth again; if the therapist is intellectually domineering, there is an implicit expectation that the patient must defer to the intellect. The patient should not have to act in any special way with his therapist; he must never feel that there are needs of the therapist he must meet, either consciously or unconsciously.

What about the professional qualifications of a Primal Therapist? He needs to know something about physiology and neurology so that he does not treat an organic brain impairment as something psychological. He must have an appreciation of scientific methodology and know what evidence consists of. He must learn not to speculate abstractly about what goes on inside people but to be open enough to allow the patient to *tell him* what is real.

He must be both sensitive and perceptive. This means, of course, he has felt all his Pains. This automatically enables him to understand others. Sensing the rhythm of his own life, he will be able to sense the disjointedness in others. He will be feeling and thus know when someone else is not. He will have, in short, qualities many of us left behind in the first few years of life: a directness, an openness, gentleness and warmth.

I do not believe that a neurotic (an unfeeling person), no matter how much theory he knows, can honestly help a neurotic patient. He cannot know when that patient is blocking feeling or expressing it if he (the therapist) is blocking feeling. To be neurotic means not to live in the present. The Primal Therapist must be with his patient every second. He must sense when feeling is on the rise and know how to help it along. He cannot do this if he is spinning elaborate explanations for his patient.

How unreal the therapist is may limit how real the patient may become, in the same way that a parent's unreality largely determines how real his child can grow to be. It is not only what the therapist does that matters, but what he is!

There are specific Primal techniques, but those techniques are of no use in the hands of a neurotic, even if that person understands physiology, sociology and psychological theories.

The Primal Therapist is not dealing with an 'analytic' patient with super-ego deficiencies or with an 'existential' patient with a life crisis; he is not, in short, dealing with categories or theoretical types. We know that when a patient comes for therapy, he is usually acting unrealistically. We see no need to classify those actions and make them something else – e.g., poor psychosexual identification. The Primal Therapist doesn't treat a compulsive or hysteric; he treats a person who covers his feelings in a certain way. He is not after the cover except as an incidental factor; he is concerned only with the reality underneath.

The predicament of the neurotic patient is that he has spent a lifetime doing unreal things and is apt to follow suit in his choice of therapist. He may seek out pseudo-psychotherapies and pseudo-psychotherapists in order to *go through the motions* of getting well without the Pain which, deep down, he often knows is necessary to really get well. The therapy is too often like the rest of his life – symbolic of the real thing, but *not* the real thing. He may take up a class in dream analysis or special group therapies run by laymen. Too often the neurotic who is in a hurry through life may gravitate towards 'quickie' therapies – weekend seminars, six-week sensitivity training sessions, or self-awareness programmes. Frequently, these programmes are aimed at making new people *out of* the individuals when the problem, in my opinion, is to change them *into* what they are.

Separating the entrance and exit of the therapeutic office is a legacy from the early days of psychoanalysis. Perhaps the fact that no patient sees another, combined with the absence of clocks in the office, has tended to make a spook show out of therapy – making the patient feel that there is something opprobrious and secretive about emotional illness.

The patient often does leave the doctor's office red-eyed and dishevelled, but I see no reason why other patients cannot see this reality. If the patient leaves angry and depressed, why hide it? Indeed, patients often report being helped by seeing others leave the office upset. In this way they learn that feeling is encouraged, not discouraged, inside those closed doors.

One may wonder why Primals often do not occur spontaneously with standard therapists. One important reason may be that an overloaded psychotherapist is not likely to take the time required with a single patient to build towards a deep feeling experience. Often the patient may be just getting into something important when the fifty minutes are over and he must leave. In a society where 'time is money', it is often difficult to find anyone with enough time to do a thorough job. Primal patients consistently remark how relaxing it is to know that they are the sole patient in individual therapy for a three-week period and that only their feelings will dictate the end of a session.

Time is not the only consideration. If something unusual, such as an incipient Primal, should occur in conventional therapy, too often the therapist will try to fit the event into some preconceived theoretical interpretation, instead of letting nature take its course. The Primal Therapist must permit himself to lose almost as much control as his patient. He must be willing to let events take place for which he has no immediate explanation. Furthermore, this unusual event is not likely to happen within the context of *psycho*therapy, where only the mind of the patient is engaged. (Take such a simple thing as putting the patient on the floor instead of having him sit in a chair.) The therapist, too, must be willing to move around, away from his easy chair.

If a therapist could stop trying to 'figure out' his patient, he might leave himself time to make an important discovery: *There is nothing to figure out.* The patient who feels his Pain will figure it out totally without help. Too many of us professionals have had too great a stake in being right, in making our theories work, and have kept too tight a rein on our patients. This is not to say that theory is not important; we produce Primals day after day because we have a theory to guide us. But theory should flow from observation.

I foresee the possibility of a major breakthrough in the treatment of psychological illness in a short space of time. The relatively short treatment period of Primal Therapy leads me to see no reason why we have to live in an age of anxiety any longer.

Since we need the co-operation and help of mental health professionals, a special caveat: Beware of the tendency to try to incorporate Primal Theory into theories therapists have become familiar with over the years. Bringing in past terminology to explain Primals, likening it to something someone said decades before, is to engage in the neurotic struggle to make old sense out of something new. Although Primal Theory does have similarities to many differing approaches, I ask that it be examined on its own terms for what it is.

Clearly, I believe there is a truth – a reality. The predictability of the Primal technique leads me to believe that the Pain principle may be one major truth which dictates human behaviour. From all evidence, there is a set of laws governing human behaviour and particularly neurotic processes which is every bit as precise as the laws of physical sciences. There are no numerous explanations for gravity, nor should there be myriad approaches to explain neurosis. I do not see how there can be any number of psychological theories, each equally valid, each contributing something important and true. If one theory is valid, and I believe the Primal notions are valid, then other approaches are invalid. When I say that neurosis is the symbolic acting out of covered feelings and that we can eliminate neurosis by uncovering feelings, and when we uncover feelings and consistently and predictably eliminate neurotic acting out, we are validating our hypotheses. I think that the reason we have come to adopt so many psychological approaches to neurosis is that we have not set up *predictive* theories.

The lack of infinite possibilities to explain behaviour may put off some people. It is in the liberal tradition to believe that there can be many sides to a question and that no one can be the exclusive holder of *the* truth. They would not question the physical laws which produce electricity in their homes, but they may want to believe that man is too intricate to be governed by scientific laws. To accept an answer means to give up the struggle to find truth. We seem more comfortable in the struggle.

Some of us prefer the neurotic never-never land where nothing can be absolutely true because it can lead us away from other personal truths which hurt so much. The neurotic has a personal stake in the denial of truth, and it is this we must face when stating that a truth has been found. To find the truth is to find freedom. It means to eliminate neurotic choice which is no more than rationalised anarchy. The neurotic who wants to be free to see all sides often cannot believe that he may proceed directly to what is true – not *my* truth, but *his*. He has only to journey inside himself, which is a lot closer than India.

Science is the search for truth, which does not preclude finding it. Too often we in the social sciences have been content with statistical truths rather than human ones, piling up cases to 'prove' our point when, it seems to me, scientific truth ultimately rests on predictability – to make a cure *happen*, not simply to build theoretical rationales to *explain* later why someone improved in this therapy or that.

We still need, and plan to do, a great deal of follow-up research on Primal Theory and Primal Therapy. Yet the results thus far are promising enough to convince me that Primal Therapy will create lasting effects with patients because it involves no more or less than making the person into what he already is. Once that happens, a person cannot retreat into his unreality even if he wanted to. To relapse into neurosis after Primal Therapy would be tantamount to losing the height one has gained, to lose the beard one has finally grown, or to have one's breasts shrink back to their pre-Primal size – not likely events and important reminders that we are curing not a mental illness, but a psychophysiological one.

My deepest hope is that professionals will consider taking a revolutionary approach to neurosis and perhaps come to see that almost a century of psychotherapy has passed now without making a significant dent in mental illness. I think we must realise that possibly patchwork methods to overthrow an unreal system do not work and have never really worked.

For the suffering neurotic who may think that Primal Therapy is too overwhelming or too difficult to go through, I would only say that the Herculean task is to be what you're not. The easiest thing to be is yourself.

APPENDIX A

Tom

'Tom' is included in the Appendix because, while at present writing his therapy has not been concluded, his treatment is the subject of a full-length documentary film about Primal Therapy. This account contains his personal observations on that treatment.

Tom is a thirty-five-year-old history teacher, now divorced. He has had what I believe to be a fairly typical American upbringing. He had no obvious neurosis. He was functioning well, was responsible, was a good parent, but felt something was missing in his life.

Tom was always searching. He had spent a great deal of time in sensitivity training and in special encounter groups. They enabled him to learn about people, but none of his own problems changed significantly. He was not, in any sense, what people consider a neurotic (though I later learned that he ground his teeth so badly at night that he had to have a special device for his mouth). Tom was polite and respectful, cared about his country, had friends, loved his children and took them on trips, and seemed to the world to be happy. Though he had made all the right motions, he himself had this feeling of not getting anything out of life. Life seemed empty for him.

Before Tom came for therapy, he classified himself as an intellectual. He was completely involved in the history of ideas, in philosophical systems, he could quote verbatim the brilliant thoughts of learned men; but he could not employ this knowledge to live his personal life intelligently.

Often, intellectuality is the mental process of repression at work just as the body armour is the physically repressive process. In Primal terms, intelligence is the ability to think what you feel and vice versa. Tom taught college, yet by his own account he was 'not smart'. 'Smart,' he told me, 'is to be free to see what is. My feelings were too hurtful to let me do that.'

Tom's value structure changed radically in a short three-week period. To understand such a rapid transformation, we need to remember that in Primal Therapy for the first time since childhood, ideas flow into the mind out of deep feeling experiences. Thus, the mind is no longer inventing value systems to cover Pain, and when the mind is no longer used to suppress feeling, one becomes real. Old values and ideas come tumbling down because they were false structures in the first place. Tom was never allowed to have his own real thoughts and feelings. He accepted his parents' and the church's views first. There was no point in going over each false idea with him and explaining how the idea may have been irrational. Having his mind come into accord with his feelings rendered those irrationalities superfluous.

Late in the afternoon of the day before my therapy was to begin I checked into a small and quiet hotel in Beverly Hills. I did not leave my room until the following morning when I left for Dr Janov's office.

Being alone in that postage-stamp room with nothing to do and no one to talk to put me on the spot. There was nothing else around. Only me. I had no real interest in the present and its drab, confining surroundings. I had no idea of what to expect in therapy. The future was blank. All I had was my past. Before long, all the major events and all of the prominent people in my life began seeping through the walls of that hotel room. To my surprise those memories and reflections were extraordinarily vivid, yet curiously unreal: I wanted to become involved with each of them just as it happened, but I couldn't. Something seemed to hold me back. Why? It was like looking at my life from a great distance through a powerful telescope. This inability to become involved confused me. I began to feel that I must not be taking all of this as seriously as I should. Shouldn't I be suffering? I tried to come up with some explanations, only to finally realise that I couldn't explain anything. I could only speculate. I went to bed.

Monday

The therapy began in typical fashion (I had plenty of therapy before). I walked into the office and was told to lie down on a big black couch on one side of the room. Then I was asked to explain why I had decided to go into therapy.

I had been very dissatisfied with my job over the past two years. I had some serious doubts about remaining in teaching. My love life had not given me the happiness I was looking for. I had been through one marriage and two affairs. When I was about halfway through explaining all of this, Art interrupted: 'That's not why you're here at all,' he observed. 'You are here because you are a loser. It won't make any difference what kind of a job you have: You'll still be miserable. You're a loser.' With one swift chop I had been busted wide open. There was no need for any more explaining.

Then he wanted to know about my father. He was a freight manager for a trucking firm. Everyone liked him because he was so good-natured and obliging. But he wasn't much of a father. He spent most of the time at the office. He rarely came home before 7 p.m. Very often it would be 8 or 9 before he got there. He never ran around or drank. He just worked at the office. He'd come home, eat supper, and then sit on the couch and fall asleep. Dad always did his work around the house. He also liked to listen to ball games on the radio. Beyond that, there wasn't much to say. We never did anything together. I played basketball and baseball in high school, but Dad would never come to see me play. One day he and Mom did drive out to watch a baseball game. I was so nervous that I booted an easy grounder in the early innings. A few minutes later I saw the car going out of the ball park. You can imagine how I felt.

Then I was taken by surprise. Art had me ask Dad for help. I didn't understand what he was doing, but I started asking Dad for help. After a few pleas I told Art that it seemed so pointless because I knew Dad wouldn't deliver. He didn't push me, and we went on to other things.

He asked me to describe my life around home when I was a kid. So I started talking about 'the programme'. The programme was a sometimes subtle, frequently transparent scheme of life devised for my edification and well-being by unknown and external forces. It made itself known through the home, the church and the school. Since my mother was the big voice around home, and the home was the closest institutional link of my early years, I came to closely associate my mother and the programme. Around home the programme was brought to my attention by continuous nagging, harping, carping, bitching and bawlings out. I could get dirty, but not too dirty when I went out to play. I was expected to behave as a 'good Catholic boy' – i.e., respect my elders, do what I am told, and no dirty thoughts. For all practical purposes our house was off limits. It was furnished with antiques. I was always told to 'be careful, you might break something'. Bringing my friends around to play was virtually unthinkable. First of all, I couldn't have but one or two; else Mother would get nervous and upset. Second, playing in the house was like being on parole: We were under constant surveillance; we couldn't jump around, bang things, or make too much noise. So if I really wanted to play or be with my playmates, I had to leave home – the farther, the better.

Mine was a good Catholic family. Of course I went to a Catholic school. I was taught by nuns for twelve years! To make matters even more difficult, my mother had two younger sisters who were in the order of nuns teaching at our school. So all the nuns knew my mother. For me it was like a giant conspiracy. The moment I stopped being a good Catholic boy, I got it from all sides. I didn't really know where family ended and church and school began. That was the programme.

When I finished describing the programme, Art asked for my reaction to this way of life that had been established for me as a child. He might just as well have dropped a match in a pool of gasoline. I exploded in a flaming tirade. The flames leaped up and lashed out at the programme, giving me an intense and angry satisfaction. I wanted to burn the programme to the ground. I repeatedly yelled out as loud as I could: 'Fuck the programme! Fuck the programme! Fuck it! Fuck it! Fuck it!' As the flames subsided, I concluded with the quiet, white anger of a glowing ember: 'And fuck you, Mom and Dad, as official representatives of the programme.'

After I lay there in silence for a while and the fire had gone out of me, Art asked me about my brother, Bill. I told him how Bill and I never had much of a relationship. He was three years older than I and didn't appreciate a little brother tagging around behind him. Unfortunately, he couldn't see our relationship in any terms but these, and so he shoved me aside because I was too young. For a brief time when I was around sixteen, Bill and I did a few things together and developed a small bundle of understanding. I remember our going to several cowboy movies, lampooning the script together and digging the barroom brawls. After the movie we would go somewhere and have a beer. But those occasions were few and the period of understanding brief. As I grew older, my image of Bill began to change. I saw him as being turned off and dead. He dampened my zest for life and my desire to do things with him tapered off.

It seemed as though I was the one who was always getting into trouble or causing some sort of disturbance. And when Mom and Dad would get down on me for these things, Bill would always join them. I never felt that I could turn to him when I got in trouble. This angered me and hurt me deeply. I felt all the more lonely because of it. So whenever he got into trouble, which wasn't very often, I would feel better – a lot less lonely. Bill was the sort of kid who would do daring feats in order to get attention and gain the affection of his peers. I remember one occasion he rode a bike along the ledge of a hundred-foot railroad bridge that spans the river on the south side of town. One wrong move and he would have been killed. I watched from the end of the bridge until he started across. Then I couldn't bear to look any longer. I thought he was crazy to try such a thing and told him so. But it didn't seem to have any effect on him. One time he made me feel a lot better. He had gone out to a dance hall with some of his friends who told him that he couldn't drink a case of beer. That's all Bill needed, and he proceeded to down twenty-four bottles of Weideman's fine beer. When they brought him home he was totally soused. To make matters worse, as he staggered up the steps and into the house, they all sat in the car and to the tune of 'Good Night, Ladies', they sang 'Good Night, Smiley, Good Night, Smiley, It's time to say good-bye'. Mom and Dad were mortified: What would the neighbours think! Well, I was scared because they got so mad at him. But inside I felt real good seeing Bill get knocked off his righteous pedestal.

I hoped that being knocked off his pedestal would bring us closer together, but it didn't. 'You were a pretty lonely kid,' Art observed. 'That's really true,' I replied. There really wasn't anyone I could turn to or be with around home. It would get so bad that I'd leave just to get away. When I was a kid, I'd go out into the woods and play. I'd find other kids to play with – anyone who would go with me – or I would sometimes just want to go out alone. We would go out and play war. We would hike around and explore. I think I knew every cave and crevice in that woods. We would go down the river to the falls, a small tributary that dropped around seventy-five feet into the river. We would swim in the river and swing on vines. Sometimes we would raid the farmers' fields, get ourselves some potatoes and corn, pack them in river mud, and cook them on a bed of hot rocks. We'd bring along a couple of cans of pork and beans. For dessert we'd pick a couple of round sweet watermelons from the fields or get some fruit from an orchard. Sometimes we would fish, hunt snakes or groundhogs or anything we could find. We'd gather berries and asparagus growing wild along the railroad tracks. In the autumn we'd go out and eat wild papaws. I remember taking another kid out one day to show him the papaws because he'd never even heard of them. Well, he ate too many and got sick. I thought that was pretty funny.

In my early teens I got away from home a lot by playing ball. I'd play ball all day long – baseball, basketball, football – whatever was in season. I could play all of them very well, and the other kids always wanted me on their team. That was such a good feeling. I had never felt wanted like that before.

Later on I would get away from home by going out at night. I would go to bars and dance halls a lot. Sometimes I would just go downtown and talk to whoever I could find. The older I got, the more I stayed away from home. During my senior year in high school not once did I bring a book home to study in the evening. I had to get away. I was gone all the time. Finally, I left for college. After that, I spent very little time at home.

When I finished, Art noted that I had been very passive and accommodating in my relationship with my parents. This seemed to fit, and I concurred. Then he asked if I ever felt like a woman or if I ever had any homosexual fantasies. He asked the questions in what seemed to be a sly, insinuating way. I answered no to both questions, but the whole scene made me uneasy and angry.

Art did not push these questions any further. Instead, he focused in on the programme again. I got nervous and had to urinate. I asked Art where the head was, but he didn't want me to go. 'You'll piss off your feelings,' he said. I held on for a while. Then I couldn't wait any longer. He said we'd have to stop whenever I took a leak. That made me mad, for I felt that he was trying to manipulate me. I went out to take a leak. When I came back, the door was locked. I knocked. He didn't open it. That really pissed me off, and I beat on the door until the walls began to rattle. 'What did you do that for?' I asked when he opened the door. 'I didn't want anyone else to get in,' he answered with a straight face. The reply thoroughly turned me off. My only reply was: 'Shit!' I went back to the couch and started in again. We went on for another half hour.

After getting home, I began to get mad over being a loser. The term seemed to fit. I even wondered if I should have been having some homosexual fantasies. Balling other men never appealed to me. Then I began to get mad at Art: Before we were supposed to begin, he had called and told me that we would have to delay our session for one day because he had 'laryngitis'. I deeply resented his sly insinuations on the homosexual issue. I was provoked by the door game he played that morning. These issues irritated me until I made up my mind to go in there tomorrow and get these games cleared up.

Tuesday

I arrived at nine fifty. The door was locked. I wanted to be alone to concentrate on my anger, so I went to the head and waited there until ten. When I arrived, the door was open. I walked in. Art asked why I was late. I looked at my watch. It was three after. I told him that I had been there earlier but that the door had been locked. He told me to lie down. I told him that I didn't want to, that I wanted to look him in the eye and talk face-to-face. He snapped his fingers and told me to lie down because we were wasting time. The sound of those snapping fingers only steeled my resolve to have a face-to-face encounter. I was numb and light-headed with rage. Instead of replying to his command, I walked straight over to the chair, sat down, faced him, and told him there were some things I wanted to get straight. I went into the games. Then I told him that I was tired of being manipulated and that I wanted to say now what I felt. He said that I was playing a game. He told me again to go over and lie down. This time I did, but with very mixed feelings.

We began with my anger. I told him that behind my anger with him I was angry at myself for being a loser. He asked what it felt like. 'Tight in my chest and a burning gut,' I answered. He told me to ask Dad to help get it out. He had me take deep breaths with a wide-open mouth. The breathing seemed to transport me to another life, but asking Dad for help didn't do anything. I told him that Dad wouldn't help. He asked me how that felt. 'Like being left alone, being left out,' I answered. It made me feel sad. He had me breathe more and told me to get the pain out. This time the breathing really took me out. I began to writhe in pain. My stomach was aflame and my chest felt like it was being crushed. He told me to go on and get it out and to ask Dad for help. I began beating the hell out of the couch and yelling at Dad to help get it out until I was exhausted.

After I had rested, Art asked what it was that I had gotten out. For a while I was so overwhelmed by the whole experience that I couldn't explain what it was. Finally, I recognised all the guilt, fear of being myself, and frustration at not being able to be myself. Suddenly I realised what asking Dad for help was all about. I had been very puzzled by this tactic, and now I couldn't wait to get it out. I told Art that it no longer seemed senseless to ask Dad for help. For now I could understand that I am talking to the dad *within* me – the dad that I wished for. 'It's a matter of getting *that* dad to accept me as I am and to help me get out the feeling of being left alone and left out,' I explained.

He asked me what I had to do next. I told him I had to first of all learn how to feel that dad within. Feel what it is like. Feel it like one feels a good golf swing or a good dance rhythm, and then later learn how to use it. Then I told him how good it felt to have a dad – one who cared and could help. It felt so good that I laughed and cried for a long time.

When I could talk again, I told him how long I had felt left alone, left out. Then I recalled the lonely Christmas child that I was one year. I remember sitting under the Christmas tree and sadly looking at the blue light in the crib after they had told me there wasn't a Santa Claus. They explained that Bill was too old for that and they knew it wouldn't matter to me. In a way they were right, for I had known for some time that Santa Claus was a put-on, and the gift thing really didn't matter that much. But the way they told me took all the love out of Christmas, and that was the only time I ever felt I really got any. All I wanted for Christmas was a real dad and mom, who would love me, care for me, help me, and stick up for me the way I am. I was a very sad and lonely Christmas child that year.

Wednesday

Today Art had me lie on the floor. I spent this session, as well as all subsequent sessions, on the floor. He asked what I had done since yesterday. I told him that I had been very tired, was still tired, and that I had spent the whole time resting. From the very first day I had established a routine. After therapy I would come home, have lunch, rest for an hour or so, write up my notes on the day's session with Art, reflect on the day's session, eat supper, write up my reflections, just sit for about an hour, and then go to bed. I found that by concentrating exclusively on my therapy, I could gain much insight and recall many helpful experiences and events from my past. But yesterday had been so exhausting that after writing up the session, I couldn't do any more. I just lay there like a dead man. Three events passed through my mind, and I narrated them.

The first event was the day Dad took Bill, our cousin, and me to a baseball game in Cincinnati. I was about five years old. I was so overwhelmed by all the sights that my head must have been turning a hundred and eighty degrees. When I got to the ball park, it locked in on the diamond like a laser. After the game Dad took us out the centrefield gate. As we walked through the gate, I turned around for one last look at the field. I wanted to stay there all night – forever! When I finally turned around, Dad and the other two were nowhere in sight. I panicked and began bawling. The people around me got all excited, and before long, Dad and the other kids were there to retrieve me. Then we got on a bus to the train station, and I had to pee so bad I couldn't stand it. I told Dad. He said that he couldn't do anything about it and that I would just have to pee in my pants. It was a very relaxing pee. But I vividly remember the discomfort of those wet, scratchy woollen short pants.

The second event involved my very early school years. Sometimes I would come home after school, and the door would be locked. I would sit on the back steps, pound the screen door in rage, and cry for Mom to let me in. Then one of the neighbours would come over and tell me that my mother wasn't at home. I would just sit there and wait until she got back.

The third event happened on a Sunday evening when I was about eight. We didn't have a car. The only time I got to go anywhere in a car was when Grandma and Pop (my grandfather) would take us somewhere. One Sunday evening I was visiting the neighbours across the street when they came over to take us to the cemetery and a drive around town. Dad and Mom told them not to wait for me, and they were pulling away just as I was running up behind them. I ran as fast I could and yelled at the top of my voice, but it was all to no avail: they turned the corner and drove away.

Art asked me why those things came up. 'Because,' I replied, 'they were times when I was left alone and left out.' He asked what it felt like. I told him how it grabbed my stomach and my chest. He had me try to breathe it up and out like I did yesterday. I was too exhausted to make it. I lay there for a long time, motionless. When I finally moved, he asked what the trouble was I told him that my back hurt. He said that it wasn't physical. He told me not to move, but just to feel it. I told him it felt like the programme: 'Don't sit on that chair with your dirty clothes. Take your shoes off. Don't touch that!'

I lay there for a long time and felt the programme get me in the back. Finally, I said, 'You know, I found a way not to get left out though. The way I found was to help people. Do things for them. One day Pop (Grandpa) found me out in the street holding a piece of paper between my teeth, and two guys with eight-foot bullwhips were cutting it in half. He made me stop. He couldn't understand why I was doing it.' 'He cared, didn't he?' Art interjected. 'Yeah, he really cared,' I added. 'Tell him,' Art said. So I told Pop how he really cared and how much it meant to me, and how it hurt when he died because he was about all I had. And I wept in torrents like I never cried before, even when he died, and that was the saddest day of my young life.

After the cry I told Art all about Pop. How he taught me all kinds of things and how he always let me watch whatever he was doing and how he always explained it all and then let me take a crack at it, too.

At the end of the session Art made an observation which surprised and confused me. He said I sounded like a Midwestern hick. I said that sounded like a put-down. 'No judgment at all,' he said. I couldn't figure out why he said it. After getting home and thinking it over, the comment sounded like another way of saying, 'You're really a loser.'

Today has been the most difficult day. Yesterday I was mad and beginning to take care of myself and stick up for myself. Today I was back on the floor – a bawling kid left out of everything. 'Like a little kid with his nose up against the glass trying to get into life,' as Art described it. It feels like I have such a long way to go. After having worked so hard, it feels like I have not yet made much progress.

I began thinking about being a loser – left out. I have felt that way at every stage of my life. I don't know how to feel any other way. I have built up an entire ethic around it. It just seems like such a monumental task to relearn all of this that I don't know how I'm going to do it.

Thursday

Today we began with my feeling dejected over the realisation
that my whole life-style had been built upon the device of being
a loser and the realisation that I had such a long way to go in
building a new lifestyle. I told Art about my reflections on his
observation that I was a Midwestern hick; it seemed to me to be
another way of saying that I'm a loser. He concurred.

Then he asked me to talk like a Midwestern hick. I said that I
couldn't really do it just for the sake of doing it; that would be a
head trip. I had to get into. 'What do you mean?' he asked. 'I
mean into where I was yesterday with Pop.' 'Did you go to the
funeral?' he asked. 'Oh, sure.' 'Tell me about it,' he said. So I
told him the whole thing: how I lived there and helped
Grandma all the while Pop was sick, how Pop had died, the
wake, the funeral.

'Did you cry much?' Naw. A little the first day and a little bit
when they put Pop in the ground. I tried to take it like a man, as
they say. I was thirteen. 'Did you say good-bye to Pop when
they put him in the ground?' Naw. Not with all those people
there. They would have had to carry me out. 'Say good-bye to
Pop now. Tell him what he means to you.'

And so I said good-bye to Pop with all the love and feeling in
my body. I cried and I talked to Pop until there wasn't anything
left. I told him how much I loved him because he cared, because
he showed me how to do things and took me under his wing. I
told him how I like to learn and do things myself because then
he could see that his love and care wasn't being wasted. I told
him how I wanted him to understand when he saw me drifting
away as I grew older, but that I had to go on according to the
new way and not the old. 'I gotta go on, Pop, I gotta go on!' Oh,
I cried it over and over again. 'I gotta go on, Pop, please understand! Please! You didn't fail, Pop. I gotta go on! Good-bye,
Pop. Good-bye!' And I cried like a young river at the spring
thaw. Like I'm crying now typing this up and like I cried when I
wrote it down the first time.

Then Art told me to tell my dad how I wanted him to be like
Pop. And I did. I told him the whole thing. I told him how I
wanted to be wanted and cared for like Pop wanted and cared
for me. Then I told Art how Mom and Dad didn't want me to
be born and how Dad said he wanted to slam the window on
his cock and cut it off when he found out Mom was pregnant
with me. Then I said, 'Dad, you know what I really want? I'd
really want you to really want the whole shot, the fuck and
everything that comes with it – 'cause that's where it's at, Dad.
I'd want you to really want Mom, really put it to her and want
me, too. 'Cause that's where I am, Dad: I'm more than just me.

I'm life! And ya gotta want it, Dad, ya gotta want it!'

Then I talked about my mother and how she acted like she never really had it – wouldn't let herself have it, always bitching, always on edge. And I started to get that pain in my back again like I did yesterday. Art had me lie there awhile and feel it. 'What's the feeling?' he kept asking. 'It arches up right in the small of my back,' I finally replied. 'Like I'm bracing myself against—' 'Against what?' 'Against being left out, left alone. It's like walking barefoot on real sharp rocks. Ya gotta keep real tensed up all the time or you'll get cut.'

So Art had me tell Mother she was cutting me. And I really let it rip. I shouted at the top of my lungs, telling her to stop 'cause she was cutting me up. Always bitching. 'And get off it! Get off my back!' When I got finished yelling, I had to piss.

When I came back from taking a leak, Art showed some surprise that I was learning so quickly. He said I was doing a real fine job. And that helped because I felt so far away from the end of the tunnel when I started this morning. When I got home, I started to think about telling Art in therapy today why I've been a loser. I've been programmed for it. The reason: If I know that I am already a loser, then I don't have to worry about being left out. I've already taken myself out of the action before they ever get a chance to cut me out.

Friday

Today was my first day at the group session. I just watched for a while. Then I got down on the floor and said good-bye to Pop again. Towards the end I got the feeling that Pop would understand that both he and I had to go our separate ways – he into death and me into manhood. I felt that we were real close together now, despite the fact that we were both going our separate ways. It was like feeling close to the earth or like being in bed with my girl and not being uptight in the slightest. Art told me to sink into it, and I did as best I could what with all the yelling and crying going on around me. I wasn't used to it, but I'll catch on.

After everyone was up off the floor, we talked. Art introduced me to the group. I told them I didn't feel like I really knew enough to contribute anything. I told them I awakened this morning knowing too I had to stop balling women because I was fucking off too many feelings. Art turned to me and said that I didn't look that sexual. He registered mild surprise that I had been balling a lot of women. Then he added that what I was really doing is covering up a latent homosexuality. It wiped me out.

By the time I got home my head was splitting with pain. My

stomach was too upset to eat anything. All I could do is just lie on the floor. I felt that if I had to be a fag all my life, latent or otherwise, fuck it. I didn't want to live. I wanted to get rid of the fag. I went back and tried to identify all the faggy feelings. The pain got so bad that I had to call Art. He was in Santa Barbara. I wanted to do a Primal and asked if he could tell me how to get into one at home. He said it wouldn't work and gave me some numbers of others who could take me. I said I wanted to know if I could get the fag out. 'No problem,' he rejoined. I cried with relief and told him I could wait until Monday for the Primal.

Monday

We had a hard time getting started today. I had shut down my feelings after talking to Art in Santa Barbara simply to be able to function. Art wanted to know what happened Saturday. I tried to recount as much as I could, but it was a head trip, and I couldn't get into it any more. 'Well, what are you feeling now?' Art asked. Like a shot I lashed out at him, wept and cried: 'Why weren't you there Saturday when I needed you? What a shitty thing to do! Drop the fag thing on me and then bug out of town! You certainly knew what kind of reaction you'd produce.'

He told me to lie down again and not worry about it, for we would get to it another way. He asked me to tell him about my life. I told him about my falling in love with Betty, my relationship with Louise, and my marriage to Phyllis. He got on the older woman thing and wanted to know about Vi. Towards the end of my account of the affair with Betty, the traumatic part, I had to piss. It had been building up since I began talking about her. I told Art. He told me just to feel it and not to move a muscle. Earlier my arms had gone to sleep as I spread them out on the floor. He asked if they were too long. I said, 'No, they just fell asleep this morning. I don't know what to do with them.' He told me not to move and just feel what was going on. So I lay there. Before long, I started to get a heaving feeling in my gut. It pushed upwards. Soon I began to flop my arms and legs on the floor and roll my head around, so intensely did the tension mount. I was an infant in the crib. I could feel it. My hands tensed up like those of a little baby when he cries. My mouth withered up like I was trying to get something out of an empty bottle. I didn't say anything or cry out. I just violently flopped and gasped for air. Finally, I got so tired that I stopped and just lay there real still. Then consciously and slowly I repeated all the motions and the drawing up of my mouth and my hands to make sure I had remembered them.

I was kind of foggy coming out of the Primal, and I'm not exactly sure how it happened. But it went something like this: Art said, 'You weren't allowed to touch it, were you?' I grabbed my cock and said, 'No, I'd always get smacked.' Then I went through it by smacking myself on the hand and telling Art about the way it was. 'You weren't allowed to have a cock, were you?' 'No.' So I sat up and rubbed my cock. I got up in front of the mirror, took my pants down, rubbed my cock, and told Mom and Dad it was okay. Then I told Art I could only have a cock in secret when I jacked off, but that I wanted my cock to be a part of all my life. 'You knew, didn't you?' he added. 'Yeah, I really knew! And that's why they were afraid. They knew that I knew, and they were real quick to put it all back in the box.' 'And you became a good little fag,' he added. 'Yeah.'

It was a wonderful feeling I got when I rubbed my cock and told Dad and Mom it was okay. 'I looked for that feeling in philosophy, religion, my work and God knows where, and I found it today in my cock! You're wonderful, Art. It's beautiful!'

After getting home I spent most of the day rubbing my cock and telling Mom and Dad it was okay. On coming out of Art's office I saw an older, prosperous-looking man coming down the corridor. My first feeling was the old one of passivity, uneasiness and inner shame upon seeing a stranger who looked more important than I. Then the feeling that I've got a cock and it's okay came over me, and my whole attitude changed. Suddenly I felt comfortable, at ease, self-accepting and open towards him. I'd never had that feeling before. It's beautiful! I got the same feeling when I passed some women in the supermarket.

I no longer have the same past. I must go back and reconstitute my entire past to bring it into accord with what I am now learning. I need to do this in order to obtain continuity in my life. Without continuity I cannot have orderly change.

In therapy I want to express more and more without the use of regular logical sequences and ordinary language patterns, complete sentences, connecting a sentence to its antecedent, etc. For I get all fouled up trying to experience and at the same time duplicate the experience in a thought pattern and a linguistic structure.

Tuesday

Today Art tried to get me to cry like a baby. I failed. I got it for just a little bit, but then I lost it. I flopped around on the floor for three and a half hours. I tried to get back through having to piss. It was a blind alley. A trap. If I pissed, I wouldn't cry because I would piss off my feelings. If I cried, I'd relax my stomach muscles and piss all over everything.

However, some insights did come out of the effort. Their value has proven to be immense. I felt my mother's anger at my squirming and crying in the crib. I couldn't face it. I hid from it. I felt what it was like never to get enough milk and what it was like to eat air. I felt the lack of love in their American Gothic faces. I wanted to hide under the couch from their cold expressions. So I crawled under the couch and cried to Art: 'What do you want to know?' I learned how to talk baby talk with my mouth all drawn up. 'Wey won't wet me cwry!' I felt my dad's distance from me – as if he had come right out and said: 'I'll help take care of you, but don't expect me to be your dad.' I felt how he always hid his cock from me and never let me see him naked. Never saw Mom naked either.

When it was over, I was completely exhausted – too exhausted even to write a complete account of it. This is all I could do.

Sometimes when I was very young, I would hide under the bed or crawl behind the couch. I liked it there, for I could be all alone and Mommy couldn't see me. It felt so free and good not to be seen. That's what I was doing under the couch today. I remember now. I'd forgotten all about that! I'd get tired of seeing her anger. So I would hide where it would be solitary and quiet and loving.

My behavioural pattern in therapy is very typical. I start out like a flash. Then something goes awry. I seem to need to make a big deal out of it, do a lot of struggling, and have failures. Then I really get down on myself until I become a helpless little boy. I don't understand it. All I see is that my attention has been diverted away from what I am actually doing and directed towards something else.

Wednesday

Today I flopped around on the floor again. I learned how rigid my upbringing had been. My body was never allowed to do what it wanted. It was kept in a straitjacket. I wasn't allowed to kick, to thrash and roll around. I never got to play with my mother. I never got to suckle at her breast. It seems as though so many of the things I wanted and needed were denied.

I learned to roll and play on the floor today. But we went through the same old pissing game. And we did not do what we have needed to do all week: get back to the fag fear I had on Saturday.

Thursday

I felt my fear today – the fear that comes with faggery. It wasn't like Saturday, when I came home with my head splitting open, but I got into it enough to feel what it is like. I was on the floor going back to the baby me. I got back to the baby and Mommy, but then I got confused. I didn't know whether I should get mad or get into the baby flopping on the floor again. I've come to call the latter my baby fit. Then I had to piss again.

This time I got angry. I raged on like a major volcano for a long time. I beat one pillow with another, fighting off Mommy for control of my body. I screamed and raged about the pressure in my gut, telling her that I wanted control of my gut. I went on like that until, to my surprise, I did get control of my gut. The pressure to piss subsided. I got control of my body with my anger! My violence obtained what properly belongs to me – my body.

Friday

Today we went into Mom and Dad again and how it was with them when I was a boy. I told Art how Dad was all but totally shut down, how what little of a relationship I did have came through Mom, how I really had no one, how lonely and fucked up I was in college with no one to counsel or advise me, how I came to marry someone so turned-off as Phyllis.

Then we went into my doubts about public school teaching. It came down to the fact that it was a safe, respectable, secure, middle-class programme, and I wanted to fuck the programme. I told Art I was afraid because I didn't know what the new me was like, and I was hesitant about turning away from the only me I knew. Then I saw that I had to turn away from that me whether I wanted to or not because if I keep the programme, I keep the fag and I don't want the fag any more!

He asked me what I had obtained from these two weeks. 'My past and my body,' I replied. He asked me what I wanted to do. I told him I wanted to teach people to experience, both individually and politically.

When I got home I was high as a kite. The urge to do something with my life – something meaningful – had really turned me on. I realised that fucking, or cigarettes, or booze, or money, or pot, or anything else could not substitute.

Saturday

They started on the floor again today in group. After several people had started to cry for their mommies, I began to get angry because I couldn't go back, because there wasn't anything to go back to. Art saw me sitting there and got me down on the floor. I began beating the floor in blind, uncomprehending anger. Then I screamed out in rage: 'I'm mad. Wey won't wet me cwry! I want my life!' Art came by, and I told him that I had been breaking away for twenty years and it was so hard to go back to Mom and Dad. 'I can cry for Pop,' I said, 'because he cared and helped!' 'Tell them you want to come back,' he said. So I told them I wanted to come back as I am, and I wanted them to care like Pop cared. I sobbed unabashedly for a brief time. Then I told Art about Uncle Mac and how Pop had put him down for wanting to be a musician and how Mac hated Pop so and killed himself drinking. 'Just like you were killing yourself,' Art said. 'But at least Mac seemed to know what he wanted. I don't know yet.' 'No,' he added, 'they put you down.'

I sank into the feeling of Mac, my favourite uncle and childhood idol, of slowly killing myself, what Mom and Dad had done. I got the big pain in my gut and my head. Then I went into my thrashing baby fit. When I came out of it, they were all looking at me. They said I frightened them with my anger.

I told them all how I had been trying to let the fear take over my body all week. One woman observed that I was not lying still when the Pain came, but instead began my thrashing baby fit. It sounded like a good idea. Moreover, my way wasn't working. Deep in the fit there just seems to be blind emotion. Everything else vanishes until I subside. It hardly seems likely that I would ever move from blind rage into paralytic fear.

When I got home, I noticed that the small of my back felt tired – like it had gone through a good workout after a long period of being inactive. It was the same spot that hurt from lying stiff on the floor!

That evening I went to a party. It was the first time I had talked with people socially in two weeks. I had no desire to drink or smoke, but I wanted to fuck, and I wanted to blow a joint or two. I felt good – rather different and new. More alive. I seemed to radiate quite a bit of vitality that people picked up on. Met a lovely, lissome blonde named Frances. Also met Eileen, a juicy brunette in a Bathsheba-like low-cut gown and gold jewellery. But I dug Frances more because she could do something with her body – many wonderful things. I watched her dance for a while. Then I tried to dance with her, but I wasn't that good. I got the old turned-off, self-effacing fag feeling. Noticed that a lot of people there seemed to have that feeling. Weren't into their bodies. Weren't into anything. Was so good fucking Frances after the party, but wished she hadn't tried so hard with her head. 'You're such a man,' and all of that bullshit. Feel this morning that I should have done something about it, like: 'Easy there, don't force it. Just relax and let your body take over. Let your body tell your head what to do. Then you won't have to do the bullshit thing.'

The next day I took a nap. Just as I was waking up, a vague awareness dawned upon me, much like we see light in the morning before we see the sun. I had felt it for several days off and on. It frightened me. It seemed to be so terrifying that this way of presenting itself was a way of preparing me for the day when I could handle it. I got the sense that the day was almost at hand and that I should prepare myself.

Monday

What I learned today must be stated generally because it was so physical.

I told Art about everything that happened over the weekend. I told him how I always felt left out at home and how even Pop would have turned against me had he lived because his way was the old way. He would have turned against me, just like he turned against Mac. So Art had me say good-bye to all of them – Pop, Dad and Mom. I told them all I had to go on and that I loved them but would not be bound to their ways. I told them not to worry because I wouldn't turn out like Mac.

I had to piss then, and Art had me start pulling it up instead of pushing it down. I did. With my breathing and voice, my cock and my hands, my stomach and legs and back, I started pulling up. I felt the pressure gradually subside to the point where my mind could let go and my body could take over. That happened when I let it feel good in my cock and when my body motion and my breathing became co-ordinated. When that happened, I realised they had been out of sync all these years. For one thing I had been breathing improperly. I had been sucking in with my stomach when I inhaled and letting out when I exhaled. The two motions collide about halfway down the abdomen. The lower half of the abdomen is shut off. All genital action is cut off from the rhythm of breathing.

As I went deeper into it, I learned the movements I wanted to make in the crib and couldn't and for which I substituted my baby fit. I felt an undulating movement in my stomach co-ordinate with my breathing and my voice in a most pleasurable way. It felt so good in my cock, and I had a bodily rhythm just like fucking, but I was on my back. How it washed away all the anger and frustration! I didn't get it all up that day. My extremities were still rigid. But they will make it, too.

Tuesday

Not very much happened today. I was too tired from the long, exhausting session yesterday. Art picked it up, and we called it a day after about half an hour. When I got home the black, brooding mood set in.

Wednesday

I told Art I wanted to deal with the black, brooding mood. 'Sink into it,' he said. So I went right into it. I told myself how no good I was, how I was wasting my time and money in therapy, and how things wouldn't be any different when I got out. Then I lamented having no opportunity to do anything except teach high school. I sadly described my inability to return to graduate school; I have no money; I'm too old; I'm not smart enough. I said I had no business reading and talking about things like Sir James Frazer and mythology. I summed up by complaining that things weren't going to change, how really helpless I am, and how useless it is to even try.

Art told me to sink into it more. I told him I was sinking into a black hole where it was dark and very lonely and where nobody cared. He told me to ask Mommy and Daddy for help. I did, but it had little effect on me. I told Art that Dad couldn't help because he was turned-off and shut-down. He told me to breathe deeply and sink farther. I did, and my gut began to hurt. I told Art that I didn't trust anyone down here in the hole. I want to be alone. When people are around and I'm in the deep, black hole, I get edgy. I become edgy because I don't know what they will do to me. I then described crawling behind the couch when I was a very little boy. I would also hide in the dark closet and a large built-in shoe box in my parents' bedroom. I liked dark and isolated places where I could be alone. He told me to breathe deeply and sink farther. I told him that the little baby was drowning, sinking. My head was reeling. I was going under! 'Ask your mommy for help,' Art pleaded. I did. She just stood there. Then Art told me to let the baby drown. I felt a huge weight on my chest. It became very difficult to breathe. Art told me to stop breathing and let the baby drown. I did it! Silently. Dry-eyed. Cold as my mother. But I don't think the baby drowned when I look at it in retrospect. He just seemed to fade out of my consciousness.

Then Art asked me to recount a few times when my mom and dad showed some warmth towards me. I told him that I had seen genuine tears in my mother's eyes when I was critically ill with pneumonia as a child. I also told him how our dad would occasionally take us for a walk up to the station to watch the train come in. We would stand around and talk with the station-master, the mailman, the Railway Expressman, the cabdriver and anyone else who might be around. As a kid I used to have a fantasy about the train coming in every night before going to sleep. I'd be right out in the middle of the tracks waiting for it to come in. I would see it coming over the horizon way out in the distance. The lacy wafts of steam gradually became massive billows as the train got closer. Then, just as the mighty black engine got right up to me, I would fall asleep. I just felt that when the train got in, I could rest. I told Art that I felt a con-nection between that dream and being in the closet. It was always dark in both instances. I was always alone. Finally, I always felt solitary and warm.

I couldn't remember being fondled or touched, much as I tried to remember some physical sign of warmth from my parents. But I remembered snuggling up with my mother and taking an afternoon nap on the couch. I remember reaching up and touching my dad's beard. I recall watching my dad shave and smelling the bay rum he used. He'd always sing a little bay rum jingle to me and laugh. I was almost afraid of touching my dad.

Thursday

I told Art how it distressed me that I had let the baby drown yesterday without even shedding a tear. 'Had it been anyone else's baby, I would have been terribly broken up about it,' I concluded.

I explained to Art that it was very difficult for me to receive any kind of favourable notice for an achievement. It secretly thrilled me to see my name on the sports page, but when anyone brought it to my attention, I became acutely embarrassed. The same was true when people found out I was going to Fordham. I preferred that they didn't know about it at all. I would not allow myself to be proud of anything I had done. In fact, I would chastise myself to guard against becoming conceited. Art asked me why I did this. 'I didn't want to be different than anyone else', I replied. 'Success would have widened the gulf between Dad and me as well as between others and me. As far as I was concerned, the gulf was already wide enough. So, like my dad, I had condemned myself to evoking people's sense of pity.'

I lay there for a long time, talking and thinking about my poor dad. Then I realised what I was doing, 'Jesus!' I ex-claimed. 'What's the matter?' asked Art. 'Here I am feeling sorry for Dad because he wasn't more of a father to *me*! Like what about me? And all the pity he got from others didn't do

Dad one bit of good either. Well, go ahead, Dad. Be that way. It doesn't matter any more. It's your problem, and you are the one who can't do anything about it. Go ahead and be that way. It doesn't make any difference to me now. It's too late now. Goodbye, Dad. It's very sad to say good-bye. You meant well. But I've got to go on.'

When I got home, I ate lunch and then took a nap. Just as I was waking up, I got the feeling of doing graduate work in psychology. The feeling brought tears of joy.

Friday

We took the day off, so I took my boy, Fred, to Lake Gregory for a swim. We had a great time, but I was restless. We lay out in the middle of the lake on a surfboard. I couldn't let go and relax all the way. It took me back to infancy – to wanting my mommy when she wasn't there. Not only was she not there physically; her soul wasn't there. Her cold, steel-walled soul that had to put everyone off when it came to loving.

Saturday – Group

I was overcome by the baby wanting his mommy. That's what the big fear dream is all about. That's what's coming, what I've been preparing myself for. I tried to get into it today, but I could only get a little way. Then I did what I always did when Mommy put me off. I threw a baby fit and pissed off my feelings.

Monday

Today I got back to Mommy. I got to feel some of the pain of being put-off, put-down, and put-out over being so alone. I got angry. I screamed. I screamed that I hated it all and that I hated Mommy for doing that to me. Then I cried bitterly in my sense of loss. I reached out for Mommy and felt nothing. I cried out for Mommy and felt nothing. I told Art how I envied other children when they received recognition and consideration from their parents. I told Mommy how it was always life on her terms or condemnation. It was very sad and very lonely.

Tuesday

'How do you feel?' Art began. 'Oh, I feel pretty blue today.' 'How come?' 'Yesterday. It was very sad to feel so left out and lonely. I always felt closer to Grandma than I did my own mom.' 'Tell me about her.' 'Oh, she was a beautiful soul. She was patient and understanding. She didn't rant and rave at me like my mother did. When I had problems. I would always go to her. She would listen and give me support. Whenever I got sick at school, I would go to Grandma because I knew she wouldn't get mad at me and would take care of me. She'd fix me some hot broth or some sassafras tea. She'd take time out from her work just for me until I was settled and cared for.

'After Pop died, she moved into an apartment. I'd go visit her and do things for her because I knew she liked to have company and I always felt so good about the way she treated me that I wanted to do all I could for her. After she fell and broke her hip, she moved right across the street from church so she wouldn't have to go far to mass. It was close to school, too, and I would drop in every day to see that everything was okay. If it wasn't, I'd take care of it. I really loved Grandma. I wish I would have been there when she died.' 'Say good-bye to her now.' And so I said good-bye to Grandma. I cried like I cried for Pop – almost as hard. I told her how much she meant to me. I thanked her for being so kind and so good to me. I told her that she would always be a part of me, that I'd always keep her close to me for the rest of my life. I told her how much I wanted to hug her and hold her close. I told her how good it felt to pour my heart out and cry because she deserved every ounce of love and affection that I could give her. 'It's easy to cry for Grandma and Pop,' I said, 'but it's so hard to cry for my own mother and father.'

'Let the baby cry for his mommy now,' Art said. 'Just cry out for her.'

I cried out. Not with words, for I had been lying on the couch the night before, and it occurred to me that words take me away from the great fear, the great feeling. Instead, I cried out with pleading non-verbal cries, and then it was all over me like a spring shower. It was pure feeling, and there were no words, no images of Pop or Dad, or Grandma or Mom. It was pure need. I cried with my whole body. My whole body cried out in need with great heaving sobs, and the tears gushed like blood from an open wound.

I was bathing in happiness after my crying subsided. Art asked why. 'Because I feel whole,' I replied. 'What do you mean?' 'Oh, there are many ways to explain it. I can go all the way back to my feelings now (what I meant by being born) without having them in conflict. I didn't have to leave any of them out to avoid the conflict. I have my whole range of feeling now. I have my baby, and I'm going to take good care of the little guy. I'm going to stick up for him and give him support when he needs it. My history has been brought up to date.'

All day long I felt like a tender shoot that had just popped out of the ground. Everything touched me tenderly. Waves of feeling rolled through me all day. That night in group a young woman cried because she felt such great pain in living. We got to talking about what we 'Primal' people would do in such a barbarous world. I was really ready for a Primal, but I didn't know how to get into it. I didn't want to make a false start and ruin the scene. I wanted to tell her with my soul that I, too, felt the Pain, but that I wanted to live, for there is warmth and joy in being able to care for the Pain we feel within us. Pain, like all other experiences, is momentary. If we learn how to handle it, how to love and care for ourselves, then our Pain, if it is authentic, will lead us to warmth, love and joy, regardless of what is happening in the barbarous world. For the Pain is not in the world; it is in our bodies, where we can care for it. And so it's all right. Living becomes a real problem that takes us towards death only when we keep the Pain out.

I didn't say any of this, for it wouldn't have done a bit of good. We all talk too much, even when what we have to say has a measure of validity. So I came home and wrote it down. But I felt I had come away empty-handed because I did not find my own way to get into the Primal when I was so deeply moved.

I am becoming whole now. I am my body. I am a great symphony of rich and varied feelings, each harmoniously running through my body to complement another. My sex, my body structure and energy, my anger, my fear, my warmth, my sadness, my joy – each of these has its time and its texture (there are textures in time), and each in its own time and way serves the others in their needs. I am becoming whole now, reborn of my own parentage. I am my own father. I am my own mother. I am my body. I am what I feel.

Wednesday

This morning I had another cry of pure need. Listening to the adagio of Beethoven's A Minor Quartet I stood in the middle of the dining-room floor and cried with the music (I have never heard another piece of music evoke such a sense of intense physical pain) just like I let the baby cry yesterday in therapy. There were no words, no images. There was pure sorrow and pain in the music, and I cried and cared for the sorrow and pain within.

Thursday

Sat down to work up my notes. Got to page 45: no mommy; sad

and lonely. Thought about the trip home I was planning to take. Would I want to see anyone but Mom and Dad? No. I'm going for therapy and not for fun and games. Oh! Yeah! Want to see Aunt Millie and Uncle Les. Millie was so good to me when I was a teenager. So was Les. Want to thank them like I thanked Grandma and Pop, because I was sad and lonely and they helped me. Such an orphan. And with parents. Bang! Into a sad and lonely Primal. Bang! That's what the A Minor Primal was: sad and lonely. Bang! I'm real again.

Friday

The first day since Sunday that I haven't had a Primal. But I feel one coming. This morning I thought about going home and what their reaction would be. No job. Long hair. Roughing it. I could see Mom pulling the 'We worry' bit. Then I thought to myself. *You know what that 'We worry' bit does, Mom? That sets me apart. Makes me a special case. Something is wrong with me. It's your way of making something wrong with me so you can stay on top of things. If something is wrong with me, then the heat is taken off of you. But you know what that did to me, Mom?* It made me an outsider. A sad and lonely little orphan with parents.

So I realised how afraid I am to go out of the bourgeois bag. Afraid that Mommy and Daddy will put me down and leave me out. I'm afraid. The BIG FEAR. The sad and lonely little boy.

Monday–Friday

Went back to Woodsville to visit with my parents. First time I had been back there in over ten years. The visit validated all the feelings about my parents that came out of therapy. They threw a big scowling scene over being interviewed on film.* Their reluctance had nothing to do with me or my past, although that is all they were asked to talk about. My mom tried to badger me about being divorced, quitting the Catholic Church and the job scene. I waited to see what Dad would do. Nothing, as usual. He let her go on. Then I put a stop to the badgering. It hurt very much: the badgering, Dad's typical nonperformance, my angry halting the badger bit. Then Mom tried to hang the 'crazy' tag on me, and I really blew up. After that, things began to improve outwardly, but inwardly nothing changed. That evening I wanted to go out just to get away for a while. After I got out of the house, I had the same orphaned feeling I knew so well as a wandering teenager. I began to wonder how I ever managed to live through it all as a youth.

* This refers to the documentary being made of Tom's treatment.

I went back to the old train station, the river, the woods, and the big bridge. All the old feelings of the young boy seeking refuge in the wilds came back. I stood on the bridge and wept for the young boy who couldn't allow himself to feel all the pain then. So I stood on the bridge and cried and let him feel it now – now that it's over. I felt so warm and grateful towards those old spots for giving the young boy some measure of what he needed so deeply.

I went down to see my uncle and aunt. I told them all about my therapy, for I knew they would be interested and understanding. It was wonderful to be with them again. It felt so good to tell them how much they meant to me, to let them know how much they did for me when I was an adolescent. It made them feel wonderful. The vibrations flowed all over the room all night.

I went down to the cemetery to visit Pop and Grandma's grave. I knelt there between their graves and told them all the things I told them in therapy. I knelt there for a long time, crying and talking to Pop and Grandma. When the crying stopped, I just knelt there for quite a while in the open silence. I had never seen Grandma's grave. It had been twenty-two years since I stood at that grave site when they put Pop in the ground. For me it was only yesterday. Uncle Mac was buried there, too. I had never seen his grave either. 'My poor Uncle Mac' was all that went through me when I turned to his grave. Then I walked over to Pop and Grandma's big stone, touched it for a while, and left.

My return home brought me closer to the warmth I want to feel, for it confirmed the reality of my Pain and my therapy. Now it is only a matter of passing through the pain. The warmth lies on the other side. Now I know where warmth and love are – on the other side of the Pain I must pass through. I have already experienced enough of the Pain to understand this. So now it is no longer necessary for me to constantly rely on my old way of searching for warmth and love. In my old way I would not function at optimum levels in order to obtain pity. (I had mistaken pity for warmth and love.) In my old way I wanted people to feel sorry for me. I wanted them to make up for the love and affection I did not receive from my parents, but which I so desperately needed. I got down on myself until I functioned erratically. Then I hoped that someone would come along, feel sorry for me (Mommy) and give me help and support (Daddy).

Conclusions

After three weeks of therapy I made several major changes.

First, prior to therapy I had been smoking about three packs of cigarettes a day. Not only did I stop smoking, but now I do not even have a desire to smoke.

Second, prior to therapy I was a moderate drinker. I frequented bars several times a week. Although rarely drinking excessively, I looked forward to belting down four or five scotches. After therapy I have no desire to continue the practice.

Third, my sexual activity has tapered off considerably. Prior to therapy I had intercourse at least three times a week. Since therapy began a month and half ago I have had intercourse three times. However, while I feel the first two changes are permanent, I am not yet clear as to my feelings about my sex life. Prior to therapy I slept with many women. I seldom slept with the same woman more than once a week. Making women was my way of hiding from my deep pain – the pain of being left out, a loser. One cannot be a successful loser if he squarely faces the fact. He must run from it. He must have a cover to hide his shame of being a loser. My cover was women. I no longer have the urge to go on like that. But my real desires have yet to be worked out. Perhaps it will just be with one woman or a few – I don't know.

Fourth, I don't have problems sleeping any more. Neither do I have headaches.

Fifth, a lot of the tension has subsided. Some still remains, but I can feel it lessening.

Sixth, my relations with people are changing. (This is a most gradual, subtle and difficult change to describe.) I no longer get the feeling of being dominated and passive – the fag feeling – with the intensity I did before therapy. Neither do I get the feeling as frequently. Sometimes I get confused in distinguishing between the fag feeling and the simple feeling of being helpless in regard to other people loving me. (I am new at identifying both feelings.) But now I can usually make the distinction by my sense of being alone. In the fag feeling I don't feel alone. I feel some ominous presence lurking in the shadows of the here and now. In the helpless feeling I feel very alone, and it doesn't hurt a bit; it's more or less exhilarating, depending upon the circumstances.

I feel more distant in my relations with people, but it is a distance which seems to be cultivating a new capacity for intimacy. It is as yet so inchoate and so new, but what it holds out for the future excites me. In its present effects, though, it merely intrigues me.

In my relations with people, as well as when I am alone, I feel the deep, indescribable hurt of all that lost love that I needed so much as a child but didn't get. Sometimes it is so great that I am all but paralysed. I still feel this more than anything else. Most of the time I am either on the verge of tears or very fearful.

To most people I would appear very sad. I am sure that my uninitiated friends privately wonder just how much good my therapy has brought about.

Lastly, my orientation is undergoing a massive transformation. Of course, this process is as yet incomplete. But it is possible to sketch some of the changes.

For one thing, I no longer feel dominated by the need for recognition in the professional world, just as I am no longer dominated by the need for the love of one or more women. I cannot honestly say that these needs have been replaced as yet. In some respects I now feel as though I am in limbo or some no-man's-land. However, this is not especially disconcerting because I can feel the newness emerging. While it may be premature to talk about it, nonetheless it is there, and it is growing.

I feel the most radical change has come in my value structure. Now I have an ever-growing awareness of values being worked out of the dynamics of my organism. My intellect does not direct this process; my body does. My intellect plays a role, but that role is ancillary. I might best describe it by saying that my intellect does not take part in the process so much as it observes and records what has taken place, much as modern science has observed the structure and dynamics of the atom and then fabricated a notational system of protons, neutrons, electrons and the like to record what it has observed.

What I am asserting is that the value concepts or ideas by which we attempt to control our behaviour and experience do not properly originate in thought. Ordering our experience in terms of ideas is the result of a sickness which cuts us off from the organic processes of the environment as well as from our own. We utter foolish and nonsensical exclamations such as: 'Mind over matter!' or 'Get in control of yourself!' These and countless other remarks reveal a deep split in our view of life, the result of which is that we become divided from the world, as well as from ourselves.

Speaking positively, I am asserting that the value concepts or ideas by which we wish to order our lives properly originate in the organism's experience of itself. They express the organism's requirements for a sustained, healthy existence, which is another way of saying they express what we really want. Ideas are involved, and these ideas play an important role. But what is important to understand is that the ideas are *derived* from the experience. For example, I do not first generate an idea about being with a group of people and then go join one. First of all I *experience* my own sense of being alone. Then I generate an idea about this. The nature of this idea is to duplicate the experience – photograph it, if you will. This enables me to identify the experience, place it in relation to other experiences, and, finally, to act upon it. For me this is of crucial importance. It means that my values and goals, what men have traditionally held to be most sacred in life, really have their source in the organic structure of *my* being. Therefore, it would be decidedly unhealthy for me to allow this value-forming process to be assumed by my or other intellects, or by some public authority or philosophical system which purports to be in possession of 'truth'.

Instructions for New Primal Patients

For Primal Therapy to be effective, you must co-operate with the following simple instructions without deviation:

1. Forty-eight hours before your therapy begins, give up all smoking and drinking of alcoholic drinks. This includes beer and wine.
2. Do not take any drugs such as aspirin, sleeping pills, tranquillisers, mood elevators, stimulants or any other drug that may affect your state of being. Stop all pills four to five days before therapy begins and continue without them until the entire treatment period is over.
3. You already know what you do to relieve tension. Stop doing it! This means to give up compulsive eating and snacking, biting nails, keeping busy and on the run, oversleeping etc.
4. Twenty-four hours prior to therapy, you are to be totally alone, preferably in a hotel room near the office. Do not make phone calls, see friends, watch TV or go to the movies. It is a time to be undistracted. Check into the hotel the afternoon before therapy begins and try not to leave the room until your appointment hour the next day.
5. When you enter Primal Therapy, do exactly as the therapist says. In no case will any harm be allowed to come to you. No trickery is used, nor are any statements made to produce a special effect. This therapy has nothing to do with Zen, hypnosis or the use of any kind of medication. It is based upon sound scientific principles already applied with success to many individuals who have gone through the treatment.
6. The initial phase of therapy is approximately three weeks. You should plan not to work or go to school during this time. Generally, this is all the individual treatment you will need except for an occasional follow-up hour now and then. You will be seen daily for the first week or two for approximately two hours. You may take all the time you need each day as the sessions are open-ended. You will be seen several times during the third week depending on your need.
7. After the third week, you will be placed in a post-Primal

group made up of people who have been through the treatment. These groups meet once a week or twice a week. These groups are a must as they are an integral part of the therapeutic plan. You should plan to attend for a period of several months. After that, therapy is over.

Bibliography

BOOKS

CUMMING, R. D., *The Philosophy of Jean-Paul Sartre*. New York, Random House, 1965.

ELLIS, ALBERT, *Reason and Emotion in Psychotherapy*. New York, Lyle Stuart, 1963.

FRANKL, VIKTOR, *Man's Search for Meaning*, rev. ed. Boston, Beacon Press, 1962.

FREUD, SIGMUND, *A General Introduction to Psychoanalysis.* New York, Tudor, n.d.

—— *The Problem of Anxiety*. New York, W. W. Norton & Co., 1936.

INHELDER, BARBEL, and PIAGET, JEAN, *The Early Growth of Logic in the Child*. New York, Harper & Row, 1964.

JACOBSON, EDMUND, *Biology of Emotions*. Springfield, Ill., Charles C Thomas, Publisher, 1967.

—— *Tension in Medicine.* Springfield, Ill., Charles C Thomas, Publisher, 1967.

KNAPP, PETER H., *Expression of the Emotions in Man*. New York, International Universities Press, 1963.

KOLODNY, A. L., and MCLOUGHLIN, P. T., *Comprehensive Approach to Therapy of Pain*. Springfield, Ill., Charles C Thomas, Publisher, 1966.

KRON, Y. J., and BROWN, E.A., *Mainline to Nowhere*. New York, Pantheon, 1965.

LAING, RONALD, *Politics of Experience*. New York, Pantheon, 1967.

LAUGHLIN, HENRY P., *The Neuroses*. London, Butterworth, 1967.

LEVINE, MAURICE, *Psychotherapy in Medical Practice*. New York, Macmillan, 1942.

LING, T., and BUCKMAN, J., *Lysergic Acid and Retalin in the Treatment of Neurosis*. London, Lombardi Press, 1963.

LOWRY, THOMAS, *Hyperventilation and Hysteria*. Springfield, Ill., Charles C Thomas, Publisher, 1967.

MARMOR, JUDD, *Psychoanalytic Therapy as an Educational Process*. New York, Grune & Stratton, 1962.

MARMOR, JUDD, *Psychoanalytic Therapy and Theories of Learning*. New York, Grune & Stratton, 1964.

MASLOW, ABRAHAM H., *Toward a Psychology of Being*. London, D. Van Nostrand Co., 1962.

MAY, ROLLO; ANGEL, ERNEST; and ELLENBERGER, HENRI, *Existence*. New York, Basic Books, 1960.

MICHAELS, JOSEPH J., 'Character Structure and Character Disorders', in Silvano Arieti, ed., *American Handbook of Psychiatry*. New York, Basic Books, 1959.

MILLER, NEAL, and DOLLARD, JOHN, *Personality & Psychotherapy*. New York, McGraw-Hill, 1950.

OFFER, DANIEL, and SABSHIN, MELVIN, *Normality*. New York, Basic Books, 1966.

PIAGET, JEAN, *The Language and Thought of the Child*. New York, Meridian, 1955.

—— *Origins of Intelligence in Children*. New York, International Universities Press, 1956.

PUTNEY, SNELL and GAIL, *Normal Neurosis: The Adjusted American*. New York, Harper & Row, 1964.

SALTER, ANDREW; WOLPE, JOSEPH; and REYNA, L. J., *Condition Reflex Therapy*. New York, Holt, Rinehart and Winston, 1965.

SCHULTZ, DUANE P., *Sensory Restriction*. New York, Academic Press, 1965.

SCOTT, JOHN PAUL, *Animal Behavior*. Chicago, University of Chicago Press, 1958.

SHAPIRO, DAVID, *Neurotic Styles*. New York, Basic Books, 1965.

SOULAIRAC, A. J.; CAHN, J.; and CHARPENTIER, J., *Pain*. New York, Academic Press, 1968.

STERNBACH, RICHARD A., *Pain: A Psychophysiological Analysis*. New York, Academic Press, 1968.

WEDDELL, A. G. M., 'Activity Pattern Hypothesis for Sensation of Pain', in R. G. Grenell, ed., *Progress in Neurobiology*. New York, Hoeber, 1962.

WITTENBORN, J. R., *The Clinical Psychopharmacology of Anxiety*. Springfield, Ill., Charles C Thomas, Publisher, 1966.

WOLBERG, LEWIS R., *The Technique of Psychotherapy*. New York, Grune & Stratton, 1954.

JOURNALS

AIKEN, L. R. JR., 'Stress and Anxiety as Homomorphisms'. *Psychological Record*, Vol. 11 (1961), pp. 365–72.

ANSBACHER, H. L., 'On the Origin of Holism'. *Journal of Individual Psychology*, Vol. 17 (1961), pp. 142–48.

AX, A. F., 'The Physiological Differentiation Between Fear and Anger in Humans'. *Psychosomatic Medicine*, Vol. 15 (1953), pp. 433–42.

—— 'Psychophysiology of Fear and Anger'. *Psychiatric Research Reports*, No. 12 (1960), pp. 167–75.

AZRIN, NATHAN, 'Pain and Aggression'. *Psychology Today*, Vol. 1, No. 1 (1967), pp. 26–33.

BARABASH, V.I., 'Kvaprosu o zapredel nykh formakh psikhicheskogo nopryahenija'. *Voprosy Psikhologii*, Vol. 14, No. 6 (1968), pp. 122–26. 'Forms of Above Normal Psychological Tension.'

BARON, NAOMI, 'Memory and Emotion'. *American Psychologist*, Vol. 17 (1962), pp. 146–48.

BEECHER, H. K., 'Generalization from Pain of Various Types and Diverse Origins'. *Science*, Vol. 130 (1959), pp. 267–68.

BERNSTEIN, ALVIN S., 'Anxiety as a Non-Directional Drive: A Test of Hull-Spence Theory'. *Psychological Reports*, Vol. 12, No. 1 (1963), pp. 87–98.

BEVAN, W., 'The Contextual Basis of Behavior'. *American Psychologist*, Vol. 23 (1968), pp. 701–14.

BHARUCHA, REID RHODABE, 'The Internal Modulating System and Stress: A Neurophysiological Model'. *Journal of General Psychology*, Vol. 66 (1962), pp. 147–58.

BLANCHARD, WILLIAM H., 'Psychodynamic Aspects of the Peak Experience'. *The Psychoanalytic Review*, Vol. 56, No. 1 (1969), pp. 87–112.

BOUL, JACK C., 'Security as a Motivation of Human Behavior'. *Archives of General Psychiatry*, Vol. 10, No. 2 (1964), pp. 105–8.

BOWERS, KENNETH S., 'Pain, Anxiety and Perceived Control'. *Journal of Consulting and Clinical Psychology*, Vol. 32, No. 5, Pt. 1 (1968), pp. 596–602.

BOWLBY, JOHN, 'Separation Anxiety, a Critical Review of the Literature'. *Journal of Child Psychology and Psychiatry*, Vol. 1 (1961), pp. 251–69.

CARLSMITH, J. MERRIL, and GROSS, ALAN E., 'Some Effects of Guilt on Compliance'. *Journal of Personality and Social Psychology*, Vol. 11, No. 3 (1969), pp. 232–39.

COHEN, IRA S., 'Rigidity and Anxiety in a Motor Response'. *Perceptual and Motor Skills*, Vol. 12 (1961), pp. 127–30.

COLLIER, REX M., 'The Role of Affect in Behavior: A Holistic-Organismic Approach'. *Journal of Individual Psychology*, Vol. 22, No. 1 (1966), pp. 2–32.

DIXON, N. F., and HAIDER, M., 'Changes in Visual Threshold as a Function of Subception'. *Quarterly Journal of Experimental Psychology*, Vol. 13 (1961), pp. 229–35.

ENGEL, G. L., 'Psychogenic Pain'. *Journal of Occupational Medicine*, Vol. 3 (1961), pp. 249–57.

EYSENCK, HANS J., 'The Effects of Psychotherapy'. *International Journal of Psychiatry*, Vol. 1 (January, 1965), pp. 97–144.

FAST, IRENE, 'Some Relationships of Infantile Self-Boundary

Development to Depression'. *International Journal of Psycho-Analysis*, Vol. 48, No. 2 (1967), pp. 259–66.

FESHBACK, SEYMOUR, 'The Effects of Emotional Restraint upon the Projection of Positive Affect'. *Journal of Personality*, Vol. 31, No. 4 (1963), pp. 471–81.

FISHER, SEYMOUR, 'Depressive Affect and Perception of Up-Down'. *Journal of Psychiatric Research*, Vol. 2, No. 1 (1964), pp. 25–30.

FOX, HENRY M.: GIFFORD, SANFORD; MURAWSKI, BENJAMIN J.; RIZZO, NICHOLAS D.; and KUDARAUSKAS, EDMUND N., 'Some Methods of Observing Humans Under Stress'. *Psychiatric Research Reports*, No. 7 (1957), pp. 14–26.

FRENKEL-BRUNSWIK, E., 'Psychoanalysis and the Unity of Science'. *American Academy of Arts and Science*, Vol. 80 (1954), pp. 271–347.

GAZZANIGA, M. S., 'The Split Brain in Man'. *Scientific American*, Vol. 217 (1967), pp. 24–29.

GESCHWIND, N., 'Disconnection Syndromes in Animals and Man'. *Brain*, Vol. 88 (1965), pp. 237–94.

GIBSON, JAMES J., 'The Useful Dimension of Sensitivity'. *American Psychologist*, Vol. 18, No. 1 (1963), pp. 1–15.

GONDA, T. A., 'Some Remarks on Pain'. *Bulletin of British Psychology and Sociology*, Vol. 47 (1962), pp. 29–35.

HARLOW, HARRY F., 'Love in Infant Monkeys'. *Scientific American*, Vol. 200, No. 6 (June, 1959), pp. 68–74.

—— 'Social Deprivation in Monkeys', *Scientific American* (November, 1952).

HAYWOOD, H. C., 'Relationships Among Anxiety, Seeking of Novel Stimuli and Level of Unassimilated Percepts'. *Journal of Personality*, Vol. 29 (1961), pp. 105–14.

HEATH, R. G.; MARTENS, S.; LEACH, B. E.; COHEN, M.; and ANGEL C., 'Effect on Behavior in Humans with the Administration of Taraxein'. *American Journal of Psychiatry*, Vol. 114 (1959), pp. 14–24.

HEATH, ROBERT G., 'Studies Toward Correlating Behavior with Brain Activity'. Pavlovian Conference on Higher Nervous Activity, *Annals of the New York Academy of Sciences*, Vol. 92 (1961), pp. 1106–22.

HERRON, WILLIAM G., and KANTOR, ROBERT E., 'Loss of Affect'. *Journal of Psychology*, Vol. 70, No. 1 (1968), pp. 35–49.

JACOBSON, E., 'Electrophysiology of Mental Activities'. *American Journal of Psychology*, Vol. 44 (1932), pp. 677–94.

—— 'Variation of Blood Pressure with Skeletal Muscle Tension and Relaxation'. *Annals of Internal Medicine*, Vol. 13 (1940), p. 1619.

KANUNGO, RABINDRA N., and DUTTA, SATRAJIT, 'Retention of Affective Material: Frame of Reference or Intensity?'

Journal of Personality and Social Psychology, Vol. 4, No. 1 (1966), pp. 27–35.

KENNEDY, WALLACE A., and WILLCUT, HERMAN C., 'Praise and Blame as Incentives'. *Psychological Bulletin*, Vol. 62, No. 5 (1964), pp. 323–53.

KEY, B. J., 'Effect of LSD on 25 Potentials Evoked in Specific Sensory Pathways'. *British Medical Bulletin*, Vol. 21, No. 1 (1965), pp. 30–35.

KNAPP, PETER H., 'Conscious and Unconscious Affects: A Preliminary Approach to Concepts and Methods of Study'. *Psychiatric Research Reports*, Vol. 8 (1957), pp. 5–74.

KUNKLE, E. CHARLES, 'Pain Unfelt or Pain Unheeded: A Distinction with a Difference'. *Archives of Neurology*, Vol. 5 (1961), p. 579.

LAING, R. A., 'An Examination of Tillich's Theory of Anxiety and Neurosis'. *British Journal of Medical Psychology*, Vol. 30 (1957), pp. 88–91.

LESHNER, SAUL S., 'Effects of Aspiration and Achievement on Muscular Tension'. *Journal of Experimental Psychology*, Vol. 61 (1961), pp. 133–37.

LEVIN, SIDNEY, 'Some Metapsychological Considerations on the Differentiation Between Shame and Guilt'. *International Journal of Psycho-Analysis*, Vol. 48, No. 2 (1967), pp. 267–76.

LIBET, BENJAMIN, and JONES, MARGARET HUBBARD, 'Delayed Pain as a Peripheral Sensory Pathway'. *Science*, Vol. 126 (1957), pp. 256–57.

MALERSTEIN, A. J., and LANGLEY, PORTER, 'Depression as a Pivotal Effect'. *American Journal of Psychotherapy*, Vol. 22, No. 2 (1968), pp. 202–17.

MASLOW, A. H., 'The Need to Know and the Fear of Knowing'. *Journal of General Psychology*, Vol. 68, No. 1 (1963), pp. 111–25.

MATSUYAMA, Y., 'Drive Discrimination Learning by Pain and Fear'. *Japanese Journal of Psychology*, Vol. 36 (1960), pp. 7–15.

MATTSON, JAMES M., and NATSOULAS, THOMAS, 'Emotional Arousal and Stimulus Duration as Determinants of Stimulus Selection'. *Journal of Abnormal and Social Psychology*, Vol. 65, No. 2 (1962), pp. 142–44.

MCCONNELL, JAMES V.; CUTLER, RICHARD L.; and MCNEIL, ELTON B., 'Subliminal Stimulation'. *American Psychologist*, Vol. 13 (1958), pp. 229–42.

MEISSNER, W. W., 'Affective Response to Psychoanalytic Death Symbols'. *Journal of Abnormal and Social Psychology*, Vol. 56 (1958), pp. 295–99.

MELTZER, H., 'Individual Differences in Forgetting Pleasant and Unpleasant Experiences'. *Journal of Educational Psychology*, Vol 21 (1930), pp. 399–409.

MELZACK, RONALD, and SCOTT, T. H., 'The Effects of Early Experiences on the Response of Pain'. *Journal of Comparative Physiological Psychology*, Vol. 50 (1957), pp. 155–61.

MERSKEY, H., 'Psychological Aspects of Pain'. *Postgraduate Medical Journal*, Vol. 44, No. 510 (1968), pp. 297–306.

MYERS, THOMAS I.; JOHNSON, EUGENE; and SMITH, SEWARD, 'Subjective Stress and Affect States as a Function of Sensory Deprivation'. *Proceedings of the 76th Annual Convention of the American Psychological Association*, Vol. 3 (1968), pp. 623–24.

NAFE, JOHN P., and KENSHALO, D. R., 'Homesthetic Senses'. *Annual Review of Psychology*, Vol. 13 (1962), pp. 201–24.

NICHOLS, D. C., and TURSKY, B., 'Body Image, Anxiety and Tolerance for Experimental Pain'. *Psychosomatic Medicine*, Vol. 29 (1967), pp. 103–110.

OKEN, DONALD, 'An Experimental Study of Suppressed Anger and Blood Pressure'. *Archives of General Psychiatry*, Vol. 2 (1960), pp. 441–56.

OLIVIER, PAUL, 'Uber die Gefühle'. *Psychiatrie, Neurologie und Medizinische Psychologie*, Vol. 9 (1957), pp. 349–57. 'On the Emotions.'

ORZECK, A. Z.; MCGUIRE, C.; and LONGENECKER, E. D., 'Multiple Self Concepts as Effected by Mood States'. *American Journal of Psychiatry*, Vol. 115 (1958), pp. 349–53.

PAPEZ, J. W., 'A Proposed Mechanism of Emotion'. *Archives of Neurology and Psychology*, Vol. 38 (1937), pp. 725–43.

PETERSEN, PREHEN B., 'La Description de réorie d'émotion vasomotrice'. *Acta Psychiatric Scandinavia*, Vol. 42, Supplement 191 (1966), pp. 188–92. Description of Lange's conditional reflexes based on his theory of vaso-motoremotion.

PETRIE, ASENATH; COLLINS, WALTER; and SOLOMON, PHILIP, 'The Tolerance for Pain and for Sensory Deprivation'. *American Journal of Psychology*, Vol. 73 (March, 1960), pp. 80–89.

PETROVICH, DONALD V., 'A Survey of Painfulness Concepts'. *Journal of Clinical Psychology*, Vol. 14 (1958), pp. 288–91.

PLATZ, A., and HONIGFIELD, G., 'Some Effects of Anxiety on the Intelligibility of Communication in Psychotherapy'. *Journal of Personality and Social Psychology*, Vol. 2 (1965), pp. 122–25.

SCHILDER, P. and STENGEL, E., 'Asymbolia for Pain.' *Archives of Neurological Psychiatry*, Vol. 25 (1931), pp. 598–600.

SCHNEIDER, S. F., 'A Psychological Basis for Indifference to Pain'. *Psychosomatic Medicine*, Vol. 24 (1962), pp. 119–32.

SCHONBAR, ROSALEA A., 'Identificación y Busqueda de la Identidad'. *Revista de Psicoanálisis, Psiquiatría y Psicologia*, No. 8 (1968), pp. 49–66. 'Identification and Search for Identity.'

SCHUMACHER, A.A.; WRIGHT, J.M.; and WIESEN, A. E., 'The Self as a Source of Anxiety'. *Journal of Consulting Psychology*, Vol. 32, No. 1 (1968), pp. 30–34.

SEARS, R. R., 'Functional Abnormality of Memory – with Special Reference to Amnesia'. *Psychological Bulletin*, Vol. 33 (1936), pp. 229–74.

SHOBEN, EDWARD J., JR., 'Love, Loneliness and Logic'. *Journal of Individual Psychology*, Vol. 16 (1960), pp. 11–24.

SINGH, LABH, "Effect of Need Tension on Time Perception'. *Psychological Researches*. Vol. 1, Nos. 1–2 (1966), pp. 28–32.

SOLLEY, CHARLES M., and LONG, JOHN, 'Affect, Fantasy and Figure Ground Organization'. *Journal of General Psychology*, Vol. 62 (January, 1960), pp. 75–82.

STELLAR, E., 'The Physiology of Emotion'. *Psychological Review*, Vol. 61 (1954), pp. 5–22.

STERNBACH, R.A., 'Congenital Insensitivity to Pain: A Critique'. *Psychological Bulletin*, Vol. 60 (1963), pp. 252–64.

SUINN, RICHARD M., and HILL, HUNTER, 'Influence of Anxiety on the Relationship Between Self Acceptance and Acceptance of Others'. *Journal of Consulting Psychology*, Vol. 28, No. 2 (1964), pp. 116–19.

THORNE, F. C., 'An Existential Theory of Anxiety'. *Journal of Clinical Psychology*, Vol. 19, No. 1 (1963), pp. 35–43.

WALDMAN, R. D., 'Pain as Fiction: A Perspective on Psychotherapy and Responsibility'. *American Journal of Psychotherapy*, Vol. 22, No. 3 (1968), pp. 481–90.

WALL, P. D., and SWEET, W. R., 'Temporary Abolition of Pain in Man'. *Science*, Vol. 155 (1967), pp. 108–9.

WALTZER, HERBERT, 'Depersonalization and Self-Destruction'. *American Journal of Psychiatry*, Vol. 25, No. 3 (1968), pp. 399–401.

WENGER, M. A., and associates, 'Autonomic Response Patterns During Intravenous Infusion of Epinephrine and Nor-Epinephrine'. *Psychosomatic Medicine*, Vol. 22 (1960), pp. 294–307.

WEST, LOUIS JOLYON, and FARBER, I. E., 'The Role of Pain in Emotional Development'. *Psychiatric Research Reports*, No. 12 (1960), pp. 119–26.

WOLFF, B. B.; KRASNEGOR, N. A.; and FARR, R. S., 'Effect of Suggestion upon Experimental Pain Response Patterns'. *Perpetual and Motor Skills*, Vol. 21 (1965), pp. 675–83.

ZUBEK, JOHN P., 'Pain Sensitivity as a Measure of Perceptual Deprivation Tolerance'. *Perceptual and Motor Skills*, Vol. 17, No. 2 (1963), pp. 641–42.

DISSERTATION ABSTRACTS

COVHRANE, CARL MURRAY, 'Reaction Time and Intensity of Response as a Function of Anxiety and Stress'. University of North Carolina, Vol. 20 (January, 1969), pp. 2899–900.

DOWLING, ROBERT MOXWELL, 'Effect of Sensorimotor and Conceptual Activity on Perceptual Functioning'. Clark University, Vol. 23, No. 9 (1963), pp. 3489–90.

FRANK, KENNETH, 'Mood Differentiation and Psychological Differentiation: Some Relationships Between Mood Variations and Witkins Research'. Columbia University, Vol. 12 (1968), pp. 5203–4.

GOLDSTEIN, ROBERT HOWARD, 'Behavioral Effects of Psychological Stress'. University of Michigan, Vol. 19 (June, 1959), p. 3364.

KISSEN, MORTON, 'A Demonstration of Certain Affects of Emotional States upon Perception'. New School of Social Research, Vol. 29, No. 5 (1968), p. 1836.

KRAUSER, EDWIN LLOYD, 'Stress as an Independent Variable in Transfer of Training'. Purdue University, Vol. 20 (January, 1960), p. 2904.

MASON, RUSSELL ELLSWORTH, 'A Study of Secondary Sensations Arising in Emotionally Loaded Situations'. Purdue University, Vol. 21 (1961), pp. 2800–1.

ROAZEN, IRWIN H., 'Effects on Pain Threshold of Concomitant Distraction and Past Distraction'. University of Minnesota, Vol. 28, No. 12 (1968), p. 5220.

RUIZ, RENE ARTHUR, 'Situational Factors in the Intensity of Anxious Response'. University of Nebraska, Vol. 24, No. 8 (1964), p. 3428.

Index

Index

Abacus now offers an exciting range of quality fiction and non-fiction by both established and new authors. All of the books in this series are available from good bookshops, or can be ordered from the following address:

Sphere Books
Cash Sales Department
P.O. Box 11
Falmouth
Cornwall TR10 9EN.

Please send cheque or postal order (no currency), and allow 60p for postage and packing for the first book plus 25p for the second book and 15p for each additional book ordered up to a maximum charge of £1.90 in U.K.

B.F.P.O. customers please allow 60p for the first book, 25p for the second book plus 15p per copy for the next 7 books, thereafter 9p per book.

Overseas customers including Eire please allow £1.25 for postage and packing for the first book, 75p for the second book and 28p for each subsequent title ordered.